AGENDA FOR EXCELLENCE
Public Service in America

Edited by

Patricia W. Ingraham
Syracuse University

and

Donald F. Kettl
University of Wisconsin–Madison

Chatham House Publishers, Inc.
Chatham, New Jersey

This book is for Charlie,
but it is also for
Elaine and Jordy Levine, his wife and son,
who were the center of his life.

Agenda for Excellence: Public Service in America

Chatham House Publishers, Inc.
P.O. Box 1 / Chatham, New Jersey 07928
Copyright ©1992 by Chatham House Publishers, Inc.

Publisher: Edward Artinian
Production editor: Christopher J. Kelaher
Cover design: Countryside Studios
Composition: Bang, Motley, Olufsen
Printing and binding: BookCrafters

Library of Congress Cataloging-in-Publication Data

Agenda for excellence: public service in America
/ edited by Patricia W. Ingraham and Donald F. Kettl
p.   cm.
Festschriften in honor of Charles H. Levine.
Includes bibliographical references.
ISBN 0-934540-86-1
1. Administrative agencies—United States—Management.
2. Civil service—United States. 3. United States—Politics
and government.   I. Ingraham, Patricia W.   II. Kettl, Donald F.
III. Levine, Charles H.
JK421.A55   1992
353.001—dc20   91-47714
                                                    CIP

Manufactured in the United States of America
10 9 8 7 6 5 4 3 2 1

Contents

Preface

Patricia W. Ingraham
and
Donald F. Kettl

This book is dedicated with deep affection, but with a profound sense of loss, to the memory of Charles H. Levine. It is a fitting tribute to Charlie's intellect and achievements that the book is one of a two-part set; it was not possible to accommodate the full range of Charlie's contributions in a single volume. The second volume, edited by B. Guy Peters and Bert Rockman, will also be published by Chatham House. We are grateful to Ed Artinian for his support of these books. They are, for all of us, an important opportunity to acknowledge the significance of Charlie and his work. As friend and colleague, he enhanced our lives immeasurably. As critic, he improved our analyses and our efforts to present them. As scholar, he simply redefined the boundaries of inquiry; none of us can recall a question to which Charlie did not have a challenging or provocative answer or an issue for which he did not have a new and interesting perspective.

Throughout his too-brief career, Charlie was as demanding of others as he was of himself. The disciplines of public administration and political science benefited from the rigor of those demands. Just as important was Charlie's determination to improve the practice, as well as the study, of government. At the end of his life, his work as the deputy director of the National Commission on the Public Service was directed toward correcting the many problems that confront the American public service in the 1990s. The title of this book, *Agenda for Excellence*, reflects Charlie's conviction that an excellent and effective public service is fundamental to good government.

Charles Levine was born 13 July 1939 in Hartford, Connecticut. He received a bachelor's degree from the University of Connecticut and an M.B.A., M.P.A., and Ph.D. from Indiana University. He held academic appointments at Michigan State University, the University of Maryland, Syracuse University, and the University of Kansas, where he was the Edward O.

Stene Distinguished Professor of Public Administration. Charlie also served as a member of the senior staff of The Brookings Institution and as a senior specialist in American national government and public administration for the Congressional Research Service at the Library of Congress. At the time of his death, he was Distinguished Professor of Government and Public Administration at the American University and deputy director of the National Commission on the Public Service (also known as the Volcker Commission).

Charlie was the founder or co-founder of the Organized Section on Public Administration in the American Political Science Association and the Section on Public Management in the American Academy of Management. He served on the editorial boards of sixteen academic journals. He was the author or editor of ten books and numerous articles and monographs across a remarkably broad spectrum of the discipline, as the list of publications at the end of this essay richly shows. In his lifetime Charlie was honored by the American Society for Public Administration, the National Association of Schools of Public Affairs and Administration, the French-American Foundation, and many others for his outstanding contributions. At his death, awards in his memory were created by the American Political Science Association and the American Society for Public Administration.

These awards mark Charlie's exceptional contribution to practice, teaching, and research in public administration. Charlie played a leading role in strengthening the intellectual fiber of the American Society for Public Administration. Many of his colleagues, moreover, saw him as the *yenta* of the discipline, a matchmaker who constantly put people together with positions. His hidden hand shaped the growth of many leading academic programs around the country. His scholarly work, especially on the civil service and on government's responses to fiscal stress, shaped the field.

At a time when cynicism dominated much of the public's view of government, and even of elected officials' view of administration, Charlie championed government's positive role and identified the new and challenging problems facing it. When commentators wondered if good government was possible, Charlie led the fight to make government work. And when a drumbeat of attacks on the public service threatened to undercut government performance, Charlie helped shape the Volcker Commission's effort to rebuild the public service. He was waging that battle when he died in 1988.

This volume thus is more than a testimonial from friends whose lives Charlie touched and who miss his companionship and energy. It is a celebration of the potential of the public service and of the ongoing search for excellence in government to which Charlie devoted his life. The authors of this book hope to infect its readers with at least some measure of the enthusiasm and hope that Charlie brought to these issues and thereby keep his work alive.

PART ONE

Foundations

I

The Founders' Unsentimental View of Public Service in the American Regime

Lloyd G. Nigro and William D. Richardson

The aim of every political constitution is, or ought to be, first to obtain for rulers men who possess most wisdom to discern, and most virtue to pursue, the common good of the society; and, in the next place, to take the most effectual precautions for keeping them virtuous whilst they continue to hold their public trust.
—*The Federalist Papers*

The Framers of the U.S. Constitution were decidedly ambivalent about the extent to which the regime they contemplated would reliably produce *disinterested* governors. On the one hand, they hoped that sufficient numbers of wise and virtuous rulers would hold elective and appointive posts. On the other, they were far from convinced that the American character would long support a classical republic (or confederation of republics) requiring widespread public virtue. In 1787, the pursuit of self-interest seemed more the American norm.[1] This latter aspect of the Framers' thinking is reflected in a constitution that diffuses and limits governmental powers, and frustrates the tyrannical propensities of "factions." These "precautions," however, do not fully mirror the Founders' aspirations, for they also expected that the regime would produce a fair number of public servants dedicated to the common good if the Constitution did what it was intended to do.

By simultaneously recognizing self-interest as the driving force of politics and reaffirming the possibility (if not the necessity) of disinterested governance by the wise and virtuous, the Founders were advancing what may be called an unsentimental view of public service in the American regime. The term "unsentimental" is used here in the same sense that Ralph Lerner uses it to describe John Adams's point of view.

> John Adams understood that self-governance needs as good a people as one could muster and as many public-spirited individuals as one could press into the public's service. But to insist on that desideratum as an everyday requirement would guarantee, not the rule of the disinterested and the saintly, but the enthronement of hypocrites and knaves. Adams's steadily unsentimental view of things did not lead him to deny that there are disinterested men, but only to insist that "they are not enough in any age or country to fill all the necessary offices." Only levelheadedness could keep the counsel of perfection in political life from turning into the triumph of madness and despotism.[2]

Like Adams, the Founders anticipated that incompetents, knaves, and hypocrites would not be strangers to our public offices. From the vantage point of the twentieth century, their fears about such officeholders would certainly seem to have been confirmed on all levels and in all branches of government. But throughout its history, the American regime has also produced many public-spirited men and women who have served the republic competently and faithfully. These contradictory results confirm the wisdom of the Founders' "levelheaded" approach to the task of writing a political constitution for the American republic. In this chapter, we attempt to show how the Founders' unsentimental view of public service in America might help us to think more clearly about a variety of contemporary issues related to the character of public administrators.

The Founding Perspective on Public Administration

It is often observed that the Constitution of the United States says very little, if anything, about *administration*. Yet there is considerable evidence that public administration was of great concern to many of the Founders, most notably James Madison and Alexander Hamilton.[3] As John Rohr points out, "if you look at the Federalist papers as an authoritative commentary on the Constitution, the word administration or its cognates are used 124 times. This is more than the words Congress, president, and Supreme Court appear."[4] In addition to contending that the federal executive should be energetic, competent, and govern in the public interest, Publius (the pseudonym under which Hamilton, Madison, and John Jay wrote) argued that public administration had an important role to play in cultivating citizen character. Emphatically rejecting the Anti-Federalists' argument for small and administratively weak governments, he asserted that a strong and competent public administration would command public support and "promote private and public morality by providing them with effective protection." [5]

The written record strongly suggests that the Founders did not think politics could or should be separate from administration. In No. 72, Publius says: "The administration of government, in its largest sense, comprehends all the operations of the body politic, whether legislative, executive, or judiciary; but in its most usual and perhaps in its most precise signification, it is limited to executive details, and falls peculiarly within the province of the executive department." [6] Elsewhere, however, Publius makes it clear that the purposes of republican government, factional politics, and the separation of powers make it impossible to remove executive details from the realm of administration in "its largest sense." [7]

Further defining the political function of public administration in the American regime, the Founders make it clear that there are no grounds for a politics-administration dichotomy in a Federalist system where "all parts of the government became rulers and representatives of the people at the same time." [8] The representative, and therefore truly political, responsibilities of public administrators under the Constitution were set forth by James Wilson and other Federalists, who argued that "all government officials, including even the executive and judicial parts of the government, were agents of the people, not fundamentally different from the people's nominal representatives in the lower houses of the legislatures.... The different parts of the government were functionally but not substantially different." [9] This aspect of Founding thought, however, has been obscured by later efforts to build a theory of public administration based on the norm of "neutral competence."

Although often credited with having prescribed a "politics-administration dichotomy," Woodrow Wilson did not actually seek to establish such a separation. Robert Miewald has characterized Wilson's point of view in the following terms:

> Regardless of what he wrote in "The Study of Administration," the implications of his later work are unavoidable: administrators were politicians; they must have the freedom to make ethical decisions. The [Wilson] lectures contain no support for the idea that politics can be removed from administration. [10]

Nevertheless, the essay and the dichotomy it implied were embraced by later generations of reform-oriented administrators, who sought to define themselves as managers who could best serve the public interest if they were (1) judged by the standards of partisan neutrality and technical competence, and (2) effectively insulated from "politics." [11]

Of particular relevance here is Miewald's observation that an important effect of the dichotomy on the study of public administration was to remove questions of character and ethics from the mainstream of the field. In his words, treating public administrators "as a special class in society not affected by ordinary human weakness produced a doctrine that effectively removed the bureaucrat from scholarly scrutiny."[12] One especially important consequence of assuming that public administrators are or can be paragons of impartial wisdom is to treat administration as a field of essentially *structural* questions, the objective being to implement arrangements that permit administrators to exercise their expertise.[13] In contrast, if the Founders' understanding of public administration as a form of politics is accepted, questions regarding the character of public administrators cannot easily be treated as secondary issues. Dwight Waldo put it bluntly: *"These are not irrelevant or captious questions. They are things we are entitled to know about our new Ruling Class."*[14] Seen in this light, public administrators should not escape the general analysis of representation and of the character of representatives offered by the Founders. Particularly in the Federalist scheme, administration is clearly best understood as a *necessary form of politics intrinsic to the regime,* and in Jeremy Rabkin's words, Hamilton, Madison, and Jay "would probably have been astonished by the contemporary notion that the 'goodness or badness' of our 'administration' can be settled by impersonal, nonpolitical standards."[15] In these terms, the contributions of Founding thought to our understanding of the virtues or excellences we may reasonably expect of one class of representatives, public administrators, seem well worth exploring.

Founding Thought and the Character of the American Public Administrator

With the bicentennial of the Constitution, the relationship of Founding thought to public administration has gotten some much deserved attention. The "administrative theories" of Hamilton, Madison, and Jefferson have received renewed scrutiny, particularly in the context of a long-running debate over the constitutional legitimacy of the federal administrative state. Structural analyses, especially those dealing with the separation of powers and representation, also have been popular.

The relevance of Founding thought to matters of administrative conduct, morality, and "ethics" has also surfaced as part of a more general concern with public administration's role in contemporary American society. The commentary in this area contains two general emphases, each of which draws on key aspects of the Founders' unsentimental perspective on public service in the American regime.

The Founders' willingness to contemplate a regime in which self-interest was likely to be a dominant motive has led some to conclude that they intended to rely primarily on constitutional and other mechanisms for "channeling" and "checking" self-interest (including that of public administrators). In its purest form, this approach requires no special or elevated character traits of either elected or appointed public officials; they need only be like everybody else—predictably self-interested *and* capable of learning the virtues of moderation and self-restraint.[16]

Others favor an interpretation that stresses the Founders' hope that their constitutional system would encourage the emergence of a "natural aristocracy" of intelligent and virtuous citizens dedicated to public service and to the preservation of the regime. In Gordon Wood's words, the Federalists "anticipated that somehow the new government would be staffed largely by 'the worthy,' the natural social aristocracy of the country."[17] The implications for public administrators are fairly obvious: They should be disinterested, honorable, and intelligent practitioners of the art and science of government.

Both positions find support in the writings of the Founders and the analyses of those who have studied the intellectual and normative wellsprings of Founding thought. Therefore, the first line of reasoning we examine has its roots in the Founders' belief that the regime would encourage the development of a disinterested and virtuous "natural aristocracy" of governors. We then trace the implications for public administration of the Founders' intention to establish "a republic which did not require a virtuous people for its sustenance."[18] Finally, we attempt to demonstrate that the Founders' realism is based on the assumption that these two perspectives need not be mutually exclusive.

The Disinterested Administrator

Must American public administrators be exceptionally virtuous in order to carry out the political functions the Founders apparently intended for them? Must they be ethically superior to the average citizen? One recent interpretation of the Founding view concludes that public administrators should be held to an elevated standard of "noblesse oblige" or benevolence.

> When one accepts the calling of the public service, it is presumed that one is committed to the American regime values. Since those values must be realized in the character of the individual, the honorable bureaucrat is automatically committed to the quest for moral nobility.... It is in the acceptance of *noblesse oblige* that effective reform and progress is built into the political system. The Founders ... believed that the success of the system would depend upon the virtue of its citizens and honor of its public

servants. An essential characteristic of the honorable bureaucrat is a devotion to *noblesse oblige* —to moral nobility.[19]

This characterization of their ideas implies that the Founders intended to establish a regime that relied heavily on the virtue of its citizens and governors. Accordingly, public administrators and elected representatives should be truly disinterested politicians or statesmen, men and women who may be expected to rise above private interest in order to identify the public interest and to seek the common good.

> The "special relationship" that must exist between public servants and citizens in a democracy is founded upon the conscious knowledge about the citizens that they are loved by the bureaucracy .... [The Founders] believed that the necessary element for the realization of a true democracy was (and is) that both citizens and public servants be possessed of an *extreme and active love for others* —in other words, they possess a sense of benevolence.... [T]he primary duty of public servants is to be the *guardians* and *guarantors* of the regime values for the American public.[20]

In fact, many of the Founders were far from opposed to the cultivation of such an ideal among an elite of political leaders. James MacGregor Burns has described their aspirations as follows:

> [T]hey wanted *virtue* in both leaders and citizens. By virtue they meant at the least good character and civic concern; at the most ... a heroic love for the public good, a devotion to justice, a willingness to sacrifice comfort and riches for the public weal, an elevation of the soul. One reason the Framers believed in representation was that it would refine leadership, acting as a kind of sieve that would separate and elevate the more virtuous elements.[21]

The Federalists' relative optimism on this question was challenged by the Anti-Federalists, who were unconvinced that such a group could effectively represent the broad spectrum of political interests, especially within the framework of an extended republic. As Gordon Wood noted:

> The prevalence of interest and the impossibility of disinterestedness inevitably became a central argument of the Anti-federalists in the debate over the Constitution. Precisely because the Constitution was designed to perpetuate the classical tradition of disinterested leadership in government, the Anti-federalists felt compelled to challenge that tradition.[22]

Thus, in certain important respects, the Founders were not "modern" men in their political thought or social attitudes. They were brought up in a tradition of social and political leadership. They saw government as an instrument for moral improvement, not simply as an institutional mechanism for articulating and compromising a broad spectrum of private interests. Madison, for example, was not a "pluralist" in the contemporary sense of that term. He wanted to see clashing interests or factions neutralize one another, thereby allowing virtuous men to step in and promote the public good—to act as disinterested "umpires" in disputes between interests.[23]

It was the liberally educated, cosmopolitan gentlemen who were generally thought most likely to possess the requisite "virtues" for such disinterested leadership.[24] As a group, the Founders saw leadership or statesmanship as an exceptional quality of "disinterestedness"—of not being influenced by considerations of private gain. "Virtue or disinterestedness, like the concept of honor, lay at the heart of all prescriptions for political leadership in the eighteenth century Anglo-American world."[25] It seems fair to say that the Founders of the American regime anticipated that at least some public administrators would reliably display the admirable traits of noblesse oblige, benevolence, and disinterestedness.

Gordon Wood has also observed that the Founders' elevated standards have influenced our thinking regarding the conduct of public administrators, judges, and elected officials.

> The Founders ... passed on ideals and standards of political behavior that helped to contain and control the unruly materialistic passions unleashed by the democratic revolution of the early nineteenth century. Even today our aversion to corruption, our uneasiness over the too blatant promotion of special interests, and our yearning for examples of unselfish public service suggest that such ideals still have great moral power.[26]

These ideals and standards are central to much of the current discussion of administrative ethics and morality. The public administrator's obligations to the law, public good, colleagues, citizens, and the Constitution are long-standing concerns. The duty to rise above narrow partisanship and self-interest is a dominant theme. Of the public administrator, Paul Appleby wrote in 1952: "Most of all his concern must be with his distinctly public responsibilities."[27]

The highest standards of conduct and an ability to reason in ethical and moral terms are often asked of the individual administrator. For example, in his 1983 argument for an American Society for Public Administration (ASPA) code of ethics, Ralph Clark Chandler observed that "the real decisions of public officials frequently involve ethical choices and the resolution of ethical dilemmas.... An enhanced and self-consciously developed capacity to engage in moral reasoning, and even an occasional glance at a modern version of the Athenian Oath, might help."[28] According to David K. Hart, "public administrators are obligated to serve the first principles upon which the Republic was founded.... This means that all those in the public service, whether through election or employment, must be completely ... committed to those regime values. All public administrators must be moral philosophers and all public administration education must begin with the consideration of regime values."[29]

A related theme, one very much reminiscent of the Founders' guarded optimism regarding the emergence of a "natural aristocracy," takes the form of an obligation to assume a leading role in enhancing the quality of citizenship in a democracy. John Rohr has summarized this prescription as follows: "I would urge the career civil servant to come to terms with his or her role as a part of a governing elite; [and] ... let the career civil servant work at broadening the base of the elite by encouraging as many of the public as possible to become citizens in the classical mold.... The task of the administrator is to invite the participant whose primary concern is quite properly his or her own interest to the higher ground of public interest."[30]

Among those who see a pervasive failure on the part of public administrators to live up to these standards, calls for "revitalization" and reform are not unusual. Hart, for example, identifies a profound "disaffection" among citizens and public servants, and attributes it to a loss of "idealism" in the public service. He states: "In American democracy, *the primary motivation for public service must be a profound commitment to the Founding values of our inception, which includes an extensive and active love of others.* That commitment must be reflected in morally appropriate policies, programs, and behaviors, as they relate to the general public, to specific constituent clients, and to colleagues as well."[31]

These and similar expressions concerning the conduct and character of American public administrators are not at odds with the Founders' belief that the American regime required and would be capable of producing its fair share of virtuous and honorable leaders, including public administrators. Also, such calls for disinterestedness, nobility, and public-spiritedness require that public administrators be held to standards higher than those applied to the average citizen. They embody, therefore, a modern version of the Federalists' belief that a functional equivalent of aristocratic politics could emerge within a democratic republic.

What was needed then, the Federalists argued, was to restore a proper share of political influence to those who through their social attributes *commanded* the respect of the people and who through their enlightenment and education knew the true policy of government.[32]

The Self-Interested Administrator

Nevertheless, there is equally strong evidence to support the conclusion that the Founders never intended to *base* the American regime on citizen virtue and the honor of its administrators. Their writings, and those of serious students of the Founding period, reveal profound reservations about the extent to which Americans could be expected to rise above self-interest and a factional inclination to dominate others. Throughout *The Federalist Papers*, Publius is quite explicit on this point: Selfish passions and interests are usually stronger than public ones—for individuals as well as groups. Publius was "too 'realistic' to believe that each citizen was moved by the idea that it would be in his true interest to do what is in the true interest of the nation."[33]

> These were no garden-variety eighteenth century ideologues flattering themselves they had an option to create a utopia. Knowing that they could neither stop history nor command it, these Founders turned their thoughts to identifying sources of danger without fancying that they might overcome those dangers once and for all.[34]

By 1787, the Federalists were convinced that the American character would not long support ‿ classical republic (or confederation of republics) *based on* widespread public virtue. The years under the Articles of Confederation had provided many reasons to doubt that proposition. The historical record, as well as the writings of those who attended the Constitutional Convention and participated in the ratification debates, reveals a pervasive *disappointment* with the results of the postrevolutionary experiment in highly democratic, legislatively dominated state governments. Throughout the Confederation, the pursuit of self-interest was the norm, and the Founders were quick to identify a potentially fatal mismatch between the optimistic assumptions regarding citizen character that underpinned the new American "republics" and the reality that had emerged since 1776.[35] They "had learned that it was *foolish* to expect most people to sacrifice their private interests for the sake of the public welfare."[36] There is no evidence whatsoever that the Founders were at all inclined to exclude public administrators from this general observation.

> [They] shared a profound distrust of man's capacity to use power wisely and well. They believed self-interest to be the dominant motive of political behavior, no matter whether the form of government be republican or monarchical, and they believed in the necessity of constructing political machinery that would restrict the operation of self-interest and prevent men entrusted with political power from abusing it. This was the fundamental assumption of the men who wrote the Constitution, and of those who opposed its adoption, as well.[37]

In this context, Morton White has observed that James Madison sought to restrain the tyrannical inclinations of administrators through the separation of powers.

> Madison's belief that this internal division of the government would be effective—to some extent—in controlling the government was ... compatible with his belief that ... the tyrannical impulses of individual administrators would not be restrained merely by the motives of prudence, reputation and conscience. The internal control which Madison thought would *not* restrain members of factious majorities was therefore quite different from the internal control he thought *would*—to some extent—restrain tyrants by preventing one part of the interior structure of the government from dominating the others.... [W]hat prudence, reputation, and conscience could not do *within the mind* of a man of factious temper, separation of powers might to some extent accomplish within the government.[38]

These are not the expressions of men who thought public administrators could be *relied on* to be disinterested. There is also little, if any, evidence here that public administrators were expected to be consistent guardians of higher virtues. This other side of the Founders' line of reasoning reveals an intention to establish a regime based, as Hamilton said, on human nature as they saw it, not as they might *wish* it to be. This low but solid foundation allowed them to envision a regime that would require very little active supervision by administrative guardians "fitted to perform the function of ruling."[39]

Wood has characterized this facet of the Founders' thinking in the following terms:

> The Federalists hoped to create an entirely new and original sort of republican government—a republic which did not require a virtuous people for its sustenance. If they could not, as they thought, really reform the character of American society, then they would somehow have to influence the operation of the society and moderate the effects of its viciousness.[40]

It seems reasonable to conclude, therefore, that the Founders anticipated that public administration in the American regime would be an enterprise conducted more often than not by self-interested citizens. The challenge was not to change this reality but to recognize it and seek institutional and other ways of channeling it into habits of mind and action that would rather consistently serve the common good and protect the republic.[41]

The Founders' unwillingness to *rely* on citizen virtue and the presence of disinterested officeholders is reflected in the literature on public administration, much of which deals with external controls. Administrative and bureaucratic theory devote much attention to matters of hierarchy, authority, accountability, and management-control systems. Politically, there is an enduring concern with questions regarding the implications for public administration of the constitutional separation of powers. As a field of inquiry, bureaucratic politics is as much concerned with the mechanisms by which interest-group pluralism limits the power of individual agencies as it is with sources of bureaucratic power. Statutory, structural, and procedural checks on the exercise of executive power and administrative discretion have received considerable attention. Judicial review, legislative oversight, open administrative rulemaking procedures, and merit-based personnel systems routinely are examined in relation to their capacities to restrain effectively the self-interested ambitions of administrators. Each of these concerns, in its own way, is an admission that Publius was correct in his assertion that "framing a government which is to be administered by men over men, the great difficulty lies in this: you must first enable the government to control the governed; and in the next place oblige it to control itself. A dependence on the people is, no doubt, the primary control on the government; but experience has taught mankind the necessity of auxiliary precautions."[42]

A related but relatively new development is the attention being paid to the functions of codes of ethics for public servants. At least by implication, such codes accept Publius's view that "men" are not "angels." In essence, codes such as the one set forth by ASPA are based on the premise that public servants should be held accountable to a set of "objective" values or standards of conduct. Moral relativism and autonomy are balanced by an *external* authority—the code of ethics and the reasoning behind it—that compensates for a potential lack of reliable *internal* virtues.

According to Chandler, codes of ethics serve two primary functions, both of which may be seen as falling within the category of necessary "auxiliary precautions." First, they provide specific criteria for judging the conduct of individual public administrators and, when violations occur, establish grounds for appropriate discipline by the professional or political community. Second, they are guides to action and choice that, if followed, are intended to help the individual better serve the common good. Character, as an attribute of the person, is not a particularly relevant concept, because *doing good* does not require that one *be good*. As Chandler puts it, "we do good acts because they have been prescribed by the requirements of virtue, good manners, the revealed word of God, tradition, the elders, the common law, the Constitution, or some other source of transcendent authority; and in the process of doing good acts, we become good."[43]

The Founders were explicit in their opposition to any effort to establish the American regime on a foundation of exemplary citizen virtue, instinctive benevolence, or reliably disinterested leadership. As Martin Diamond has observed, the Founders were distinctly modern in their approach:

> [F]or modern political thought—because making the motives better, that is forming the human excellences, was no longer the primary end of politics [as it had been for the ancients]—a different prospect was opened. The chief political end had become commodious self-preservation, with the higher human matters left to the workings of society. It thus became possible to conceive of interested behavior as a general substitute for the too-hard-to-come-by "better motives."[44]

To the extent that constitutional, organizational, legal, political, and other ways of improving the chances that public servants will act in a manner that advances the public good have been central concerns, American public administration has conformed to Founding precepts. Similarly, its often noted failure to become a social class or "natural aristocracy" is not, in and of itself, an apparent threat to the relatively "solid but low foundation" of the regime established by the Founders.[45]

At its worst, the public service in America has employed a disproportionate number of "the selfish, the interested, the narrow, the vulgar, and the crassly economic."[46] During the best of times, it has employed large numbers of moderate, honest, hard-working, decent persons who have learned, in Alexis de Tocqueville's terms, to practice "self-interest properly understood."[47] This, as well, is a logical outcome of the Founders' success in creating a republic capable of restraining the pursuit of self-interest and of channeling it toward socially beneficial consequences. Of course, neither condition approaches governance by the truly disinterested and benevolent.

The Realism of the Founders

What, then, do the Founders have to teach us about the ethical foundations of public administration in the American regime? On the one hand, they seem to be saying that a "natural aristocracy" of talent and virtue should govern and, at least by implication, that public administrators should be important members of that elite. Is the American regime at an impasse, in moral crisis, because we have not cultivated, or have lost, a class of administrators who are consistently benevolent, public spirited, and disinterested? Is a radical reformation of the public administrator's character required?

On the other hand, they are even more adamant in their insistence on a regime that, once established, should not require for its maintenance anything approaching this elevated standard. Is the current situation one that the Founders would have judged acceptable, perhaps even commendable? After all, by the standards of its past and in comparison to its counterparts in many other nations, the American public service is relatively well educated and trained, nonpartisan, hard-working, honest, and technically competent. Should efforts at improvement therefore concentrate on a further elaboration of the system of separation of powers, checks, balances, and other shrewd "devices" upon which the Founders relied to control and moderate the actions of self-interested citizens and governors?

One way to approach these questions is to reconstruct in general terms how the Founders dealt with them and, in so doing, framed a constitution designed to preserve liberty, prevent tyranny, and "encourage virtue among both leaders and followers."[48] The keys to their logic appear to be the following: First, elites as well as majorities, being often selfish and inclined to tyrannize others, pose a constant threat to domestic tranquility, liberty, and justice. Second, given that it is the norm for people to be self-interested, any republic created as the moral or ethical "instrument" of an elite or faction is likely to become a tyranny as that group seeks to eliminate different interests and opinions, and to control the process of character formation. Third, as a consequence, any American elite or leadership aristocracy that arises must do so in the context of a republic framed by a Constitution that establishes justice and protects liberty.

Therefore, if disinterested or morally elevated administration was to emerge in the American regime, the Founding perspective required that it be deeply rooted in both the normal operation of the regime and the existing character of its citizens. Martin Diamond addressed this point in a critique of Richard Hofstadter's argument that the Founders' idea of human nature should be revised along "humanistic" lines, thereby allowing the establishment of a more ennobling political system.

> Hofstadter's entire criticism of the American Founding rests upon his apparent certainty that it is going to be possible 'to change the nature of man to conform with a more ideal system.' ... He seems to take from the Aristotelian enterprise something of the elevation to which virtue is thought capable of reaching but strips it of its corollary severity and inegalitarianism; and this 'high toned' expectation regarding virtue he apparently combines with the democracy and commodious well-being of Madison's enterprise, but strips it of *its* corollary, the foundation in the system of opposite and rival interests. Such complacent synthesizing or combining of irreconcilables is the hallmark of contemporary utopianism.[49]

For American public administration, the implications seem fairly clear. Whatever excellences of character are asked of the administrator, or asked by the administrator of the citizen, must rest squarely on the regime's foundation. More precisely, they should *visibly* be connected to the expectations comprising that foundation and to a political constitution intended "to obtain for rulers men who possess most wisdom to discern, and most virtue to pursue, the common good.... " Clearly, some of the Founders were optimistic that such a natural aristocracy would be "obtained" within the framework of the Constitution. Thomas Jefferson, for example, is particularly well known for his belief that an aristocracy of merit could be developed and that Americans would consent to be governed by this elite.[50] Their concept of democracy "never denied the unequal existence of human virtues or excellences; it only denied the ancient claim of excellence to *rule as a matter of right.*" In America, merit (broadly defined) would often be rewarded with public office (far more so than it was in societies ruled by "artificial aristocracies"). But in the American regime, excellence—a natural aristocracy—could rule only through popular consent.[51]

Seen in this light, contemporary calls for public spiritedness, honor, and noblesse oblige are responses to an apparently increasing reluctance to believe that public administrators have "earned" the people's trust. Terrence Mitchell and William Scott have observed that the modern administrative state creates conditions under which the public "has had to rely on administrative *noblesse oblige* in the sense that the positions administrators hold will impose on them obligations to discharge faithfully and justly their stewardship responsibilities.... The crisis in confidence may indicate that the public no longer believes that administrators are responsibly exercising their stewardship."[52] Thus, as Mitchell and Scott suggest, calls for moral reform are not so much arguments for an elevation above what the Founders sought as they are efforts to preserve (and perhaps extend) the basis of the administrator's authorization to govern within the institutional system established under the Constitution. There would seem to be, accordingly, no compelling reason for the authors of calls for ethical or moral reform to disassociate them (fully or in part) from Founding precepts or the purposes of the Constitution.

Remaining within the Founders' framework requires that efforts to justify administrative power and discretion be balanced fully by a concern with "effectual precautions for keeping them [administrators] virtuous whilst they continue to hold their public trust." The most effectual precaution, of course, is to assume that people are self-interested and moved by a variety of motives, only some of which are likely to be realized through serving the public good.[53] Public administrators are not—must not be—excluded from this assumption. Otherwise they pose, at least potentially, a grave threat to the regime. Thus, a wide array of effective institutional, legal, procedural, professional, and popular restraints (including a healthy skepticism) is necessary.

It is, however, important to recognize that the Founders did not see their efforts to channel and restrain the exercise of self-interest as an essentially negative enterprise. They sought precautions that would do far more than simply *control* "knaves" and "beasts" because they believed most Americans often were capable of much better. Probably the best way to describe their purpose is indirect and rather gentle "encouragement" or "support" of those virtues and habits that promote the common good. Paul Appleby reflected this point of view when he wrote the following about the individual public administrator:

> If our concern with moral performance were to take the exclusive form of insisting upon moral quality on the part of all individuals engaged in the public service, we could not thereby ensure the quality of performance we had sought. It is also true that if we had the most admirable system of organized performance, but permitted it to be operated by the weak and corrupt, our system would produce very inferior performance. Individuals with moral purpose and strength are important, and systematic organizational structure and processes in support of moral performance are important.[54]

Conclusion

The Founders of the American regime were stubbornly unsentimental in their insistence that the survival of the republic not be *dependent* on a highly virtuous citizenry led by disinterested governors. They were optimistic that the regime would produce many virtuous citizens and leaders, but did not seek to impose a political elite to oversee that process. Character formation was left to the workings of institutional arrangements, representative democracy, and the realms of family, school, and community. The Founders' America, in other words, is one in which public administrators are *encouraged* to be disinterested and benevolent servants of the public interest. It is not *assumed* that they will be. Also, it seems fair to conclude that the Founders *hoped* that those who held public office would seek to promote (not command) the moral elevation of the citizenry. They did not *depend* on it. In the final analysis, the Constitution was intended to be both the elevating device and the means of assuring that all who seek to govern—including public administrators—must do so with popular consent, no matter how virtuous or benevolent they might be.

The contemporary concern with administrative ethics and the role of public administrators under the Constitution is an important development, in part because it focuses attention on a fundamental question that has been a part of the study of public administration since Wilson's 1887 essay, namely, Is it possible to meaningfully separate the enterprise of public administration from that of politics?

In "The Study of Administration," Wilson asserts that "administrative questions are not political questions."[55] He goes on, however, to note that the line of demarcation between constitutional and administrative "questions" is more difficult to draw.[56] Nonetheless, he tries to draw that line. First, "no administration, however perfect and liberal its methods, can give men more than a poor counterfeit of liberty if it rest upon illiberal principles of government."[57] Second, public administration is the detailed execution of public law. Third, public administration may assist constitutional study by "discovering" efficient as well as effective ways of distributing constitutional authority, but this is only an "overlap" of two distinct fields of study.[58] Wilson then proceeds to argue that the comparative study of public administration is "safe" because of the distinction between administration and politics. Safe, that is, from the risk that we might "blindly borrow something incompatible with our principles."[59] Finally, Wilson essentially repudiates the dichotomy he has, in this essay, labored to establish as a foundation for a science of administration.

> We can borrow the science of administration with safety and profit if only we read all fundamental differences of condition into its essential tenets. We have only to filter it through our constitution, only to put it over a slow fire of criticism and distil away its foreign gases.[60]

After saying that we may learn to sharpen knives "cleverly" without "borrowing" murderous intent, he states: "Our own politics must be the touchstone for all theories. The principles upon which to base a science of administration for America must be principles which have democratic policy very much at heart."[61]

"The Study of Administration," considered by some to be the Founding document of a self-aware study of public administration, contains a series of irreconcilable statements about the separability of politics and administration. Wilson later disavowed any such dichotomy, but in certain respects the field is still in the grip of his 1887 puzzlement: How can the study of public administration be distinguished from the study of politics and constitutions without producing a "science" that is trivial or is disconnected from the foundations of the regime?[62] Current treatments of administrative ethics and character are no exception. To the degree that they do not squarely confront the challenge of the Founders' clear-eyed refusal to split politics from administration, they allow public administrators to escape the logic and the requirements of the Constitutional design. From the Founding perspective, the Constitution and the regime it frames must be the "touchstones" for any meaningful inquiry into this vital area. Otherwise, we will continually be at risk of "blindly borrow[ing] something incompatible with our principles."

Notes

1. Gordon Wood, "Interests and Disinterestedness in the Making of the Constitution," in Richard Beeman, Stephen Botein, and Edward C. Carter II, *Beyond Confederation: Origins of the Constitution and American National Identity* (Chapel Hill: University of North Carolina Press, 1987), 82.

2. Ralph Lerner, "The Constitution of the Thinking Revolutionary," in Beeman et al., *Beyond Confederation*, 59.

3. *The Federalist Papers* (New York: New American Library, 1961). As used in this work, "Founders" is intended to include both "Federalists" and "Anti-Federalists." In short, we are drawing on the works of individuals who could be perceived as having had a significant influence on the issues discussed at the Constitutional Convention, whether they were on the "winning" (Federalist) side or not. For a treatment of the significance of this approach, see Herbert J. Storing, *What the Anti-Federalists Were For: The Political Thought of the Opponents of the Constitution* (Chicago: University of Chicago Press, 1981). Additionally, we want to emphasize that the present study seriously attempts to understand what the Founders thought about public services *and* to use that understanding as a standard to assess contemporary issues associated with such service.

4. John Rohr, "The Constitution and Public Service," in *The Constitution and the Administration of Government, Proceedings of the National Academy of Public Administration*, ed. Gary C. Bryner (Washington, D.C.: NAPA, April 1988), 58.

5. *Federalist Papers*, nos. 1–4; and Storing, *What the Anti-Federalists Were For*, 42–43.

6. *Federalist Papers*, 435.

7. J. Rabkin, "Bureaucractic Idealism and Executive Power: A Perspective on the Federalists' View of Public Administration," in *Saving the Revolution: The Federalist Papers and the American Founding*, ed. C. Kesler (New York: Free Press, 1987), 196–98.

8. Gordon Wood, *The Creation of the American Republic, 1776–1787* (New York: Norton, 1969), 546.

9. Ibid., 598.

10. R.D. Miewald, "The Origins of Wilson's Thought—The German Tradition and the Organic State," in *Politics and Administration: Woodrow Wilson and American Public Administration*, ed. J. Rabin and J.S. Bowman (New York: Dekker, 1984), 24–25.

11. D.W. Martin, "The Fading Legacy of Woodrow Wilson," *Public Administration Review* 48 (March/April 1988): 634–35; and Dwight Waldo, *The Administrative State* (New York: Ronald Press, 1948), 97–100.

12. Miewald, "Origins of Wilson's Thought," 27–28.

13. Ibid., 27.

14. Waldo, *Administrative State*, 102. Italics in original.

15. Rabkin, "Bureaucratic Idealism," 202.

16. Robert Goldwin, "Of Men and Angels: The Search for Morality in the

Constitution," in *The Moral Foundations of the American Republic,* 2d ed., ed. Robert Horwitz (Charlottesville: University Press of Virginia, 1979), 9–12.

17. Wood, *Creation of the American Republic,* 508.

18. Ibid., 475.

19. David K. Hart, "The Virtuous Citizen, the Honorable Bureaucrat, and 'Public' Administration," *Public Administration Review* 44 (March 1984): 118.

20. H. George Frederickson and David K. Hart, "The Public Service and the Patriotism of Benevolence," *Public Administration Review* 45 (September/October 1985): 549–51.

21. James MacGregor Burns, *The Vineyard of Liberty* (New York: Vintage Books, 1983), 62.

22. Wood, "Interests and Disinterestedness," 101.

23. Ibid., 92.

24. Ibid., 85.

25. Ibid., 84.

26. Ibid., 109.

27. Paul Appleby, *Morality and Administration* (New York: Greenwood Press, 1952), 40.

28. Ralph Clark Chandler, "The Problem of Moral Reasoning in American Public Administration: The Case for a Code of Ethics," *Public Administration Review* 43 (January/February 1983): 37.

29. David K. Hart, "The Honorable Bureaucrat among the Philistines," *Administration and Society* 15 (May 1983): 44.

30. John Rohr, "Civil Servants and Second-Class Citizens," *Public Administration Review* 44 (March 1984): 139–40.

31. David K. Hart, "Public Administration, The Thoughtless Functionary, and Feelinglessness," in *The Revitalization of the Public Service,* ed. Robert B. Denhardt and Edward T. Jennings (Columbia: University of Missouri–Columbia Extension Publications, 1987), 78.

32. Wood, *Creation of the American Republic,* 508. Italics added.

33. Morton White, *Philosophy, The Federalist, and The Constitution* (New York: Oxford University Press, 1987), 122.

34. Lerner, "Constitution of Thinking Revolutionary," 65.

35. Wood, "Interests and Disinterestedness," 81.

36. Ibid., 82. Italics added.

37. Cecilia M. Kenyon, "Men of Little Faith: The Anti-Federalists on the Nature of Representative Government," in *The Formation and Ratification of the Constitution,* ed. Kermit Hall (New York: Garland, 1987), 383.

38. White, *Philosophy,* 202–3. See also Hamilton's unambiguous assessment of men in L. Caldwell, *The Administrative Theories of Hamilton and Jefferson* (Chicago: University of Chicago Press, 1944), 13.

39. Waldo, *Administrative State,* 100.

40. Wood, *Creation of the American Republic,* 475.

41. Martin Diamond, "Ethics and Politics: The American Way," in *The Moral Foundations of the American Republic,* 2d ed., 47.

42. *Federalist Papers,* 322.

43. Chandler, "Problem of Moral Reasoning," 37.

44. Diamond, 58.

45. Ibid., 59.

46. Ibid.

47. Alexis de Tocqueville, *Democracy in America* (New York: Anchor Books, 1969), 525–28.

48. Burns, *Vineyard of Liberty,* 60.

49. Diamond, 62. Italics added. Cf. David K. Hart, "A Partnership in Virtue among All Citizens: The Public Service and Civic Humanism," *Public Administration Review* 49 (March/April 1989): 101–5.

50. Thomas Jefferson, *Notes on the State of Virginia,* ed. William Peden (New York: Norton, 1972), 146–49. For a discussion of Jefferson's plan for annually selecting and educating a small number of "geniuses" for public service, see William D. Richardson and Lloyd G. Nigro, "Administrative Ethics and Founding Thought: Constitutional Correctives, Honor, and Education," *Public Administration Review* 47 (September/October 1987): 373.

51. Diamond, 67.

52. Terrence R. Mitchell and William G. Scott, "Leadership Failures, the Distrusting Public, and Prospects of the Administrative State," *Public Administration Review* 47 (November/December 1987): 450.

53. White, *Philosophy,* 98–99.

54. Appleby, *Morality and Administration,* 220.

55. Woodrow Wilson, "The Study of Administration," in *Public Administration: Politics and the People,* ed. Dean Yarwood (New York: Longman, 1987), 24.

56. Ibid., 24–25.

57. Ibid., 25.

58. Ibid., 25–26.

59. Ibid., 28.

60. Ibid.

61. Ibid., 29.

62. John Rohr, *Ethics For Bureaucrats,* 2d ed. (New York: Dekker, 1989), 30–34.

PART TWO

Political Issues

2

The Hatch Act and the Contemporary Public Service

PETER M. BENDA AND DAVID H. ROSENBLOOM

The first Hatch Act (1939) has been controversial ever since its incubation began in the U.S. Senate in 1935. The act's constitutionality was upheld over significant dissent in *United Public Workers v. Mitchell* (1947) and in *Civil Service Commission v. National Association of Letter Carriers* (1973), but over the years it has been modified and subject to many calls for fundamental revisions. Today, the act is once again the topic of substantial legislative debate. Although examining the act's history and present status is intrinsically interesting for those concerned with public administration, it is an exercise that yields much more because the Hatch Act is based on particular concepts of what a public employee and a public service should be. Analyzing the act in its broader political and administrative contexts, as well as the contemporary debate surrounding it, provides a better understanding of the models on which a public service for the twenty-first century might be based. At a time when "rebuilding the public service" is very much on the political agenda, such an understanding is clearly of great potential importance.

The Public-Service Concept Embodied in the Act

The Hatch Act originally was based on a reasonably coherent concept of what a public service should *not* be. When Senator Carl Hatch (D-N.M.) introduced his bill, the purposes were "to prevent the use of Federal official patronage in elections and to prohibit Federal officeholders from misuse of positions of public trust for private and partisan ends."[1] He feared, in particular, that the expansion of federal employment during the New Deal could be used to weaken intraparty competition: "When I look out over the country, and observe the vast, vast numbers of Federal employees who reach out and extend to every county and to every precinct in the United States, I realize that some ... [presidential] administration ... could absolutely control any political convention in which Representatives, Senators, or even a President were to be nominated."[2] He also thought that a partisan-based public service would distribute federal largesse to its own advantage. Thus, it was his "firm judgment and belief that if we build up a system by which we can use funds from the Public Treasury to control the votes of the people of the Nation it is no exaggeration to say that the moment that is done democracy in American is dead."[3]

Thus Senator Hatch wanted to prevent public employees and the public service from reverting to the status of an arm of the dominant political party, as they had been from 1829 to 1883 when the spoils system reigned supreme. In this respect, Hatch's model of the public service was a logical extension of that developed by nineteenth-century civil service reformers. The reformers' chief concern was preventing political machines and bosses from using the public service for their own partisan ends. As George William Curtis, a leader of the reformers, expressed it, "the tap root of the evils and abuses which reform would destroy is the partisan prostitution of the civil service."[4] The reformers were successful in encouraging Presidents Hayes, Cleveland, and Theodore Roosevelt to propound executive orders for political neutrality. The most important of these was Roosevelt's amendment of Civil Service Rule I, in 1907, which was very similar in wording to the language incorporated into the Hatch Act: "persons who by the provisions of these rules are in the competitive classified service, while retaining the right to vote as they please and to express in private their opinions on all political subjects, shall take no active part in political management or in political campaigns."[5] Section 9(a) of the Hatch Act essentially restated Civil Service Rule I (the qualifying "in private" language was deleted) and extended its coverage to the entire federal service.[6]

Modifying the Act: A Frequent Quest

Over the years, the Hatch Act has been subject to much criticism, two major constitutional challenges before the Supreme Court,[7] and a variety of legislative efforts to modify its restrictions. In 1976, the act was given a reprieve in the form of President Gerald Ford's veto of a bill that would have substantially reduced its restrictions on the political activities of federal employees. A decade later, new legislative initiatives to revise it began to make serious headway. Why has the Hatch Act been problematic?

In 1966, Congress established a Commission on Political Activity of Government Personnel to study the Hatch Act and related laws that "discourage the participation of Federal or state officers and employees in political activity."[8] The commission concluded that the Hatch Act's attempt to balance two competing objectives dictated that it would always be subject to substantial opposition:

First, a democratic society depends for strength and vitality upon broadly based citizen participation in the political processes of the Nation, and governments are responsible for granting their citizens the constitutional rights of free speech and association.

Second, to assure the honest, impartial, and efficient transaction of the public's business, a democratic society equally needs a government that functions with a permanent system of employment under which persons are hired, paid, promoted, and dismissed on the basis of merit rather than political favoritism. Some conflict is inevitable between these two goals since neither can be fully achieved without some loss to the other.[9]

Additionally, the commission noted that the Hatch Act was vulnerable to criticism because of its vagueness:

Employee uncertainty as to what is right and wrong under the law governing political activity is hardly surprising since the Hatch Act incorporates by a single sentence all of the Civil Service Commission rulings and decisions issued prior to adoption of the act. This means that a working knowledge of the law requires one to be familiar with the approximately 3,000 decisions issued by the Civil Service Commission between 1907 and 1939. With such a mass of information, few public employees can be sure about their status under the law. Civil Service Commission Pamphlet No. 20 purports to be a compilation and summary of this information, but its language is unclear at several points. Certainly, the pamphlet assumes too much when it states that each employee "is presumed to be acquainted with the legal provisions applicable to him, and his ignorance of them will not excuse a violation."[10]

Based on these observations, the commission concluded that the time had come "to expand, within limits, the area of political activity permitted for Federal employees."[11] But the commission's proposed bill was never adopted, and some two decades later, the basic issues it addressed have yet to be resolved in favor of change.

Today, as in the 1960s and 1970s, calls for fundamental change of the Hatch Act are based on the belief that it is too restrictive and ambiguous in its proscriptions. But nowadays there is also a serious underlying concern with the plight of unionized federal employees. Unlike workers in the private sector and many nonfederal public jurisdictions, most federal employees cannot bargain over wages and hours—postal workers are a major exception—and none of them can legally strike. The narrow scope of bargaining, coupled with the lack of "muscle" that a right to engage in concerted job activity provides, has encouraged unions representing federal employees to focus much of their effort on lobbying Congress for better working conditions and higher pay. The unions could benefit greatly if their federally employed members were turned loose to campaign on behalf of or, less likely, against congressional incumbents. As Representative Patricia Schroeder (D-Colo.), long a leading proponent of Hatch Act reform, observed in 1988: "The last seven years have demonstrated just how politically weak Federal employees are. Their wages have not kept pace with the private sector. Whenever deficit reduction comes up, cuts in civil service pay adjustments, reductions in health benefits, and delays in civil service retirement COLAs are the first things to be placed on the table. *Permitting Federal employees to participate in politics might make politicians think twice before going after them for more budget cuts.*"[12]

This is a major political matter underlying the contemporary debate on the Hatch Act. No wonder that two Republican presidents—Ford and Ronald Reagan—were arch opponents of reform ("pro-Hatchers"), while union leaders and members of Congress whose districts include large numbers of federal employees have been major proponents of change ("un-Hatchers"). Even if much of the issue is about partisan or political advantage, however, the pro-Hatchers and un-Hatchers couch their perspectives in terms that promote a better understanding of how contemporary public officials and political activists view federal employees and the federal service.

Alternative Models of Political Neutrality

From a contemporary perspective, it is somewhat surprising that the primary justification for the Hatch Act, in the view of its sponsor, was neither the promotion of efficiency nor the constitutional desirability of having a politically neutral public service at the service of the public as a whole. Although the efficiency criterion was a secondary concern for the reformers and Senator Hatch, it was later considered primary by the U.S. Supreme Court. In *United Public Workers,* the first challenge to the Hatch Act to reach it, the Court reasoned that the statute "forbids only the partisan activity of federal personnel deemed offensive to efficiency."[13]

Yet an efficiency argument, coupled with a commitment to promoting the public interest in a narrowly tailored fashion or by the means least restrictive of individuals' constitutional rights, could well yield a different statute. For example, banning all partisan displays at work or on federal property could easily prevent partisan exhibitions from interfering with the efficiency of the service, while leaving federal employees free to campaign on their own time for the parties of their choice.

By contrast, a constitutional model of the public service might yield a result that is closer to the Hatch Act, but not identical to it. Such a model was first articulated by President Jefferson in 1801. Jefferson issued a circular declaring that "it is expected that [public officers] will not attempt to influence the votes of others [members of the public], nor take any part in the business of electioneering, that being deemed inconsistent with the spirit of the Constitution and his duties to it."[14] A constitutional model of the public service is at ease with banning all overt displays of partisanship by federal employees, whether on the job or off duty. It might also make distinctions with regard to the level and functions of employees. Certainly not all federal employees are equally situated to do damage to the Constitution's interest in a public service not tinged with partisanship or merely the extension of a political party. For example, in *United Public Workers,* one employee challenging the Hatch Act was a roller in the mint. It is an open question whether a constitutional model can reasonably justify preventing such an employee from exercising political rights deemed highly virtuous when exercised by ordinary citizens. At any rate, the constitutional model is certainly less convincing in this regard than the justification for the Hatch Act based on the fear that federal employees might form the basis of a giant political machine or that their partisan displays might interfere with working relationships and efficiency.

There is another dimension to these differences. If one adopts the political machine perspective of Hatch and the civil service reformers before him, it is perfectly logical to outlaw federal employee participation in partisan electioneering and campaigning on the ground that such a proscription is the best (and only effective) means of protecting civil servants from being coerced into performing partisan acts, including donating money. In contrast, if efficiency or the constitutional model forms the basis for political neutrality, one would not necessarily begin from the premise that such coercion would be a genuine problem. Under the constitutional model especially, public policy could determine which groups of federal employees should be allowed to engage in partisan activity and then deal with the potential problem of coercion directly, by effectively outlawing coercion itself rather than the political activities. The constitutional model, like the political machine model, might prohibit federal employees from making financial contributions to parties on the ground that any deviation from strict neutrality could impair the service's dedication to the public interest. But it is difficult to see why, in the absence of coercion, efficiency would be reduced if employees were voluntarily to donate money to parties, even in the workplace, if this was not done in an overt display of partisanship.

The Act Today

Of the three rationales for political neutrality discussed above, that of preventing the rise of a giant political machine based on the coerced partisan activity of federal employees fares least well today. Senator Hatch was looking at a political landscape that included a strong president supported by Congress and relatively strong political parties. Since 1969, however, it has been far more common for the nation to have a Republican president and a Democratically controlled Congress. Under such conditions, support for, and the reality of, a strong presidency in domestic affairs is very difficult to sustain. Could Presidents Nixon or Reagan have attempted to turn the federal service into a political machine for the election of Republicans without inviting a swift and devastating response from a Congress dominated by Democrats? Could Bush do so now? Yet there is good reason to believe, along with Morris Fiorina, that "the Decline of Collective Responsibility" caused by the partisan split between the president and Congress is now a normal condition of American politics.[15]

Even should the presidency and Congress be controlled by the same party, as was true under President Carter, the prospects for the development of a giant political machine are very much dimmed by the weak condition of both political parties. Walter Dean Burnham argues that the decline in voter turnout is not merely evidence of the weakening of political parties but part of an overall "decomposition of the American political regime."[16] The vast weakening of party identification and loyalty since the 1930s also makes it unlikely that political machines could be resurrected on the backs of federal employees. More likely, old-style machine-based political parties are truly passé. Partisanship is far less important to the public and to members of Congress, whose incumbency is now less tied to programmatic policy stands than to constituency service and the pork barrel.[17]

Taken together, the decline of collective responsibility and political parties makes the partisan coercion of federal employees to engage in political activities and form a giant machine very unlikely—indeed, almost absurd. But the prospects for such coercion are weakened even further by two additional developments. First, based on the Supreme Court's rulings in *Elrod* v. *Burns* (1976)[18] and *Branti* v. *Finkel* (1980),[19] patronage dismissals from the vast majority of federal jobs would be unconstitutional and would potentially subject those engaging in attempts at coercion to discipline. Second, and perhaps more important, the administrative mechanisms available today, such as elaborate adverse action hearing systems and the Special Counsel at the Merit Systems Protection Board (MSPB), are far stronger and more sophisticated than anything available in 1939.[20] (In fact, the extension of rudimentary but modern due process protections to federal employees in dismissals did not begin until the enactment of the Veterans Preference Act of 1944.) The availability of these elaborate procedural safeguards against arbitrary dismissals and other "prohibited personnel practices" alone would seem to cast considerable doubt on the claim that relaxation of the Hatch Act's proscriptions on partisan activity might issue in the re-creation of old-style political machines. Representative Stephen Solarz

(D-N.Y.) delivered a persuasive rejoinder to the argument offered in recent testimony by Constance Horner, Office of Personnel Management director during Reagan's second term: "While one could conceive that there may be an isolated instance here or there where somebody is forced to participate in a campaign against their [*sic*] will, it is literally inconceivable, given all of [the] restrictions and prohibitions against coercion [now in place], that anybody who wanted to could possibly transform the Federal Civil Service into a political machine."[21]

In sum, the original rationale for the Hatch Act has been weakened substantially by political and administrative developments over the intervening half century. A statute as invasive of constitutional rights as the Hatch Act is not now necessary to assure that federal employees will not be organized into a giant political machine.[22]

There is almost no prospect of that, and there are other adequate defenses against whatever prospect there may be. Whether a persuasive case can be made for the Hatch Act today would seem to depend on the development of a different concept or model of what federal employees and the public service should or should not be.

The Pro-Hatcher Model: Additional Rationales for the Act

If the political-machine perspective is no longer apposite, neither are there substantial grounds for concern today that lifting prohibitions on public employees' off-duty partisan political activities would adversely affect governmental efficiency. To their credit, for latter-day defenders of his handiwork, as for Senator Hatch, the efficiency criterion has been, at best, a secondary concern. But contemporary pro-Hatchers have made little headway toward filling the resulting void by attempting to elaborate a more fleshed-out constitutional or other model of political neutrality that might withstand critical scrutiny. They have instead offered a series of discrete arguments against an easing of the act's restrictions, several of which seem to rest on empirical propositions (projections or predictions) only slightly less dubious than the political-machine argument.

One important such proposition, closely related to, but logically distinguishable from, the machine argument, is the claim that federal employees would be considerably more vulnerable to supervisor coercion were current restrictions on their partisan political activities relaxed. In the eyes of pro-Hatchers, it is illusory to suppose that the safeguards now in place—or even the more specific prohibitions and the tougher sanctions reformers have proposed[23]—would provide a sufficient deterrent in this context. As one prominent Reagan administration official put it, "an absolute ban on party electioneering and politicking is the only genuine protection employees have against the subtle pressures that are outside the reach of any anti-coercion statute."[24]

From the point of view of three senators opposed to reform, the reasons for this are rooted in "human nature":

> Once employees are free to engage in partisan political activity, it will only be human nature for them to believe that it would please their politically appointed superior to exercise their new political rights ... in a manner that pleases the superior. It will only be human nature for employees to aspire to promotions and salary increases. It will only be human nature for employees to try to get an edge on their competition by engaging in the partisan politics of their superior. It will only be human nature for other employees who had not engaged in the partisan politics of the superior to feel it is necessary to do so to eliminate the edge of their competitors.[25]

These irreducible predilections of human nature suggest that the Supreme Court was correct in supporting the historic judgment that the Hatch Act provides the only reliable means of shielding government employees from "express or tacit invitation to vote in a certain way or perform political chores in order to curry favor with their supervisor rather than to act out of their own belief."[26] If the un-Hatchers fail to appreciate this point, the same cannot be said of many whose cause they purport to champion. As the general counsel of the Civil Service Commission noted in commenting on an earlier reform bill, "many Federal employees read the Hatch Act very broadly in order to protect themselves from what they perceive to be political pressure. They are able to say 'I'm Hatched' even in circumstances in which the Act may not apply, and by so doing to ward off attempts to have them engage in political activity."[27]

To these arguments, un-Hatchers might respond that while the Hatch Act has no doubt served a useful prophylactic purpose at times, there is simply no evidence to support the claim that relaxation of its prohibitions would leave federal employees significantly more exposed (or at risk) to greater levels or new, more insidious forms of supervisor coercion.[28] Evidence gleaned from recent experience at the state level, where a trend toward relaxation of political activity restrictions has occurred,[29] suggests that political coercion has not been a substantial problem. In 1987, the Subcommittee on Civil Service of the House Committee on Post Office and Civil Service sent questionnaires to the attorneys general of thirteen states that had liberalized political neutrality restrictions since 1974, inquiring (among other things) whether there had been any increase in the coercion of state employees. Of the eleven attorneys general who responded, only one reported receiving any allegations of coercion.[30] This evidence, though limited,[31] and other factors strongly suggest that there is little cause for concern that the pro-Hatchers' more dire projections would be borne out in practice.

Recent experience at the state level is also cited by un-Hatchers to rebut another important claim (empirical projection) offered by pro-Hatchers. Many of the latter have weighed in against relaxation of prohibitions on the partisan political activity of public employees on the ground that the mere *appearance* of involvement could, and in their estimation inevitably would, drastically undermine civic confidence that the laws were being administered in an "impartial" fashion. Here again, the arguments of contemporary pro-Hatchers echo those adduced by the Supreme Court in *Letter Carriers*, where the Court held that the appearance of impartial administration is critical if the public's "confidence in the system of representative Government is not to be eroded to a disastrous extent."[32]

This line of argumentation has been criticized by William L. Magness, who notes that

> in some respects the use of "public confidence" as a weight in the Court's balance is dubious. The Court does not explain the relationship between public confidence and the specific Hatch Act provisions that it upholds and presents no evidence that confidence is any lower where political activity restrictions are less stringent. As a weight on government's side of the balance, public confidence is difficult to quantify and the assertion of its absence is impossible to rebut. It adds little to the clarity of the analysis whether employee political activity restrictions are proper public policy.[33]

As Magness and others have observed, there is in fact little to suggest that public confidence in the integrity of the public service has been negatively affected in states that have less stringent political activity restrictions on the books.[34] Even were one to grant that there may be a more compelling rationale for attempting to preserve an appearance of neutrality where certain members of the federal service are concerned, this could hardly be said to justify the blanket prohibitions contained in the Hatch Act. To return to the example of the roller in the federal mint, it is difficult to imagine that civic confidence in the impartial administration of the law would in any way be jeopardized were steps taken to un-Hatch officials exercising purely ministerial functions of this kind.

In short, while a constitutional or other model might provide a firmer foundation on which political neutrality restrictions might be laid, contemporary pro-Hatchers rest their case for the Hatch Act on sweeping claims positing an indissoluble link between its prohibitions, on the one hand, and the furtherance of certain objectives that may or may not to be apposite, on the other. By and large, however, they have resolutely refused to acknowledge that any significant modification in the act's regime may be in order, insisting that remedial measures intended to do more than clarify implementing regulations would, as former Office of Personnel Management Director Horner put it, open up a "Pandora's box."[35] As the foregoing discussion has suggested, the rationales and arguments advanced in defense of the status quo have tended to track closely those of Justice Byron White's opinion for the Court in *Letter Carriers,* which cited four "undoubtedly important interests" furthered by the act.[36] In addition to the somewhat dubious status of the asserted state interests, the *Letter Carriers* decision has been roundly and justly criticized for its "inattention to the nature and importance of the public employee's interest in free speech and association, as well as its disregard for the public's interest in hearing from a large segment of the electorate with special insights and interests regarding the workings of politics."[37] Would-be defenders of the Hatch Act can ill afford to follow *Letter Carriers'* lead in "brush[ing] these interests aside,"[38] particularly given the Court's acknowledgment that Congress was "free to strike a different balance than it has."[39]

Although they might yet prevail in the immediate political battle,[40] this could well prove a pyrrhic victory. In any event, the challenge of grounding political neutrality principles in a revamped model of the federal service—a model that fits the circumstances and has external as well as internal credibility—remains.

The Un-Hatcher Model

It would seem a matter of some importance that pro-Hatchers rise to this challenge because while un-Hatchers have had the upper hand in the recurrent debates over the act's revision, it is far from clear that they are substantially better positioned to point the way toward a fully satisfactory model of the federal service. Insofar as the un-Hatchers have a model to offer, it would appear to be a constitutional one, albeit a radically different constitutional model than that which President Jefferson had in view—indeed, one that in effect denies there is anything peculiar about the status of *any* member of the federal career service that would justify restrictions on his or her taking an active part in "the business of electioneering." This claim is no less sweeping in its scope, and for that same reason no less vulnerable to criticism, than many of those advanced by the pro-Hatchers.

Although the contention that intervening developments have long since outstripped the original rationale for the act has been a consistent (and effective) theme, the more fundamental objection entered by modern un-Hatchers is what might be called the "second-class citizenship" argument. This argument proceeds on the assumption that, as Justice Hugo Black succinctly put it, "there is nothing about federal ... employees as a class which justifies depriving them or society of the benefits of their participation in public affairs."[41]

By denying federal employees the same participation rights enjoyed by other citizens, the Hatch Act—or so its critics allege—symbolically consigns an important sector of the electorate to a subordinate role in the political process in a manner that is out of keeping with contemporary notions of how constitutional democracies ought to function, to say nothing of elementary principles of equal protection and "fair play."[42]

This argument had an obvious appeal even in 1947, but it has struck a particularly responsive chord among those who share the commitment to "opening up" government and creating new avenues for citizen participation that became so pronounced during the 1960s and 1970s. Opponents of the Hatch Act clearly have sought to capitalize on these sympathies by, for example, analogizing their campaign to "emancipate" the federal workforce to earlier efforts to extend the franchise to women, as well as more recent efforts to expand opportunities for blacks, other minorities and 18–20 year olds, to make their presence felt in the political process. That their allegations regarding the act's putative "disenfranchisement" of public employees has had the intended effect is reflected in the statement of purpose accompanying the reform legislation passed in 1989 by the House, which reads (in significant part): "to restore to Federal civilian employees ... their right to participate voluntarily, as private citizens, in the political activities of the Nation."[43]

Nevertheless, the effort to analogize the situation of federal employees to that of other groups in society is plainly misleading insofar as it exaggerates the Hatch Act's evisceration of political rights.[44]

It also ignores a basic premise that has undergirded Supreme Court analysis of the public employment relationship for at least the past two decades. The Court has been quite clear in holding that the government has an interest in regulating the conduct and "the speech of its employees that differ[s] significantly from those it possesses in connection with the regulation of speech of the citizenry in general."[45]

On occasion, un-Hatchers seem to neglect this important distinction. In general, however, they plainly appreciate that while several important rulings during the past two decades have favored the interests of the public employee, the Supreme Court decision in *Pickering* [46] and other cases left open the possibility that a sufficiently compelling governmental interest might justify an infringement on First Amendment or other constitutional rights. The un-Hatchers' general claim is that even if the government has a legitimate interest in promoting the objectives allegedly served by the act, far less drastic means to their realization can be found. In particular, they insist that the "'supposed evil of political partisanship by classified employees of Government' [cited by the Court in *United Public Workers* v. *Mitchell*] is neither so imminent nor so apparent as to justify an intrusion into [First Amendment] rights . . . as profound as the Hatch Act imposes."[47]

This argument has a powerful appeal. Pro-Hatchers might respond, however, that the un-Hatchers appear to regard the government's interest in preventing the "supposed evil of political partisanship" from infecting the workforce (or interfering with the conduct of official business) to be essentially no greater than that which a private employer might have. So much would appear to be implicit in the "black and white" approach adopted in pending Hatch Act reform legislation: "no partisan political activities on the job, any otherwise legal activities off the job."[48] Although there clearly is something to the un-Hatchers' claim that their proposed legislation is in certain respects "more restrictive than what we have now,"[49] it is not enough, argue the pro-Hatchers, to ban the wearing of campaign buttons and other overt on-the-job displays of partisanship by federal employees.[50]

Measures of this kind fail adequately to recognize the needs of the government as employer, which has a special obligation to ensure that those charged with the administration of public policies and programs carry out their responsibilities in accordance with the dictates of law, without regard to partisan considerations. Equally important is the public's *expectation* that official authority not be abused for partisan purposes, an expectation that likewise cannot be satisfied by the simple expedient of banning all partisan activities (or displays) from the workplace.

It would be erroneous to suppose that un-Hatchers are oblivious to concerns that easing restrictions on federal employees' off-duty partisan political activities might give rise to conflict-of-interest problems, jeopardize public confidence in the impartial administration of government programs, or both. They agree that "any form of political activity that creates the *appearance* of possible favoritism or conflicts of interest must be kept illegal."[51] Thus, for example, in addition to banning all on-the-job political solicitation, provisions incorporated into the House and Senate bills stipulate that it shall be unlawful for any employee to "knowingly solicit, accept, or receive a political contribution from, or give a political contribution to" any person who has (or is seeking to obtain) contractual or other business with the agency for which the employee works, conducts activities regulated by that agency, or "has interests which may be substantially affected by the performance or nonperformance of the employee's official duties."[52] These and other provisions clearly reflect the un-Hatchers' desire to proscribe those (off-duty) partisan political activities that might have an adverse effect, not only "on the integrity of Government" but on "*the public's confidence*" in that integrity as well.[53]

From the point of view of pro-Hatchers, the problem with these and other provisions designed to preserve at least an appearance of political neutrality is that they simply do not go far enough. In particular, pro-Hatchers argue that the un-Hatchers fail to appreciate the extent to which federal employees' involvement in partisan politics will adversely affect public confidence in the impartial administration of federal laws and programs. Although it was suggested earlier that these claims are overdrawn, there would appear to be a compelling rationale for making distinctions with regard to the level and functions of employees and circumscribing, more narrowly than would the un-Hatchers, the *range* of permitted activities for those in certain positions.

In 1966, the Civil Service Commission described the purpose of the Hatch Act as that of preventing those subject to it from becoming "prominently identified with any political movement, party, or faction, or with the success or failure of any candidate for election to public office."[54] No doubt the danger to be apprehended from the "prominent identification" of most members of the federal service with partisan politics or candidates for office today is minimal at best. The same cannot as readily be said, however, of the relatively small percentage of the federal workforce whose duties involve the exercise of significant discretionary authority—in rulemaking, grant and contract making, adjudication, and law enforcement. With respect to governmental activities of this kind, there is legitimate cause for concern that the narrow line between the "appropriate exercise of discretion under the law and political expediency"[55] might be crossed. Career officials entrusted with law enforcement or grant-making authority have a special responsibility to ensure that this does not occur. The prominent identification of these officials with partisan politics could give rise to suspicions, however unfounded, that decisions of vital importance to private citizens—decisions to confer or withhold a grant, contract, or license, for example—were "tainted" by partisan considerations. While the pending Hatch reform bills incorporate provisions designed to protect against the misuse of official authority for partisan reasons,[56] pro-Hatchers argue with some persuasiveness that if, for example, the supporter of an unsuccessful candidate is denied a contract by a contracting official who served as treasurer of the winning candidate's campaign, the *perception* of favoritism or retribution will be impossible to rebut. In short, a compelling case can be made that in order to ensure public confidence in the fair and impartial administration of certain laws or programs, *some* restrictions on the off-duty partisan political activities of certain federal employees must be preserved.

Indeed, it seems not unreasonable to expect that federal employees entrusted with significant rulemaking, grant or rate making, adjudicatory or law enforcement authority be prepared to accept certain restrictions on their active participation in "the business of electioneering." The intrusion on First Amendment rights need not be nearly as profound as the Hatch Act imposes. Given the importance of the responsibilities entrusted to them, however, it is not too much to ask that such officials relinquish the right to run for partisan office and sacrifice as well their right to engage in activities that would "prominently identify" them with a particular party or candidate in a partisan election. When the federal employee takes an oath to support the Constitution, he or she in effect enters into a compact that may at times necessitate giving up certain liberties enjoyed by others in the interest of effective government.

A Look Ahead (and an Immodest Proposal)

In reflecting on the most recent round of disputation over Hatch Act reform, one cannot but be struck by the extreme positions staked out by participants in the debate. Pro-Hatchers regularly and adamantly insist that lifting the prohibition on federal employees' taking "an active part in political management or in political campaigns" would court disaster, perhaps paving the way for a return to a full-fledged spoils system.[57] Un-Hatchers are no less adamant in their insistence that nothing less than a complete scuttling of this prohibition will suffice to vindicate federal employees' First Amendment rights to freedom of speech and association, and in their insistence that more-than-adequate safeguards are now in place to prevent the various potential problems of concern to pro-Hatchers from materializing. With rare exceptions, spokespersons for neither side seem seriously prepared to entertain the possibility that there might be some acceptable middle ground, some reasonably satisfactory way of balancing the many competing factors and interests at stake in this dispute.[58]

The foregoing analysis has outlined one potentially promising means of attempting to achieve this balance. It was suggested earlier that under a constitutional model of the public service, public policy could determine which groups of federal employees should be permitted to engage in partisan activity and which not—the idea being that the government's interest in ensuring that its workforce is (or appears to be) politically neutral is not equally compelling for all employees and that distinctions can and should be made between them with regard to level and function. In support of this point, it was argued that (1) the traditional rationales and arguments adduced by supporters of the Hatch Act are insufficient to justify its sweeping curtailment of public employees' First Amendment rights to freedom of speech and association, but that (2) a persuasive case can be made that *certain* of the Hatch Act's restrictions on the partisan political activities of federal employees should be retained for those employees exercising significant discretionary authority. With regard to this latter group, the government's interest in preserving an appearance of political neutrality seems sufficiently compelling to justify some infringement on employees' First Amendment (participation) rights.

No serious effort has ever been made by parties to the recurrent debates over Hatch Act reform to differentiate federal employees according to level or function in seeking to determine whether or to what extent the act's prohibitions on partisan campaigning and electioneering are justifiable. The potential utility of this general approach, however, is illustrated by Supreme Court rulings in three post- *Letter Carriers* cases, which, while not directly on target, likewise implicated the First Amendment rights of public employees: *Elrod* v. *Burns* (1976),[59] *Branti* v. *Finkel* (1980),[60] and *Rankin* v. *McPherson* (1987).[61]

Both *Elrod* and *Branti* involved patronage dismissals. In *Elrod*, the Supreme Court held that patronage dismissals can be unconstitutional infringements on public employees' First Amendment rights to freedom of association and freedom of political belief. This judgment was subsequently affirmed in *Branti*, which involved the patronage dismissal of public defenders in Rockland County, New York. Yet while both these decisions vindicated the right of most public employees not to be terminated on the basis of their political affiliations, the Court in each case carved out exceptions, indicating that in certain circumstances such dismissals might be justified.

In *Elrod*, the Court held that patronage dismissals from confidential and policy-making positions could be squared with the First Amendment when they serve the public interest in preventing "tactics obstructing the implementation of policies of the new administration, policies presumably sanctioned by the electorate."[62] Although this formulation appeared to signal considerable deference to the prerogatives of the hiring authority, Justice William Brennan's plurality opinion emphasized that intrusions on public employees' First Amendment rights would not lightly be tolerated. Any requirement that employees support the party in power, he argued, must be shown to "further some vital government end by a means that is least restrictive of freedom of belief and association in achieving that end, and the benefit gained must outweigh the loss of constitutionally protected rights."[63]

The fact that *Elrod* lacked a majority opinion left somewhat unclear just how much deference was due the party in power or how heavy a burden would be necessary to justify a patronage dismissal. The majority opinion in *Branti*, however, clarified the *Elrod* decision in both respects. The majority pointedly warned that the Court would not be duped by labeling games; merely designating those dismissed as "policy makers" or as employees in "confidential" positions would not suffice to rebut a claim that their discharge constituted an unconstitutional infringement of First Amendment rights. In fact, *Branti* carved out a more limited exception than had *Elrod* by holding that patronage dismissals from policy-making positions would be sustained if, and only if, the hiring authority could "demonstrate that party affiliation is an appropriate requirement for the effective performance of the public office involved."[64]

Elrod and *Branti* are both taken to signal increased Supreme Court solicitude for constitutional rights of employees as against the competing claims of the state. Certainly the Court's ruling in each of these instances betrayed far less deference to the interests of the government as employer, and far greater concern for public employees' First Amendment rights, than did the ruling in *Letter Carriers*. It is noteworthy, however, that in each case the Court regarded the question of whether the dismissed employee occupied a policy-making or nonpolicy-making position as a relevant, indeed key consideration to be considered in assessing the relative weight of the employees' and employers' competing claims. In effect, the distinction between policy making and nonpolicy making "guarantees to nonpolicy-making public employees the First Amendment right to belong to the political party of their choice,"[65] but allows the removal of policy-making employees on the basis of their partisan affiliation if the hiring authority can "demonstrate that party affiliation is an appropriate requirement for the effective performance of the public office involved."

Rankin v. *McPherson* is a later illustration of the Court's insistence that the nature of the public employee's position be taken into account in determining whether an employer's alleged infringement of First Amendment rights (in this case, to freedom of speech) may be justified. McPherson was a probationary employee in a constable's office whose duties entailed no policy-making responsibilities and only very limited opportunity for contact with the public. She was in the company of a fellow employee (her boy friend, as described by the Court) when she learned of the Hinckley assassination attempt on President Reagan. At this point, McPherson was overheard by another employee to say, "If they go for him again, I hope they get him." Her statement, made privately to her boy friend in the context of a discussion about Reagan's policies, upset the third employee, who reported the incident to Constable Rankin. After questioning McPherson about the remark, Rankin fired her. In ruling that McPherson's remark was constitutionally protected, the Court's majority first reasoned that it was on a matter of "public concern," as that term had been defined in earlier cases, and hence fell within the protective rubric of the First Amendment's free speech guarantee. The majority went on to observe:

> in weighing the State's interest in discharging a public employee on any claim that the content of the statement made by the employee somehow undermines the mission of the public employer, some attention must be paid to the responsibilities of the employee within the agency. The burden of caution employees bear with respect to the words they speak will vary with the extent of authority and public accountability the employee's role

entails. Where, as here, the employee serves no confidential, policymaking, or public contact role, the danger to the agency's successful functions from that employee's private speech is minimal.[66]

Although the Court was badly divided in this case (5 to 4), the *Rankin* ruling may carve "out a new and very large class of employees—i.e., those in 'nonpolicymaking' positions—who ... can never be disciplined" for making statements that fall within its definition of public concern.[67]

The Supreme Court decisions in these three cases serve to underscore the utility of focusing on the position occupied by the public employee in attempting to ascertain whether or to what extent the public employer's effort to regulate employee conduct constitutes an unconstitutional infringement on First Amendment rights. Though none of the cases addressed the constitutionality of political neutrality restrictions, they serve to reinforce the central claim made here, namely, that there is little justification for imposing such restrictions on all employees because the benefit gained does not compensate for the loss of constitutionally protected rights, but that nevertheless the public employer may have a legitimate claim to make adherence to political neutrality restrictions a condition of employment for those in specific positions, such as "policy-making" positions. The coercion of any public employee to engage in partisan activities should, of course, be prohibited. Moreover, the public employer should be required to observe the standard suggested by Justice Brennan in *Elrod:* to demonstrate that political neutrality restrictions "further some vital government end by a means that is least restrictive of freedom of [speech] and association in achieving that end, and [that] the benefit gained ... outweigh[s] the loss of constitutionally protected rights." In a regime dedicated to the preservation of individual rights, there is great force to the argument that government should not be allowed to infringe on the rights of its citizens, including public employees, unnecessarily.

Fleshing out a "policy-making/nonpolicy-making" distinction (or other categorization) and translating it into a workable legislative scheme assuredly would not be an easy undertaking. Policy makers might readily balk at the prospect of undertaking to determine, in case-by-case fashion, whether or not particular agencies or levels or kinds of employees should be permitted to engage in partisan political activity and, where they conclude that some "vital government end" would in fact be served by imposing political neutrality restrictions, what kinds of restrictions might be appropriate. Assuming this imposing hurdle could be crossed, a massive educational effort surely would be required to ensure that employees and the public at large would understand and appreciate the rationale for treating cases differently. If this effort were to go even partway toward alerting the citizenry to the dangers of making sweeping generalizations about a supposedly monolithic federal bureaucracy or public service, it would have accomplished something very important. Neither the federal bureaucracy nor the federal service is all of a piece. Recognition of the fact that we need *models*, rather than *a model*, to guide us may be a sine qua non if we are to succeed in the "rebuilding" effort on which we have embarked.

Notes

1. *Congressional Record*, 75th Cong., 3d sess., vol. 83 (pt. 4), 4458 (31 March 1938), S.847.
2. Ibid., 4459.
3. Ibid., 7964.
4. George W. Curtis, *Civil Service Reform under the Present National Administration* (New York: National Civil Service Reform League, 1885), 14. The Pendleton Act (Civil Service Reform Act) of 1883 stipulated that no person in the competitive service should be under any obligation to render any political support or service and should not be prejudiced for refusing to do so. It also prohibited those in the competitive service from using their official authority or influence to coerce political action.
5. U.S. Civil Service Commission, *Annual Report* 24 (1907): 9.
6. Section 9(a) made it "unlawful for any person employed in the executive branch of the Federal Government, or any agency or department thereof, to use his official authority or influence for the purpose of interfering with an election or affecting the result thereof. No officer or employee in the executive branch of the Federal Government, or any agency or department thereof, shall take an active part in political management or in political campaigns. All such persons shall retain the right to vote as they may choose and to express their opinions on all political subjects."
7. *United Public Workers* v. *Mitchell*, 330 U.S. 75 (1947), and *Civil Service Commission* v. *National Association of Letter Carriers*, 413 U.S. 548 (1973), granted considerable deference to the intent of Congress, as understood by the majority opinions, to promote the efficiency of the federal service. While these decisions permit restrictions on the political activities of federal employees, they do not require them or identify any constitutional basis for such a requirement. Both cases have been exhaustively analyzed in the legal literature. For a brief review that places them in a general constitutional setting, see David H. Rosenbloom and Jennifer Gille, "The Current Constitutional Approach to Public Employment," *University of Kansas Law Review* 23 (Winter 1975): 249–75. Because they are so well known, our discussion integrates these cases into the text and does not rehearse them in a separate section.
8. Commission on Political Activity of Government Personnel, *A Commission Report*, vol. 1, *Findings and Recommendations* (Washington, D.C.: Government Printing Office, 1968), 1.
9. Ibid., 15.

10. Ibid., 21.

11. Ibid., 3.

12. See *Proposed Federal Employees' Political Activities Legislation: Pro and Con* (Washington, D.C.: Congressional Digest, January 1988), 16. Italics added.

13. 330 U.S. 75, 99 (1947).

14. J. Richardson, *Messages and Papers of the President*, vol. 10 (1899), 98–99.

15. Morris Fiorina, "The Decline of Collective Responsibility in American Politics," in *Classic Readings in American Politics*, 2d ed., ed. P. Nivola and D. Rosenbloom (New York: St. Martin's Press, 1990), 156–78.

16. Walter Dean Burnham, "The Turnout Problem," in *Elections American Style*, ed. James A. Reichley (Washington, D.C.: Brookings Institution, 1987), 97–133.

17. See, e.g., Morris Fiorina, *Congress: Keystone of the Washington Establishment* (New Haven: Yale University Press, 1977).

18. 427 U.S. 347 (1976).

19. 445 U.S. 507 (1980).

20. Robert Vaughn, "The Performance of the United States Merit Systems Protection Board: The Foundation for Future Regulation," *Policy Studies Journal* 17 (Winter 1988–89): 352–69.

21. U.S. House of Representatives, *Federal and Postal Employees' Political Activities Acts of 1987: Hearings before the Subcommittee on Civil Service of the House Committee on Post Office and Civil Service*, 100th Cong., 1st sess., 1987, 162–63. Hereafter cited as *1987 House Hearings*.
A number of other post-Hatch Act developments strongly militate against the contemporary plausibility of this scenario. Perhaps the most important of these developments is the growth of federal employee unions, whose presence affords employees an additional safeguard against supervisor coercion. Another development of potential relevance in this context is the enactment of the Whistleblowers Protection Act of 1989 (P.L. 101-12, signed into law on 4 April 1989), which lowers the burden of proof federal employees carry in attempting to sustain a charge that an agency or a supervisor took action against them on the basis of some "prohibited personnel practice."

22. A contrary conclusion was reached by the Supreme Court in the 1973 *Letter Carriers* case, in which the Court cited concern that federal employees "not be employed to build a powerful, invincible, and perhaps corrupt political machine" as one of four "obviously important interests" furthered by the Hatch Act. The Court found that Congress was justified in concluding that "substantial barriers should be raised against the party in power—or the party out of power, for that matter—using the thousands or hundreds of thousands of federal employees, paid for at public expense, to man its political structure and political campaigns" (413 U.S. 548, 564–65 [1973]).

23. The reform legislation recently passed by the House bill (H.R.20) would specifically prohibit federal employees from intimidating any person's

exercise or nonexercise of political rights (7323(a)(2)) or from soliciting contributions from subordinates or handing over political contributions to a superior (7324 (a)(3),(4)). Reprisals after an election are also specifically prohibited in H.R.20. The companion Senate bill (S.135) does not include any similar specific prohibitions. Both bills, however, would toughen sanctions on those found to have violated its prohibitions. Under the Hatch Act, penalties for violation of the statute range from a 30-day suspension without pay to removal from the service (secs. 7323 and 7325). Under the House-passed bill, by contrast (and the Senate-proposed bill follows suit), the full range of penalties in 5 U.S.C. 1207 would apply to violations of the statute. These include fines, suspension, and debarment from employment; removal; and reprimand.

24. Letter dated 26 October 1987 from James C. Miller III, Director, Office of Management and Budget, to the Minority Leader of the House of Representatives, concerning H.R.3400, the Federal Employees' Political Activities Act of 1987. Reprinted in Congressional Digest, *Proposed Federal Employees' Political Activities: Pro and Con* (Washington, D.C.: Congressional Digest, January 1988), 15, 17.

25. U.S. Senate, *Hatch Act Reform Amendments of 1988: Report of the Senate Committee on Governmental Affairs to Accompany H.R.3400,* Sen. Report 100–417, 100th Cong., 2d sess., 1988, 20–21 (minority views of Senators Roth, Rudman, and Trible). Hereafter cited as *1988 Hatch Act Reform Amendment.*

26. *Civil Service Commission v. National Association of Letter Carriers,* 413 U.S. 548, 565 (1973). See also 566: "For many years the joint judgment of the Executive and Congress has been that to protect the rights of federal employees with respect to their jobs and their political acts and beliefs it is not enough merely to forbid one employee to attempt to influence or coerce another." Unlike Senators Roth, Rudman, and Trible, the *Letter Carriers* Court did not believe this policy to be rooted in "human nature," acknowledging that "perhaps Congress at some time will come to a different view of the realities of political life and Government service." Ibid., 567.

27. See Congressional Research Service, Issue Brief, *Hatch Act Amendments: Political Activity and Civil Service,* by Barbara Schwemle (Government Division), 16 May 1989, 6.

28. As for the claim that most federal employees *want* the (additional) protection afforded by the Hatch Act, un-Hatchers can plausibly argue that the evidence is at best ambivalent on this score. As Representative Solarz observed, "They [federal employees] are not coming before us saying, 'Don't pass this legislation; we will be subjected to the whip and the lash and obligated to do things we don't want to do, in spite of all the protections in the bill.' On the contrary, they are saying, 'Pass the bill; we want to be able to participate, and we are not really worried that we are going to be forced to participate over our objections.'" *1987 House Hearings,* 162.

29. See "Developments in the Law—Public Employment," *Harvard Law Review* 97 (May 1984): 1611–1800 (authors unidentified), 1659 n.68, which lists 19 state statutes permitting most off-hours political activities that do not

interfere with public employees' job performance and 10 other state statutes "significantly less restrictive than the Hatch Act."

30. U.S. House of Representatives, *Federal Employees' Political Activities Act of 1989, Report of the House Committee on Post Office and Civil Service (together with Minority Views)*, House Report 101–27, 101st Cong., 1st sess., 1989, 11–12. Hereafter cited as *1989 House Report.* The exception was Alabama. It is important to note, however, that six of the eleven states responding to the subcommittee's questionnaire "were unable to provide any information of the effects of the changes in their state laws" (p. 12).

31. Above and beyond the "small sample" problem (see note 30), pro-Hatchers might argue that the lack of *allegations* of coercion provides no assurance that such coercion is not taking place. It may simply reflect employees' recognition of the difficulty involved in attempting to make a charge of coercion against a supervisor "stick," their fear of potential reprisals, or both. The problem with this line of argument, of course, is that it is essentially irrebuttable. One would want to know what *would* count as evidence that coercion is not taking place.

32. 413 U.S. 565 (1973).

33. William L. Magness, "Un-Hatching Federal Employee Political Endorsements," *University of Pennsylvania Law Review* 134 (1987): 1497–1529.

34. See, e.g., the statement of Stephen Solarz, *1987 House Hearings* : "My impression is that in those States [which have eased political activity restrictions] the confidence of the public in the integrity of their State service has not been significantly impaired, nor is it significantly less, as I understand it, in comparison to those States which have prohibitions on partisan political activities similar to those which now exist with respect to Federal employees"(p. 163).

35. *1987 House Hearings,* 134–35.

36. In White's view, the Hatch Act's restrictions served the government's interest in ensuring that federal employees (1) "administer the law in accordance with the will of Congress, rather than in accordance with their own will or the will of a political party"; (2) not "appear to the public" to be making politically influenced decisions, lest "confidence in the system of representative Government ... be eroded to a disastrous extent"; (3) not "be employed to build a powerful, invincible, and perhaps corrupt political machine"; and (4) be free "from express or tacit invitation to vote a certain way or perform certain chores in order to curry favor with their superiors...." 413 U.S. 564–65.

37. "Developments in the Law—Public Employment," 1656.

38. Ibid.

39. 413 U.S. 564.

40. Pro-Hatchers can draw comfort from the fact that the Hatch Act to date "has shown remarkable resiliency in the face of reams of critical comment." "Developments in the Law—Public Employment," 1651. More important, the Bush administration, like its predecessor, has taken a firm stand in opposition to reform legislation and may successfully block it.

41. *United Public Workers* v. *Mitchell*, 330 U.S. 75, 111 (Black, J., dissenting).

42. As one federal employee union president recently put it (statement of Kenneth Blaylock, president of the American Federation of Government Employees, AFGE): "Employees subject to the Hatch Act are disenfranchised. They have been subordinated in status to another class of citizenship and we submit this egregious state of affairs is wholly without validity." *1987 House Hearings*, p. 44. Proponents of reform now and in the past have pointed to the example of other (especially European) nations to support their contention that the restrictions placed on the voluntary political activities of federal employees in the United States are unduly limiting for a democratic nation.

43. *1989 House Report*, 2.

44. After all, employees covered by the Hatch Act retain the right, among other things, to (1) register and to vote; (2) contribute money to partisan political campaigns; (3) express their views in private and in public (though not in a concerted way to elicit support for a candidate or party); (4) attend political conventions and rallies; (5) assist in nonpartisan voter registration drives; (6) campaign for or against political referendum questions; (7) attend political fund-raising functions; (8) wear political buttons (off duty or, subject to certain agency restrictions, on duty); and (9) participate in nonpartisan campaigns. Given the scope of these permitted activities, the Justice Department has argued that "it is hard to view [the pending House and Senate reform bills] as the 'restoration' of political rights their sponsors claim them to be." Letter dated 16 May 1988 from Thomas M. Boyd, Acting Assistant Attorney General, Department of Justice, to Senator John Glenn, Chairman, Senate Governmental Affairs Committee, re: Hatch Act Reform Amendments of 1988, 6.

45. *Pickering* v. *Board of Education*, 391 U.S. 563, 568 (1968).

46. It was in the context of the landmark *Pickering* case that the Court first articulated a "balancing test" to be used in attempting to mediate the tension between "the interests of the [public] employee, as a citizen, in commenting upon matters of public concern and the interest of the State, as an employer, in promoting the efficiency of the public services it performs through its employees." 391 U.S. 563, 568 (1968). Employing this test, the Court in *Pickering* found the state's legitimate interest in (inter alia) maintaining discipline and harmony in the workplace insufficient to justify the discharge of a public school teacher for speaking out on matters of public interest. See also *Rankin* v. *McPherson*, 97 L. Ed. 2d 315 (1987).

47. *1989 House Report*, 4.

48. *Congressional Record*, 17 April 1989, H1248 (statement of Congresswoman Constance Morella).

49. *1987 House Hearings*, 159 (statement of Representative Frank Horton).

50. Sec. 7325(a) of H.R.20 would prohibit federal employees from engaging in any political activity (1) while on duty; (2) in any room or building occupied by individuals engaged in the performance of official government business; (3) while wearing a uniform "or other official insignia identifying the office or

position of the employee"; or (4) while using any vehicle owned or leased by the Federal government "or any agency or instrumentality thereof." (The same prohibitions are set forth in Sec. 7324 of S.135.)

51. *1987 Senate Hearings,* 28 (opening statement of Senator Carl Levin). Italics added.

52. H.R.20, 7324(*b*)(1)(A), (B), (C).

53. H.R.20, Sec.7324(*b*)(3). Special Counsel of the MSPB can grant exceptions to the general prohibitions itemized in text "in situations where the acts and circumstances indicate there would not be any adverse effect on the integrity of Government or the public's confidence in that integrity."

54. *1987 House Hearings,* 163 (statement of Mary F. Wieseman, Special Counsel, Office of Special Counsel).

55. Robert Vaughn, "Restrictions on the Political Activities of Public Employees: The Hatch Act and Beyond," *George Washington Law Review* 44 (May 1976): 516–53.

56. H.R.20, Sec. 7323, prohibits the abuse of official authority by federal employees, including, in the case of those outside government, "promising to confer or conferring any benefit (such as any compensation, grant, contract, license or ruling)."

57. In the view of Senators Roth et al., the Hatch Act represents "the only effective remedy for the spoils system this nation has known." *1988 Hatch Act Reform Amendments,* 21.

58. As the above overview suggests, the debate over the Hatch Act presents a number of thorny questions. Policy makers are challenged to balance a number of competing interests and considerations: federal employees' rights to freedom of speech and association, which must be weighed against their interest in protection against coercion; the interest of the public at large in hearing the views of a large sector of the American electorate with special insights into the workings of government, balanced against the public's expectation that federal employees will not allow partisan considerations to color the exercise of official authority; and the interests of the government in promoting efficiency, protecting federal employees against coercion, and assuring both the reality and the appearance of integrity in the administration of governmental affairs, all of which must be balanced against the government's duty not to abridge the constitutional rights of its employees lightly.

59. 427 U.S. 347 (1976) (plurality opinion).

60. 445 U.S. 507 (1980).

61. 97 L. Ed. 2d 315 (1987).

62. 427 U.S. 347, 367 (1976).

63. Ibid., 371.

64. 445 U.S. 507, 518 (1980).

65. "Developments in the Law—Public Employment," 1749.

66. 97 L. Ed. 2d 315, 328 (1987).

67. Ibid., 331.

3

Political Appointees and Career Executives:
The Democracy-Bureaucracy Nexus

James P. Pfiffner

The balance between presidential appointees and career executives in governing the United States is a fundamental question of who shall rule.[1] But it is also a question of governmental and organizational mechanics. The democratic principle that the president along with political appointees ought to direct policy in the executive branch is not in question, but judgments about the most effective way to organize that political control have been changing. In recent years the balance has shifted toward using more political appointees to assure tighter White House control of administration.

The Western European democracies of France, Britain, and Germany allow only 100 or so new political appointees to each new administration to establish its control of the government.[2] In contrast, a new administration in the United States fills thousands of political positions with its own appointees. Major reasons account for this. The United States has a separation of powers rather than a parliamentary form of government, and it does not have the party discipline in Congress that parliamentary systems often enjoy. Neither does it have the same governmental and administrative traditions that matured in Europe over the centuries.

In the United States the spoils system developed to assure that a new president's programs were implemented by those sympathetic to his policies. This was done with the Jacksonian assumption that government jobs were so simple that virtually anybody could handle them. The legacy of the reform movement removed most federal government jobs from the spoilsmen by expanding appointment by merit (often by "blanketing in") but still left the top tier of positions to presidential discretion.[3] After the high-

NOTE: Reprinted, with minor editorial changes, from *Public Administration Review* (January-February 1987, 57–65) © 1987 by the American Society for Public Administration, 1120 G Street NW, Suite 500, Washington DC 20005. All rights reserved.

water mark of the merit system was reached in the 1940s, the pendulum reversed directions, and the proportion of political appointees began to increase again, particularly in the 1970s and 1980s.

Though little danger exists that the scale of personnel spoils will be approached again, this chapter argues that the balance in the United States has shifted too far toward a greater number of political appointees. It argues that recent presidents have come to office with distrust and hostility toward the career bureaucracy and that this attitude has been reflected initially in their political appointees. Evidence is offered that this distrust of career executives is misplaced and that most administrations experience a "cycle of accommodation" with the career bureaucracy. The conclusion will be that the "in and outer" system is a good one that has served this country well, but that the balance should be shifted back toward fewer presidential appointees. The number of political appointees can be reduced without reducing the responsiveness of the permanent government to legitimate political leadership.

Presidential Mistrust and Increasing Control

Presidential candidates in the United States have increasingly come to office distrusting the career bureaucracy. They suspect it to be salted with holdovers from the previous administration and to be unsympathetic to their priorities. They believe this will lead to foot dragging, if not outright sabotage. Running against the Washington bureaucracy also has potent political appeal to the voters. It is inevitable that the appointees recruited to join an administration are affected by this rhetoric, particularly those with no prior experience in the federal government.

This attitude is certainly not a new phenomenon, but it has been increasing in recent years. When President Eisenhower came to office after twenty years of Democratic rule, Schedule C positions were created to allow the Republicans to place their own appointees at lower levels in the bureaucracy, GS-18 and below. President Kennedy felt that the career bureaucracy tended to be too stodgy and would not be able to move vigorously enough to "get the country moving again." He used temporary task forces instead of relying exclusively on traditional bureaucratic structures.[4] He also began the centralization of policy making in the White House instead of relying heavily on his cabinet secretaries as had Eisenhower. Lyndon Johnson was an exception to the trend of distrust toward the bureaucracy, but not to the trend of centralizing control in the White House.

President Nixon had a legendary distrust and hostility toward the bureaucracy, which he called "dug-in establishmentarians fighting for the status quo."[5] His administration began with the attitude that there would be, in John Ehrlichman's words, "guerrilla warfare" with the bureaucracy.

This distrust led that administration to establish a White House "counter-bureaucracy" in the Domestic Council, to propose a major reorganization of the executive branch, to place White House political appointees as "spies" in the departments and agencies, and to attempt illegal political placements through the career merit system.[6]

Jimmy Carter ran as an outsider against the establishment. He asserted that "our government in Washington now is a horrible bureaucratic mess. . . . We must give top priority to a drastic and thorough reorganization of the Federal bureaucracy."[7] Carter and many of his appointees adopted an attitude of moral superiority toward Congress and the bureaucracy.[8]

The Reagan administration probably was more distrustful of the bureaucracy than any previous one. Reagan also ran as an outsider against Washington, declaring that government is part of the problem, not part of the solution and promised there would be no more business as usual. In office, the Reagan administration forced severe cutbacks on the domestic side of the government and reduced nonmilitary employment by reductions in force, leaving about 92,000 fewer employees in domestic agencies in 1983 than in 1981.[9] Reagan appointees began their terms by systematically excluding career executives from policy-making deliberations based on the fear that they would try to undercut the administration's policies if they were included.[10]

More Appointees

This trend of increasing distrust of the bureaucracy was accompanied by an increasing centralization of control of personnel and policy in the White House. This change arose from the greater numbers of political appointees available to an administration and tighter control of appointments by the White House. At the upper levels the number of presidential appointments requiring Senate confirmation has increased. In 1933 there were 71 such positions; by 1965 there were 152; and President Johnson made 237 appointments to these top positions.[11] By 1984 there were 523 of these appointments.[12]

In addition to these presidential appointments, department and agency heads can make numerous political appointments. Each administration can appoint up to 10 percent of the Senior Executive Service (SES) at the top management level (GS-16 to Executive Level IV). This amounts to about 700 of 7,000 total SES positions. The SES regulations also increased political control of the bureaucracy by allowing agency heads to transfer executives throughout the agency and to place political appointees in any position that is not "career-reserved." In addition, "limited-term" and "limited-emergency" appointments can be appointed for terms up to three years.

Schedule C positions are reserved for confidential or policy-related functions at the GS-15 level and below. Schedule C positions have steadily increased in number since their creation in the 1950s, with the Reagan administration increasing their numbers significantly over the number used by the Carter administration.[13] In 1985 there were 1,665 Schedule C positions governmentwide, up from 911 in 1976.[14] In addition, immediately after a transition a new administration can appoint up to 25 percent more Schedule Cs to assist with the transition for the first 120 days of an administration. In 1981 this time period was extended for an additional 120 days by Office of Personnel Management Director Donald Devine.[15]

The total number of allocated, noncareer employees in the executive branch increased from 2,794 in 1979 to 2,951 in 1984 (excluding White House staff, military, Coast Guard, Foreign Service, and Public Health Service).[16] The number of appointees is not fixed and varies depending on who does the counting and how positions are defined. The specific numbers are not important; what is important is the *trend* toward more political appointees for each presidential administration. The direction of this trend is not in dispute.

Increasing Control

The increasing number of political appointments available to presidents over the past several decades has been accompanied by increasingly tighter control of them by the White House. While subcabinet appointments (associate and assistant secretaries) are presidential appointments, Schedule C and SES appointments are made by agency heads and departmental secretaries. Since the 1950s, presidents have usually allowed agency heads to appoint their own teams below the subcabinet level; at the subcabinet level presidents have generally given agency heads and departmental secretaries wide discretion. A Brookings Institution study in 1965 concluded that the selection of assistant secretaries was "a highly decentralized and personalized process revolving around the respective department and agency heads," with the president generally delegating selection to his cabinet secretaries. "Where the secretary and White House staff conflicted over an appointment, the secretary generally won."[17]

This practice has been reversed since the 1950s with increasing control of all political appointments being drawn into the White House.[18] The Reagan administration took this trend to the extreme by insisting on White House control or clearance of each noncareer appointment in the government. According to Pendleton James, the director of Reagan's Presidential Personnel Office, "We handled all the appointments: boards, commissions, Schedule C's, ambassadorships, judgeships ... if you are going to run the government, you've got to control the people that come into it."[19] Edwin Meese argued: "The president has to decide right off the bat that there will be one central control point. And that while you encourage department heads to develop names, the ultimate approval is to be that of the president."[20]

Politicization

The tight White House control of political appointees by the Reagan administration was accompanied by an attitude of tight control of career executives by the White House appointees. This approach entailed an attempt strictly to separate policy issues from administrative ones and to exclude career executives from policy deliberations.

The most extreme defense of this approach to government has been put forth by Michael Sanera of the Heritage Foundation, a conservative think tank that had high-level access to the Reagan administration.[21] Sanera argues that big government is "inefficient" and "destructive" and that career bureaucrats will actively try to sabotage any administration that is trying to achieve significant change.

To counter this type of subversion Sanera recommends several tactics for political appointees. One of these is "jigsaw puzzle management" in which

> career staff will supply information, but they should never become involved in the formulation of agenda related policy objectives.... Once controversial policy goals are formulated, they should not be released in total to the career staff. Thus the political executive and his political staff become "jigsaw puzzle" managers. Other staff see and work on the individual pieces, but never have enough of the pieces to be able to learn the entire picture.[22]

Sanera also encourages political appointees to promote conflict and uncertainty among their subordinates in order to ensure a rich flow of information. These precepts flow directly against accepted management theory and practice in the private sector. But Sanera feels that what is lost in efficiency will be made up by greater political control.[23] Another analysis of political control of the bureaucracy, or "politicization," is made by Terry Moe.[24] Moe argues that the incongruence between public expectations for presidential performance and the actual resources available to presidents drives presidents to embrace politicization and centralization in order to gain as much control as they can in order to implement their priorities.

Arguments by reformers and public administration scholars in favor of treating the bureaucracy as neutral experts are beside the point, according to Moe, because they do not address the underlying systemic pressures on presidents. He argues that these reformers will inevitably fail and that it would not be a good thing if they succeeded.

Reagan did much more than continue a historical trend. In moving ambitiously down the paths of politicization and centralization, he built a set of administrative arrangements that by past standards proved coherent, well integrated, and eminently workable ... future presidents ... will have every reason to learn from and build upon the Reagan example in seeking to enhance their own institutional capacities for leadership.[25]

Once an area of administration has been politicized it is virtually impossible to reverse the process. Each new administration feels it is entitled to the same political controls as its predecessor, and members of Congress and political parties resist any reduction in their opportunities for influence. In the nineteenth century this dynamic of political control through the spoils system did not abate until the Pendleton Act began a period of major reform.

The Politics/Administration Dichotomy

In its simple form the politics/administration dichotomy holds that a distinction exists between policy and administration. Political leaders make decisions about what policy should be and those in the bureaucracy merely carry out policy and follow orders from their political superiors. Those who have argued for the strict separation of politics from administration have based their reasoning on Woodrow Wilson and Max Weber.

Wilson argued: "Administration lies outside the proper sphere of politics. Administrative questions are not political questions." [26] Weber characterized the contrasting roles of the politician and the bureaucrat: "To take a stand, to be passionate ... is the politician's element ... indeed, exactly the opposite, principle of responsibility from that of the civil servant. The honor of the civil servant is vested in his ability to execute conscientiously the order of the superior authorities.... Without this moral discipline and self-denial, in the highest sense, the whole apparatus would fall to pieces." [27]

But in the modern, industrialized, technocratic state these simple distinctions break down. Just as a legislature cannot specify all the details of complex programs, neither can political appointees give precise and complete orders about how their policy decisions must be implemented. They cannot because they do not have the time, but more important, they do not have the expertise. Career civil servants have made their careers managing the details of programs and may even have helped write the legislation that established them. They have the information upon which programmatic decisions must be made. In addition, they are experts at applying bureaucratic rules and regulations to particular programs: oiling the budget, personnel, and paper flow parts of the machine.[28] The simple version of the politics/administration dichotomy "assumes a degree of hierarchy of authority, of simplicity of decision, and of effective political supremacy that now seems unrealistic to students of modern government." [29] As a practical matter, this type of division of labor is impossible.

Because of this many social scientists have declared the politics/administration dichotomy to be hopelessly naive. According to Moe, "the politics-administration dichotomy has been firmly rejected as a naive misunderstanding of the inherently political context and nature of the administrative process." [30] But despite the impossibility of a simplistic dichotomy between politics and administration, it remains a highly important normative ideal. It is from Weber's normative sense, rather than from Wilson's empirical claim, that we should derive the contemporary meaning of the politics/administration dichotomy.

"Modern critics have scored points by mistaking social science theory for what was actually a normative political doctrine," Hugh Heclo argues. [31] This normative doctrine stresses that the legitimate authority for administration policy making derives from the president and is delegated to his appointees in the government. Despite the fact that career bureaucrats are, of necessity, involved in policy decisions, they ought not to lose sight of the democratic imperative that presidential appointees are the legitimate locus of decision making in the executive branch. The appropriate posture of the civil servant is to carry out faithfully legitimate policy decisions, despite personal preferences. Without this chain of legitimacy the democratic linkage between the electorate and the government would become unacceptably attenuated. [32]

In addition to these normative distinctions, differences of background and style distinguish bureaucrats and politicians, each set of officials making different contributions to the formulation of public policy. Appointees' political skills are needed to identify goals and mobilize support for them. The strength of civil servants, on the other hand, lies in designing programs to implement those goals. [33] These differences reflect contrasting roles and are rooted in institutional positions. Political appointees are in-and-outers. That is, they are recruited to serve a particular president and rarely stay longer than a president, usually much less. The average tenure of a political appointee in a position is about two years. This rapid turnover is often motivated by the desire of presidential appointees to make their mark quickly and move on, either to a higher position in the government or back to the private sector to make more money. Much of the appointees' agendas are driven by the mandate to reelect a president or to leave a good record to run on for the partisan heir-apparent.

Career executives, in contrast, have a longer-term perspective. They will still be operating programs and administering agencies after the political birds of passage have left. This causes them to pay attention to the health of institutions and to the integrity of the processes that assure non-partisan implementation of the laws. The rules and regulations designed to do this can also be used to insulate and protect civil servants from either legitimate or illegitimate political controls. This longer-term perspective makes them less willing to upset long established practices quickly. But "bureaucratic inertia" is not a sufficiently subtle description of this type of behavior. Hugh Heclo describes the elements of bureaucratic dispositions as gradualism, indirection, political caution, and a concern for maintaining relationships.[34] Bureaucrats are concerned about the institutions they manage as well as the current policies of those institutions. Politicians tend to see organizations as convenient tools to achieve their policy objectives.[35]

The basic dilemma that underlies government in the United States is that the permanent bureaucracy must be responsive to the current president, yet it must maintain the necessary professionalism in its career managers to be able to accomplish missions effectively and efficiently.

The Cycle of Accommodation

Despite initial distrust of career executives, political appointees usually develop over time a trust for the career executives who report to them. This is a predictable cycle that has operated in all recent presidential administrations, even if not in all political appointees. The cycle is characterized by initial suspicion and hostility, which is followed by two or three years of learning to work together. This results in a more sophisticated appreciation of the contribution of the career service and a mutual respect and trust.

To take an extreme case, John Ehrlichman, who had characterized relations with the bureaucracy as "guerrilla warfare," later felt that it was a "big mistake" for the Nixon administration to exclude career executives from policy deliberations, both because of their expertise and because of their ability to develop support for the administration's programs. "I did not encounter devastating problems with the bureaucracy." You have to remember that the career service is not a "faceless, formless enemy."[36]

Other high-level White House officials have come to similar conclusions about the career service. Theodore Sorensen recalled his White House experience with the bureaucracy: "The career services are a vastly underused resource, particularly by new presidents who come in suspicious of the career services and confident that they can run everything themselves with their political hired hands. That's a mistake. I don't think that a president needs to have a vast number of political appointees going well down into the agencies. I believe the career services will respond to a president who has some confidence and trust in them, and who knows how to tap their expertise."[37]

After serving in the Carter White House for four years, Jack Watson had strong feelings about the career bureaucracy. "I honestly believe that the career bureaucracy for the most part are professionals, civil servants in the positive sense, who want to serve the new administration.... I never experienced some sinister counter force out there seeking to undermine and sabotage our administration. A president should go into office with an operating assumption, a rebuttable presumption, that the people of the government are there to serve him and to help him succeed."[38] "One good careerist is worth ten campaigners," declared Harrison Wellford, Carter's top management person at OMB.[39]

Craig Fuller of the Reagan White House said, "My experience in the four years that I've been here is that ... the relationship between the political appointee and the career people in the departments is very much a partnership.... I don't come at this with some notion that we have some norm of behavior among the career staff that is totally at odds or variance with the ideals of the political appointee."[40]

These attitudes of White House aides are shared by the vast majority of presidential appointees in recent administrations. In a survey sent by the National Academy of Public Administration (NAPA) to all presidential appointees between 1964 and 1984, each appointee was asked to characterize how *responsive* and *competent* the career employees of their agencies were. Those who responded that career employees were "responsive" or "very responsive" (4 or 5 on a 5-point scale) are reported in table 3.1.

Thus the evidence is overwhelming that experienced political appointees, regardless of administration, party, or ideology, believe that career executives are both competent and responsive.

TABLE 3.1

PRESIDENTIAL APPOINTEES' PERCEPTIONS OF CAREER
EMPLOYEES' COMPETENCE AND RESPONSIVENESS

Administration	Competence	Responsiveness
Johnson	92%	89%
Nixon	88	84
Ford	80	82
Carter	81	86
Reagan	77	78

SOURCE: National Academy of Public Administration, Presidential Appointees Project, *Leadership in Jeopardy: The Fraying of the Presidential Appointments System* (Washington: NAPA, 1985). All presidential appointees who were still alive and whose addresses could be verified were polled. The response rate was 56 percent.

More personal reflections of presidential appointees from different administrations reinforce these statistical data.[41]

The Johnson Administration—John Gardner, Secretary of Health, Education and Welfare:

> I would strongly urge any incoming top official to come in with the recognition that he has a lot of potential allies around him.... People who would be glad to help if they got the chance. One of the great mistakes people make in coming in is developing a we/they attitude toward their own staff.... Big mistake. There are a lot of potential teammates out there, and you have to find them. And the faster you do the better.... I fairly soon found the people who could keep me out of the beartraps and could advise me.... I found that immensely helpful, and I think any newcomer will.

The Nixon Administration—Elliot Richardson, Secretary of Commerce, Defense, HEW, and Attorney General:

> I did find them easy to work with. I did find them competent.... they saw their own roles in a manner that virtually required political leadership. They didn't want to have to make the choices on competing claims that are the function of the political process.... People who had devoted a lifetime or significant part of it to expertise in their field are entitled to be listened to with respect.... many presidential appointees make the gross mistake of not sufficiently respecting the people they are dealing with ... and get themselves into trouble as a result.

The Carter Administration—Walter McDonald, Assistant Secretary of Treasury:

> Without exception I never found an administration as it was leaving office that had anything but praise for the career service in general, and respect.... I think a learning process takes place. I think politicals learn after they're burned a few times that careerists are really there to serve them. They're not wedded to any party.... And it's very hard for the politicals to understand that.... and it takes four years to convince them of this. How you do this, god, I don't know.

The Reagan Administration—Richard Lyng, Secretary of Agriculture:

> In every case, I found career people that were absolutely splendid. Their experience was absolutely invaluable. I needed them, it was essential. The

career people kept me from shooting myself in the foot.... The way you get them (career bureaucrats) with you is to treat them like equals, point out I need you to help me. These people want the job done right. I never cared if a fellow was a Democrat or a Republican, because ... all of them are nonpartisan.... A presidential appointee who doesn't work with the career people will not make it.

The ways in which career executives are critical to the success of their political superiors are many. They are highly educated and they know the intricacies of the laws and regulations governing programs they implement. They are the repositories of organizational memory. They remember who were allies and enemies in past turf battles. They know whom to go to for help in central management agencies or in Congress. Their personal intelligence and communication networks have been built up over many years dealing with the same organizations, people, and issues.

One political appointee described the importance of the memory of career executives. "Those same people keep you out of trouble. You get a decision, someone recommends this, and some special interest group comes in and says 'do this,' or some agency in the government or the White House. You bring in the staff and say, what if we do this? They'll say well, if you do that, this is what will happen, and these guys will get mad. Or they'll say, yeah, that was tried in 1931 and again in 1938 and here's what happened. You've got to have those guys with you." [42] To ignore this source of advice and expertise is shortsighted and self-defeating.

Not only are career executives responsive, but they perform functions that are essential to the proper operation of the government and to the success of the political appointees for whom they work. While we expect career executives to be responsive to political leadership, at the same time we expect them to resist illegal or unethical direction from above. For instance, we would expect career bureaucrats to resist orders to allocate grants based on illegal or political criteria at variance with the established laws and regulations governing the grant process. We would also expect them to blow the whistle rather than cover up illegal activities by their colleagues or political superiors. One example of appropriate bureaucratic resistance was the refusal of the Internal Revenue Service (IRS) to audit George McGovern's campaign aides' tax returns at the order of the Nixon White House.[43] Thus we expect bureaucrats to be responsive, but not *too* responsive.

In legitimate matters career executives should be expected to do more than passively carry out orders. A "yes, boss" attitude is not merely inadequate, it may be downright dangerous. One career executive remembers warning his newly appointed political boss that a sole-source contract granted to the boss's former colleagues "would not pass the smell test" in

Washington. His boss did not grant the contract and later thanked him for the warning.[44] In contrast, one "responsive" bureaucrat followed orders without questions and "left my ass in one of the biggest slings in town by letting me redecorate the office," according to one political appointee.[45] These contrasting examples illustrate the types of responsiveness that may make or break a new political appointee.

True neutral competence is "loyalty that argues back," according to Hugh Heclo.[46] One appointee of President Reagan described his relations with career civil servants: "They were responsive to clear, rational guidance. They wouldn't always agree, I would have been concerned had they always agreed with me; but I was always the boss, that was never in doubt."[47] Having "my own person" in the job is not enough, that person must have the requisite knowledge and skills to make the bureaucratic machine work and the good judgment to warn the boss about impending trouble.

That the responsiveness of career employees will not prevent turf battles or the frustration of presidential initiatives must be stressed. Bureaucratic warfare and turf battles always plague presidents, but the cleavages run along agency and programmatic lines, with political appointees and bureaucrats on the same sides of the barricades. Incidents like end runs to Congress and leaks to the press surface in every administration, but as likely as not they are instigated by a president's own political appointees.

Resistance to presidential directives is inevitable, but it is important to keep in mind that this resistance stems from members of Congress, interest groups, and the leadership of executive branch agencies. Career bureaucrats may be a part of these opposing forces, but they are seldom the instigators or even the most influential participants. Using the career service as a scapegoat for all resistance to presidential desires may be comforting, but it does not represent an accurate analysis of power in Washington.

The Tradeoff Between Responsiveness and Effectiveness

The United States' system of executive branch leadership was designed to maximize responsiveness to the electorate by ensuring that many top positions throughout the government are filled by supporters of the president. But there is a tradeoff in efficiency and effectiveness for responsiveness. Just as the separation of powers system undercuts efficiency, the political appointee system often results in inefficiencies, with rapid turnover of positions and reversals of policy direction. But this is a small price to pay for a system that brings with it the ability to respond rapidly to the wishes of the electorate.

In addition to providing this democratic link, the "in-and-outer" system has other virtues. It brings into the bureaucracy fresh ideas and "new blood" to try them out. It brings in people who have not been worn down by the system and who can afford to work at full speed for the president's program for several years and return to their previous careers when they approach the burnout stage. It brings in people who are working on the cutting edge of new technologies or management practice, people who can transfer new ways of doing things to the government.

But the increasing number of political appointees and the increasingly deep penetration of them into the bureaucratic machinery may have reached the point of diminishing returns. Is there a point at which increasing political control no longer enhances the effective implementation of presidential priorities? Some would suggest that this point was passed in the United States in the 1980s. Patricia Ingraham has concluded: "The end result is *not* enhanced presidential direction or control but a political management void." [48]

In comparing the United States to western European democracies, Hugh Heclo has observed: "the foreign studies suggest that accountable political control of the bureaucracy is not necessarily a function of the number of political appointees in the bureaucracy. In fact the relationship may be inverse." [49]

Drawbacks of this shift of balance toward a larger number of political appointees are several. First, it is difficult to recruit high-quality political appointees for some of the lower subcabinet positions. Elliot Richardson observed in 1985:

> I think this Administration has tried to cut too deep into the system by turning jobs traditionally held by career people over to appointees. The price paid is I think significant ... the lower level the job, the less attractive it may appear to one coming from the outside. The consequence of this is that a lot of people recruited as political appointees for that sort of job have not had outstanding competence. This Administration is full of turkeys who have undercut the quality of public service in their areas. [50]

Filling high-level appointive positions is not a major problem, but the lower levels of the subcabinet (for instance, deputy assistant secretaries) are increasingly filled with those who are relatively young and inexperienced. While these people may be talented, they may not have the maturity or experience needed in positions of great responsibility. They may be merely "ticket punchers" looking for experience to allow them to get good jobs when they leave the government.

Second, the skills and motivation of the career service are undermined. According to John Gardner, "There are far more political appointees, and the political tests of those appointees are narrower and sharper, certainly more deeply partisan over the past 15 years. Also, the degree to which they subordinate the career people under them, diminishing the integrity and dignity of the career people, is increasing. You can't have an effective government with people who are cowed and dumped on." [51]

Another problem with layering too many political appointees over career bureaucrats is that it closes off career options to career executives. According to Elliot Richardson, "You reduce the opportunities for career people to rise to positions of responsibility. You have amputated the career level and thus reduced the attractiveness of the career service." [52] Shutting off career paths too soon may let the career service "go to seed.... And so it is that by not being consulted, senior careerists over time become less worth consulting, less worth appointing to the more responsible departmental positions." [53]

Third, the short tenure of political appointees aggravates the problem. It takes considerable time to master the operations of high-level positions in huge organizations. And only after the job itself has been mastered can the incumbent work at maximum effectiveness. But the tenure of political appointees has fallen to about two years.[54] Such short terms encourage many appointees to think about their own careers rather than the interests of the organization they are running. They may be tempted to sacrifice "long-term working relations and procedural norms for immediate policy objectives." They have enough time to make mistakes, but not enough time to learn from them.[55]

Finally, layering political appointees, particularly in staff positions, diffuses legitimate political authority and attenuates the link between the responsible political official and the career implementors of policy. Frederic Malek, who had broad experience as an appointee of President Nixon and who headed the White House Personnel Office, makes a convincing argument for fewer political appointees:

> The solution to problems of rigidity and resistance to change in the government is *not* to increase the number of appointive positions at the top, as so many politicians are wont to do.... This task is difficult for an administration and is seldom done effectively.... In many cases, the effectiveness of an agency would be improved and political appointments would be reduced by roughly 25 percent if line positions beneath the assistant secretary level were reserved for career officials.[56]

These observations are even more relevant in the 1990s than they were in the late 1970s when fewer political appointees were available to presidents.

Conclusion

Recent presidents have tried to increase control of the executive branch by increasing the number of political appointees and by tightening White

House control over political appointments and career executives. This chapter has argued that career executives are responsive to legitimate political control and that increasing politicization is counterproductive to effective government. The trend toward more political appointees should be reversed for the following reasons:

1. A democratic government needs the capacity to change directions when a new president and Congress are elected. The ability to change means that the institutional capacity to do so must be available to a new administration. The bureaucratic machine must be there and ready to respond. This capacity is impaired if the bureaucracy is completely decapitated with each change of administration. Thus, career executives must be able to operate at the upper levels of the government and gain experience with "the big picture." But along with this power comes the duty to embrace the normative ideal of the politics/administration dichotomy, even as they are involved in policy formulation and high-level decision making.

2. Each president needs a capable and effective governmental apparatus to carry out the administration's policy priorities. It is particularly important for new presidents to "hit the ground running" with their policy initiatives in order to take advantage of the election mandate and the honeymoon with Congress.[57] They will be able to do this only if the bureaucracy is ready to move. But the longer it takes new political appointees to establish working relationships with the career bureaucracy, the longer it is before the bureaucracy can work effectively for a president. The more political appointees there are and the more layers which separate the agency head and career executives, the longer it will take to establish effective control.

3. The present large number of political appointees strains the capacity of the White House to do effective recruitment and selection. According to Frederic Malek, President Nixon's presidential personnel assistant, "If you try to do everything, I'm not so sure you can succeed. It's an awfully difficult job just to handle the *presidential* appointees. I'm concerned that if you try to do too much, you may be diluted to the point where you're not as effective."[58]

The argument here is not to discard the in-and-outer system that has served government well. The argument is that the capacity of the White House is being strained and the effectiveness of the government is being undermined by the present trend toward increasing numbers of political appointees. Reversing this direction would increase the capacity of the government to function efficiently and effectively without sacrificing political accountability or responsiveness.

Notes

1. The author would like to thank the following colleagues for comments on an earlier draft: Edie Goldenberg, University of Michigan; Michael Hansen, American University; Charles Levine, Congressional Research Service; Nancy Lind, Illinois State University; Terry Moe, Stanford University; Alana Northrop, California State University, Fullerton; Paul Quirk, University of Pennsylvania; Lester Salamon, the Urban Institute; and Richard Stillman, George Mason University.

2. See James W. Fesler, "The Higher Civil Service in Europe and the United States," in *The Higher Civil Service in Europe and Canada,* ed. Bruce L.R. Smith (Washington, D.C.: Brookings Institution, 1984). In France the total number is 500, but most of these come from the career civil service.

3. On the development of public personnel policy in the United States, see Frederick C. Mosher, *Democracy and the Public Service* (New York: Oxford University Press, 1984).

4. For an argument that this undermined bureaucratic capacity, see Garry Wills, *The Kennedy Imprisonment* (New York: Atlantic/Little Brown, 1982).

5. *Public Papers of the Presidents, 1971,* 448–65.

6. See U.S. House of Representatives, *Violations and Abuses of Merit Principles in Federal Employment, Hearings before the Subcommittee on Manpower and Civil Service of the House Committee on Post Office and Civil Service,* 94th Cong., 1st sess., 10 April 1975.

7. Quoted in James Sundquist, "Jimmy Carter as Public Administrator," *Public Administration Review* 39 (January/February 1979): 8.

8. See Charles Jones, "Keeping Faith and Losing Congress: The Carter Experience in Washington," *Presidential Studies Quarterly* 14 (Summer 1984): 437; and James Sundquist, "Jimmy Carter as Public Administrator," *Public Administration Review* 39 (January/February 1979): 3.

9. Edie N. Goldenberg, "The Permanent Government in an Era of Retrenchment and Redirection," in *The Reagan Presidency and the Governing of America,* ed. Lester Salamon and Michael Lund (Washington, D.C.: Urban Institute, 1985), 390. The number of full-time equivalent positions eliminated came to about 75,000.

10. See James D. Carroll, A. Lee Fritschler, and Bruce L.R. Smith, "Supply-Side Management in the Reagan Administration," *Public Administration Review* 45 (November/December 1985): 805.

11. David Stanley, Dean Mann, and Jameson Doig, *Men Who Govern* (Washington, D.C.: Brookings Institution, 1967), 4; and Linda Fisher, "Fifty Years of Presidential Appointments," in *The In-and-Outers,* ed. G. Calvin Mackenzie (Baltimore: Johns Hopkins University Press, 1987).

12. Patricia W. Ingraham, "Political Direction, Control and Abuse: The Administrative Presidency and the Significance of the Fine Line." Paper presented at the 1986 American Political Science Association convention, 21.

13. See Bernard Rosen, "Effective Continuity of U.S. Government Operations in Jeopardy," *Public Administration Review* 43 (September/October 1983): 383.

14. Ingraham, "Political Direction, Control and Abuse," 22.

15. *Federal Register* 46, no. 115 (16 June 1981): 31405; *Federal Personnel Manual Bulletin* 213–32 (24 April 1980, "Temporary Schedule C Appointing Authority").

16. Ingraham, "Political Direction," 21.

17. Dean Mann with Jameson Doig, *The Assistant Secretaries* (Washington, D.C.: Brookings Institution, 1965), 99, 265.

18. For an analysis of this trend, see James P. Pfiffner, "Nine Enemies and One Ingrate: Presidential Appointments During Transition," in Mackenzie, *The In-and-Outers.*

19. National Academy of Public Administration, "Recruiting Presidential Appointees," Conference of Presidential Personnel Assistants, December 1984, 10.

20. Interview with Edwin Meese, Attorney General's Office, 2 July 1985.

21. Michael Sanera, "Implementing the Agenda," in *Mandate for Leadership II,* ed. Stuart M. Butler, Michael Sanera, and W. Bruce Weinrod (Washington, D.C.: Heritage Foundation, 1984).

22. "Implementing the Agenda," 514–15.

23. For a detailed critique of Sanera's position, see James P. Pfiffner, "Political Public Administration," *Public Administration Review* 45 (March/April 1985): 352.

24. "The Politicized Presidency," in *The New Direction in American Politics,* ed. John E. Chubb and Paul E. Peterson (Washington, D.C.: Brookings Institution, 1985).

25. Ibid., 271.

26. "The Study of Administration," *Political Science Quarterly* 2 (June 1887): 197–222, reprinted in Frederick C. Mosher, ed., *Basic Literature of American Public Administration, 1787–1950* (New York: Holmes and Meier, 1981).

27. "Politics as a Vocation," in *From Max Weber,* ed. H.H. Gerth and C.W. Mills (New York: Oxford University Press, 1946), 95.

28. See Edie Goldenberg, "The Permanent Government in a Time of Retrenchment and Redirection," in *Reagan Presidency,* ed. Salamon and Lund.

29. Joel D. Aberbach, Robert D. Putnam, and Bert Rockman, *Bureaucrats and Politicians in Western Democracies* (Cambridge: Harvard University Press, 1981), 6.

30. Terry M. Moe, "The Politicized Presidency," in Chubb and Peterson, *New Direction in American Politics,* 265.

31. "The In and Outer System: A Critical Assessment," in *The In-and-Outers, in Mackenzie, The In-and-Outers.*

32. For a discussion of several different interpretations of the role of civil servants, see Goldenberg, "Permanent Government in a Time of Retrenchment." See also Paul Light, "When Worlds Collide: The Political/Career Nexus," in Mackenzie, *The In-and-Outers.*

33. See Richard Rose, "Steering the Ship of State: One Tiller But Two

Pairs of Hands," Centre for the Study of Public Policy, University of Strathclyde, 1986, 8.

34. Hugh Heclo, *A Government of Strangers* (Washington, D.C.: Brookings Institution, 1977), chap. 4.

35. See Hugh Heclo, "Executive Budget Making," in *Federal Budget Policy in the 1980s*, ed. Gregory Mills and John Palmer (Washington, D.C.: Urban Institute, 1984).

36. Interview with John Ehrlichman, Santa Fe, 3 June 1983.

37. Interview with Theodore Sorensen, New York City, 25 March 1985.

38. Interview with Jack Watson, 17 June 1983.

39. Interview with Harrison Wellford, 7 July 1983.

40. Quoted in *P A Times*, 1 January 1985.

41. Each of these quotations is taken from the transcripts of interviews of the NAPA Presidential Appointees Project. The interviews were conducted by Jeremy Plant and Michael Hansen.

42. NAPA, Presidential Appointees Project, interview with Richard Lyng, assistant secretary of agriculture for President Nixon and secretary of agriculture for President Reagan.

43. See Richard Nixon, *RN* (New York: Grosset and Dunlap, 1978), 676; and H.R. Haldeman, *The Ends of Power* (New York: Times Books, 1978), 150.

44. Interview with Al Zuck, Washington, 1983.

45. Quoted in Heclo, *Government of Strangers*, 177.

46. Hugh Heclo, "OMB and the Presidency—The Problem of Neutral Competence," *Public Interest*, no. 38 (Winter 1975): 80–82.

47. NAPA, Presidential Appointees Project, interview with Erich Evered, administrator, Energy Information Administration, 1981–84.

48. Ingraham, "Political Direction, Control and Abuse," 16.

49. "A Comment on the Future of the U.S. Civil Service," in Smith, *Higher Civil Service in Europe and Canada*.

50. NAPA, Presidential Appointees Project, interview with Elliot Richardson.

51. *New York Times*, 4 July 1985, A14.

52. NAPA, Presidential Appointees Project, interview with Elliot Richardson.

53. Hugh Heclo, "The In and Outer System: A Critical Assessment," in Mackenzie, *The In-and-Outers*.

54. See Linda Fisher, "Fifty Years of Presidential Appointees," in Mackenzie, *The In-and-Outers*.

55. Heclo, "The In and Outer System: A Critical Assessment," in Mackenzie, *The In-and-Outers*.

56. Frederic V. Malek, *Washington's Hidden Tragedy* (New York: Free Press, 1978), 102–3.

57. For an analysis of the need for presidents to move quickly upon taking office, see James P. Pfiffner, *The Strategic Presidency: Hitting the Ground Running* (Chicago: Dorsey, 1988).

58. NAPA, "Recruiting Presidential Appointees: A Conference of Former Presidential Personnel Assistants," 13 December 1984. Italics added.

4

The Consequences of a Minimalist
Paradigm for Governance:
A Comparative Analysis

COLIN CAMPBELL, S.J., AND DONALD NAULLS

This chapter* argues that the decline of the federal public service stems from a minimalist perspective of government advanced by the public-choice view of bureaucracy that took root in the late 1960s and early 1970s. It starts with a brief assessment of the approach of a major proponent of this school—William Niskanen—who introduced the term *budget-maximizing bureaucrat* to the lexicon of political economy.

We probe whether the public-choice view is minimalist both in its conception of what government should be doing and in its assumption of the worst of government officials' motives. Further, we explore the issue of whether it becomes a self-fulfilling prophecy in that bureaucracies serving politicians and citizenries who have adopted a "meanness" of mind increasingly assume the motivational psyche of their masters. In systems that have proven relatively successful in constraining the expansion of budgets, the introduction of a strongly minimalist ideology can work acutely deleterious effects on the very fabric of governance.

Limitations of Public-Choice Theory

Niskanen chooses as the unit of his analysis the bureau. He delineates these organizations from others according to two criteria: (1) the owners and employees of bureaus do not derive personal income from the profits of the organization; (2) at least part of the revenues of the bureau accrue from appropriations or grants, rather than simply sales.[1]

---

* The analysis in this chapter builds on and substantially expands a chapter titled "The Limits of the Budget Maximizing Theory: Some Evidence from Officials' Views of Their Roles and Careers," in *The Budget Maximizing Bureaucrat: The Empirical Evidence,* ed. Andre Blais and Stephane Dion (Pittsburgh: University of Pittsburgh Press, 1991).

Many organizations might satisfy the criteria Niskanen employs. But he centers his attention on governmental bureaucracies and the orientations of the people who operate these institutions.[2] Significantly, he includes among bureaucrats both those who have dedicated themselves to a permanent career in the civil service and those who received their appointments from the elected executive.

Niskanen was writing in a period of governmental expansion. Thus the tendency in that epoch for bureaucracies to seek and usually gain enhanced budgets absorbs Niskanen's attention. He asserts that bureaucrats demonstrate a deep-seated inclination toward budget maximization.[3] This phenomenon owes to the strength of the link between individual officials' personal utility and the benefits that a robust budget can advance. These include an adequate salary, perquisites, public reputation, power, patronage, and the output of the bureaucrats' organization.

This chapter assesses this approach from the standpoint of what we know about the motives of senior civil servants. Before moving to our data analysis, we first offer some reflections on the applicability of Niskanen's work to Anglo-American systems other than the United States, especially in the light of developments in bureaucracy since 1971. This section, in effect, proposes some caveats about the portability of the budget-maximization theory.

Problems with Portability

Niskanen's *Bureaucracy and Representative Government* obviously has had a tremendous impact on thinking about bureaucracy both in the United States and elsewhere. For instance, the monograph *Bureaucracy: Servant or Master? Lessons from America* and the fact that Margaret Thatcher made it required reading at the outset of her government point up the influence of Niskanen's thought in the United Kingdom.[4] Indeed, Niskanen's approach, along with other public-choice-oriented theories, has contributed to the development of programs designed to inculcate in senior officials a greater ability to clarify their objectives and minimize their claims on resources. With the emergence of such "managerialism" in the United Kingdom, Canada, Australia, and New Zealand, we find that Whitehall-style bureaucratic systems increasingly evaluate the performance of senior officials on the basis of how effectively and efficiently they utilize their resources.[5]

Notwithstanding Niskanen's and others' impact, any scholar who has attempted a cross-national comparison of bureaucratic cultures has to question how readily a theory developed to describe the behavior of bureaus in the United States might accommodate a similar task in a "Whitehall/Westminster" system of government. The upper levels of the American public service differ substantially from those in Whitehall/Westminster systems.

In the United States, political appointees penetrate down four levels in administrative hierarchies below the cabinet-level head of a department of agency. This contrasts sharply with the practice in Whitehall/Westminster systems where permanent heads serve as the deputy to the cabinet-rank minister and career civil servants fill all the remaining slots in the administrative hierarchy.

Permanent officials in the United States tend to spend the bulk of their careers within highly specialized offices and bureaus without moving between units, let alone departments.[6] In Whitehall/Westminster systems, officials move frequently both within and between departments. Indeed, some studies of career routes in the Canadian public service suggest that the more frequently officials change departments, the more rapidly they rise to the most senior posts.[7]

The tendency for U.S. permanent officials to focus their careers in one relatively narrow field of government contributes greatly to the ossification of relationships between civil servants, congressional staff, and interest groups in U.S. policy sectors. Scholars have characterized the institutional sclerosis[8] originating from rigid client-patron relationships in the United States variously as "subgovernment," rule by "iron triangles," and "atomization."[9]

We might expect that the infusion of political appointees to U.S. departments and agencies would offset the tendency of career officials to follow overly specialized career routes. But if we differentiate between "politicos" and "amphibians" among appointees, it becomes clear that the latter often become intensely specialized. Politicos obtain appointments mostly on the basis of their adeptness at political operations, whereas amphibians usually draw both on detailed knowledge of some substantive policy field and some previous experience working in that area within government.[10] Hugh Heclo has maintained that amphibians—he terms them "public careerists"— constitute a de facto higher civil service in the United States.[11]

Niskanen posits a symbiosis between the interests of top-level officials and legislative committees that cannot be assumed in Whitehall/Westminster systems. Even if it did exist, it would not work anywhere near the same effects toward budget maximization. Niskanen asserts that the members of legislative committees seek to maximize the net benefits of specialized areas of government activity to their constituents.[12] They therefore share a mutual interest with bureaucrats in the expansion of programs.

Two conditions must prevail in order for this symbiosis to operate as a major factor in executive-legislative relations. To begin, legislators must have the power to form specialized committees that enjoy mandates going beyond the term of a parliamentary session. They also must be able to determine the membership of these committees without interference from the political leadership of the executive branch. In the U.K., Canadian, Australian, and New Zealand systems, none of the legislatures satisfied these criteria in 1971. While all of these systems have made some progress toward security of mandate and tenure in the past twenty years, they currently have achieved, at best, fledgling status when compared to congressional committees in the United States.

The second condition for symbiosis between bureaucrats and elected politicians builds on the first. It requires that what the legislative committee does in the policy process makes a difference.[13] That is, the committee's hearings and deliberations actually exert consistent and substantive sway over the formulation and implementation of policies and the allocation of resources to competing programs. Nelson Polsby terms legislatures whose committees possess a capacity—independent of the political executive—to mold and reshape laws and budgets "transformative."[14] No Whitehall/Westminster legislature has attained this position. At best, we can posit only limited symbiosis between Whitehall/Westminster bureaucrats and legislators because any linkages that have developed would still fall far short of producing transformative consequences.

As James B. Christoph has put it, Whitehall departments enjoy monopolies over administrative resources in most policy sectors that make it very difficult for ministers and groups alike to contest their received wisdom.[15] But even the substantial leverage of career public servants in the United Kingdom does not necessarily translate into budget-maximizing behavior. This largely owes to the immense power of H.M. Treasury in reviewing the expenditure plans of individual departments. Some important institutional features buttress the Treasury's role. Since 1974, an increasing proportion of government programs have come under a "cash limit" regime. This discipline has greatly reduced cost overruns based on special pleading about unexpected events or higher-than-anticipated inflation. Second, Treasury officials work closely with the financial officers of departments to reach agreement on the guidelines for making bids for new money or identifying savings through the Public Expenditure Survey (PES). Finally, an informal body—termed the Star Chamber and chaired by a senior cabinet minister—settles the handful of disputes that remain after the fall round of bilaterals between the Treasury and departments.

Political executive/bureaucrat/interest-group relationships in Canada contrast sharply with those in the United Kingdom. The high degree of regional, economic, and cultural segmentation of Canadian society has since the beginning of Confederation imposed an array of representational imperatives on the cabinet that does not exist in Britain.[16] The fact that Parliament functions as a nontransformative legislature exacerbates societal pressures that would make legitimation of the federal government's role difficult even if the country had a Congress-like legislature. Fear of the consequences of divisive public discourse tends to make party discipline in

Canada even stricter than that in the United Kingdom. In many cases, working out agreements between contesting groups in secret cabinet sessions becomes the only way in which to resolve key issues without divisive controversy.[17] In the transaction, Canadians expect that they will have spokesmen in the cabinet—especially individuals who will express the views of their region, province, or locality and their ethnic/cultural group.

Such representational imperatives have tended at least since the turn of the century to inflate the size of the cabinet and the complexity of the public service.[18] Beginning with Lester B. Pearson in 1963, successive governments have attempted to bring greater control to the budgetary process.[19] They have tried several major reorganizations of cabinet processes and supporting central coordinating agencies. Yet few of these efforts have had appreciable effects. In fiscal year 1982-83, after the most intense period of institutional reform, the federal government's expenditures exceeded its revenues by fully 50 percent. The deficit for 1988-89 was some $29 billion. Those who blame the budget-maximizing bureaucracy on the symbiosis between legislatures and the absence of central guidance systems in the executive branch might well reflect on the Canadian experience.[20]

It becomes clear that the exact conditions that give rise to budget-maximizing behavior among bureaucrats in the United States do not pertain in the United Kingdom and Canada. In Canada, however, the representational imperative works on the cabinet—its size, structure, and dynamics—to mimic the circumstances of the U.S. budgetary process, without, of course, the presence of a transformative legislature. We now turn to an examination of whether differences in public servants' reports of their motives and aspirations for their departments and agencies relate to the nature of their bureaucratic cultures.

Different Bureaucratic Cultures

One of us, in an article with B. Guy Peters and a subsequent review essay,[21] has attempted to point up the degree to which bureaucratic cultures differ. Without giving due regard to various systemic patterns, we cannot make any valid comparisons of officials' motives and behavior. This assertion rests largely on what scholars have found over the past two decades about the applicability of the policy/administration dichotomy across executive-bureaucratic systems—even between types of units within them.

The salience of the policy/administration dichotomy strikes at the heart of any treatment of budget-maximizing bureaucracy. Niskanen's theory simply highlights one way in which, it is alleged, officials have put themselves in the driver's seat so that they—not elected authorities—determine agendas, rank priorities, and establish the contours and extent of implementation.

Such a condition—where officials influence policy as much as politicians—would fly in the face of the received wisdom on the role of bureaucrats that dominated thinking about public administration through the first half of this century. It claims little currency these days. Since World War II, political scientists have beat a gradual retreat from this purist notion.[22] In the 1950s, the view emerged that officials involve themselves in policy but confine their interventions to relevant facts and knowledge.[23] By the 1960s, scholars increasingly accepted that bureaucrats engage themselves in political calculation and manipulation, although they respond to a narrower band of concerns and with less passion or ideology than do politicians.[24]

Aberbach, Putnam, and Rockman have identified a third view of bureaucracy along the path away from the policy/administration dichotomy.[25] They adduce some recent literature suggesting that some civil servants—usually at the highest levels or in the most strategically located units—do develop and employ a full range of behind-the-scenes political skills and passionately commit themselves to assuring specific policy outcomes.

Aberbach, Putnam, and Rockman note how these "pure hybrids" have made their presence felt in the interlocking career ladders of politicians and career civil servants in France and Japan;[26] in the assumption of positions specially created for "outsiders" in Britain and Germany;[27] and in interventionist central agencies that foster a "superbureaucratic" mentality.[28]

Campbell and Peters, and Campbell alone, further developed the pure-hybrid thesis by positing three broad types of politically oriented officials: (1) reactive career bureaucrats (i.e., traditional officials in whose case only incrementalism and intransigence betrays deeper political commitments than their aura of detached competence suggests); (2) proactive permanent civil servants, who engage collegially with the political authorities of the day and work to comprehensive policy agendas; and (3) party-political officials, who owe their positions to overt party connections but occupy hierarchical positions within the bureaucracy and style themselves as policy professionals.[29]

The Case of Central Agents

In several studies we, along with George J. Szablowski of York University and John Halligan of the University of Canberra, have conducted a series of in-depth interviews designed to ascertain the role perceptions, behavioral orientations, and social-demographic backgrounds of officials in central agencies. Our research has centered on systems in the United States (1979 and 1982-83), United Kingdom (1978 and 1986-87), Canada (1976), Australia (1988), and Switzerland (1978). For the purposes of this chapter, we focus our current analysis on U.S. political appointees under the Carter and Reagan administrations, career officials under Carter, U.K. permanent officials in 1978, and Canadian civil servants in 1976.

Central agencies are departments or offices that take or share the lead in five functions with overarching importance in any executive-bureaucratic complex. These concern the development of strategic plans for a government/administration and making substantive policy decisions that reflect these, devising and integrating economic and fiscal policies, allocation of budgets and setting policies for the management of government resources, management of senior personnel, and—in federal systems—conducting federal-provincial relations. Those working in central agencies normally base their leverage within the governmental apparatus on close proximity to the chief executive or head of government, a special role regarding support of the cabinet or one of its committees, or association with a minister who enjoys a privileged relationship to the president or prime minister in connection with an overarching function.

In 1976, Canadian central agencies included the Prime Minister's Office (supporting the prime minister), the Privy Council Office (the prime minister and cabinet), the Federal-Provincial Relations Office (the prime minister and cabinet), the Treasury Board Secretariat (serving a cabinet committee), and the Finance Department (the finance minister). In 1979, U.K. central agencies took in No. 10 Downing St. (supporting the prime minister), the Cabinet Office and the Central Policy Review Staff (the prime minister and cabinet), the Civil Service Department (the prime minister as the minister responsible for the civil service), H.M. Treasury (the chancellor of the exchequer). In both 1979 and 1982-83, U.S. central agencies consisted of the White House Office and the Executive Office of the President—with the latter including the Office of Management and Budget (supporting the president), the Office of Personnel Management (the president), and the Department of the Treasury (the treasury secretary). The numbers of respondents in the four groups are Canada, 92; United Kingdom, 41; and United States (1979), 63 appointees and 69 career, and (1982-83) 60 appointees.

Allowing for overlap along the margins, we might expect British central agents to fit more the reactive career bureaucrats' mold discussed in the preceding section. Their Canadian counterparts served, especially at the time of the interviews (1976), almost as exemplars of the more up-front and aggressive proactive permanent civil servant. U.S. appointees, of course, are party-political officials. This leaves us with U.S. career central agents. To be sure, these officials perch in strategically placed departments. Nevertheless, two features of the U.S. bureaucratic culture caution us against assuming that the career central agents there would more likely resemble the Canadians than the British. First, U.S. officials—working at least five levels down in their organizations—function somewhat more remotely from the highest level of political authority than do Canadians. This is especially the case when we consider that Canadian central agents frequently attend and participate in cabinet-level meetings. Second, U.S. central agents—due largely to their relative lack of mobility between units —tend more than their Canadian counterparts to become impregnated with the approach and agenda of their specialized policy cadre.

Measure of Budget Maximization

We derived a simple additive measure of budget maximization based on responses to a series of questions attempting to ascertain officials' views of how well their agencies function within their policy sector. The items started off with an inquiry as to whether the agency role is being adequately performed. Weight was given to strongly negative, negative, and neutral responses.

Next, we asked those interviewed to diagnose the sources of any problems. We gave further weighting to those pinpointing a need for more budgetary and/or personnel resources. We then requested to focus on whom/what they blamed for their problems. We assessed additional points if they placed some of the fault at the feet of politicians—cabinet members and/or legislators—and if they associated their problems with the magnitude and complexity of the difficulties they faced.

We then asked officials how they thought the problems with their agency could be remedied. We assigned an additional point if they prescribed increased budgets or personnel. The final items through which respondents could receive further weighting consisted of whether they indicated that they believed change in their department's situation should be sought and whether they in fact believed that it would actually come about.

The scale results in a range from zero for those who failed to obtain a single point for budget maximization to 11 for the three respondents who received weightings on each item. The mean for all 325 cases was 2.77 (standard deviation, 2.61). A total of 30.5 percent of respondents scored zero on the scale. Among the five groups, career civil servants under Carter attained the highest mean—3.42 (S.D. 2.89)—followed by Carter appointees—3.06 (S.D. 2.65), Canadian respondents—2.92 (S.D. 2.42), U.K. officials—2.46 (S.D. 2.29), and Reagan appointees—1.70 (S.D. 2.46). The scale's reliability of alpha .66 is relatively strong (standardized alpha is .65). The omission of any single item but one would reduce alpha rather than raise it.

These results fit pretty well with what we might expect from the five groups. We might anticipate that the Carter career officials would score higher than any other group for two reasons: The fragmentation of the U.S. bureaucracy engenders budget maximizing; and the permanent bureaucracy in 1979 operated under a Democratic administration that still held a relatively expansive view of the role of government. The Canadian central agents exceed the maximizing tendency of their British counterparts probably because of the degree to which the representational imperative in Ottawa impinges on executive-bureaucratic politics. Given the philosophic underpinnings of their administration, it makes sense that Reagan appointees showed only a very weak interest in maximization.

Influences on Adoption of Maximizing Orientations

We have selected a number of variables that might help us ascertain what contributes to adoption of budget-maximizing roles in our five groups. These divide into three blocks. The first takes in respondents' views of their responsibilities and their stylistic approach to their work; the second probes officials' orientations toward government service; the third looks at individuals' placement and experience in government. Table 4.1 summarizes, for each group, the mean scores of respondents—with various orientations or characteristics—on the maximization scale.

Examining the relationships between responsibilities and styles, and maximization, we come first to officials' views of their roles. Here we have collapsed responses into three categories: officials who stress strategic and policy planning, allocation of resources, and/or economic and fiscal policy (individuals were allowed more than one response). In all five groups, those who relate their work to allocation of resources register the strongest orientations toward maximization, although the gap in the Carter appointee group between those involved with the role and those engaged in economic and fiscal policy is minute (3.26 vs. 3.25). This suggests that the gamekeepers believe that they require increased resources adequately to curtail the incursions of poachers!

With regard to work style, we had three categories: policy and priority planning, management and implementation, and communicating (both within and outside one's agency). A similar result to the one that emerged in the preceding cluster suggests itself here. Those who style themselves as managers and implementors rate the highest as maximizers, except in the Canadian group in which they are slightly edged out by those who see themselves as involved in setting policies and priorities (2.95 vs. 2.93). In all cases but the Carter appointee group, those whose approach involves communication within and outside their agency attained the lowest maximizer scores.

The next cluster of variables, "mandate focus," concerns officials' perceptions of the span of their agencies' responsibilities for which they bear some obligations. Again allowing for multiple responses, individuals could mention one part, several related parts, or the entire mandate as coming in some way under their purview. The results in this cluster come out less straightforwardly than in the previous two. We had anticipated that the narrower the officials' focus, the more they would lean toward maximiza-

TABLE 4.I

BUDGET-MAXIMIZING BUREAUCRAT: DESCRIPTION OF GROUPS

	Carter appointees N = 63	Carter career N = 69	Reagan appointees N = 60	United Kingdom N = 41	Canada N = 92
Mean, all respondents	3.06	3.42	1.70	2.46	2.92
Standard deviation, all respondents	(2.65)	(2.89)	(2.46)	(2.29)	(2.42)
			Mean (standard deviation/n)		
I. Responsibilities and style					
Agency responsibilities					
Strategic and policy planning	3.05	3.54	1.89	2.40	2.29
	(2.72/39)	(2.73/22)	(2.65/39)	(2.37/20)	(2.47/45)
Allocation of resources	3.26	3.66	2.00	2.64	3.14
	(2.54/23)	(2.85/39)	(2.57/26)	(2.31/17)	(2.19/58)
Economic and fiscal policy	3.25	3.40	1.71	1.87	2.58
	(2.42/20)	(3.08/32)	(2.53/28)	(1.58/16)	(2.42/34)
Work style					
Policy and priority planning	3.00	3.47	1.81	2.46	2.95
	(2.59/60)	(2.89/67)	(2.54/54)	(2.29/41)	(2.47/84)
Management and implementation	3.68	3.60	2.00	2.80	2.93
	(2.71/22)	(3.12/25)	(3.40/24)	(2.25/10)	(2.93/33)
Communications	3.32	2.93	.85	1.80	2.42
	(2.73/25)	(3.10/16)	(1.29/28)	(2.94/5)	(2.47/35)

TABLE 4.1 — Continued

	Carter appointees	Carter career	Reagan appointees	United Kingdom	Canada
Mandate focus					
Entire mandate	1.85 (2.41/7)	0.00 (0.00/1)	2.14 (3.00/14)	3.00 (2.58/13)	3.30 (3.19/13)
Part of mandate	3.34 (2.91/29)	3.56 (2.90/55)	1.42 (2.47/33)	2.64 (2.17/14)	3.13 (2.22/61)
Several parts of mandate	3.17 (2.63/29)	2.66 (2.84/15)	1.80 (2.15/21)	2.00 (2.17/17)	2.39 (2.47/38)
II. Orientation to governmental service					
Motive for government service					
Idealism, public service	3.00 (3.22/16)	4.50 (3.17/22)	1.77 (2.04/9)	2.33 (2.25/15)	3.12 (2.83/24)
Special scholastic training	2.78 (3.11/14)	3.86 (2.88/23)	1.71 (2.83/32)	2.54 (2.25/11)	2.72 (1.84/11)
"Where the action is"	2.16 (1.72/6)	4.54 (3.67/11)	1.85 (2.79/20)	3.37 (2.26/8)	3.60 (2.61/25)
Previous career experience	2.75 (2.34/24)	2.75 (2.49/8)	1.55 (2.12/9)	2.62 (2.26/8)	3.28 (3.19/14)
Specific policy interest	4.42 (2.29/7)	3.25 (2.50/4)	3.00 (0.00/1)	0.00 (0.00/1)	3.21 (2.51/14)
Career opportunity	3.19 (2.63/21)	2.88 (2.67/42)	1.18 (1.88/27)	1.93 (1.94/15)	2.91 (2.38/58)
Partisan/political commitment	3.00 (2.82/29)	6.66 (1.52/3)	1.52 (1.54/17)	2.85 (3.07/7)	2.14 (2.47/7)

Tried to accomplish in government					
To make government responsive	3.10 (2.71/20)	3.05 (3.13/18)	1.63 (1.80/11)	3.57 (3.25/7)	2.86 (3.02/15)
To improve planning/decision making	2.80 (2.31/21)	4.15 (3.28/20)	2.16 (3.39/18)	2.92 (2.23/14)	2.89 (1.93/29)
To improve specific policy	2.95 (2.28/20)	3.33 (3.16/27)	1.79 (2.46/29)	2.17 (2.06/17)	3.48 (2.76/31)
To improve personnel	4.00 (3.60/9)	4.40 (2.83/10)	3.60 (3.04/5)	2.40 (2.07/5)	4.15 (3.07/13)
To give best possible advice	2.16 (2.20/12)	3.47 (3.01/23)	1.18 (1.90/32)	2.30 (2.35/13)	3.09 (1.64/11)
To general overarching goals	4.57 (3.90/7)	1.00 (1.00/3)	2.18 (3.31/11)	2.50 (2.12/2)	1.83 (2.08/12)
To have an impact	3.00 (2.92/8)	4.33 (3.50/6)	2.11 (3.51/9)	0.50 (0.70/2)	3.45 (1.96/11)
For personal satisfaction	2.88 (2.71/9)	3.00 (2.78/9)	1.71 (1.88/7)	6.00 (1.41/2)	3.04 (2.02/21)
Facilitate policy/decision making	1.40 (2.06/10)	4.50 (3.53/2)	0.81 (1.16/11)	3.00 (3.16/4)	3.40 (3.40/10)
Miss if left government					
Impact in specific policy sector	3.11 (2.36/17)	3.14 (2.96/7)	2.25 (2.01/24)	0.00 (0.00/00)	2.16 (2.78/6)
General policy impact	2.90 (2.60/21)	4.03 (3.08/32)	1.58 (2.20/17)	2.66 (2.64/12)	3.68 (2.44/35)

TABLE 4.1 — *Continued*

	Carter appointees	Carter career	Reagan appointees	United Kingdom	Canada
Atmosphere and challenge	2.88 (2.60/43)	3.00 (2.67/37)	1.59 (2.28/32)	1.91 (1.99/23)	2.83 (2.47/55)
Variety of problems	3.00 (3.21/7)	3.85 (4.14/7)	1.50 (2.12/2)	3.60 (2.70/5)	3.53 (2.77/15)
High-caliber, stimulating colleagues	2.33 (3.82/6)	3.33 (3.07/6)	1.80 (1.75/10)	3.11 (2.61/9)	2.42 (2.41/19)
Sense of public service/teamwork	3.35 (3.77/14)	3.93 (3.47/15)	2.62 (3.15/16)	3.15 (2.60/13)	2.87 (1.99/16)
Intellectual challenges	2.85 (1.77/7)	3.33 (4.16/3)	2.50 (4.27/6)	2.50 (1.30/8)	5.00 (2.44/6)
Instrumental opportunities of job	2.60 (3.28/5)	2.66 (2.93/12)	1.40 (2.26/32)	3.25 (2.98/4)	2.68 (1.66/16)
III. Governmental position and experience					
Finance/Treasury	3.12 (2.55/31)	3.64 (2.85/57)	1.34 (1.55/23)	2.43 (2.12/23)	3.25 (2.30/60)
Other central agencies	3.00 (2.78/32)	2.33 (2.90/12)	1.91 (2.88/37)	2.50 (2.54/18)	2.31 (2.55/32)
Decision to enter government					
Before university	2.57 (2.43/7)	2.88 (2.84/9)	1.80 (2.04/5)	3.20 (2.77/5)	1.40 (1.94/5)
After university	3.50 (3.14/22)	3.45 (2.83/44)	1.64 (2.61/28)	2.20 (1.82/20)	2.90 (2.13/22)

Mid-career	2.88 (2.37/34)	3.62 (3.20/16)	1.74 (2.44/27)	2.92 (2.73/14)	2.94 (2.54/63)
Years in government					
1–5	3.00 (2.42/44)	4.50 (2.94/6)	1.59 (2.51/22)	3.83 (3.06/6)	2.63 (2.85/19)
6–10	3.00 (3.35/9)	4.55 (2.55/9)	2.18 (2.83/16)	7.00 (0.00/1)	3.33 (2.64/33)
11–20	3.42 (3.35/7)	2.80 (3.08/30)	1.10 (1.66/10)	2.68 (1.76/19)	2.81 (2.11/26)
21 or more	3.33 (3.51/3)	3.65 (2.62/23)	2.57 (2.93/7)	1.33 (1.98/15)	2.57 (1.82/14)

tion. The figures for both Carter groups bear out this expectation. In the other three groups, however, those citing some responsibility toward the entire sweep of their agencies' mandate scored highest as maximizers.

The next block of clusters, "orientation toward government service," includes variables based on respondents' renderings of why they entered government, what they have derived a sense of accomplishment from during their careers, and what they would miss if they left public service. In the cluster tapping respondents' motives for coming into government, their responses fell into seven categories: idealism and a desire to serve the public, cognate scholastic training, being where the "action" is, congruent experience in a previous career, a specific policy interest, an opportunity for advancement, and partisan/political commitments. Multiple responses were allowed in this and the other career orientation clusters.

Similar patterns emerge from the maximization scores of those registering various reasons for entering public service as appeared under the responsibility and style block. Career officials in the United States, United Kingdom, and Canada who came into government because they wanted to be close to the "action"—that is, they wanted to obtain a sense of having an influence in government—produced relatively high average maximization scores (respectively, 4.54, 3.37, and 3.60). As groups, Carter and Reagan appointees and Canadian officials who cited a specific policy interest as motivating their entrance to government all rated high as maximizers (respectively, 4.42, 3.00, and 3.21). The Carter career officials yielded two especially interesting findings. Those claiming a general interest in public service ranked high as maximizers (4.50). The data associated with motives for seeking a government career, thus, point to deep commitments to public service, a desire to be in the thick of things, and/or an interest in a specialized policy field.

A look at maximization scores among those giving various responses to our question on what officials have tried to accomplish during their careers uncovers some very strong results. In all respondent groups with the exception of the British respondents, officials who have placed a high priority on the development and management of personnel strongly favor maximization. In two groups, Reagan appointees and Canadian officials, those who made some mention of a personnel orientation yielded the highest scores; in the two Carter groups, such officials ranked second in maximization.

In work published just before his death, Charles Levine registered concern that stringent cuts in government have induced an "erosion" of human resources necessary even for minimalist governance.[30] We see in our officials' emphasis on personnel management the degree to which practitioners believe that a relationship exists between the staff efficiency and effectiveness and their compensation and resources.

Moving to what officials would miss if they left public service, the data present one strongly counterintuitive finding. As we have noted, Niskanen's budget-maximizer theory rests heavily on the assertion that officials view the expansion of the resources in their policy field as serving their personal utility. In their responses to our question about what they would miss if they left, government officials gave responses that we coded into eight categories. Among these, we devised a variable, "instrumental opportunities of the job," which encompassed responses that related directly to respondents' personal utility. These included the prospect that they would miss the opportunity to manage a large number of people, relatively free access to the facilities and materials available for conducting research or carrying out one's responsibilities, reasonable security of life style, career satisfaction denied in other sectors (e.g., professional advancement for women or minorities), and an outlet for a profession not well represented in the private sector.

With respect to the instrumental opportunities variable, the U.S. data suggest the exact opposite from what we might expect with those whose personal utility becomes entwined with the resource situation of their organization. Those who would miss their jobs due to loss of instrumental opportunities score lower than any other motivation group in maximization. That is, those seeking optimal personal utility come out as budget minimizers.

Fully 53 percent of Reagan appointees would miss the instrumental opportunities connected with their being in government, whereas only 8 and 17 percent of Carter appointees and career officials, respectively, gave responses that fit into this category. An equal proportion of Reagan appointees took a cue from the movie *Being There* and dwelt on how they would miss the atmosphere—the challenge and excitement—of working in government. These officials scored a bit higher on maximization than those stressing personal utility (1.59 vs. 1.40). But they still fell short of their group mean.

A proactive/passive split between the two administrations begins to take shape when we look at what officials scored high as maximizers. With both political groups, those who would miss the feeling that they were serving the public lean the strongest toward maximization, although Reagan respondents' scores fall considerably short of Carter appointees' (2.61 vs. 3.35). The Carter career officials registering the highest (4.03) on maximization were the 46 percent of respondents who would miss the sense that they were having an impact on policy. In the U.S. groups, those who presented themselves as actively engaged with the project of governance come out as maximizers. In contrast, those simply sopping up the atmosphere and seeking instrumental opportunities prove to be minimizers.

The final group of variables, "governmental position and experience," probes whether respondents' location in the bureaucracy and career experience relates to their assumption of budget-maximizing orientations. Three variables served as the basis of this group: (1) whether the agency in which the official works focuses on economic policy and/or budgeting or in one of the other central-agency fields; (2) when they decided to enter government (i.e., before receiving university degrees, after they completed their degree work, or mid-career); and (3) how many years they have served in government—five or less, six to ten, eleven to twenty, or more than twenty.

When we examined the relationship between respondents' views of their agencies' responsibilities, we found that those who emphasized roles associated with the allocation of resources came out as the strongest maximizers in all five samples. Our analysis suggests that this finding did not carry over evenly to the relationship between whether officials work in the economics/budget agencies and their scores as maximizers. Nevertheless, Carter appointees and Canadian respondents based in economics/budget agencies do register stronger orientations toward maximization (3.64 vs. 2.33 and 3.25 vs. 2.31, respectively).

Regarding when officials decided on their career and how long they have served in government, we might expect those who chose early and have served long to manifest clearly tendencies toward maximization. That is, they might have become more strongly entrenched in their units or policy networks and, therefore, more likely to view these as extensions of their personal utility. In fact, the analysis produces mixed findings. Carter appointees who decided to enter government shortly after leaving the university, Carter and Canadian career officials who made up their minds either after university or in mid-career, and Britons who elected public service before leaving university all came out relatively strongly as maximizers.

The maximizing scores for the variables based on how long officials have served in government again do not correspond with what we might expect. No clear differences suggest themselves among the Carter appointees. A washboard effect appears among Reagan appointees with those serving five or less and eleven to twenty years yielding low scores on maximization. Among career officials under Carter, the five-or-less and six-to-ten groups prove to be markedly stronger maximizers than the more experienced cohorts. The U.K. figures provide the opposite to what we might expect, with the relatively short tenured rating higher as maximizers. The Canadian respondents resemble the Carter appointees in that scores for the four groups suggest no pattern.

Regression Analysis

Table 4.2 summarizes the results of analysis of variance for regression of the dependent variable—maximization—on the influences discussed in the above section for each of our five respondent groups. This analysis assesses the effects of three blocks of independent variables: "responsibilities and

TABLE 4.2
ANALYSIS OF VARIANCE FOR REGRESSION ANALYSIS

Group of independent variables	Carter appointees	Carter career	Reagan appointees	United Kingdom	Canada
Zero order effects: budget maximization					
Responsibilities and style	10.4	8.1	18.8	14.2	11.8
Orientation to governmental service	21.7	18.4	32.3	35.3	23.3
Governmental position and experience	1.9	7.0	6.3	17.1	5.3
Total explained by all variables	32.4	31.7	49.1	60.2	40.8
Unique effects: budget maximization[a]					
Responsibilities and style	7.8	4.2	9.2	5.8	11.8
Orientation to governmental service	20.0	13.8	26.6	27.4	22.8
Governmental position and experience	2.9	4.2	6.6	12.5	9.4

a. Equal to the additional variance explained by each set of variables after all other variables are in the equation.

style," "orientation to governmental service," and "governmental position and experience." The figures under "zero order effect" represent the variance in respondents' orientations toward maximization when an influence block is entered alone in a regression equation. The results under "unique effects" account for the variance explained by a given block when the others are held constant.

The zero order regressions reveal some fairly strong findings. In all five respondent groups, the joint effects of the blocks explain over 30 percent of the variation in "maximization." The 60 and 49 percent figures attained by the British and Reagan politico groups, respectively, suggest especially consistent patterns between individuals' responses to the independent variables and their scores on the maximization scale in those two samples. We should remember, however, that the British group—with only 41 respondents—is relatively small.

In all but one group, the variables tapping officials' orientations toward public service do about twice as much work as the next block. The exception is "responsibilities and style" in the Reagan appointee group, which comes somewhat more than a strong second in relation to "orientation to governmental service" block. Interestingly, officials' governmental position and experience edges out their responsibilities and style as the second most important block in the U.K. group. The unique effects on maximization of the individual blocks—that is, while holding the others constant—suggest a remarkable consistency between the two types of regression for all five respondent groups.

Table 4.3 presents the effects of each constituent element of the influence blocks on officials' adoption of budget-maximizing orientations in each of the five groups. Standardized coefficients depict the relative weight of each variable when the dependent variable is regressed on it while controlling for the effects of the other variables in each block.

In the case of variables based on when respondents decided to enter government, how many years they have served, and whether they work in a "finance/treasury" or "other" agencies, the indicators that make up the subset of a cluster derive from mutually exclusive categories. According to regression protocol, we therefore excluded from our equations for each group the category into which the largest proportion of respondents fit. For example, among Carter appointees, the largest number of respondents said that they decided to seek a career in government at mid-career. Thus, for the Carter appointees "mid-career" becomes the "reference" category.

In some instances, the results for variables for which the categories were not mutually exclusive proved heavily skewed. For instance, only one Carter career civil servant believed that his role encompassed the entire mandate of his agency. Since there were only two remaining categories for this variable and very few multiple responses, we deemed the category

TABLE 4.3
REGRESSION ANALYSIS FOR "BUDGET MAXIMIZER"

Independent variables	Carter appointees N = 63	Carter career N = 69	Reagan appointees N = 60	United Kingdom N = 41	Canada N = 92
I. Responsibilities and style					
Agency responsibilities					
Strategic and policy planning	.454[a]	-.133[b]	.091	.152	-.181
Allocation of resources	.222	.070	.191	-.102	-.112
Economic and fiscal policy	.272	-.023	.084	-.176	-.198
Work style					
Policy and priority planning	-.176	.100	.083	—	.152
Management and implementation	.200	-.085	.194	.335	.075
Communications	.140	-.116	-.111	-.231	-.057
Mandate focus					
Entire mandate	—	—	.133	.168	.254[b]
Part of mandate	.079	refer.	-.004	refer.	.011
Several parts of mandate	.082	-.174[b]	.183	-.410[b]	-.107
II. Orientation to governmental service					
Motive for government service					
Idealism, public service	-.075	.200	-.007	-.569	.080
Special scholastic training	-.087	.061	-.263[b]	-.372	.020
"Where the action is"	—	.119	.050	.107	.095

TABLE 4.3— Continued

Independent variables	Carter appointees	Carter career	Reagan appointees	United Kingdom	Canada
Previous career experience	.055	.024	-.085	-.090	-.095
Specific policy interest	—	—	—	—	.048
Career opportunity	-.094	-.164	-.179	-.281	-.035
Partisan/political commitment	.203	—	-.244	-.064	—
Tried to accomplish in government					
To make government responsive	-.085	-.018	-.114	.185	.093
To improve planning/decision making	-.234[b]	.059	.060	.060	.067
To improve specific policy	.124	-.007	.125	.220	.141
To improve personnel	.129	.082	—	.139	.133
To give best possible advice	-.297[b]	.087	-.305[b]	-.352	.091
To general overarching goals	—	—	.082	—	-.272[b]
To have an impact	-.011	—	.005	—	.196
For personal satisfaction	-.094	-.062	.073	—	.183
Facilitate policy/decision making	-.395[b]	—	-.108	—	—
Miss if left government					
Impact in specific policy sector	-.042	—	.357[b]	—	—
General policy impact	-.071	.124	.007	-.044	.196
Atmosphere and challenge	-.076	-.053	-.127	-.117	-.097
Variety of problems	—	—	—	.039	.043
High-caliber, stimulating colleagues	—	—	.175	.141	-.124
Sense of public service/teamwork	.073	.065	-.360[b]	.394	-.108
Intellectual challenges	.086	.061	—	-.119	—
Instrumental opportunities of job	.042	-.088	.018	—	-.127

III. Governmental position and experience					
Finance/Treasury	.219	refer.	-.550[b]	refer.	refer.
Other central agencies	refer.	-.114	refer.	-.399	-.255[b]
Decision to enter government					
Before university	—	refer.	—	—	—
After university	.221	—	refer.	refer.	.025
Mid-career	refer.	-.064	.057	-.309[b]	refer.
Years in government					
1–5	refer.	—	refer.	.309	-.261[b]
6–10	.085	.117	.202[b]	—	refer.
11–20	—	refer.	.001	refer.	-.367[a]
21 or more	—	.204	—	-.523[a]	-.163

LEGEND: refer. = reference category; — = too few cases.
a. Significant at .01 level
b. Significant at .05 level

drawing the highest proportion of respondents the reference category. We should note as well that the numbers of respondents under some categories, while not minuscule, was so low that meaningful regression analysis could not be conducted. We have marked such instances with a dash (—).

The results of the various regressions suggest some findings that did not emerge from table 4.1's summarization of the average maximization scores of individuals fitting within various categories. With respect to the "responsibilities and style," the regression of "maximization" on "strategic and policy planning" for the Carter appointees—controlling for the other variables in the block—yields a very strong standardized regression coefficient of .454 (significant at the .01 level). This suggests that Carter appointees who viewed themselves as involved in keeping sight of the big picture and advancing major policy initiatives might have shown a greater tendency toward maximization than the group's average score on maximization indicated. Among the career officials under Carter, we find a stronger negative relationship between respondents citing "strategic and policy planning" as one of their agency's roles and maximization than had been suggested by the scores in table 4.1 (−.133, .05 level). The other significant result for Career officials under Carter—the negative relationship between those claiming responsibility for several dimensions of their agency's mandate (as opposed to a single part) and maximization—fits with the scores reported in table 4.1 (−.174, .05 level).

No dramatic results suggest themselves for the Reagan appointees under the responsibilities and style block. The findings for the British respondents correspond with what we might have expected based on the average scores in table 4.1. Those claiming responsibilities toward several parts of their agency's mandate reveal consistently low maximization scores when we control for other variables in the block (−.410, .05 level). We find a relatively modest but noteworthy carryover in the case of officials who style themselves as managers and implementors, and score high on maximization (.335). In the Canadian regression, we discover that the high maximization scores attained by those characterizing their roles as covering the entire compass of an agency's mandate carry over quite strongly when the other variables are controlled (.254, .05 level).

Turning to the regressions of maximization on the "orientation to governmental service block," three variables from the middle cluster, "tried to accomplish in government," seem to work the most sustained effects in the Carter appointee group. Those who have tried to improve planning and decision making while in government appear to score high as maximizers when we control the other career orientation variables (.234, .05 level). In contrast, those who have sought to give the best possible advice or facilitate the policy process and decision making—the two categories of respondents with the weakest maximization averages—yield regression coefficients that suggest very low maximization scores when we take the other orientation factors into consideration (respectively: −.297, .05 level; −.395, .05 level).

The regression of maximization on the government-service orientation variables for the Carter career group produces no coefficients of special note. But the regression for Reagan appointees yields a number of relatively strong results. The coefficients indicate that those who pointed to a special scholastic training as one factor motivating their careers and those who would miss the sense of service and teamwork that exists in government if they left both scored especially low on maximization when we control the other variables (respectively: −.263, .05 level; −.360, .05 level). In contrast, the findings indicate a stronger relationship between Reagan appointees' reporting that they would miss having an impact in a specific area of government and maximization than appeared when we looked at the average scores of various groups (.357, .05 level).

Several of the British coefficients are quite high, but the small size of the group appears to preordain an absence of statistically significant results. The tendency of Canadian respondents who count among their accomplishments in government the achievement of some overarching goal to score low on maximization proves most resilient under the closer scrutiny of regression analysis—with a coefficient of −.272 (.05 level).

The regressions of maximization on the variables from the "governmental position and experience" block for the two Carter groups all fall short of statistical significance. But we find that the disinclination of Reagan appointees based in the Treasury Department or Office of Management and Budget (OMB) to maximization stands up exceptionally well to regression analysis (−.550, .05 level).

When we move to the British group, we discover further confirmation of the propensity of officials who have served for over twenty years to eschew maximization (−.523, .05 level). We similarly find further evidence of the tendency for those who decided upon their careers at mid-career to eschew maximization (−.309, .05 level).

The Canadian results indicate once again that officials in central agencies other than the Finance Department and the Treasury Board Secretariat are chary of maximization (−.255, .05 level). Under "years in government," we find that on either side of the strongest maximizing group—that is, those in government six to ten years—respondents come out as fairly adverse to maximization when we control for the other variables (respectively: −.261, .05 level; −.367, .05 level).

Conclusion

A chapter that Charles Levine wrote with Peter M. Benda for a book assessing Ronald Reagan's legacy cuts to the heart of the problems that minimalist approaches to governance pose to the future of the public service in the United States.[31] Their observations resonate with our own view that public-choice theorists in many respects appear to long for a simpler governmental era in which bureaucrats styled themselves as simply the people who implemented the policy attentions of their political masters.

Benda and Levine asserted that the top-down, control-oriented nature of the Reagan administration's approach ran counter to the views of management reform that prevail in the best-performing elements of the private sector.[32] They argue that, in fact, the very measures that sought to control public service added to overload and deepened ungovernability. They adduce the *Challenger* disaster and the Iran/*contra* scandal as the two extreme examples:

> The high-tech, high-finance, high-risk worlds of space travel and international intrigue are only symptomatic of similar problems throughout government as it turns toward increasingly intricate organizational arrangements to conduct public business. Perhaps that is appropriate because complex problems require complex solutions. Real fiascos occur when complexity is mistaken for simplicity.[33]

This chapter has argued that the pursuit of the minimalist view can prove overzealous because it misconstrues the motives of officials and underrates institutional factors that serve as checks on bureaucratic expansionism. We have centered our critique on a test of Niskanen's budget-maximizing-bureaucrat theory. With respect to its applicability in Anglo-American systems other than the United States, we have cautioned that differences in both the structure of bureaucratic careers and the nature of power relationships—between the political executive, the bureaucracy, the legislature, and interest groups—make it highly unlikely that the conditions that lead to a high degree of budget maximization in the United States will prevail elsewhere. Nevertheless, the Canadian system attains an approximation of some U.S. conditions largely through the auspices of cabinets' laboring under the burden of the representational imperative.

Regarding officials' role perceptions, career motives, and governmental position and experience, we found that maximizers tend to be committed to public service as a value and dedicated to relatively specialized fields. In view of the fact that our officials work in central agencies, we were surprised to find the degree to which those focusing their work on allocation of resources throughout the bureaucratic system proved inclined toward maximization. We also came upon the especially remarkable discovery that those who viewed their careers from the standpoint of personal utility came out as minimizers, not maximizers. But the most obvious finding from the scores on maximization achieved within the five bureaucratic cultures was the fact that each of them differed in very substantial ways.

This point was brought home when we employed regression analysis to assess further the effects of blocks of variables and the constituent items within them when other blocks/variables were controlled. First, the results suggested that officials' career motives work considerably greater effects on their association with maximization than do their views of their and their agency's roles, and their governmental position and experience. Second, the regression analyses provided data that accentuate the fact that some variables work almost idiosyncratic effects on assumption of maximization within some of the bureaucratic cultures. These two facts should remind us to use extreme caution when making assertions about officials' career motives as associated with their views of their organization's budget. That is, we do not even find much consistency between the three American groups, let alone the five cultures examined in this study.

Notes

1. William A. Niskanen, *Bureaucracy and Representative Government* (New York: Aldine-Atherton, 1971), 15–16.

2. Ibid., 21–22.

3. Ibid., 38.

4. William A. Niskanen, *Bureaucracy: Servant or Master? Lessons from America* (London: Institute of Economic Affairs, 1973).

5. Peter Aucoin, "Contraction, Managerialism and Decentralization in Canadian Government," *Governance* 1 (1989): 144–61; Jonathan Boston, "Transforming New Zealand's Public Sector: Labour's Quest for Improved Efficiency and Accountability," *Public Administration* 65 (1987): 423–42; Mark Considine, "The Corporate Management Framework as Administrative Science: A Critique," *Australian Journal of Public Administration* 47 (1988): 4–17; Geoffrey K. Fry, "The Thatcher Government, the Financial Management Initiative and the 'New Civil Service,'" *Public Administration* 66 (1988): 1–20; Geoffrey K. Fry, Andrew Flyn, Andrew Gray, William Jenkins, and Brian Rutherford, "Symposium on Improving Management in Government," *Public Administration* 66 (1988): 429–45. See as well the special issue of *Governance* on managerial reform in the United Kingdom, Canada, Australia, and New Zealand in vol. 3 (April 1990).

6. Hugh Heclo, *A Government of Strangers: Executive Politics in Washington* (Washington, D.C.: Brookings Institution, 1977), 116–20.

7. P.J. Chartrand and K.L. Pond, *A Study of Executive Career Paths in the Public Service of Canada* (Chicago: Public Personnel Associates, 1970), 48–49; Audrey Doer, *The Machinery of Government* (Toronto: Methuen, 1981), 46, 63; Sanford Borins, "Management of the Public Service in Japan: Are There Lessons to Be Learned?" *Canadian Public Administration* 29 (1986): 175–96.

8. Mancur Olson, *The Rise and Decline of Nations: Economic Growth, Stagflation, and Social Rigidities* (New Haven: Yale, 1982), 50–52.

9. Joel D. Aberbach, Robert A. Putnam, and Bert A. Rockman, *Bureaucrats and Politicians in Western Democracies* (Cambridge: Harvard University Press, 1981), 94–100; Randall B. Ripley and Grace A. Franklin, *Congress, the Bureaucracy, and Public Policy* (Homewood, Ill.: Dorsey, 1980); Richard Rose, *Managing Presidential Objectives* (New York: Free Press, 1976), 161; Hugh Heclo, "Issue Networks and the Executive Establishment," in *The New American Political System,* ed. Anthony King (Washington, D.C.: American Enterprise Institute, 1978), 102–5.

10. Colin Campbell, S.J., *Managing the Presidency: Carter, Reagan and the Search for Executive Harmony* (Pittsburgh: University of Pittsburgh Press, 1986), 200–201.

11. Hugh Heclo, "In Search of a Role: America's Higher Civil Service," in *Bureaucrats and Policy Making: A Comparative Overview,* ed. Ezra N. Suleiman (New York: Holmes and Meier, 1984), 18–20.

12. Niskanen, *Bureaucracy and Representative Government,* 159.

13. Nelson W. Polsby, "The Institutionalization of the U.S. House of Representatives," *American Political Science Review* 62 (1968): 144–68.

14. Nelson W. Polsby, "Legislatures," in *Governmental Institutions and Processes,* vol. 5 of *Handbook of Political Science,* ed. Fred I. Greenstein and Nelson W. Polsby (Reading, Mass.: Addison-Wesley, 1975), 277.

15. James B. Christoph, "Higher Civil Servants and the Politics of Consensualism in Great Britain," in *Mandarins of Western Europe: The Political Roles of Top Civil Servants,* ed. Mattei Dogan (New York: Halsted, 1975), 32–36. See also Colin Campbell, *Governments under Stress: Political Executives and Key Bureaucrats in Washington, London and Ottawa* (Toronto: University of Toronto Press, 1983), 57, 128–30.

16. Colin Campbell, "Cabinet Committees in Canada: Pressures and Dysfunctions Stemming from the Representational Imperative," in *Unlocking the Cabinet: Cabinet Structures in Comparative Perspective,* ed. Thomas T. Mackie and Brian W. Hogwood (London: Sage, 1985).

17. Arend Lijphart, *Democracy in Plural Societies: A Comparative Exploration* (New Haven: Yale University Press, 1977), 118–29; W.A. Matheson, *The Prime Minister and Cabinet* (Toronto: Methuen, 1976), 22–25; R.M. Punnett, *The Prime Minister in Canadian Government and Politics* (Toronto: Macmillan, 1977), 65–70.

18. James R. Mallory, *The Structure of Canadian Government* (Toronto: Macmillan, 1971), 103; V. Seymour Wilson, *Canadian Public Policy and Administration: Theory and Environment* (Toronto: McGraw-Hill Ryerson, 1981), 329.

19. Richard Van Loon, "Kaleidoscope in Grey: The Policy Process in Ottawa," in *Canadian Politics in the 1980s: Introductory Readings,* ed. Michael Whittington and Glen Williams (Toronto: Methuen, 1981), 256; Richard D. French, *How Ottawa Decides: Planning and Industrial Policy-Making, 1968–1980* (Toronto: Lorimer, 1980); and Campbell, *Governments.*

20. Niskanen, *Bureaucracy and Representative Government,* 221–22.

21. Colin Campbell and B. Guy Peters, "The Politics/Administration Dichotomy: Death or Merely Change?" *Governance* 1 (1988): 79–99; and Colin Campbell, "The Political Roles of Senior Government Officials in Advanced Democracies," *British Journal of Political Science* 18 (1988): 242–72.

22. Aberbach, Putnam, and Rockman, *Bureaucrats and Politicians*, 2–20.

23. Herbert A. Simon, *Administrative Behavior* (New York: Macmillan, 1957), 57–58.

24. Martin Landau, "The Concept of Decision-Making in the Field of Public Administration," in *Concepts and Issues of Administrative Behavior*, ed. Sidney Mailick and Edward H. Van Ness (Englewood Cliffs, N.J.: Prentice-Hall, 1962), 10; Matthew Holden, "Imperialism in Bureaucracy," *American Political Science Review* 60 (1966): 943–51; Herbert Kaufman, "Administrative Decentralization and Political Power," *Public Administration* 29 (1969): 4–5.

25. Aberbach, Putnam, and Rockman, *Bureaucrats and Politicians*, 16–23.

26. Ezra N. Suleiman, *Politics, Power, and Bureaucracy in France: The Administrative Elite* (Princeton: Princeton University Press, 1974); Ezra N. Suleiman, "From Right to Left: Bureaucracy and Politics in France," and T.J. Pempel, "Organizing for Efficiency: The Higher Civil Service in Japan," in *Bureaucrats and Policy Making*, ed. Ezra N. Suleiman.

27. Christopher J. Pollitt, "The Central Policy Review Staff," *Public Administration* 52 (1975): 375–92; Campbell, *Governments*, 63–67; Renate Mayntz and Fritz Scharpf, *Policy-Making in the German Federal Bureaucracy* (New York: Elsevier, 1975), 85–86; Renate Mayntz, "German Federal Bureaucrats: A Functional Elite Between Politics and Administration," in Suleiman, *Politics, Power, and Bureaucracy*; Hans-Ulrich Derlien, "Repercussions of Government Change on the Career Civil Service in West Germany: The Cases of 1969 and 1982," *Governance* 1 (1988): 50–78.

28. Colin Campbell and George J. Szablowski, *The Superbureaucrats: Structure and Behaviour in Central Agencies* (Toronto: Macmillan, 1979).

29. Campbell and Peters, "Politics/Administration Dichotomy"; and Campbell, "Political Roles."

30. Charles Levine, "Human Resource Erosion and the Uncertain Future of the U.S. Civil Service: From Policy Gridlock to Structural Fragmentation," *Governance* 1 (1988): 119; and Michael G. Hansen and Charles H. Levine, "The Centralization-Decentralization Tug-of-War in the New Executive Branch," in *Organizing Governance: Governing Organizations*, ed. Colin Campbell, s.j., and B. Guy Peters (Pittsburgh: University of Pittsburgh Press, 1988), 270–78.

31. Peter M. Benda and Charles H. Levine, "Reagan and the Bureaucracy: The Bequest, the Promise, and the Legacy," in *The Reagan Legacy: Promise and Performance*, ed. Charles O. Jones (Chatham, N.J.: Chatham House, 1988), 102–42.

32. Ibid., 137.

33. Ibid., 138.

5

Micromanagement: Congressional Control and Bureaucratic Risk

DONALD F. KETTL

Political scientists have traditionally argued that congressional oversight of administration is infrequent and, when it occurs, ineffective. Analysts for a generation were unanimous in decrying "Congress's neglected function."[1] Congress has even been sharply critical of itself.[2] Ironically, however, a rising chorus of voices has criticized congressional oversight for being *too* effective. Especially in defense policy, critics ranging from government officials to outside policy experts have with surprising unanimity criticized congressional "micromanagement": too much control of too many details of administrative activities. The results, they argue, are higher defense costs, long delays, loss of administrative flexibility, and ineffective programs and weapons systems.

Congress thus is criticized both for not overseeing the bureaucracy enough and for overseeing it in obsessive detail. In one sense, both sides are right. Congress often does not control administrative activities very effectively, and sometimes when it tries to exert control, it only makes things worse by dealing with micro-level details instead of macro-level policy. Some of the dispute arises because the relations between the branches have changed since some political scientists' earlier studies. Tensions between the branches have grown, while Congress has strengthened its own ability to scrutinize executive branch activities. In a broader sense, however, oversight is a much more complex function rooted in the subtle relationships between the executive and legislative branches in our constitutional system. Oversight in fact is a much more pervasive and complex phenomenon than its earlier critics recognized. Its exercise is caught up in never-ending separation-of-powers questions that critics of micromanagement fail to acknowledge. The debate between critics of too little oversight and too much micromanagement reflects tradeoffs that can never be satisfactorily and permanently made.

The dispute over congressional oversight, moreover, raises a dilemma that echoes one of the most lasting puzzles of public administration. If oversight is effective, is it doomed to interfere excessively with the efficient and effective execution of the laws Congress passes? Put differently, is effective and efficient administration incompatible with democratic control?

The Many Faces of Congressional Oversight

This debate is, in part, definitional. Students of congressional-executive relations have referred to oversight in different ways—some very narrowly and some taking a more encompassing view—that reflect different views of what congressional control ought to be.

Perspectives on Oversight

The classical studies of congressional oversight of administration define the activity as the review by the legislature of actions taken by administrators in the implementation of law.[3] Moreover, students of oversight who have been most disappointed with congressional oversight have relied on the narrowest definitions, with oversight limited to formal reviews of administrative activities through such vehicles as oversight hearings and General Accounting Office audits.[4] With narrow boundaries around the phenomenon, it is little wonder that observers have seen little and have not been impressed by much.

The formal lines have served a useful purpose. They have helped define the phenomenon for study and have enabled congressional scholars to develop theoretical propositions about when and how such oversight was likely to occur. For example, they argued that oversight was more likely when different parties controlled the presidency and the Congress; when members of Congress sought to pressure reluctant administrators or protect favored programs; when Congress itself became more decentralized; and when scandals offer inviting targets for expressing outrage.[5]

There is unquestionably much merit in these propositions. Especially since the Nixon administration, many disputes between the parties have been played out through oversight hearings. The tradition of divided party control, of the presidency and Congress held by different parties, has undoubtedly increased tensions in the oversight process. The problem with the propositions is not that they are wrong but that they are too limited; they miss much that is important and interesting about congressional oversight. Indeed, oversight is pervasive through congressional action.[6] Lawmaking is part of a seamless web: past problems partially solved; previous administrative action that produced some positive effects but that left other difficulties behind; hearings designed to define problems and build support and provide money for new solutions; new laws designed to solve these problems; and yet more hearings to discover what effects the laws produced. Congress cannot write new law without first considering, implicitly or explicitly, what results existing law has produced. It cannot authorize programs or appropriate money to fund them without appraising the results of earlier outlays. Policy making is impossible without considering, at least implicitly, previous policy execution. Oversight thus inevitably "can lead Congress into every facet of administration," as Dodd and Schott have pointed out.[7] Oversight cannot be separated into a distinct part of the congressional policy cycle. It pervades all parts of it.

Furthermore, oversight occurs in a multifaceted policy world where competing issues are always struggling for a place on the agenda and where only a few of them will make it. It also occurs in a complex environment of conflicting political pressures by political parties and interest groups. Oversight thus is a question of which issues will surface when, with whose support and opposition. Oversight is a two-way street: of getting the right information to legislators to attract their attention; and of sending the right signals from legislators to influence administrative behavior.

We would expect, therefore, that nonlegislative participants, from interest groups to administrators, would marshal the information that maximizes their chances of winning a place on the crowded congressional agenda and defines issues in a way they believe will be most favorable for them. We would expect that members of Congress would seize on issues that best enhance their chances for influencing bureaucratic behavior, and hence public policy, in the direction they most prefer. We would expect, not incidentally, that members would calculate the effect of such actions on their own prestige within Congress and on their reelection chances,[8] although members have sometimes shown remarkable insulation from short-term political calculations. We would expect that members of Congress would communicate with administrators through a wide variety of signals, from the most subtle to the most direct, to match their motives. Finally, we would expect that administrators would respond to these signals after calculating how the congressional signals, along with the threats and inducements behind them, fit into their own political calculus, especially their overall balance of political support. Oversight is thus one ingredient in a soup, constantly bubbling with new ingredients and continually stirred by complex political forces. Defined this way, the oversight phenomenon is much more difficult, but infinitely more interesting, to study.

Congressional Microcontrol and Macrocontrol
What kind of oversight would we expect to emerge from this policy gumbo? First, we would expect oversight to be a two-sided game of give and take. Legislation inevitably involves delegation of authority to administrators, and the exercise of administrative discretion invites a congressional

response. We would not expect everything—perhaps anything—to work right the first time. Public problems are usually not easily tractable. Moreover, the very nature of lawmaking produces legislation that is vague, often confusing, and sometimes internally contradictory. Oversight thus is part of the process of gradual definition and redefinition of administrative discretion.

This first proposition suggests that congressional oversight is an inextricable part of lawmaking. Only in administration can congressional goals be brought to life, but administration is inevitably a process that produces some mismatch between congressional goals and administrative results. Administrators often test the limits of their discretion. Members of Congress must repair the fences to bring wide-ranging administrators back within the corrals legislators have in mind. Members of Congress, furthermore, sometimes discover that their goals change along the way; legislative "intent" frequently is a gradually evolving concept. Oversight thus is about error definition, detection, and correction—with error defined by the eye of the member of Congress, a vision often not universally shared. Legislative strategies for signaling desired behavior and administrative strategies for resisting them are nearly endless.

Second, since it is a system based fundamentally on communication, we would expect that the participants would develop means for processing information in which the formal patterns of communication, such as laws, are only a part. In fact, members of Congress have developed many ways of signaling, often subtly, to administrators. Committee and subcommittee hearings, and the questions asked at them, are often intended to send messages about desired administrative behavior. Many members of Congress and their staffs are trained in law and know well the first law of cross-examination: Never ask a question unless one knows the answer. Members rarely ask questions at hearings without anticipating their answers, and they rarely query witnesses without clearly recognizing the signals that questions send. The same is true of public statements, news conferences, letters to administrators, and requests for casework assistance. Requests for General Accounting Office investigations, advance review and clearance of administrative actions by committees and subcommittees, legislative vetoes, and other more subtle forms of communication provide legislators with a remarkable variety of ways to send signals from the Hill.[9]

This second proposition suggests that legislators have many ways to involve themselves in administration, and they quite naturally take advantage of them. Legislative delegation of power to administrators is often vast, but the string controlling discretion is often short and, when tugged, highly effective. As long as legislators have the ultimate weapons, control of authorizations and appropriations, administrators ignore hints and signals from Congress at their peril.

Third, since it is but a subsystem that is part of a much larger and more complex governmental system, all the participants in the oversight process always have competing demands on their time. As earlier students of oversight suggested, therefore, oversight is likely to be episodic. In fact, Matthew D. McCubbins and Thomas Schwartz distinguish between regular, direct, centralized, and systematic oversight, which they call "police-patrol" oversight, and "fire-alarm" oversight, which is more decentralized and periodic. They argue that members of Congress have little incentive to devote their time to regular patrols looking for administrative misbehavior. Instead, they engage in oversight when alarms ring to suggest problems and opportunities.[10]

This third proposition suggests members of Congress will give only sporadic attention to administrators, often at unpredictable times. Oversight can be triggered by many things: disasters that attract attention by the news media; studies conducted or charges raised by interest groups; program analyses by Congress's own support agencies, such as the General Accounting Office or the Office of Technology Assessment; detailed investigation by a member's or a committee's staff; or an agency's own internal studies and documents.

From the legislative side, this means that outside demands for oversight in all its forms are insatiable and eternal. Oversight occurs when members of Congress calculate it is worthwhile to do it, and tends not to happen otherwise. The key to making it happen is getting the attention of key members, and that in turn depends on uncovering and delivering the right nuggets of information. From the administrative side, this means that congressional intervention, when or on what, is very difficult to predict. Administrators must therefore always behave as if congressional oversight on any detail were imminent. From both perspectives, finally, it means that oversight is likely to focus on the narrow phenomenon that triggers it. Oversight therefore is likely to occur on small details, not broad policy.

These three propositions, put together, suggest that legislative relations with the executive branch are likely to be extremely complex, unpredictable, subtle, rarely sustained on individual issues, but continuous across the broad range of policy. Furthermore, they suggest that sporadic oversight of administrative details is as much a part of the legislative policy fabric as filibusters, spittoons, reporters, senatorial courtesy, and the American flag hanging at the front of each chamber. It is the inevitable result of the separation of powers created by the framers of the Constitution. The question, therefore, is not whether members of Congress should oversee, often in microscopic detail, administrators and their programs, for it is inevitable that they will do so. The question is what effects micromanagement has on the policy process, and how in the end the process can be adjusted to achieve better the results its participants desire.

Micromanagement and Congressional Control

In no other part of the policy process has micromanagement been more criticized than in defense policy. Nearly every expert who has examined congressional involvement in defense affairs has criticized Congress for its overinvolvement in the details of weapons policy. The verdict is harsh and nearly unanimous: "Congress devotes great amounts of energy to defense but often devotes it to the wrong things," as a Common Cause analysis put it.[11] The President's Blue Ribbon Commission on Defense Management, better known as the Packard Commission, argued in June 1986,

> Congressional focus ... is myopic and misdirected. Only the upcoming budget year gets real attention, and this attention is directed at the budget's microscopic pieces, its line items.... The Commission believes that both the number and the magnitude of changes resulting from congressional review of the defense budget are excessive and harmful to the long-term defense of the country.[12]

Nevertheless, "micromanagement," used typically as a derisive term, means different things to different critics. It is, in part, congressional obsession with short-term decisions over the long term. It is congressional budgeting of very small details in a very large defense budget. It is congressional mandating of narrow administrative details. It is a huge appetite for reports, studies, and testimony on minute details of defense programs. In short, it is both traditional oversight, understood as after-the-fact review of administrative actions, and before-the-fact legislation of management minutiae.[13]

Varieties and Costs of Micromanagement

Such micromanagement, critics claim, produces several dangerous results.

1. Demands on managers' time. The Packard Commission found, for example, that Congress in 1985 alone directed the Defense Department to conduct 458 different studies, "from the feasibility of selling lamb products in commissaries to the status of retirement benefits for Philippine scouts."[14] In just eight months in 1983, Congress held 407 hearings and collected 5,000 hours of testimony from 1,200 defense officials. During the year, the Pentagon received 84,148 written inquiries and logged 592,150 phone calls from Congress.[15] Preparing so much testimony and so many reports requires an enormous amount of time. As Norman R. Augustine, a former undersecretary of the Army, put it, officials are called before Congress "with such frequency that many seemingly have little time to do anything but tell what they would have been doing if they had not been too busy testifying."[16]

2. *Focus on the short term.* In overseeing the defense budget, critics claim, Congress too often seeks accountability by budgeting in too much detail. A Senate Armed Services Committee staff report, for example, concluded that Congress tends "to sacrifice long-term goals in the face of short-term pressures." The annual budget process continually reopens budgetary questions to new, detailed scrutiny, so conclusive decisions are rarely made.[17] The result often is erratic changes in program funding that make long-term planning impossible and that increase the cost of weapons systems. In 1973, for example, the Senate Armed Services Committee cut $100 million from the B-1 bomber program because the committee was unhappy with the air force's management. In the end, one study suggests, the cut worsened management problems, further stretched out the bomber's production, and drove up its costs.[18]

The result is "a nightmare from the standpoint of administrative efficiency": Micromanagement through detailed budget decisions reduces the autonomy of Pentagon managers, encourages them to emphasize procedures over performance, slows production, increases costs, and worsens relations among Congress, the Defense Department, and private industry.[19] One study, for example, estimates that improved congressional oversight, along with better program auditing and clearer regulations, could save as much as $16 billion in the defense budget over the next ten years.[20] Worst of all, critics contend, micromanagement "removes decision making from the manager on the scene and puts it into the hands of those who cannot possibly know the nitty-gritty of their choices." It "is a primary cause of the defense procurement mess."[21]

3. *Diversion of programs to the pork barrel.* Congressional meddling in the details of both defense budgeting and administration produce enormous temptations for steering some programs to favored political interests. When budget cuts threaten, members seek to protect projects in their own districts by legislating details in defense authorization and budget bills. That, in turn, "encourages the intrusion of narrow political considerations into the determination of matters that ought ideally to be resolved by professional experts."[22] Micromanagement also creates similar incentives within the Defense Department and its contractors to spread defense contracts around among congressional districts to help insulate programs from attack. When the Reagan administration started up the B-1 bomber program again after the Carter administration canceled it, Rockwell International, the prime contractor, bought itself insurance against another cancellation by scattering the bomber's subcontracts among forty-eight different states.[23]

Shifting the Balance of Power

Congressional micromanagement had grown markedly since the mid-1970s.[24] One wag, in fact, calls it possibly "America's fastest growing industry."[25] The Vietnam war and Watergate increased congressional suspicion about the exercise of executive power.[26] Micromanagement, however, also has its roots in Congress's changing structure and patterns in policy making.

The decentralization and professionalization of Congress. The proliferation of congressional subcommittees and the growth in congressional staffs increased Congress's potential for delving into the details of Pentagon budgets and operations. One study estimated that twenty-nine committees and fifty-five subcommittees in both houses oversee defense activities, and that the bodies are supported by more than 20,000 staffers directly dealing with defense policy.[27] The lines between the committees and subcommittees, meanwhile, weakened, so several committees could claim jurisdiction over many issues and programs.[28] As the potential for oversight increased, so naturally did the practice.

The executive-legislative mismatch in defense policy. Congressional micromanagement is also the product of the different role that the legislative and executive branches play in defense policy. Congress is inevitably reactive to executive branch policy. The Defense Department has the initiative in proposing new systems and an overwhelming advantage in technical information. Congress, moreover, is much more decentralized and cumbersome in structure and operation than is the executive branch, especially the Pentagon. Defense planners think in system-wide, multiyear terms. Congress, especially in preparing the budget, operates in the very short term, and members of Congress rarely have the time, expertise, or information to take more than small bites of defense issues. As James W. Reed concludes in a trenchant analysis, "in a very real sense, Congress finds itself dealing only on the margins of military policy with those issues most susceptible to domestic pressures."[29] On defense issues, Congress is much more likely to take microsize bites of defense issues, compared with the president's and the Defense Department's macrosize bites. For Congress, digesting those bites occurs in a more politically hot-blooded system.

The budgetary process. The congressional budgetary process increases the pressures to focus on the short term. Because the defense budget is the second largest part of the budget, after social security, the defense budget is a tempting target indeed for budgeteers seeking money to fund other programs. Programs are most easily cut in their infancy, before sunk costs and political constituencies have grown. Cutting them at that stage often yields relatively small savings, however. Once programs have become more established, they become much more resistant to pruning, especially in the short-term world of deficit estimates. Thus, members of Congress seeking budgetary savings dwell on micro- instead of macro-level details, since that is often the only place where money can be found in the short term. Micro-level attention also offers the best ongoing chance for steering programs to favored constituencies, since major weapons decisions come along infrequently.[30]

Defense technology. The increasing complexity of defense technology also fosters a micro-level focus by Congress. Analysts have developed an S-curve that explains the effect of increasing complexity on time and expense of developing new systems (see figure 5.1). The more mature technology becomes, the more expensive improvements are and the longer it takes to make them. Therefore, the more mature defense systems become, the more importance that initial decision becomes, since that decision creates large financial demands for a long time. Moreover, the larger the sunk costs in any system, the harder it is to make any but micro-level changes. Maturing technologies and older programs thus increase micromanagement.[31] With defense systems, in particular, becoming more mature, it is little surprise that congressional micromanagement has increased.

FIGURE 5.1

THE S-CURVE OF TECHNOLOGY GROWTH

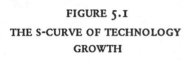
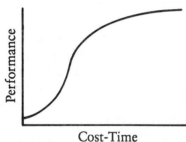

Performance

Cost-Time

SOURCE: Thomas L. McNaugher, *New Weapons, Old Politics: America's Military Procurement Muddle* (Washington, D.C.: Brookings Institution, 1989), 89. Used by permission.

Micromanagement and Bureaucratic Risk

Micromanagement also subtly affects the behavior of bureaucrats. By its very nature, micromanagement is both highly focused and unpredictable. No program administrator can know when congressional attention might be focused on his or her actions, but when that attention does come, it can shine with intense light on the smallest details. In a system that buys millions of spare parts for thousands of pieces of military equipment, who could have guessed in advance that members of Congress would investigate in close detail the procurement of small plastic caps used on the legs of a stool, which in turn was used as a part of a manual backup system for electronic navigation in the AWACS (Airborne Warning and Control System) aircraft? When NBC News discovered that Boeing was charging the air force $1,118.26 apiece for the small pieces of plastic, the story hit the national media.[32] So did similar tales about $5,000 coffeepots, $2,000 pliers, $1,000 Allen wrenches, and $600 ashtrays.[33]

To be sure, common sense would suggest that these are outrageous tales that demand congressional investigation. They, in turn, illustrate why many program administrators are becoming more and more risk averse. If nearly any official's actions, no matter how detailed or lowly, can subject the official and the agency to scathing attack and potential loss of political support and appropriations, the tendency to avoid risk increases: to check and double-check, to obtain advance clearance far up the hierarchy, and to read Congress's legislation very narrowly to limit exposure. It is little wonder, therefore, that paperwork and red tape proliferate. Forms and rules not only play an important part in administering programs but also in preparing a defense for administrators who can unexpectedly find themselves under attack. The danger of oversight, furthermore, can make administrators reluctant to stick their necks out, because Congress has a multitude of ways of chopping off necks stuck out too far. Norman Augustine sarcastically contends that

> Any bureaucrat worthy of the name will soon strategize that a fail-safe way to guard against criticism is *never* to take risk, even when that risk may be very prudent and may have significant probable payoff. Extrapolating the theory that the only people who never make bad decisions are those who never make any decisions, we can logically conclude that the only people whose work cannot be criticized are those who produce no work.[34]

Many administrators thus take the view, "If the law does not specifically tell me I can, I won't," as Robert B. Costello, former undersecretary of defense for acquisition, put it.[35]

The result is not so much paralysis as administrative sluggishness. Checking and cross-checking slow down the administrative process. Administrators become more circumspect in making decisions, less likely to take chances that could improve production or save money, and more likely to avoid making decisions at all if they can be avoided. Administrators become more likely to pass decisions up the chain of command, and progress slows. Members of Congress discover that the programs they created are not administered as well or as quickly as they would like, so they attempt to ferret out why. Investigating the details uncovers instances of bad administration or nonadministration which quickly become the focus of congressional attention. That makes administrators take even fewer risks and administration even more reactive to congressional initiatives. Such a closed loop, with its inbred obsession with details, encourages micromanagement and stimulates a "no risk" attitude among administrators.[36]

Members of Congress employ micromanagement because few other tools of oversight offer the same leverage over administrative action. Risk-averse administrative behavior, however, can sow the seeds that court even more micromanagement. The process thus threatens to become an accelerating, ever tightening choking spiral. And that is precisely the danger that most defense analysts have identified.

Congressional Oversight and Effective Management

To the issue of congressional micromanagement, many of those who have studied the situation have a common recommendation: "Stop!" They argue that Congress should stop meddling in the details of administration; should authorize programs for longer periods in larger packages; should appropriate money for at least two years at a time to allow administrators a longer lead time; and, in general, should spend more time setting broad strategy and less time dealing with individual weapons systems. They urge, in short, that Congress delegate broader authority to program managers. As one critic put it, members of Congress "are simply too far from the scene and often lack the engineering and industrial management talent for the kind of detailed decisions they are making."[37]

It is unquestionably true that Congress can pass the line from productive oversight to intrusive meddling, and the consensus among defense experts is that Congress indeed intrudes excessively into the details of defense policy. It is not true that simply asking the Congress to back off will solve the problem or that congressional nit-picking stems totally from a desire by members of Congress to stick their noses too far into another branch of government. Why, then, do members engage in oversight? Why are they driven to micromanage? The answer must be understood as part of a reciprocal process based in the balance of powers between the legislative and executive branches.

For micromanagement even to happen, the perception of problems must cross a minimum threshold: Administrative problems must loom larger in some members' minds than the many other things competing for their time and attention. Members are not likely often to seek out administrative problems. Instead, through the complex issue networks that stretch through Washington and around the country, problems seek them out. Interest groups, disaffected administrators, reporters, committee staffs, and even unhappy constituents all press problems and demands on members, who then pursue those that seem to offer an acceptable payoff. This does not mean that some members of Congress are not sometimes entrepreneurial in pursuing oversight and micromanagement, for of course there are members who eagerly seek to make their mark in steering administrative details, especially in whose district money should be spent. It does mean that most congressional micromanagement is reactive. There usually are too many other items on a member's agenda to make proactive oversight politically worthwhile.

Oversight in its many forms thus is principally a mechanism through which Congress attempts to ensure its leverage over the laws it enacts, in programs that technically are ever more complicated. Indeed, as Allen Schick argued, "control of administration means control of government."[38] It is little wonder, then, that members of Congress find themselves driven to investigate detailed administrative actions. These "details" are the core of government, and controlling them means winning the power that matters most.

Is Micromanagement Inevitable?

Despite the many tensions between the branches, congressional micromanagement is not inevitable. Executive branch officials can minimize the invitation to micromanagement by running programs in consonance with the sometimes vague intentions of Congress. As Fisher argues, "agencies that maintain trust with their oversight committees can be expected to retain substantial discretion and relative freedom from legislative intervention."[39] The tensions of divided party government make it tempting to pick fights on partisan or programmatic grounds, and administrators have sometimes asserted an absolute right, once a program has been enacted, to steer it according to the president's and not the Congress's will, which naturally provokes members of Congress to intervene. Simply asking Congress not to micromanage will scarcely end the tensions of divided party control unless Congress abdicates its constitutional role. Administrative discretion is, in large part, the result of the balance struck in the never-ending struggle between the branches of government.

Smooth-running programs, moreover, are unlikely to court micromanagement. Risk-averse administrators, however, are unlikely to produce effective programs. In his struggle to reform defense procurement during the Reagan years, Undersecretary Costello pressed contract administrators constantly "at least to use all authority contained within the intent of the law." Too often, he said later, he found that administrators read the narrowest possible interpretation into the law as a way of minimizing their exposure. That made their administration of programs more reactive and, in turn, courted congressional micromanagement. Costello, instead, exhorted, "We need to take charge and be managers, not administrators."[40] A narrow administrative approach to program management, he believed, discouraged people from making decisions.

He argued that managers needed to seize the discretion present in their jobs and manage more aggressively. For example, Costello gave some base commanders in the military a unified budget for their bases, with broad discretion over how to allocate their money, instead of a line-item budget, which specified the amount to be spent for every object. The actual flexibility provided by the change was only about 2 or 3 percent of the budget, since predictable and uncontrollable expenses such as electricity, water, and supplies dominated base spending. Nevertheless, Costello reported, every base commander was able to improve his base's productivity by 10 to 15 percent. Increased budget flexibility—and more important, the trust in the commander's management that it embodied—allowed commanders truly to manage.[41]

The argument against encouraging managers to take more risks is that it potentially jeopardizes political support. Anyone who assumes risk can make mistakes, and administrative mistakes invite congressional intervention and political attack. In such a system, everyone is reactive: members of Congress who respond to problems that emerge; top agency officials who fear budgetary and programmatic retribution; and lower-level administrators who avoid rocking the boat. The result, of course, is that nothing happens quickly or well. This approach ignores the fact that "one way to get political support is to do the right thing."[42] While asking Congress to reduce its micromanagement is sound advice, the tactic must be matched by more confident and aggressive management by program officials, at all levels.

Indeed, micromanagement must be understood as part of the struggle between the legislative and executive branches over political power, as embodied in the details of administration. It is, in its less benign form, a process in which everyone is reactive: members of Congress, to perceived wrongs committed by administrators; administrators, to unpredictable incursions by members of Congress into the exercise of their discretion; presidents, to worries that accommodations by administrators to congressional demands will weaken their own leverage over the executive branch; and interest groups, to opportunities to slide questions of keen interest onto the policy agenda in a form that best presents their points of view. Micromanagement, at its core, is a central part of the "collision between the branches."[43] Only careful and confident administration, coupled with accommodation between the branches, can minimize the impact.

Notes

NOTE: The preparation of this chapter was generously supported by a grant from the Earhart Foundation, whose support is gratefully acknowledged.

I am indebted to Robert B. Costello, James W. Fesler, Louis Fisher, and Erwin C. Hargrove, who provided valuable suggestions for improving the chapter.

1. J.F. Bibby, "Oversight—Congress's Neglected Function: Will Watergate Make a Difference?" paper presented at the 1974 meeting of the Western Political Science Association, quoted by Joel D. Aberbach, "Changes in Congressional Oversight," *American Behavioral Scientist* 22 (May/June 1979): 494. See also Lawrence C. Dodd and Richard L. Schott, *Congress and the Administrative State* (New York: Wiley, 1979). And see, among others, Seymour Scher, "Conditions for Legislative Control," *Journal of Politics* 25 (August 1963): 526–51; and Morris Ogul, *Congress Oversees the Bureaucracy* (Pittsburgh: University of Pittsburgh Press, 1976). For a brief, excellent history of congressional oversight, see Allen Schick, "Congress and the 'Details' of Administration," *Public Administration Review* 36 (September/October 1976): 516–28.

2. See U.S. House of Representatives, Select Committee on Committees (Bolling Committee), *Committee Reform Amendments of 1974, Report to Accompany H.Res.988,* 93rd Cong., 2d sess., H. Report 93–916.

3. See, for example, Joseph P. Harris, *Congressional Control of Administration* (Washington, D.C.: Brookings Institution, 1964), 1–2.

4. Joel D. Aberbach, for example, defines oversight as a "review that takes place *during* program and policy implementation as well as afterwards, but excludes much of what Congress now does when it considers proposals for new programs or even for the expansion of current programs." See "Changes in Congressional Oversight," *American Behavioral Scientist* 22 (May/June 1979): 494.

5. Ibid., 495–98. See also Scher, "Conditions for Legislative Control"; and Ogul, *Congress Oversees the Bureaucracy.*

6. See Christopher H. Foreman, Jr., *Signals from the Hill: Congressional Oversight and the Challenge of Social Regulation* (New Haven: Yale University Press, 1988), 12; Dodd and Schott, *Congress and the Administrative State,* 156; Lawrence D. Brown, *New Politics, New Politics: Government's Response to Government's Growth* (Washington, D.C.: Brookings Institution, 1983); National Academy of Public Administration, *Congressional Oversight of Regulatory Agencies: The Need to Strike a Balance and Focus on Performance* (Washington, D.C.: National Academy of Public Administration, 1988), 1; and Louis Fisher, "Micromanagement by Congress: Reality and Mythology," in *The Fettered Presidency: Legal Constraints on the Executive Branch,* ed. L. Gordon Crovitz and Jeremy A. Rabkin (Washington, D.C.: American Enterprise Institute, 1989), 143.

7. Dodd and Schott, *Congress and the Administrative State,* 156.

8. Foreman, *Signals from the Hill,* 14.

9. The phrase is Foreman's, in *Signals from the Hill.* See also Fisher, "Micromanagement by Congress," 143.

10. Matthew D. McCubbins and Thomas Schwartz, "Congressional Oversight Overlooked: Police Patrols versus Fire Alarms," *American Journal of Political Science* 28 (Fall 1984): 165–79.

11. Mark Rovner, *Defense Dollars and Sense: A Common Cause Guide to the Defense Budget Process* (Washington, D.C.: Common Cause, 1983), 51.

12. The President's Blue Ribbon Commission on Defense Management (Packard Commission), *A Quest for Excellence: Final Report to the President* (Washington, D.C.: Government Printing Office, 1986), 21.

13. The latter, of course, does not fit the traditional view of oversight.

14. Packard Commission, *Quest for Excellence*, 21–22.

15. J. Ronald Fox with James L. Field, *The Defense Management Challenge: Weapons Acquisition* (Boston: Harvard Business School Press, 1988), 75–76.

16. Norman R. Augustine, *Augustine's Laws* (New York: Viking Press, 1986), 331. See also Rovner, *Defense Dollars and Sense,* 57; William H. Gregory, *The Defense Procurement Mess* (Lexington, Mass.: Lexington Books, 1989), 55; and U.S. Senate, Committee on Armed Services, *Defense Organization: The Need for Change,* staff report, 99th Cong., 1st sess., 1985, 592.

17. Senate Armed Services Committee, *Defense Organization,* 589.

18. Nick Kotz, *Wild Blue Yonder: Money, Politics, and the B-1 Bomber* (New York: Pantheon, 1988), 126.

19. Fox with Field, *Defense Management Challenge,* 83–84. See also Kotz, *Wild Blue Yonder,* 241; David C. Hendrickson, *Reforming Defense: The State of American Civil-Military Relations* (Baltimore: Johns Hopkins University Press, 1988), 33; and Center for Strategic and International Studies (CSIS), *U.S. Defense Acquisition: A Process in Trouble* (Washington, D.C.: Center for Strategic and International Studies, 1987), 39. The phenomenon is common in Great Britain as well as in the United States. See Andrew Cox and Stephen Kirby, *Congress, Parliament and Defence* (New York: St. Martin's Press, 1986), 4.

20. CSIS, *U.S. Defense Acquisition,* 59.

21. Gregory, *Defense Procurement Mess,* 3.

22. David C. Hendrickson, *Reforming Defense: The State of American Civil-Military Relations* (Baltimore: Johns Hopkins University Press, 1988), 33. See also Thomas L. McNaugher, *New Weapons, Old Politics: America's Military Procurement Muddle* (Washington, D.C.: Brookings Institution, 1989), 121–22.

23. Kotz, *Wild Blue Yonder.*

24. Senate Armed Services Committee, *Defense Organization,* 589, 592.

25. Augustine, *Augustine's Laws,* 324.

26. Fox with Field, *Defense Management Challenge,* 80–83; McNaugher, *New Weapons, Old Politics,* 56–69.

27. CSIS, *U.S. Defense Acquisition,* 15.

28. Senate Armed Services Committee, *Defense Organization,* 573–80; Fox with Field, *The Defense Management Challenge,* 80–83; and McNaugher, *New Weapons, Old Politics,* 56–69.

29. James W. Reed, "Congress and the Politics of Defense Reform," in *The Defense Reform Debate: Issues and Analysis,* ed. Asa A. Clark IV, Peter W. Chiarelli, Jeffrey S. McKitrick, and James W. Reed (Baltimore: Johns Hopkins University Press), 235–47, esp. 236.

30. Compare McNaugher, *New Weapons, Old Politics,* 123. Cox and Kirby point out that similar phenomena characterize British budget making for defense as well. See *Congress, Parliament and Defence,* 300.

31. For example, in jets, engine and airframe technologies are entering maturity, as are tank-armor and engine technologies. See McNaugher, *New Weapons, Old Politics,* 89–90.

32. A. Ernest Fitzgerald, *The Pentagonists: An Insider's View of Waste, Mismanagement, and Fraud in Defense Spending* (Boston: Houghton Mifflin, 1989), 156–58.

33. Gregory, *Defense Procurement Mess,* chap. 6.

34. Augustine, *Augustine's Laws,* 328.

35. Interview with the author, 10 July 1989.

36. Ibid.

37. Gregory, *Defense Procurement Mess,* 193. Compare Senate Armed Services Committee, *Defense Organization,* 612; and CSIS, *U.S. Defense Acquisition,* 49.

38. Schick, "Congress and the 'Details' of Administration," 516.

39. Fisher, "Micromanagement by Congress," 151.

40. Interview with the author, 19 July 1989.

41. Ibid.

42. Ibid.

43. Fisher, "Micromanagement by Congress," 151.

PART THREE

Management Issues

6

Building Public Management
Research and Practice

HAL G. RAINEY AND JAMES L. PERRY

Many people remember Charles Levine for his remarkable combination of attention to both scholarship and practice. No part of his work illustrates that combination better than his efforts relating to the nature of management and organizations in the public sector. He played leading roles in two main streams of activity whose development we describe here: first, research and professional activity regarding the distinctive characteristics of public organizations and management; second, management in the federal government. In connection with the latter he published insightful articles and worked with the Volcker Commission on the Revitalization of the Public Service in the United States.

The former stream of research increasingly identifies public management as subject to intense influences from the political processes in which it operates. In the latter, Charles Levine pointedly illustrated the practical impacts of these generalizations from the research. He wrote and acted in response to his and others' conviction that the political climate of the times had brought the public service of the United States to a point of crisis.

Research and Professional Activity on
Public Management

Research on organizations and their management has burgeoned during this century. An interesting divergence in this research came increasingly into focus in the late 1970s. The main body of this literature sought to develop generic theories about organizations and managers, applicable to all sectors of economic and social activity. This approach draws on formidable justifications, such as the blurring of the boundaries between the public and private sectors in the United States. Sophisticated versions of these observations[1] provide valuable counterpoints against invidious stereotypes about differences between public and private management.

Even so, prominent economists have for decades depicted public bureaucracies as sharply different from private firms and markedly inferior in efficiency and innovativeness because their outputs have no economic markets.[2] In various ways they argue that without the discipline of the market, managers have little incentive to control costs and therefore make decisions without regard to productive returns, which are not easily measured. Aggressive managers leave for greener, private pastures, and the public agencies fill up with cautious and rigid conservers. Lower-level administrators distort information reported up to higher levels. Red tape proliferates.

Not necessarily so wedded to the markets-make-things-better school, a group of political scientists shows a similar tendency to depict public bureaucracies as subject to unique external political influences. Until recently, however, both the economists and political scientists paid little attention to the managerial characteristics of those bureaucracies or to the other topics that organization and management theorists analyze so intensively in their more-generic approaches.[3]

This divergence over the distinctiveness of public organizations has both practical and theoretical significance. Nations throughout the world struggle with difficult choices between political and market-based controls, and whether functions should be public or private in this sense. During the 1980s in the United States and many other countries, privatization of governmental organizations and services was intensely debated. Earthshaking changes in the socialist countries late in the decade turned in part on concerns about the performance of government-controlled organizations. If public organizations and management processes closely resemble those in the private domain, all these policy makers and experts have been misguided and need to be disabused. The disagreements in the academic literature, just mentioned, indicate the theoretical significance of the issue. If the policy makers turn to the academics for guidance, they find that most general management and organization theory literature implies or asserts that their question has little importance. The disciplines of political science and economics embrace the issue, but have had little to say about its implications for management.

In the past decade, however, numerous books and articles noted this divergence between managerial theory and theory in political science and economics;[4] more and more relevant research has appeared. The need to substantiate this distinction persists, however. Charles Levine, recognizing this need, played a central role in preparing one of the contributions to the articles and books, mentioned above, that called for such work.[5]

The Growing Body of Research

Table 6.1 (pages 115–23) summarizes selected works and illustrates that relevant material has appeared in highly diverse forms and places.

TABLE 6.1

SUMMARY OF SELECTED RESEARCH ON THE
PUBLIC-PRIVATE DISTINCTION

Author(s) (year)	*Methodology*	*Findings and conclusions*
*Positive and deductive theories of public bureaucracy and related social control processes*		
Banfield (1975)	Propositions about corruption in "typical" government agencies and typical business firms.	Government agencies have (a) greater fragmentation of authority and weaker requirements to avoid "selling" outputs below cost of production; (b) greater vagueness, multiplicity, and conflict among objectives and products; (c) stronger requirements to adhere to external laws and administrative procedures; and (d) less reliance on pecuniary incentives. Therefore, they spend more on reducing corruption than is gained in return, and are less able to reduce corruption through strong central control.
Dahl & Lindblom (1953)	Theoretical analysis of societal decision and allocation mechanisms.	"Agencies" under governmental control have more intangible goals, less incentive for cost reduction, more dysfunctions of bureaucracy (red tape, rigidity) than do "enterprises" controlled by markets.
Downs (1967)	Conceptual/theoretical model of bureaucracy.	Due to the absence of the economic market, public bureaucracies tend toward more elaborate hierarchies. The political environment is more important and influences internal decisions. Agencies become rigid over time.
Wamsley & Zald (1973)	Conceptual/theoretical analysis of public organizations.	Public ownership and funding subjects public organizations to unique political and economic environments and unique public

Continued . . .

TABLE 6.1 — *Continued*

Author(s) (year)	Methodology	Findings and conclusions
		expectations. For example, political sentiment toward the agency becomes more important.

Typologies and taxonomies of organizations that include a public-private distinction

Author(s) (year)	Methodology	Findings and conclusions
Blau & Scott (1962)	Deductive typology.	Four-category typology of organizations: Commonweal, Business, Service, and Mutual Benefit. Commonweal organizations (public agencies) benefit the general public, and public accountability is the central organizational issue. Businesses benefit owners, and productivity is the central issue.
Haas, Hall, & Johnson (1966)	Empirically derived taxonomy.	Constructed nine taxonomic categories. Public and private organizations were mixed among categories, so the study did not support a public-private distinction.
Mintzberg (1979)	Typology of organization structure based on review of research.	"Public machine bureaucracies" are posited as one subcategory within "machine bureaucracies" because public agencies tend toward highly bureaucratized form due to external constraints.
Pugh, Hickson, & Hinings (1969)	Empirical taxonomy of structural dimensions of 52 organizations in Great Britain, 8 of which were government organizations.	Most of the public organizations were unexpectedly low on measures of internal structure but high on concentration of authority at the top, with personnel procedures highly centralized or externally controlled. Noting that the government organizations were not typical government agencies but local "workflow" organizations, such as a water department, the researchers suggested that the

Continued ...

TABLE 6.1 — *Continued*

Author(s) (year)	Methodology	Findings and conclusions
		size and technological develop-ment determine internal structure, whereas concentration of author-ity is determined by government or other external auspices.

Anecdotal observations by practitioners with experience in the public and private sectors

Author(s) (year)	Methodology	Findings and conclusions
Blumenthal (1983)	Experienced practi-tioner's views on similarities and differ-ences between public and business manage-ment.	Federal executives have less con-trol over their organizations than business executives. Federal orga-nizations are more conglomerated and diverse. Congress and the press are more influential. The de-cision process is more cumber-some.

Empirical research on public bureaucracy and public administrators

Author(s) (year)	Methodology	Findings and conclusions
Hood & Dun-sire (1981)	Empirical taxonomy of British central govern-ment departments us-ing archival data.	Arguing that public bureaucracies are a distinct set of organizations, the researchers developed a three-category empirical taxonomy of British central government depart-ments.
Kaufman (1981)	Descriptive study of six federal bureau chiefs.	Much of bureau chiefs' work is generic management (motivating, communicating, decision making), but the political environment and congressional relations are highly significant.
Meyer (1979)	Empirical study of structural change us-ing a national sample of state and local finance agencies.	Public bureaucracies are particu-larly open to external pressures for changes. Their hierarchies are stable, but there is frequent change in subunit composition. Their personnel systems are in-creasingly formalized over time due to federal emphasis on civil service rules. External pressures

TABLE 6.1 — *Continued*

Author(s) (year)	*Methodology*	*Findings and conclusions*
		are mediated by political processes. Public bureaucracies have no alternative to Weberian hierarchy, and they are evaluated in terms of conformity with higher authority.
Warwick (1975)	Case study of U.S. Department of State.	Public organizations are heavily influenced by external political and institutional factors. They are prone to elaborate hierarchies and rules. Their internal structures are often imposed externally. They are resistant to change and to delegation of authority. Employees are security-conscious, especially in relation to potential political controversy.

Empirical research comparing samples of public and private organizations and managers

Boyatzis (1982)	Study of managerial competencies in four federal agencies and 12 Fortune 500 firms.	Private managers were higher on "goal and action" competencies. This is attributed to absence of clear performance measures, such as profits and sales, in the public sector. Private managers were also higher on leadership competencies of "conceptualization" and "use of oral presentations." This is attributed to more strategic decision making in the private sector and greater openness and standard procedures in the public sector.
Buchanan (1974, 1975)	Compared questionnaire responses from managers in four "typical" federal agencies and four large business firms.	Public managers were lower on job satisfaction, job involvement, organizational constraints and rules. Findings reflected weaker hierarchical authority, greater diversity of personnel, and weaker commitment expectations due to

TABLE 6.1 — *Continued*

Author(s) (year)	Methodology	Findings and conclusions
		civil service rules, political interventions, diffuse goals, and complex bureaucratic procedures.
Kilpatrick, Cummings, & Jennings (1964)	Survey of work-related values and attitudes at all levels in federal agencies and in business from 22 metropolitan sampling units. Includes sample of 273 federal executives and 27 business executives.	Federal executives were comparable to business executives on job satisfaction, but federal scientists, engineers, and college graduates were lower than their private counterparts. Public sector respondents in all these groups were more favorably disposed to work in the other sector than were private respondents. There were conflicts between the public image of the federal service and the occupational values of highly educated, higher occupational status groups in the United States.
Lau, Pavett, & Newman (1980)	Compared U.S. Navy civilian executives to executives from a number of service and manufacturing firms.	Found general similarities in the work of the two types of managers, although the public managers devoted more time to "fire drills" and crisis management.
Paine, Carroll, & Leete (1966)	Compared managers in one federal agency to managers in industry who were comparable in age and level.	Federal managers were lower on all 13 items in Porter need satisfaction scale, with greatest difference on job security, autonomy, and self-actualization.
Rainey (1979, 1983)	Compared questionnaire responses from middle managers in four state agencies and a defense installation to middle managers in four private firms.	Public managers were lower on satisfaction with co-workers and promotion, relations of extrinsic rewards (pay, promotion, firing) to performance, perceived value of monetary incentives, and perceived organizational formalization (rules, channels). There were no differences on role conflict and ambiguity, task variability and analyzability, goal clarity, and self-reported motivation and job involvement.

TABLE 6.1 — *Continued*

Author(s) (year)	Methodology	Findings and conclusions
Rhinehart, Barrell, De-wolfe, Griffin, & Spaner (1969)	Compared supervisory personnel in one federal agency to managers in a large sample from industry, with management level as a control variable.	Federal managers were lower on all 13 items on Porter need satisfaction scale, especially on social and self-actualization need satisfaction. Among higher level managers, federal managers were lower on autonomy and self-actualization. Results confirmed Paine et al. (1966).
Smith & Nock (1980)	Comparison of results from 1976 General Social Survey of 1,499 adults by National Opinion Research Center and 1973 Quality of Employment Survey of 1,496 employed persons by Survey Research Center, University of Michigan.	Blue-collar, public-sector workers were more satisfied with most aspects of work than blue-collar, private-sector workers. White-collar, public-sector workers were much less satisfied with co-workers, supervision, and intrinsic aspects of work (interest, etc.).

Empirical research comparing samples of public and private organizations in similar functional categories

Chubb & Moe (1985)	Mail questionnaire survey of 11,000 principals and teachers in 450 public and private (Catholic, other private, and elite private) high schools.	Public school members perceived stronger influence by outside authorities, weaker parental involvement, more managerial and less professional orientations of principals, less emphasis on academic excellence, less clarity of goals and disciplinary policy, more formal constraints on personnel policy, weaker faculty influence on curriculum.
Savas (1982)	Review of numerous studies of private vs. public provision of services.	Reviews findings of greater cost-efficiency of private delivery systems for solid waste collection, fire protection, transportation, health care, custodial services, landscaping, data processing, and

TABLE 6.1 — *Continued*

Author(s) (year)	Methodology	Findings and conclusions
		legal aid. Comparisons of hospitals and utilities have been mixed and inconclusive.
Solomon (1986)	Compared 120 Israeli public-sector top managers to 120 Israeli private-sector top managers on questionnaire responses. Both samples were evenly divided between manufacturing and service organizations, and they represented a broad range of Israeli work organizations.	Private-sector managers were much higher on perception that rewards were contingent on performance, that policies promoting efficiency were more prevalent in their organizations, and on personal satisfaction with various dimensions of their work. On the latter two dimensions, differences between public and private service organizations were particularly strong.
Spann (1977)	Reviewed empirical studies of public vs. private provision of five types of services.	Private producers can provide airline, garbage collection, fire protection, and electric utility services at the same or lower costs than can public producers. Results for hospitals indicate little cost or quality difference.

Organizational research in which the public-private distinction serves as a significant moderator

Hickson, Butler, Cray, Mallory, & Wilson (1986)	Intensive longitudinal study of strategic decision processes in 30 public and private service and manufacturing organizations.	For both service and manufacturing organizations, public ownership increases tendency toward a "vortex-sporadic" mode of decision processes and the tendency toward higher levels of formal and informal interaction in strategic decisions. Both public/private ownership and purpose (service/manufacturing) showed important relations to decision processes.

TABLE 6.1 — *Continued*

Author(s) (year)	Methodology	Findings and conclusions
Holdaway, Newberry, Hickson, & Heron (1975)	Analyzed structures of 16 public and 4 private colleges in Canada, using procedures similar to Aston studies (Pugh et al., 1969)	Higher degrees of public control were related to higher levels of bureaucratic control (formalization, standardization of personnel procedures, centralization). The public colleges were higher than the private on degree of public control.
Kurke & Aldrich (1983)	Replication of Mintzberg (1972) study, observing four executives, including a school and a hospital executive representing the public and "quasi-public" sectors.	Mintzberg's findings were replicated and supported. Public managers spent much more time in contact with directors and outside groups. The school administrator spent much more time in formal activity (e.g., formal meetings).
Mintzberg (1972)	Observational study of five executives from a variety of organizations, including a hospital director and superintendent of a large school system.	There were marked similarities in work roles of the five executives. The managers in public and "quasi-public" organizations—the school administrator and hospital administrator, respectively—spent more time in contact with directors and with external interest groups. The contacts were more structured and formalized (e.g., formal meetings), and the public administrators received more "status" requests.
Tolbert (1985)	Analysis of data on 167 public and 114 private colleges and universities from Higher Education General Information Survey.	For public colleges and universities, higher levels of private funding were related to existence of more administrative offices for private-funding relations. For private colleges and universities, more public funding was related to more offices for public-funding relations. The results support a

TABLE 6.1 — *Continued*

Author(s) (year)	Methodology	Findings and conclusions
		combined institutionalization and resource dependence interpretation.

SOURCE: James L. Perry and Hal G. Rainey, "The Public-Private Distinction in Organization Theory: A Critique and Research Strategy," *Academy of Management Review* 13 (1988): 182–201.

Definitional Issues

Perry and Rainey discuss many continuing issues in this research, such as the definition of *public* and *private*.[6] Most researchers have either left the definition implicit, with public management generally involving some muddle of governmental, nonprofit, and quasi-public domains, or have equated public management with governmental ownership. These are reasonable responses to a very complex problem. A variety of potential approaches to definition actually conflict with one another. Benn and Gaus point out that one can distinguish the two domains on the basis of public or private access, whether public or private interests are affected, and whether or not persons or organizations act as agents for the public.[7] These approaches conflict with one another in various ways, and definitions on the basis of access and interest do not work very well. Some of the most significant governmental activities deny public access, and concepts of the public interest have proven notoriously hard to specify. Most researchers employ a variant of an agency approach by referring to governmental auspices or ownership, which indicates formal responsibility to act as agent of the public.

This use of simple public versus private dichotomies, based on governmental versus private ownership, has provided a convenient alternative for researchers. Such comparisons have kept this topic alive by continuing to produce empirical findings of differences, as entries on table 6.1 illustrate. Researchers have also shown increasing impatience with inadequacies of such approaches. Such dichotomizations often remain unclear or inconsistent with their use in other studies. For example, some researchers include government-owned enterprises in the public category, some do not. This impedes cumulation of the research. In addition, many of the studies announce exploratory intent, that is, they look at whether public versus private ownership makes a difference for some dependent variables, with no particular attention to theoretical rationales for the comparisons. This impedes theory development and analysis of how and why public auspices make a difference.

Simple dichotomies also overlook a fairly long-standing recognition, in political science and public administration, of the complex interstices between the two categories. Years ago, Dahl and Lindblom noted the hybrid forms of organization, but argued that one could still distinguish governmental agencies from enterprises that are privately owned and purportedly controlled by economic markets.[8] Later, Wamsley and Zald further developed this distinction by differentiating two major dimensions related to governmental control: ownership and funding.[9] They designated a core category of public organizations that are owned and funded by government. Private organizations are owned by nongovernmental individuals or groups and are funded mainly through market exchanges or other private means. Of course, this leaves aside the hybrid categories of government organizations funded through user charges and private organizations that get most or all of their funding from government. These approaches specify that, in defining a set of public and private organizations for comparative research, one must take care to attend to both ownership and funding.

In more recent developments, researchers focus on how we can introduce the complexities of the public-private continuum into research designs and better analyze how they influence organization and management. For example, Bozeman conceives the public-private distinction as a complex, multidimensional continuum, along which organizations can be arrayed according to their level of "publicness."[10] Publicness depends on the mixture of *political authority* and *economic authority* by which the organization is externally constrained and with which it is endowed. Less public organizations face greater constraints of economic authority and less of political authority, and more public organizations lie toward the other end of the continuum. Bozeman argues that one can locate organizations along such a continuum and relate the degree of publicness to organizational characteristics.

Perry and Rainey also call for more attention to the complexities of the public-private continuum, and suggest the following emphases for future research:[11] (1) elaborate the public-private dimension by employing more of the intermediate or hybrid categories in comparative research, using a typology proposed in Perry and Rainey;[12] (2) employ other independent and control variables such as size, function, and technology in the design of comparative research; (3) further elaborate and analyze the processes of governmental, political, and market influences on organizations.

Perry and Rainey[13] discuss additional useful developments including work on the ways governments can exert influence,[14] and on the choice between markets and governmental action.[15]

Research Design Issues

This topic also raises challenges in research design, such as controlling for numerous rival explanatory variables, including organizational size, life cycle, and task or function.[16] The research approaches illustrated in table 6.1 confront these challenges in different ways. Organizational task or function obviously makes a big difference, since clearly a public hospital, university, or utility more closely resembles its functional counterparts in the other sector than the different functional types in the same sector. So, as table 6.1 shows, many researchers conduct what we call *within-function comparisons*. They compare public and private versions of the same functional type. In addition to purportedly offering some control for task or function, this approach attracts researchers analyzing the privatization of public services. Many of these studies suffer from dubious handling of the public-private distinction, however. Some compare government-contracted services, as the private category, to government-provided services. Such comparisons may provide useful information, but they may confuse conclusions about public versus private auspices, since government-contracted activities represent a hybrid form of control.

Within-function comparisons, moreover, may not generalize to other functional categories, and they concentrate on the points where the two sectors most resemble each other. For these reasons, researchers also conduct what we call *across-function comparisons*. They try for large, diverse samples of organizations or managers from the two sectors. Such studies require large resources, so researchers conduct them only occasionally,[17] and sometimes only with relatively small groups of diverse organizations.[18]

Research Findings, Directions, and Observations

These challenges have not prevented a steady accumulation of theory, case observation, and structured empirical research, which shows Levine's prescience in turning attention to this topic when he did. The accumulating research has built a fairly common picture of the major distinctions between the two categories, although intense controversy surrounds certain key points, such as whether or not public agencies perform poorly in comparison to private firms. Over a decade ago, Rainey, Backoff, and Levine compiled over sixty references that in some way addressed the public-private distinction, and compiled a summary of the most common observations in that literature, similar to the summary provided by table 6.2 (*pages 126–29*).[19]

The original table drew largely on case observations, observations by experts, positive theory by economists, and a small handful of systematic empirical studies. Since then more research has accumulated, and table 6.2 updates the earlier table to reflect new findings. The table lumps together

(*Text continues on page 129.*)

TABLE 6.2

DISTINCTIVE CHARACTERISTICS OF PUBLIC MANAGEMENT
AND PUBLIC ORGANIZATIONS: A SUMMARY OF COMMON
ASSERTIONS AND RESEARCH FINDINGS

I. Environmental factors

I.1. Absence of economic markets for outputs. Reliance on governmental
      appropriations for financial resources.
      I.1.A. Less incentive to cost reduction, operating efficiency, and
              effective performance.
      I.1.B. Lower allocational efficiency (weaker reflection of consumer
              preferences, less proportioning of supply to demand).
      I.1.C. Less availability of relatively clear market indicators and infor-
              mation (prices, profits, market share) for use in managerial
              decisions.

I.2. Presence of particularly elaborate and intensive formal legal constraints,
      due to oversight by legislative branch, executive branch hierarchy and
      oversight agencies, and courts.
      I.2.A. More constraints on domains of operation and on procedures
              (less autonomy of managers in making such choices).
      I.2.B. Greater tendency to proliferation of formal administrative
              controls.
      I.2.C. Larger number of external sources of formal authority and
              influence, with greater fragmentation among them.

I.3. Presence of more intensive external political influences.
      I.3.A. Greater diversity and intensity of external informal, political
              influences on decisions (political bargaining and lobbying, pub-
              lic opinion, interest group and client and constituent
              pressures).
      I.3.B. Greater need for political support from client groups, constitu-
              encies, formal authorities, in order to attain appropriations and
              authorization for actions.

II. Organization-environment transactions

II.1. Public organizations and managers are often involved in production of
       public goods or handling of significant externalities. Outputs are not
       readily transferable on economic markets at a market price.

II.2. Government activities are often coercive, monopolistic, or unavoidable.
       Government has unique sanctions and coercive powers and is often

Continued . . .

sole provider. Participation in consumption and financing of activities is often mandatory.

II.3. Government activities often have broader impact and greater symbolic significance. There is a broader scope of concern, such as for general public interest criteria.

II.4. There is greater public scrutiny of public managers.

II.5. There are unique public expectations for fairness, responsiveness, honesty, openness, and accountability.

III. Organizational roles, structures, and processes

(The following distinctive characteristics of organizational roles, structures, and processes have been frequently asserted to result from the distinctions cited in I and II above. More recently, distinctions of this nature have been analyzed in research with varying results. . . .)

III.1. Greater goal ambiguity, multiplicity, and conflict.

 III.1.A. Greater vagueness, intangibility, or difficulty in measuring goals and performance criteria: the goals are more debatable and value-laden (e.g., defense readiness, public safety, a clean environment, better living standards for the poor and unemployed).

 III.1.B. Greater multiplicity of the goals and criteria (efficiency, public accountability and openness, political responsiveness, fairness and due process, social equity and distributional criteria, moral correctness of behavior).

 III.1.C. Greater tendency of the goals to be conflicting, to involve more "trade-offs" (efficiency vs. openness to public scrutiny, efficiency vs. due process and social equity, conflicting demands of diverse constituencies and political authorities).

III.2. Distinctive features of general managerial roles.

 III.2.A. Recent studies have been finding that public managers' general roles involve many of the same functions and role categories as managers in other settings, but with some distinctive features: a more political, expository role involving more meetings with, and interventions by, external interest groups and political authorities, more crisis management and "fire drills," more of a challenge to balance external political relations with internal management functions.

III.3. Administrative authority and leadership practices.

 III.3.A. Public managers have less decision-making autonomy and

Continued . . .

flexibility due to elaborate institutional constraints and external political influences. More external interventions, interruptions, constraints.

III.3.B. Public managers have weaker authority over subordinates and
lower levels, due to institutional constraints (e.g., civil service
personnel systems, purchasing and procurement systems) and
external political alliances of subunits and subordinates (with
interest groups, legislators).

III.3.C. Higher-level public managers show greater reluctance to
delegate authority, a tendency to establish more levels of review and approval and make greater use of formal regulations
to control lower levels.

III.3.D. More frequent turnover of top leaders due to elections and
political appointments causes more difficulty in implementing
plans and innovations.

III.3.E. Recent counterpoint studies describe entrepreneurial behaviors
and managerial excellence by public managers.

III.4.   Organizational structure.

III.4.A. Numerous assertions that public organizations are subject to
more "red tape," more elaborate bureaucratic structure.

III.4.B. Empirical studies report mixed results, some supporting the assertions about red tape, some not supporting them. Numerous
studies find some structural distinctions for public forms of
organizations, although not necessarily more bureaucratic
structuring.

III.5.   Strategic decision processes.

III.5.A. Recent studies show that strategic decision processes in public
organizations can be generally similar to those in other settings
but are more likely to be subject to interventions, interruptions,
and greater involvement of external authorities and interest
groups.

III.6.   Incentives and incentive structures.

III.6.A. Numerous studies show that public managers and employees,
as compared to counterparts in private organizations, perceive
greater administrative constraints on administration of extrinsic incentives such as pay, promotion, and disciplinary action.

III.6.B. Recent studies indicate that public managers and employees
perceive weaker relations between performance and extrinsic
rewards such as pay, promotion, and job security. The studies
indicate that there may be some compensating effect of service
and other intrinsic incentives for public employees, and show

Continued ...

no clear relation between performance and the differences in perceived reward-performance relations.

III.7. Individual characteristics, work-related attitudes and behaviors.

    III.7.A. A number of studies have found different work-related values on the part of public managers and employees, such as lower valuation of monetary incentives and higher levels of public service motivation.

    III.7.B. Numerous highly diverse studies have found lower levels of work satisfaction and organizational commitment among public, as compared to private, managers and employees. The level of satisfaction among public sector samples is generally high, but tends consistently to be somewhat lower than private comparison groups.

III.8. Organizational and individual performance.

    III.8.A. There are numerous assertions that public organizations and employees are cautious and noninnovative. The evidence for this is mixed.

    III.8.B. Numerous studies indicate that public forms of various types of organizations tend to be less efficient in providing services than private counterparts, although results tend to be mixed for hospitals and utilities. (Public utilities have somewhat more often been found to be more efficient). Yet other authors strongly defend the efficiency and general performance of public organizations, citing various forms of evidence.

SOURCE: Hal G. Rainey, "Public Management: Recent Research on the Political Context and Managerial Roles, Structures, and Behaviors," *Journal of Management* 15 (1989):229–50. Copyright 1990 by the Southern Management Association. (Adapted and revised for that work from Rainey, Backoff, and Levine [1976]).

theoretical postulates, expert justify observations, and findings from empirical research, and thus covers diverse territory. The statement of an observation on the table therefore does not imply that it has received empirical substantiation. The table indicates those entries based largely on empirical research.

The table employs a framework developed for the earlier article, which has held up fairly well, in that the important research issues have fallen into the same categories. The general consensus about public organizations and managers remains roughly intact, that is, that the absence of economic markets, the consequent importance of political oversight, the attendant vagueness and multiplicity of goals, and related influences create unique features. These include particularly complex organizational structures and constraints on managers, and related effects on attitudes, behaviors, and performance at the organizational and individual level indicated on the table. This broad picture represents only very general consensus, however. Actually, sharp disagreements play out in this literature in various ways, over such issues as these: whether public managers enjoy much autonomy or struggle with entwining red tape and the badgering of political officials; whether the circumstances described above make public management inherently inferior to private forms; whether public employees enjoy privileged compensation or suffer a disadvantage in comparison to private employees. The table reflects some of these disputes, but cannot capture them all.

Environmental Factors

The analysis of public management virtually always begins with references to the environment in which it plays out. In spite of the long-standing recognition that the public-private distinction represents not a dichotomy but a complex continuum, controversy over whether the distinction has any importance has led many researchers to conduct simple comparisons of organizations or managers under public and private ownership. These comparisons have accumulated over the past decade, quite frequently finding differences between the two categories, although in relation to diverse variables and with diverse designs. This has kept the topic alive by building the body of research on issues discussed below and in table 6.1. As described above, however, some of the important directions move beyond the simple dichotomies.

For example, Bozeman and colleagues test the dimensional approach described earlier, in analyses of a large national sample of research and development laboratories, and find that the dimensions of publicness relate fairly systematically to dimensions of the labs' structure, organization and planning, and products and outputs.[20] Bozeman and Bretschneider find that governmental funding relates to certain structural aspects of the lab, while governmental auspices relates to other structural dimensions, such as personnel procedures.[21] Evidence of such separate effects of public auspices and funding has been implicitly turning up in the literature in various ways for some time, as indicated in research about organizational structure described below.[22] Bozeman and Bretschneider nail down the hypothesis more explicitly and substantively than research heretofore reported.

Other interesting developments include recent empirical studies on how variations in the political environment relate to variations in public agencies.[23] They report national surveys of state and local agency managers, which show variations in their perceptions of the influence on their agencies of external political actors such as those listed above. They also provide evidence of the role of such variations as level of government, institutional characteristics of the jurisdiction, and type of agency. This set of studies helps clarify the relations between public managers and other political entities (e.g., the state agency managers rate the legislature as most influential, while local managers see the mayor as such, both groups rate interest groups as much less influential but often valuable as contributors to decision making).

Other researchers have used archival data to develop measures of political environments of public agencies. Hood and Dunsire developed indicators of numerous external dimensions of agencies, such as budgetary success as reflected in budget documents and political salience as indicated in newspaper coverage.[24] Ripley and Franklin had earlier conducted a similar study.[25]

Occasionally management researchers study public managers in ways that reflect on the nexus between politics and management.[26] Kotter and Lawrence, for example, use an elaborate conception of mayors' political networks to analyze how mayors coalign this network, their own characteristics, city characteristics, and their policy agendas.[27]

Just as difficult to summarize briefly is a great deal of work by organizational sociologists who have studied external controls on organizations, organizational ecologies, and external institutionalization processes. Some of these researchers typically treat a public-private distinction as minor or irrelevant. Those interested in institutional effects, however, have reported evidence of the way government plays a role in institutionalization of organizational values and structures, and often find a form of public-private comparison useful in this process.[28]

Organization-Environment Transactions

This category includes widely repeated observations about the basic nature of public organizations. Actually, people often advance them as antecedent to the environmental factors (section 1), citing them, for example, as reasons why governmental control often replaces market controls. Surprisingly little research directly addresses them, although a good bit of relevant evidence exists. For example, numerous comparisons of services provided by public and private entities, described later, tend to find public providers less efficient. Critics of government sometimes attribute this to monopolistic practices by government.[29] Yet proponents of privatization of public services also argue that government provides many services which the private sector can provide, thereby suggesting that government may behave monopolistically, but that many government activities are not inherently monopolistic.

As for public scrutiny and expectations, executives with government and business experience testify that press relations figure more significantly in public management.[30] Public opinion surveys fairly regularly find that citizens have different expectations and evaluations of public and business administrators.[31] These usually involve unfavorable attitudes toward government and public employees, and increasing intensity of these unfavorable views helped to fuel tax revolts, government cutbacks and reforms, and attacks by politicians, ultimately damaging morale in the public service.[32] Much of the research mentioned in sections below also bears on the observations in this section.

Organizational Roles, Structures, and Processes

Do the differences in context produce differences in managerial roles and organizational characteristics (see sec. 3 of table 6.1)? Over the last decade, the body of evidence has expanded a great deal, but in diverse forms and places.

Goal Ambiguity, Multiplicity, and Conflict

By far the most frequent observation in all the relevant literature emphasizes the greater multiplicity, vagueness, and conflict of goals and performance criteria in the public sector. Little comparative research directly addresses this question. Rainey and Baldwin asked managers in government and business organizations to rate the clarity of the goals of their organizations and found little difference between the two groups.[33] This makes for promising opportunities for comparative research on how managers in public, private, and hybrid organizations perceive objectives and performance criteria, and whether these do in fact coincide with the sorts of distinctions assumed to exist in our political economy.

General Managerial Role Characteristics

In the past decade, numerous relevant studies of managerial roles have appeared. In his frequently replicated study of managerial roles, Mintzberg found that the work of all the managers fell into his now well known role categories.[34] The public manager in the sample (a school administrator) and the quasi-public manager (a hospital administrator) spent more time in contacts and formal meetings with external interest groups and governing boards and received more external status requests than did the managers from private organizations. Recently, Kurke and Aldrich replicated the study, including the findings about public management.[35] Lau, Pavett, and Newman, also using a technique based on Mintzberg, find the roles of civilian managers in the Navy Department comparable to those of private manufacturing and service firm managers.[36] They add, however, a role of "technical expert" to the role categories for the navy managers, and note that they spend more time in crisis management and "fire drills" than the private managers. Other recent studies of managerial roles also show that public managers' work shares many commonalities with that of private managers, but find significant effects of the political and governmental contexts.[37] A number of testimonials from executives who have served in public and private settings, and other expert observers, echo results of these studies.[38]

Administrative Authority and Leadership Practices

More studies have appeared on the related topic of how public managers compare to private managers in the way they lead and manage their organizations. Various studies, including many described in other sections, show more constraints, interruptions, interventions, and external contacts in the public sector. Porter and Von Maanen compare city government administrators to industrial managers and find that the city administrators feel less control over how they allocate their own time, feel more pressed for time, and regard demands from persons outside the organization as a much stronger influence on how they manage their time.[39] Experienced executives and observers stress a similar picture of public management, due to various political and administrative constraints and controls.[40] Academic research and theory on strategy, structure and other dimensions, cited in following sections, emphasizes a similar picture.

In a similar vein, the National Academy of Public Administration[41] lamented the complex web of controls and rules over managerial decisions in federal agencies, and their adverse effects on federal managers' capacity and motivation to manage their units. Other observers also worry that the constraints and political processes lead to bad consequences. High-level political appointees, they say, play politics or preoccupy themselves with public policy issues; when they do undertake to manage their organizations, they issue excessive rules and clearance requirements, and avoid delegating authority. Middle managers are so constrained, yet also so protected by career service strictures, external political alliances, and the short tenure of political superiors, that they manage poorly.

Controversies over the accuracy of this view have heated up over the past decade. A growing literature, mostly case descriptive and therefore hard to summarize briefly, on *entrepreneurial* behavior by public managers emphasizes active, effective public management, and spurns the overgeneralizations about abdication of management in the public sector.[42] Similarly, a growing list of authors, citing empirical evidence, aggressively argue that public managers and organizations do better than critics realize.[43]

The debates suggest research questions. Do external pressures by legislators and others invoke such responses? Do public managers rely more on rules and directives than private managers? Too few studies have analyzed the ways in which public managers balance attention to politics, policy, and managing their units, even though the issue is crucial to the conception of effective public management. Some recent studies do look explicitly at how public managers allocate time and attention among these obligations.[44]

Organizational Structure

Time-honored observations about excessive red tape, bureaucratic structure, and overstaffing in public bureaucracies have been sanctified as social theory by various economists and political scientists.[45] Yet organization theorists from the fields of sociology and business administration have shown both more skepticism and more ambivalence about these propositions. Some early taxonomic efforts found no particular structural differences between public and private forms, and the rejection of simple public-private distinctions as crude stereotypes became a standard introduction to organizational typology.[46] Various studies and theories over the years have concluded that public and private organizations differ little on major dimensions of organizational structure.[47] Yet others find that public organizations tend toward some of the distinctive structural characteristics one would predict from the classic depiction of the public bureaucracy—more elaborate hierarchies and rule structures, for example (see many references in table 6.2).[48]

A close look at these studies shows that research results depend on the dimension of structure measured, whether it is measured with a subjective/perceptual procedure or an objective measure, and, again, on design issues such as the location of the organization on the public-private continuum, level of government, relation to central government institutions, and controls for task and other important variables. The provocative evidence suggests the value of further studies sorting out these issues with more careful designs and larger samples.

Strategic Decision Processes

Recent attention to strategic decision making in government shows that while some of the issues and variations among agencies might have uniquely governmental characteristics,[49] general frameworks for strategic decision making certainly apply.[50] A study of strategic decisions in British organizations suggests some of the distinctive ways in which the public-sector environment may influence such processes. Hickson et al. analyze strategic decision processes in thirty public and private manufacturing and service organizations.[51] In both the service and manufacturing categories, the public organizations follow a "vortex sporadic" mode of decision making, involving more turbulence, shifting participation, delays, interruptions, and more formal and informal interaction among participants. The finding conforms with other observations concerning the effects of public auspices.[52]

Incentives and Incentive Structures

One of the most consistent empirical findings about public organizations is that organizations more fully under public auspices consistently show more highly structured, externally imposed personnel procedures,[53] not just in central government agencies but also in schools, universities, and various other forms within the public category.

Public employees and managers also report greater structural constraints on administration of extrinsic rewards such as pay, promotion, and disciplinary actions, and weaker relations between performance and extrinsic rewards than do private-sector counterparts.[54]

Interesting questions remain about how such impressions form and how they influence behavior and performance. It also remains to be conclusively established as to whether circumstances really differ so markedly in public and private organizations. Even in advance of resolving these questions, however, concerns about these conditions in the public bureaucracy contributed to civil service reforms at federal and other levels. These reforms often focus in substantial part on improving motivation and performance through merit pay or bonus systems. Yet the pay reforms have foundered and debate continues on whether prospects can be improved or pay constraints are an inherent feature of government.[55]

Individual Characteristics, Work-Related Attitudes, and Behaviors

Do such differences in incentive systems result in different attitudes and behaviors? Over the years, a number of studies have found that public employees tend to have different values, often placing a lower value on financial rewards as an ultimate end of work, and a higher value on altruistic and service-oriented outcomes.[56] Such responses vary widely in the highly diverse public sector, overlapping with areas of the nongovernmental sector. Obviously, extrinsic incentives never lose significance to organizational employees, but if such distinctions hold, pay constraints of the sort mentioned above may not affect public employee motivation and performance.[57] Some of the available studies report no differences between public and private samples on availability of intrinsic rewards,[58] but little research addresses this question. More work on service-oriented motives in organizations would benefit the management literature in general.[59]

The significance of the public-private continuum for employee motivational variables remains unresolved, in spite of stereotypes about the differences. Rainey finds no differences between middle managers in public and private organizations on self-reported motivation and interest in innovation.[60] Baldwin also finds none.[61] Very large samples of public employees and managers report high levels of work effort and involvement, of perceived importance of their organizations, and of general work satisfaction; they show roughly comparable levels on such responses to private-sector samples, based on comparisons to large-scale surveys of private respondents.[62] In occasional studies, public-sector samples show higher need for achievement, flexibility, dominance and other apparently positive traits.[63]

Yet numerous comparisons of work satisfaction of public and private respondents, especially at managerial levels, report somewhat lower satisfaction for the public-sector respondents.[64] Buchanan finds lower organizational commitment and job involvement among federal managers, as compared to managers in private firms.[65] Smith and Nock, analyzing results of a large social survey, find that as compared to private-sector counterparts, public-sector blue-collar workers show more satisfaction with most aspects of work, but public-sector white-collar workers show less satisfaction with co-workers, supervision, and intrinsic aspects of work.[66] Chubb and Moe find generally lower sense of control and commitment among members of public schools as compared to private-school respondents.[67]

The different studies use widely varying samples and varied measures of satisfaction and other attitudes, making it hard to assess them precisely. Of course, some of the findings may be spurious due to sample characteristics or design weaknesses. Yet the accumulation of numerous findings, with better and better designs as time goes on, showing more unfavorable attitudes within public-sector organizations justifies further inquiry. The pattern may not indicate lower performance or quality of life in public organizations—the evidence, in fact, is that, if anything, they are marginally lower and not abysmally so. Rather, the findings may result from particular kinds of constraints and frustrations of the sort already indicated, and related differences in the climate or cultures of the organizations. The problems may be no worse than in private or hybrid forms of organizations, they may simply be different.

Organizational Performance

Whether public organizations perform as well as private organizations has been a fundamental issue in the relevant literature for at least a century. Interest has increased recently, with more attention to the pros and cons of privatizing government activities in many countries of the world, and ideologues voicing foregone conclusions about the inferiority of governmental organizations.

As noted earlier, one time-honored assertion, advanced repeatedly by prominent authors, characterizes public bureaucracies as more rigid and change resistant than private firms.[68] Some case analyses of public organizations support such assertions.[69] Golembiewski describes a "Dr. No" syndrome he has frequently encountered in public agencies, in response to proposals for doing things in new and different ways.[70]

Yet in attitude surveys, public employees and managers report an interest in change and an openness to it.[71] Golembiewski reviews 270 organizational development efforts in public organizations and concludes that over 80 percent of them were apparently successful.[72] Roessner notes scant evidence on the relative innovativeness of public and private organizations, but finds that available evidence (e.g., technological diffusion rates among public and private sectors) indicates no particular superiority on the part of the private sector.[73] Evidence reviewed in earlier sections suggests that governmental, nonmarket organizations have a *tendency* (i.e., not an absolute imperative) toward elaborate constraints. Yet examples of successful innovation or change in public organizations[74] and of innovative behaviors on the part of governmental executives[75] show that many assertions about rigidity in the public sector overgeneralize harmfully.

The relative efficiency of public and private organizations attracts even more attention. Researchers have conducted numerous comparisons of public versus private provision of services, including studies of solid-waste collection, fire protection, transportation, health care, custodial services, landscaping, data processing, legal aid, and others.[76] Most find the private form of provision more efficient. Some studies, however, particularly of hospitals and utilities, show no difference. Studies of utilities more often find public utilities more efficient.[77] Methodological problems with some of the studies make it appear that occasional researchers, usually economists, seem virtually determined to find governmental activities inferior to market-based activities. Some researchers do report more comprehensive comparative studies related to performance. Chubb and Moe report evidence that public-school members, compared to private-school counterparts, perceive weaker parental involvement, less emphasis on academic excellence, less clarity of goals and disciplinary policy, and weaker faculty influence on the curriculum.[78]

On the other hand, a number of authors mount strong defenses of government organizations. They point to various kinds of evidence that government agencies often perform quite well and at least as well as private firms, and stress the different kinds of performance expectations imposed on government organizations.[79]

Developments in the Conception and Practice of Public Management

This research accumulated during a period of rapid developments in academic disciplines related to public management, and in the practice of it. The very term "public management" came more frequently into use, by people citing deficiencies in public-sector administrative education and practice, who called for more emphasis on management as a remedy. The prescriptions involve some subtle distinctions. Very effective managerial activities abound in all levels of government in the United States. The term itself and the attendant issues have a long history in the field of public administration.

Still, during the 1970s and into the 1980s, numerous books and articles began emphasizing this theme. Typically, they stated or implied a sharp critique of the literature in public administration and public policy. They characterized the public administration literature as information rich but skill poor, and too broadly discursive and philosophical to guide public managers. The public policy literature concentrates on policy formulation and implementation, with a deemphasis on the managerial practices within those processes. They also argued that the general management literature, for its part, concentrated on business management and treated public management as indistinct from it. Consequently, they said, a scarcity of public-sector managerial research findings and training cases impeded education for the role.[80]

A sampling of many related activities echoes a similar theme. The director of the U.S. Office of Personnel Management organized a prominent conference on public management research at the Brookings Institution in 1979. The introductory statement in the conference proceedings cited the widespread concern among practitioners and researchers over "the lack of depth of knowledge in this field."[81]

Under the auspices of the National Association of Schools of Public Administration and Affairs (NASPAA), Garson and Overman conducted an extensive survey of public management research projects.[82] They found very little funded research on general issues that might broadly apply across public management contexts and described the projects as highly disparate. They called for a national effort to promote more coherent research.

NASPAA also initiated a peer-review process for NASPAA schools, which later became an accreditation program. The accreditation program aimed in part to introduce more skill-oriented and management-oriented courses into public administration curricula, and to limit the dominance in some curricula of typical political science courses, to make the M.P.A. degree more recognizable as a meaningful distinction.

Having taken a position with the Congressional Research Service, Charles Levine became increasingly concerned with the closely related theme of how management is conceived and practiced in the federal government. He mentioned to colleagues his concern over the incoherence of federal policies on organizational and managerial issues such as structural reform, executive and other human-resource development activities, and managerial support technologies and resources. He began to produce insightful papers on federal management. With Peter Benda, he traced the wayward history of management activities and policies, as weakly institutionalized in the Office of Management and Budget.[83] They reviewed the fitful attention to management issues, reinventions of the wheel by presidential administrations, and prospects, however unlikely, for a separate office of management. They pointed out, as have others, that the political and institutional context of federal management raises obstacles to generous investments in improving management. Presidents and their high-level appointees commonly lack the tenure, prospects for tenure, personal inclinations, and political incentives to invest heavily in the long-term development of managers and managerial systems. So, too, with many congressmen and senators. When elected officials and their appointees sporadically turn their attention to management, they typically emphasize top-down control and accountability, which ironically penalizes proactive and creative managers at lower levels. Levine lamented the irony that federal managerial initiatives pressed this conception of management even as the literature on business management more and more depicted successful business corporations as practitioners of decentralization and participation.[84]

Levine's concern over how public management could prosper heightened as the federal government and those who staff it became targets of political brickbats in the late 1970s and during the Reagan administration. Increasingly, Presidents Carter and Reagan, and other political actors, attacked the federal government as bloated and overbearing, with employees to match. Levine followed the progress of the historically significant civil service reforms in the later years of the Carter administration, expressing concern that positive features such as the creation of the Senior Executive Service suffered under faulty implementation and damaged morale in the federal career service.

President Reagan took aim even more aggressively at the federal government, and "bureaucrat bashing" entered the lexicon of public administration to describe the widespread political exercise of fulminating against federal bureaucrats as lethargic, bumbling, and subject to a long list of additional shortcomings. Levine joined an intense discussion of the apparent effects of the Reagan administration's forceful efforts to control the federal bureaucracy and diminish the authority of career executives, in part by increasing the numbers of loyal political appointees in the upper levels of the agencies.[85]

Benda and Levine examined the administrative legacy of the Reagan years.[86] They concluded that a strong top-down control orientation in the early years of the administration, emphasizing efficiency and cost control, may leave a valuable legacy of improved managerial systems which reduce administrative overhead. On balance, however, they felt that this management orientation only aggravates the long-standing problems of elaborate, inflexible, negative controls that impede enlightened management develop-ment. Later, having established considerable control, the administration shifted to an opposite course of devolvement and deregulation of federal management, especially through privatization or private-sector involvement in public services and policy making. This strategy played a part in what Levine and Benda see as the most significant administrative legacy of the Reagan years, the reshaping of the dialogue about the proper role and scope of the public, private, and nonprofit sectors. Yet it also seriously complicated lines of accountability and further undercut the authority and responsibility of the career service.

The harshly threatening and demeaning climate for many federal man-agers created intense concern among many public administration special-ists, including present and former officials in the legislative and executive branches. Newspaper articles, surveys of the managers themselves, and knowledgeable experts all reported evidence of serious disenchantment among federal executives and increasing departures from the service or plans to depart. The Volcker Commission formed, bringing together a dis-tinguished panel of public servants to work toward revitalization of the public service. Levine, as staff director, poured his immense energies into the work of the commission. In that work his life ended, flaming out in his driving determination to write and act in defense of the ideals of public service that his life so richly illustrated.

Notes

1. Barry Bozeman, *All Organizations Are Public* (San Francisco: Jossey-Bass, 1987); and Robert T. Golembiewski, *Humanizing Public Organizations* (Mt. Airy, Md.: Lomond, 1985).

2. Anthony Downs, *Inside Bureaucracy* (Boston: Little, Brown, 1967); and William A. Niskanen, *Bureaucracy and Representative Government* (Chicago: Aldine, 1971).

3. Francis E. Rourke, *Bureaucracy, Politics, and Public Policy* (Boston: Little, Brown, 1984); Harold Seidman and Robert Gilmour, *Politics, Position, and Power*, 4th ed. (New York: Oxford University Press, 1986); Kenneth J. Meier, *Politics and the Bureaucracy* (Monterey, Calif.: Brooks/Cole, 1987); and Graham T. Allison, "Public and Private Management: Are They Fundamentally Alike in All Unimportant Respects?" in *Public Management*, ed. J.L. Perry and K.L. Kraemer (Palo Alto, Calif.: Mayfield, 1983).

4. Donald P. Warwick, *A Theory of Public Bureaucracy* (Cambridge: Har-vard University Press, 1975); and Marshall W. Meyer, *Change in Public Bu-reaucracies* (London: Cambridge University Press, 1979).

5. Hal G. Rainey, Robert W. Backoff, and Charles L. Levine, "Comparing

Public and Private Organizations," *Public Administration Review* 36 (1976): 233-46.

6. James L. Perry and Hal G. Rainey, "The Public-Private Distinction in Organization Theory: A Critique and Research Strategy," *Academy of Management Review* 13 (1988): 182-201.

7. S.I. Benn and G.F. Gaus, *Public and Private in Social Life* (New York: St. Martin's Press, 1983).

8. Robert A. Dahl and Charles E. Lindblom, *Politics, Economics and Welfare* (New York: Harper & Brothers, 1953).

9. Gary L. Wamsley and Mayer N. Zald, *The Political Economy of Public Organizations* (Lexington, Mass.: Lexington Books, 1973).

10. Bozeman, *All Organizations Are Public.*

11. Perry and Rainey, "Public-Private Distinction."

12. Ibid.

13. Ibid.

14. Christopher Hood, *The Tools of Government* (London: Macmillan, 1983); and Eugene B. McGregor, "Administration's Many Instruments: Mining, Refining, and Applying Charles Lindblom's *Politics and Markets*," *Administration and Society* 13 (1981): 347-75.

15. Charles E. Lindblom, *Politics and Markets* (New York: Basic Books, 1977); and Charles Wolf, *Markets or Governments: Choosing between Imperfect Alternatives* (Cambridge: MIT Press, 1988).

16. Perry and Rainey, "Public-Private Distinction."

17. David J. Hickson, Richard J. Butler, David Cray, Geoffrey R. Mallory, and David C. Wilson, *Top Decisions: Strategic Decision-Making in Organizations* (San Francisco: Jossey-Bass, 1986).

18. Hal G. Rainey, "Public Agencies and Private Firms: Incentive Structures, Goals, and Individual Roles," *Administration and Society* 15 (1983): 207-42; and Richard E. Boyatzis, *The Competent Manager* (New York: Wiley, 1982).

19. Rainey, Backoff, and Levine, "Comparing Public and Private Organizations."

20. See references in Hal G. Rainey, "Public Management: Recent Developments and Current Prospects." In *Public Administration: The State of the Discipline,* ed. Naomi Lynn and Aaron Wildavsky (Chatham, N.J.: Chatham House, 1990).

21. Barry Bozeman and Stuart Bretschneider, "The 'Publicness Puzzle' in Organization Theory: A Test of Alternative Explanations of Differences between Public and Private Organizations," *TIPP Working Paper,* Maxwell School, Syracuse University, 1989.

22. David S. Pugh et al., "An Empirical Taxonomy of Work Organizations," *Administrative Science Quarterly* 14 (1969): 115-26; and E. Solomon, "Private and Public Sector Managers: An Empirical Investigation of Job Characteristics and Organizational Climate," *Journal of Applied Psychology* 71 (1986): 247-59.

23. Glenn Abney and Thomas Lauth, *The Politics of State and City Ad-*

ministration (Albany: State University of New York Press, 1986); Jeffrey L. Brudney and F. Ted Hebert, "State Agencies and Their Environments: Examining the Influence of Important External Actors," *Journal of Politics* 49 (1987): 186–206; and Richard C. Elling, "The Relationships among Bureau Chiefs, Legislative Committees, and Interest Groups: A Multi-State Study," paper presented at the annual meeting of the American Political Science Association, Washington, D.C., 1983.

24. Christopher Hood and Andrew Dunsire, *Bureaumetrics: The Quantitative Comparison of British Central Government Agencies* (University, Ala.: University of Alabama Press, 1981).

25. Randall B. Ripley and Grace A. Franklin, *Policy-Making in the Federal Executive Branch* (New York: Macmillan, 1975).

26. David N. Ammons and Charldean Newell, *City Executives: Leadership Roles, Work Characteristics, and Time Management* (Albany: State University of New York Press, 1989); and Lyman W. Porter and John Von Maanen "Task Accomplishment and the Management of Time," in *Public Management,* ed. Perry and Kraemer.

27. John P. Kotter and Paul R. Lawrence, *Mayors in Action* (New York: Wiley-Interscience, 1974).

28. Frank R. Dobbin et al., "The Expansion of Due Process in Organizations," in *Institutional Patterns and Organizations,* ed. Lynne Zucker (Cambridge, Mass.: Ballinger, 1988); Paula S. Tolbert and Lynne G. Zucker, "Institutional Sources of Change in the Formal Structure of Organizations: The Diffusion of Civil Service Reform, 1880–1935," *Administrative Science Quarterly* 28 (1983): 22–39.

29. E.S. Savas, *Privatization: The Key to Better Government* (Chatham, N.J.: Chatham House, 1987).

30. Allison, "Public and Private Management."

31. Seymour M. Lipset and William Schneider, *The Confidence Gap: Business, Labor, and Government in the Public Mind* (Baltimore: Johns Hopkins University Press, 1987).

32. National Commission on the Public Service, *Leadership for America: Rebuilding the Public Service* (Washington, D.C.: National Commission on the Public Service, 1989).

33. Rainey, "Public Agencies"; and J. Norman Baldwin, "Public versus Private: Not That Different, Not That Consequential," *Public Personnel Management* 16 (1987): 181–93.

34. Henry Mintzberg, *The Nature of Managerial Work* (New York: Harper & Row, 1972).

35. Lance B. Kurke and Howard E. Aldrich, "Mintzberg Was Right: A Replication and Extension of the Nature of Managerial Work," *Management Science* 29 (1983): 975–84.

36. Alan W. Lau, Cynthia M. Pavett, and Allen Newman, "The Nature of Managerial Work: A Comparison of Public and Private Sector Jobs," *Academy of Management Proceedings,* 1980, 339–43.

37. Herbert Kaufman, *The Administrative Behavior of Federal Bureau*

Chiefs (Washington, D.C.: Brookings Institution, 1981); and Boyatzis, *Competent Manager.*

38. Perry and Kraemer, eds., *Public Management.*

39. Porter and Von Maanen, "Task Accomplishment."

40. Allison, "Public and Private Management"; and Perry and Kraemer, eds., *Public Management.*

41. National Academy of Public Administration, *Revitalizing Federal Management* (Washington, D.C.: National Academy of Public Administration, 1986).

42. Eugene B. Lewis, *Public Entrepreneurship* (Bloomington: Indiana University Press, 1980); and Jameson W. Doig and Erwin C. Hargrove, *Leadership and Innovation* (Baltimore: Johns Hopkins University Press, 1987).

43. Golembiewski, *Humanizing Public Organizations;* and Charles T. Goodsell, *The Case for Bureaucracy* (Chatham, N.J.: Chatham House, 1983).

44. Ammons and Newell, *City Executives.*

45. Dahl and Lindblom, *Politics, Economics and Welfare;* and Niskanen, *Bureaucracy.*

46. J. Eugene Haas, Richard H. Hall, and Norman J. Johnson, "Toward an Empirically Derived Taxonomy of Organizations," in *Studies of Behavior in Organizations,* ed. Robert V. Bowers (Athens: University of Georgia Press, 1966).

47. Pugh, "Work Organizations"; and Bruce Buchanan, "Red Tape and the Service Ethic: Some Unexpected Differences between Public and Private Managers," *Administration and Society* 6 (1975): 423–38.

48. Rainey, "Public Management."

49. Peter S. Ring and James L. Perry, "Strategic Management in Public and Private Organizations: Implications of Distinctive Contexts and Constraints," *Academy of Management Review* 10 (1985): 276–86; Barton Wechsler and Robert W. Backoff, "Policy Making and Administration in State Agencies: Strategic Management Approaches," *Public Administration Review* 46 (1986): 321–27.

50. John M. Bryson, *Strategic Planning for Public and Nonprofit Organizations* (San Francisco: Jossey-Bass, 1988); and Paul C. Nutt and Robert W. Backoff, "A Strategic Management Process for Public and Third-Sector Organizations," *Journal of the American Planning Association* 53 (1987): 44–54.

51. Hickson et al., *Top Decisions.*

52. Porter and Von Maanen, "Task Accomplishment."

53. Pugh et al., "Work Organizations"; Edward A. Holdaway et al., "Dimensions of Organizations in Complex Societies: The Educational Sector," *Administrative Science Quarterly* 20 (1975): 37–58; Meyer, *Change;* Tolbert and Zucker, "Sources of Change"; and J.E. Chubb and Terry M. Moe, "Politics, Markets, and the Organization of Schools," *American Political Science Review* 82 (1985): 1065–88.

54. Rainey, "Public Management."

55. James L. Perry, "Merit Pay in the Public Sector: The Case for a Failure of Theory," *Review of Public Personnel Administration* 7 (Fall 1986): 57–69.

56. Hal G. Rainey, "Perceptions of Incentives in Business and Government: Implications for Civil Service Reform," *Public Administration Review* 39 (1979): 440–48.

57. Baldwin, "Public versus Private."

58. Rainey, "Incentives"; and Rainey, "Public Agencies."

59. Hal G. Rainey, "Reward Preferences among Public and Private Managers: In Search of the Service Ethic," *American Review of Public Administration* 16 (1982): 276–86; and James L. Perry and Lois R. Wise, "The Motivational Bases of Public Service," *Public Administration Review,* 50 (1990): 367–73.

60. Rainey, "Public Agencies."

61. Baldwin, "Public versus Private."

62. Nancy Hayward, *Employee Attitudes and Productivity Differences between the Public and Private Sectors* (Washington, D.C.: Productivity Information Center, National Technical Information Center, U.S. Department of Commerce, 1978); and U.S. Office of Personnel Management, *The Federal Employee Attitude Survey* (Washington, D.C.: Office of Personnel Management, 1979).

63. Boyatzis, *Competent Manager.*

64. Rainey, "Public Management."

65. Bruce Buchanan, "Government Managers, Business Executives, and Organizational Commitment," *Public Administration Review* 35 (1974): 339–47; and Buchanan, "Red Tape."

66. Michael P. Smith and Stephen L. Nock, "Social Class and the Quality of Life in Public and Private Organizations," *Journal of Social Issues* 36 (1980): 59–75.

67. Chubb and Moe, "Politics, Markets."

68. Dahl and Lindblom, *Politics, Economics and Welfare;* Downs, *Inside Bureaucracy;* and Warwick, *Public Bureaucracy.*

69. Warwick, *Public Bureaucracy.*

70. Golembiewski, *Humanizing Public Organizations.*

71. Office of Personnel Management, *Employee Attitude Survey;* Rainey, "Public Agencies."

72. Golembiewski, *Humanizing Public Organizations.*

73. J. David Roessner, "Incentives to Innovate in Public and Private Organizations," in *Public Management,* ed. Perry and Kraemer.

74. Golembiewski, *Humanizing Public Organizations.*

75. Doig and Hargrove, *Leadership.*

76. Wolf, *Markets or Governments;* and Savas, *Privatization.*

77. Scott E. Atkinson and Robert Halversen, "The Relative Efficiency of Public and Private Firms in a Regulated Environment: The Case of U.S. Electric Utilities," *Journal of Public Economics* 29 (1986): 281–94.

78. Chubb and Moe, "Politics, Markets."

79. George W. Downs and Patrick D. Larkey, *The Search for Government Efficiency: From Hubris to Helplessness* (New York: Random House, 1986); and Goodsell, *The Case for Bureaucracy.*

80. Allison, "Public and Private Management"; and Perry and Kraemer, eds., *Public Management*.

81. Office of Personnel Management, *Setting the Public Management Research Agenda: Integrating the Sponsor, Producer, and User* (Washington, D.C.: Government Printing Office, 1980).

82. G. David Garson and E. Sam Overman, *Public Management Research Directory*, vols. 1 and 2 (Washington, D.C.: National Association of Schools of Public Affairs and Administration, 1982).

83. Peter M. Benda and Charles H. Levine, "The 'M' in OMB: Issues of Structure and Strategy," presented at the annual meeting of the American Political Science Association, Washington, D.C., 1986.

84. Charles H. Levine, *The Unfinished Agenda for Civil Service Reform: Implications of the Grace Commission Report* (Washington, D.C.: Brookings Institution, 1985).

85. Patricia W. Ingraham and Carolyn R. Ban, "Models of Public Management: Are They Useful to Public Managers in the 1980s?" *Public Administration Review* 46 (1986): 152–60; and Rainey, "Public Management."

86. Peter M. Benda and Charles H. Levine, "Reagan and the Bureaucracy: The Bequest, the Promise, and the Legacy," in *The Reagan Legacy*, ed. Charles O. Jones (Chatham, N.J.: Chatham House, 1988).

7

The Dynamics of Employee Commitment

BARBARA S. ROMZEK

There has been a shift in the conventional wisdom about where work fits into the life of the typical American employee. For most of this century, the prevailing viewpoint was that of the Protestant work ethic, namely, that hard work was virtuous, built strong character, and was a valued commodity. According to this perspective, fortunate individuals found employment in organizations where they fit into the work culture, had long-term employment prospects, and developed a sense of loyalty toward their employer. This vision was captured in William F. Whyte's *The Organization Man.*[1]

This work ethic is so pervasive that even the feminist movement, which challenged some very basic notions about societal roles, accepted the premise that work (employment outside the home) was a positive experience. Proponents of women's increased participation in the workforce argued that women were being systematically excluded from the benefits of the world of work, including a sense of identity and purpose, status, and financial rewards. Recent research has confirmed that positive mental health effects accrue to women who work outside the home.[2]

Nonetheless, the American work ethic has changed in recent years, as seen in the shifting attitudes and expectations of American workers.[3] Today, employees are generally less willing to suspend or sacrifice personal needs for their employers. Now employees expect work that provides more than a regular income and job security. Now they expect a regular and *fair* income and a secure job *in a safe working environment.* Employees want the opportunity to hold jobs that allow them to fulfill their needs as human beings while they fulfill their obligations to their employers.[4] In short, they want to be able to be well-rounded human beings and good employees at the same time.

Unfortunately, at the same time that employee expectations are broadening, employer responses have become more constrained. Recent trends in revenue shortfalls, cutback management, and corporate mergers serve as stark evidence to public- and private-sector employees that their traditional expectations for income, security, and loyalty will not always be met.[5]

These broader employee expectations and constrained employer responses are linked. Employees whose work expectations are not met are not likely to develop strong ties to their employers.[6] Those who have developed strong emotional ties to their workplaces but find their employers no longer meet their expectations are at risk of feeling disillusioned. Such an experience can erode employee ties to the organization.

Employee Ties to the Organization

Employees can develop ties to the organization based on investments they have made in the workplace or on important values they share with the agency. The nature of the tie will depend on what the employee wants out of work and what the agency has to offer its employees. Feelings of *investment* in the organization result from an exchange relationship. Feelings of *commitment* result from shared values.[7]

These ties are not exclusive; investment and commitment can be complementary. An employee can develop one or both or neither of these ties to the workplace. The following discussion takes some care to clarify the distinction between these two different ties to one's work organization. There is a tendency in everyday parlance to lump the two together.

Employee Investment in the Organization[8]

Some employees take an investment approach to their workplace. Employees who feel they have invested a lot of time and energy in an agency often feel "committed" to their employer.[9] They feel tied to the organization because of their "sunk costs," not because they feel any sense of emotional attachment or loyalty. Such employees make career decisions based on whether they have more to gain by staying with the agency than by taking another job elsewhere.

Employees calculate their investments in an agency based on what they have put into the organization and what they stand to receive if they stay there. For example, an individual might hesitate to change employers because of the time and money tied up in the organization's retirement plan. Although retirement plans are the most obvious form of investment employees can develop in their employer, investment holdings are not always in monetary form. Investments also can take the form of time devoted to a particular career track or cultivating work-group and friendship networks. For example, an employee who has invested a lot of time in a particular career track in one agency, say, as a bank examiner for the Federal Deposit Insurance Corporation, may be hesitant to switch employers because of the "sunk costs" that would be wasted if he or she moved. If the individual took a job as an auditor for the Securities and Exchange Commission, the employee would have to start anew demonstrating abilities, building a work-group network, and earning the confidence of superiors.

Employees with an investment approach to their employers care what happens to the organization because they have a lot invested in the agency. The greater the investment in a particular work organization, the greater the likelihood an employee will stay with that employer.[10] Changing agencies might mean starting over on some key investments. Starting over is something that most employees with substantial investments in one work organization are hesitant to do.

Getting employees to feel they have a big investment in the organization is not very complicated. To foster these ties the organization has to offer opportunities and working conditions that are competitive with other prospective employers. Some of the more progressive corporations do this through liberal stock option and bonus plans. In the public sector, typical investment factors include promotion prospects, development of work-group networks, performance bonuses, and the accrual of vacation, sick leave, and retirement benefits.

Once employees have accrued investments in an organization, the employer need only remain competitive with alternative employers regarding the returns on investments it offers employees. But investment ties are often expensive to develop and maintain, requiring regular infusions of funds to underwrite promotions, bonuses, merit pay, and other returns on investment. Such resources are essential to avoid the development of the "what have you done for me lately?" syndrome. Equally important, programs that nurture investment ties generally require great managerial care to ensure equitable administration. If employees perceive favoritism in the allocation of such programs, morale problems are likely.

Often, employee investments are transferable within the particular level of government. For example, most federal employees can retain any accrued credits toward retirement, sick leave, and vacation time when they take a different job in another federal agency. Historically this has been known as "golden handcuffs" among federal employees because the benefits were not portable if the employee left the federal service before retirement age. Similar rules apply to state employees who work under a unified personnel system. Investments in state retirement systems are usually portable; they can be transferred when the employee moves to another state agency job. Sick leave often is transferable. Although the employee may be making a career shift, in the sense of undertaking a job that has an entirely new set of responsibilities and tasks and requires very different skills, he or she does not have to start at "zero" in the investment category.

Without a competitive stance on investment opportunities, agencies run the risk of losing investment-oriented employees who calculate they have more to gain from changing employers than by staying where they are. Investment-oriented employees can be lured away by competitors who offer a higher "rate of return," in the form of higher salaries, greater promotion opportunities, more office perks, better bonus opportunities, and the like.

Sometimes the accrual of such investments can work against the public employer in that the investments can be "cashed in" for employment opportunities in the private sector. The revolving-door problems among federal employees, especially among individuals who work in defense contracting, are a result of individuals developing extensive work-group networks with private contractors. Recent proposals to limit such individuals' nongovernmental employment options in the defense and aerospace industries has had extremely detrimental effects on retention of higher-level staff in NASA and the Defense Department.[11]

Having employees who only have an investment approach to their jobs can be a disadvantage to the employing organization. To the extent that an agency emphasizes investments as a tie for its employees, it is subject to the vagaries of the marketplace. As such, its ability to attract and retain qualified employees may be influenced by what its competitors offer employees. In essence, the agency's recruitment and retention patterns may be influenced by some circumstances that are beyond its control. Recruitment and retention problems in the federal government have been documented by the Volcker Commission. These problems are in part due to the number of federal employees who feel their job investments in the federal service are yielding a poor return compared to their private-sector counterparts.[12]

Agencies that emphasize investment ties among their employees run the risk of giving employees an incentive to stay with the agency even if they have mentally "retired" on the job. We see this among employees who take a minimalist approach to their jobs while they are waiting (sometimes two, three, or five years) until they qualify for retirement. Such employees have more to gain by merely putting in their time until they can retire than by changing to a more challenging or interesting employer.

This distinction between investments and commitments is particularly salient for public-sector workers, especially at the state and federal levels where many of the investments are transferable within level of government. Commitment is not so easily elicited nor transferred.

Employee Commitment to the Organization

Employee commitment is based on a psychological attachment to the work organization. Committed employees identify with and feel loyal toward the agency; they share the values of the organization and have a personal sense of importance about the agency's mission.[13] Employee commitment can become a vehicle by which individuals manifest loyalty to and identification with an individual, perhaps a respected supervisor or a charismatic chief executive officer. Commitment among public-sector employees can also be a way to fulfill a public-service motivation.[14]

Employees who feel committed to their agencies are likely to perceive that their employers expect them to feel loyal. Committed employees also are likely to feel that their job responsibilities are compatible with their personal ethics, professional standards of performance, and personal values. And their family and friends are likely to support their affiliation with the organization.[15] Employees who have low levels of commitment are not likely to perceive that organizational commitment is expected. Nor are they likely to feel that their job responsibilities are compatible with their personal standards. And their family and friends are unlikely to support their affiliation with the work organization.

Committed employees care what happens to their organization because they share the organization's goals and values. For example, employees who feel committed to the U.S. Civil Rights Commission share the agency's value of advancing the cause of civil rights. Similarly, employees who are committed to a state highway department share that organization's values of building and maintaining safe and convenient roadways throughout the state. In essence, committed employees are self-motivated to do their best for the organization because doing what is good for the organization is consistent with their personal values.

Employees who feel committed to their agency do not base their actions on calculations of what they have invested or on what they stand to gain or lose. They continue to stay with an organization because working for an organization that promotes values they share provides them with a sense of personal satisfaction. As such, commitment is much less susceptible to influences outside the organization (such as alternative employers) than are employees whose ties are based on investments. Commitment requires fewer financial resources to sustain but greater managerial attention. In particular, managers must understand the importance of and nature of employee commitment and recognize the diversity of levels of commitment likely within their work group.

In general, employee commitment is a positive factor for both agencies and individuals. Committed employees tend to have substantially more positive attendance records and are much less likely to quit.[16] While attendance and turnover are important managerial concerns, other important benefits from employee commitment are much less tangible. With commitment, organizations and managers essentially harness the individual's conscience for the purposes of the agency. Committed individuals are willing to perform "above and beyond" the call of duty to accomplish these shared purposes or promote these common values. Employees who identify with and feel loyal to their workplace are more likely to make decisions consistent with the organization's best interests.[17]

Committed employees do what is good for the agency because, in the process of advancing the interests of the organization, they are also advancing values that are important to them personally. Employees who feel committed to their agencies develop a sense of belongingness and are able to fulfill the human need for meaningful work. Feeling committed to their work organizations allows employees to find worth and meaning in their work activities. Even if their particular jobs are not especially challenging and/or complex, committed employees can derive personal meaning from their activities because they value the organized effort of which they are a part. Employees feel an attachment to something bigger than themselves. They feel that the forty hours (or more) of their work efforts are for something meaningful.

Employee commitment is much harder for agencies and managers to elicit than are employee ties based on investments. Because employee commitment is a two-way street, organizations and managers must demonstrate commitment *to* their employees in order to get commitment *from* their employees. Once employees feel committed to an agency, they are much less susceptible to being lured away by competitors because the basis of the attachment is shared values, not self-interested investments.

Organizational Factors That Affect Commitment

Whether or not organizations manage to elicit employee commitment depends on a number of factors within the organization: (1) the agency's culture, (2) the effectiveness of the organization's socialization programs, and (3) the extent to which the agency meets the employee's work expectations. Each of these three dimensions of the employee-employer relationship play an important role in the dynamic of employee commitment.

The organizational culture can foster or discourage commitment. If the organization has a culture that encourages and reinforces commitment, then that organization is more likely to have employees who feel committed to the organization. Of course, managers do not have complete control over an agency's culture. They inherit most of it. Nonetheless, it is important that managers understand organizational culture and seek to influence those aspects of the culture that are subject to their influence.

An organization also needs a socialization program that effectively communicates important organizational values to its employees. Employees cannot be expected to share the important values of the organization if they do not know what they are. Some people may choose to join an agency because they are predisposed to share the values of the organization, such as an environmentalist who goes to work for the Environmental Protection

Agency or an epidemiologist who goes to work for a state health agency. Others who lack a normative interest in agency programs may be attracted by the investment opportunities. One hopes that both groups of employees are candidates for commitment once they are employed by the agency.

Beyond culture and socialization, the expectations and experiences of employees once they are in the agency can have a substantial impact on their organizational commitment. The agency must meet employees' implicit expectations about their work experiences if it hopes to elicit employee commitment. If employees' expectations are met, then they are more likely to develop and sustain organizational commitment. The discussion that follows elaborates on these factors affecting commitment.

Culture

For employees to feel committed to their work organizations, those agencies must have cultures that allow commitment to develop. Under optimal circumstances, an organization's culture would not only *allow* commitment to develop but would actually *encourage* employees to feel committed to the organization.

When we think of an agency's culture, the images brought to mind are usually the artifacts of a culture, those physical manifestations of the agency's way of coping with its survival needs.[18] Organizational values are less tangible components of an organization's culture that reflect the collective judgment of members as to how the organization "ought to" function and beliefs about what the organization "ought to pursue." We can find the values of an organization's culture in its explicit ideology, slogans, oral histories, and goals.

Not all organizational values are of equal importance to the agency and to commitment among employees.[19] Pivotal values, those that are essential to the successful functioning and survival of the organization, are the ones that committed employees share. In an agency that has a high degree of interdependence among tasks, such as a government printing office with an assembly-line operation, interdepartmental cooperation or punctuality may be pivotal values. Similarly, in a state revenue office where citizen trust is essential to the long-term viability of the operation, honesty is likely to be a pivotal value.

In addition to artifacts and values, an organization's culture reflects the most basic shared beliefs and assumptions by which individuals operate within the agency. Most cultural assumptions are so fundamental and widely shared that organizational members cannot even conceive of pursuing strategies inconsistent with such assumptions. For example, in the U.S. Postal Service, the concept of free delivery to all homes, whether urban or rural, is a basic assumption. Although the Postal Service needs to cut its costs as much as possible, eliminating rural free delivery is not an acceptable way to do so. Similarly, an agency that has a basic assumption that employees are not to be trusted may tend to emphasize employee monitoring devices such as time clocks, random drug tests, and polygraph tests.

Because employee commitment is a two-way street, agencies and supervisors must demonstrate commitment to get commitment. For example, an agency that uses layoffs or reductions-in-force only as a last resort demonstrates by its actions that it is concerned about the well-being of its employees. In contrast, an organization that gives very little notice of staff cutbacks and fails to provide outplacement help for those released demonstrates little commitment and concern for the welfare of its employees. Such an employer will likely have a hard time eliciting commitment from its employees—even among those who survive a substantial layoff.[20]

The content of an organization's cultural assumptions are not always accurate. Nor does the lack of confirming evidence necessarily keep people from making basic assumptions. For example, the Flat Earth Society is an organization founded on the basic assumption that the earth is flat. In this era of space probes, we have ample physical evidence that the earth is not flat. Yet some people still cling to this unfounded assumption.

An example of a faulty assumption in the public sector came to light in 1989 in the scandals surrounding the role of private consultants in awarding development contracts from the Department of Housing and Urban Development (HUD). The Reagan administration operated on a policy of promoting privatization as a way to greater efficiency in program management; it assumed the private sector could do things more efficiently. The HUD scandals demonstrate the faultiness of that assumption. Current estimates put the value of private-sector abuse and lax public-sector management of these programs in the billions of dollars.[21]

We see the importance of employee commitment manifested in managers' continual efforts to recruit people who "fit in" to the organization. That is, they seek individuals who can accept the basic assumptions and who already hold key organizational values as their personal values. Of course, not all new employees fit in so readily. Organizational socialization programs are especially important for these employees.

Socialization

The process of transmitting the organizational culture to new members, especially pivotal values and basic assumptions, is an ongoing one. Socialization programs can be highly structured or fairly informal, but they all have the same purpose of integrating the individual into the organization.[22] Socialization programs are specifically geared to communicating the important agency assumptions and values to individuals. The hope is that if employees do not already share these assumptions and values, they will accept them as their own in time.

Usually the employment interview is the beginning of the organization's socialization program. It provides prospective employees with a glimpse of the agency's programs and values. Formal orientation programs follow for those hired; they introduce new employees to some of the obvious facets of the agency's culture. Usually, orientation programs emphasize organizational policies and employee rights; these policies indirectly communicate cultural assumptions and organizational values to employees.

Most formal organization socialization programs are relatively short lived, lasting from a few hours to several days. In extreme cases, formal socialization programs may last a few weeks or months. The armed services boot-camp model is probably the most widely known example of an organization socialization program. In addition to the number of recruits who have gone through these programs and have experienced them firsthand, the programs have been portrayed extensively in the entertainment media.

Agency socialization processes do not stop once an individual has passed his or her probationary period. The organization's culture continues to be transmitted to newcomers and old-timers through formal documents, direct conversations, and indirect means. The more subtle and deep-seated messages are transmitted through informal organizational socialization programs that involve direct supervisors and co-workers. Through these various encounters employees get a sense of the basic assumptions of the organization.

For example, such casual comments as "Nobody worries about how long your coffee break is around here. What matters is that you get the job done, not how long you sit at your desk" tell the new employee that this particular office does not worry about close accounting for time, but instead emphasizes output. The agency assumes you are doing your work unless it sees a drop in your output. Similarly, when a co-worker indicates that the agency accounting procedures dictate an extraordinarily strict accounting of expenses, then the employee knows that the agency assumes fiscal integrity (and maybe untrustworthy employees).

When organizational socialization processes have been relatively successful, employees will have a good "feel" for the culture and values of the agency. Employees must be aware of the agency's values before they can develop a sense of commitment to it. If the agency's culture encourages commitment and employees are aware of important organizational assumptions and values, then the potential for commitment exists.

Employee Expectations

Beyond culture and socialization programs, an individual's potential for commitment can be affected by a more particularistic factor at work. Each individual develops a unique relationship with the organization where he or she works based on unvoiced expectations about the work experience. Our particular interest in this unique relationship is with the set of implicit expectations employees bring to the work setting, called *psychological contracts.*

A psychological contract is an unwritten set of expectations that both the individual and the organization bring to their relationship.[23] We refer to these expectations as psychological because they focus on more subtle aspects of the work relationship than those covered in explicit employment contracts. They reflect unarticulated hopes and feelings about what each will give and get from the relationship, rather than concrete demands. These expectations constitute a contract because both parties consider their expectations to be part of the bargain struck when they mutually agreed to form a relationship. Employees whose expectations are met in the workplace are likely to have higher levels of commitment than those with unmet expectations.

The implicit expectations that constitute psychological contracts are often fairly straightforward.[24] Employees usually have expectations about how much effort they will have to exert as a member of the agency. For example, individuals may accept jobs thinking that they will have to work extra hours just to do their assigned tasks. Under other circumstances, people may accept jobs thinking that the organization will require little effort from them. For example, employees may expect to give the organization long hours in exchange for job experiences that will help them move on to another job or move up the career ladder. People may expect a certain kind of treatment from supervisors or have hopes for promotion opportunities or meeting interesting people. Another common employee expectation is that employees will gain valuable experience that will help them advance their careers when they move to other organizations. Similarly, employees may have expectations that they will have jobs that afford a sense of meaning or purpose and expectations that their work will be challenging. Most employees expect to be treated with dignity by supervisors.

The terms of psychological contracts can change over time. As organizational environments and personal circumstances change, the implicit needs and expectations of agencies and employees can change as well. People who once found jobs acceptable because of the opportunities for promotion may later feel a need for better treatment from their supervisors or the need to work in a more stimulating environment.

As needs and expectations change, psychological contracts must be renegotiated. Such renegotiations are most likely to occur during times of change for the organization or the individual. For example, if the organization is threatened by some outside force, employees may be willing to work harder or work longer hours than before in the interests of helping the agency cope with the threat. Changes in an employee's personal situation, such as divorce or a lengthy illness of a family member, may also initiate renegotiations of the psychological contract for the affected individual. Under the stress of such changes in their personal lives, people may not be willing or able to bring the same level of intensity or effort to their work. For example, a newly divorced parent may reorient his or her priorities away from work because of increased family responsibilities.

If the adjustment in expectations is not mutual, then there may be a feeling of betrayal similar to that of a breach of contract. In other words, if the agency's expectations for its employees change (say, it needs increased effort from them), but its employees do not adjust their expectations accordingly (they do not share the expectation that they contribute greater effort), then the psychological contract is strained. As a result, the organization may feel let down because its employees do not adjust accordingly. Or the employees may feel that the organization has changed the "rules of the game" because it now expects behaviors from them that they never agreed to contribute. A breach of the psychological contract can be just as serious a breach of trust as a failure to comply with the employment contract. Employees who feel this breach are not likely candidates for organizational commitment; those who feel committed may begin to question their commitment.

When the organizational culture encourages employee commitment, the potential for commitment exists. When agency socialization processes have been relatively successful, employees will be aware of the organization's pivotal values. Effective socialization is also likely to bring about adjustments in psychological contracts. Employee expectations are more likely to be in line with agency expectations when employees know the values and expectations of the organization.

Some employers are more successful than others in providing a good fit between its employees' expectations and the agency's expectations. They are the ones more likely to elicit commitment among their employees. When the socialization processes are inadequate or psychological contracts include a number of mismatches on expectations, the employee commitment levels are likely to register on the lower end of the continuum.

Different Levels of Employee Commitment

The results of the dynamic process surrounding employee commitment are not uniform within any one organization or among agencies. Employers differ in the levels of commitment they are able to elicit among their employees. Most agencies find themselves with a wide range of levels of employee commitment. In fact, most managers find individuals with differing levels of commitment within their own small group of subordinates.

Employee commitment can range from extremely high to extremely low. The differences are reflected in the varying degrees to which individuals share the agency's values. People who are at the extremes of the commitment continuum can experience some negative effects themselves and bring some negative effects to their workplaces.[25] The brief sketches that follow outline the differences among the levels of commitment and some behaviors associated with each.

Zealots

Zealots are individuals who have the highest possible level of employee commitment. Zealots share all the pivotal values of the agency and are willing to go beyond the call of duty for the good of the organization. They feel a very strong sense of loyalty to the agency and have strong beliefs in the worth or importance of the work their organization is doing. Nevertheless, zealots' loyalty and beliefs are extreme, out of proportion. Individuals with such commitment are often unwilling to entertain even constructive criticism of the agency.

Zealots are so strongly committed to the organization that they are often blind to any shortcomings in the organization. Zealots do not have a sense of balance in their commitments; they may be excessively absorbed in their work. In turn, this can lead to negative consequences for their personal lives. This kind of individual lives for the organization and may be difficult for less than true believers to be around.

Negative organizational consequences can arise because zealots have the potential to overstep the bounds of acceptable behavior (sometimes even legal bounds) in their pursuit of agency interests. A good example of excessive commitment in the public sector emerged in the Iran/*contra* congressional hearings. During that widely publicized investigation, Marine Lt. Colonel Oliver North, a former member of President Reagan's national security staff, testified about his conduct. In defense of his role in the affair, North dramatically stated that "this Lt. Colonel would stand on his head in a corner" if ordered to do so by his commander-in-chief, the president of the United States. Such a defense was roundly criticized by other military officers as being contrary to the military code of conduct.

Highly Committed

Highly committed employees share the pivotal values of the agency but retain their sense of balance and proportion about them. Like zealots, these individuals are anxious to engage in facilitative behaviors at work, but their sense of employee commitment can be balanced with other life commitments. High-commitment types will express support for the agency, but they also are willing to question organization policies. They trust the agency and are willing to support it, but not blindly.

Moderately Committed

Moderately committed employees share some of the important agency values, but not all. In other words, they have a partial value congruence and may experience partial inclusion in the organization. While there is some overlap between organizational values and their personal values, the overlap may not be on values pivotal to the agency. For example, employees may feel a sense of pride because they are part of an agency that provides the best service in snow removal in the metropolitan area. But they may not feel passionate about snow removal. In the private sector, the organization may be the best producer of soap, buttons, computers, or airplanes; but employees may have a difficult time seeing their employer as making any important contribution to the world. As one private-sector employee noted, he had a hard time getting excited about devoting his life to "the soap that floats." Moderately committed employees will engage in facilitative behaviors, but, unlike high-commitment people, they need to be asked to do so. For the moderately committed, their life outside the agency may be of more importance than their work.

Indifferent Employees

Marginally committed employees do not feel any particular sense of attachment to the organization, either positive or negative. They are essentially indifferent to the organization. Such employees find their personal values irrelevant to their agency roles and the organization's values. Similarly, agency values are irrelevant to their personal roles and values. Indifferent employees are not likely to engage in facilitative behaviors. In fact, they are likely to resist efforts and requests for them to go beyond the call of duty. Indifferent employees are likely to use up their leave time as they accrue it.

The Alienated

Alienated employees encounter situations where their personal values conflict with those of the work organization. Consequently, they feel hostile to organizational imperatives, are likely to distrust agency representatives, and avoid responsibilities. Alienated employees are likely to push to the limit agency policies about personal leave, absenteeism, and tardiness. Alienated employees face high personal costs because of their negative attitudes toward their workplace. They have a difficult time generating any sense of personal meaning from their work.

Managers face different supervisory challenges when they have employees with different levels of commitment. Supervisors must begin to sort out the differences in the commitment levels among their subordinates. And managers who have a diverse workforce face the challenge of treating their employees equitably while recognizing the need for treating their individual employees according to their particular needs and attitudes.

Summary

Employee ties to the organization can be based on investments or commitments. Most personnel policies that tap into an investment orientation (such as pay) are set by legislative mandate. Hence, individual agencies and managers have little latitude in this area. They can only make the best of the investment opportunities available to their workforces.

Agencies and their managers cannot completely control the employee commitment process either. Nonetheless, they can nurture and encourage such psychological involvement. Commitment is not something that can be commanded from individuals. The ultimate level of employee commitment rests on employees' reaction to their agency's culture, values, socialization processes, and work experiences.

For a commitment relationship to develop, the agency must have a culture that at least tolerates (and optimally encourages) commitment. The socialization processes must be successful enough to communicate effectively and inculcate pivotal agency values to employees. And the employee's side of the psychological contract must be met. If the agency's culture is compatible with commitment, its socialization efforts are successful, and employee needs are met, then the conditions are ripe for employee commitment to develop.

The process of fostering employee commitment largely depends on whether the agency demonstrates commitment to employees. While some aspects of these factors are difficult for managers to influence (such as an employee's personal values), sensitivity to the dynamics surrounding the commitment process will enable managers to take advantage of the opportunities for commitment that present themselves.

Notes

1. See W.F. Whyte, *The Organization Man* (Garden City, N.Y.: Doubleday, 1956).

2. See G. Staines, K. Pottick, and D. Fudge, "Wives' Employment and Husbands' Attitudes toward Work and Life," *Journal of Applied Psychology* 71, no. 1 (1986): 118–28.

3. See R.P. Quinn and G.L. Staines, *The 1977 Quality of Employment Survey* (Ann Arbor: Institute for Social Research, 1977); and D. Yankelovich, *New Rules: Searching for Self-Fulfillment in a World Turned Upside Down* (New York: Random House, 1981).

4. The phrase used to capture these new expectations is "quality of work life." See T.G. Cummings and E.D. Molloy, *Improving Productivity and the Quality of Work Life* (New York: Praeger, 1977); L.E. Davis and A.B. Cherns, *The Quality of Working Life*, vols. 1 and 2 (New York: Free Press, 1975); and J.L. Suttle, "Improving Life at Work," in *Improving Life at Work: Behavioral*

Science Approaches to Organizational Change, ed. J.R. Hackman and J.L. Suttle (Santa Monica: Goodyear, 1977), 1–29.

5. See J. Braham, "Dying Loyalty: Companies, Employees Both Less Faithful," *Industry Week* 233 (1987): 15–16; see also a follow-up piece, "Is Anyone Loyal Anymore?" *Industry Week* 234 (1988): 75–85. For a more scholarly treatment of the same issue as it applies to public-sector organizations, see C.H. Levine, I.S. Rubin, and G.A. Wolohojian, *The Politics of Retrenchment* (Beverly Hills, Calif.: Sage, 1981). For an overview of the private-sector perspective, see Marilyn L. Taylor, *Divesting Business Units* (Lexington, Mass.: Lexington Books, 1988), chap. 1.

6. See R.M. Steers, "Antecedents and Outcomes of Organizational Commitment," *Administrative Science Quarterly* 22 (1977): 46–56.

7. This distinction between investments and commitments corresponds to Etzioni's utilitarian and normative involvements, respectively. Utilitarian involvements are based on calculative types of authority. Normative involvements are based on moral authority. See A. Etzioni, *A Comparative Analysis of Complex Organizations* (New York: Free Press, 1975).

8. The term *commitment* is often used imprecisely. Many times, the same word is used by different people to refer to different phenomena. This discussion relies on the term *investment* for stylistic reasons to refer to what Etzioni (1975) has labeled "utilitarian involvement." The intention is to minimize confusion for readers unfamiliar with the intricacies of the commitment literature, which uses *commitment* to refer to two different phenomena. In this discussion, *commitment* is used to refer to psychological involvement based on shared values. The *investment* perspective refers to the perceived utility of continued participation in the organization; as such, it has a self-interested, calculative orientation, rather than an emotional, affective attachment.

9. For empirical research based on investment definitions of commitment, see H.S. Becker, "Notes on the Concept of Commitment," *American Journal of Sociology* 66 (1960): 32–40; and G.R. Salancik, "Commitment and the Control of Organizational Behavior and Belief," in *New Directions in Organizational Behavior,* ed. B.M. Staw and G.R. Salancik (Chicago: St. Clair, 1977), 1–54.

10. See Becker, "Notes on the Concept of Commitment"; and J. March and H. Simon, *Organizations* (New York: Wiley, 1958).

11. See the Report of the Task Force on Recruitment and Retention to the National Commission on the Public Service, *Leadership for America: Committing to Excellence: Recruiting and Retaining a Quality Public Service* (Washington, D.C.: National Commission on the Public Service, 1989), 69–112.

12. Ibid., 85.

13. See R.T. Mowday, L.W. Porter, and R.M. Steers, *Employee-Organization Linkages* (New York: Academic Press, 1982); and B.S. Romzek, "The Effects of Public Service Recognition, Job Security and Staff Reductions on Organizational Involvement," *Public Administration Review* 45 (1985): 282–91; and B.S. Romzek, "Personal Consequences of Employee Commitment," *Academy of Management Journal* 32, no. 3 (September 1989).

14. See A. Downs, *Inside Bureaucracy* (Boston: Little, Brown, 1967).

15. For a discussion of these various dimensions of psychological attachment to an agency, see B.S. Romzek and J.S. Hendricks, "Organizational Involvement and Representative Bureaucracy: Can We Have It Both Ways?" *American Political Science Review* 76 (1982): 75–82.

16. See Mowday, Porter, and Steers, *Employee-Organization Linkages.*

17. See H. Simon, *Administrative Behavior* (New York: Free Press, 1976).

18. For a discussion of this topic, see E. Schein, *Organizational Culture and Leadership* (San Francisco: Jossey-Bass, 1985).

19. See E. Schein, *Organizational Psychology,* 3d ed. (Englewood Cliffs, N.J.: Prentice-Hall, 1980).

20. See J. Brockner, S. Grover, T. Reed, R. DeWitt, and M. O'Malley, "Survivors' Reactions to Layoffs: We Get By with a Little Help for Our Friends," *Administrative Science Quarterly* 32 (1987): 526–41.

21. See C.D. May, "Kemp Suspends Housing Program and Plans an Overhaul of Others," *New York Times,* 7 July 1989, 1, 9; and J. Gerth, "Losses Twice as High as Thought Are Found in an FHA Program: Amount Soars to $1 Billion as Inquiry Broadens," *New York Times,* 13 July 1989, 1, 8.

22. See J. Van Maanen, "Breaking In: Socialization to Work" in *Handbook of Work, Organization and Society,* ed. R. Dubin (Chicago: Rand-McNally, 1976).

23. See C. Argyris, *Understanding Organizational Behavior* (Homewood, Ill.: Dorsey Press, 1960); and Schein, *Organizational Psychology.*

24. For empirical research on psychological contracts, see J.P. Kotter, "The Psychological Contract: Managing the Joining-Up Process," *California Management Review* 15, no. 3 (Spring 1973): 91–99.

25. See Downs, *Inside Bureaucracy.* See also Mowday, Porter, and Steers, *Employee-Organization Linkages* ; and G.R. Salancik, "Commitment and the Control of Organizational Behavior and Belief," in Staw and Salancik, *New Directions in Organizational Behavior,* 1–54.

8

The Federal Government in the Year 2000: Administrative Legacies of the Reagan Years

CHARLES H. LEVINE

Historians writing in the future are likely to regard the two terms of the Reagan administration as a watershed period in the development of the American administrative state. This period is likely to be seen as a time when some issues of governance and public administration that had been brewing for quite a while were finally brought to the surface of political debate. At the center of this debate is the issue of the desirability of government intervention in the nation's social and economic affairs. An airing of this issue in the 1980s is particularly compelling because it is obvious to even the most casual observer that the United States is in the midst of a long-term technological, economic, and demographic transformation that is creating problems and opportunities for its people and government at a rapid pace.

The technical and economic changes are closely interwoven. The nation is moving from an industrial era when the United States dominated the world economy through durable goods manufacturing and financial dealing toward what some have labeled a "postindustrial," "technoservice," or "knowledge-intensive" society.[1] In this new era, the world economic system is quickly becoming considerably more complex than before, with the movement of money and the production of goods and services more "internationalized" than in the past. In the process, the economic dominance of the United States has become more problematic than at any time since World War II, reflecting a change in America's ability to control international markets and their importance in the economic health of the nation.

NOTE: This chapter is a revision of a paper prepared for the conference on "Governing Under Stress" at Centro de Estudios Constitucionales, Madrid, Spain, 12–14 December 1985. The views expressed in this paper are those of the author only and do not reflect those of the Congressional Research Service. [Reprinted from *Public Administration Review* 40 (May-June 1986):195–206.]

To complicate this picture further, the demographic shape of the nation itself is changing. At least four dimensions of this demographic shift are cause for concern: (1) the growth in our aged population—the population of people over age sixty-five is expected to rise from 27 million in 1983 to about 35 million by the year 2000—that will generate new demands on private resources and the federal treasury by way of pension, social security, and health care costs; (2) the aging of the "baby boom" generation—those born between 1945 and 1959—who will also be expected to place heavy demands on government but may also produce pressure for conservative social and fiscal policies; (3) the rise of immigration—both legal and illegal—from Asia and Latin America, which will cause new problems and expenses for our social service organizations, school systems, and other government institutions; and (4) the continued shift of population from the "frostbelt" to the "sunbelt," which will put greater pressure on the federal government to ameliorate some of the deterioration of the Northeast and Midwest and help fund the building of an expanded infrastructure in the South and Southwest.

In combination, the forces of technological change, economic shifts, and a changing population are bound to create new problems and opportunities for the federal government over the next decade and a half. How it will respond is hardly clear. This uncertainty is based on three closely related aspects of contemporary public policy making: (1) the disappointing results of recent attempts to shape the future through government action; (2) a corresponding change in public attitudes about the desirability of government action; and (3) the success of the Reagan administration through its own words and actions and through its links to conservative "think tanks" and thinkers in stimulating public discussion and debate over the three main dimensions of the administrative state: what the government should do, how it should do it, and who should do it.

In other words, whatever its policy successes or failures, the Reagan administration's primary legacy to succeeding presidencies has been to reopen the debate over: (1) the role and reach of government in America's mixed economy; (2) the organizational and administrative apparatus that is used to carry out government's role; and (3) the role of government employees—career civil servants and political appointees—in the policy process. How this debate is likely to be resolved in the next decade and a half is the subject of the remainder of this chapter.

What Will Government Do?

In his history of the foundations of the American administrative state, Steven Skowronek outlines the rapid movement of the American polity from social simplicity to social complexity. Between 1879 and 1920, the isolated local communities that had previously characterized the United States were tied together into one interdependent nation and, as a consequence, state building caught up with the industrial revolution. The outcome of these four decades of political and administrative reform was that American government took on the organizational qualities of a modern state: (1) Authority became more concentrated at the national center of government; (2) institutional controls from the government center penetrated more extensively throughout the territory; (3) authority within the national government became more centralized; and (4) institutional tasks and individual roles within the government became more specialized.[2]

In the process, the national government of the United States overcame the organizational fragmentation imposed both by a federal structure that guarantees the states some sovereignty and by the separation of powers between its executive, legislative, and judicial branches, expanding its powers to cope with the new demands that have confronted the American people.

The 1980s provide an especially fruitful context in which to take stock of these developments and their implications because the Reagan administration has vowed to reverse some of the instrumental trends whereby the organizational features of the modern state identified by Skowronek took form and were institutionalized. The basic impulse underlying this campaign was reflected in President Reagan's first inaugural address, when, after citing a litany of economic problems, the president said:

> In this present crisis, government is not the solution to our problem; government is the problem. . . .
>
> It is time to check and reverse the growth of government which shows signs of having grown beyond the consent of the governed.
>
> It is my intention to curb the size and influence of the Federal establishment and to demand recognition of the distinction between the powers granted to the Federal government and those reserved to the States or the people. All of us need to be reminded that the Federal government did not create the States; the States created the Federal government.
>
> Now, so there will be no misunderstanding, it's not my intention to do away with government. It is rather to make it work—work with us, not over us; to stand by our side, not ride our back. Government can and must provide opportunity, not smother it, foster productivity, not stifle it.[3]

During his presidency, Ronald Reagan has attempted to live up to his words in his first inaugural address by reversing the trend of government growth.[4] Yet, despite President Reagan's persistence and his popularity, the federal government's budget continues to grow and its workforce has actually increased since 1981. This has occurred despite a reduction of 75,000 employees in the domestic agencies, an extensive effort to reduce the government's regulation of business activity, the elimination and/or reduction of several intergovernmental grant programs originally intended to aid states and local governments, a broad campaign to reduce costs in the administrative functions of federal agencies and departments, and continual pressure on administrative agencies from the White House and OMB to contract-out more work to the private sector.

The modest results of the Reagan administration's efforts to redirect the role of American government reflect the problems that confront reformers of all political persuasions in this system of government. Because it is cumbersome and complicated, our system of policy making generally does not (barring crisis) take or reverse direction quickly. This helps to explain why, after five years in office, Reagan's successes in attempting to redirect the role of government, while significant in a few policy areas, must be considered to be marginal in the aggregate. A look at government programs and legislation passed since his inauguration in January 1981 shows that the great preponderance of programs inherited by the Reagan administration are still in place and that their funding levels, while smaller in places, are similar to those of the Carter administration. There are several notable exceptions, of course, but generally speaking, few significant program terminations have occurred.

The Reagan record with respect to the role of government illustrates several important aspects of American government and political culture that are likely to continue to shape the landscape of American politics into the next century. Probably the most significant is "interest-group liberalism" and the dependency of well-organized groups on the funds and power of the federal government.[5] Behind every federal program stands a network of these groups ready to defend their pet projects by lobbying Congress and the executive to spare them budget cuts. No matter how strongly an administration professes to want to cut back programs, the combined weight of these interest groups, often expressed by their PACs and voting power, normally discourages anything more than incremental reduction at the margins of programs. Furthermore, many of the older programs, like social security, agricultural subsidies, and real estate tax incentives, are deeply woven into the fabric of American social and economic life. Families have made investment decisions based on the expectation that these programs will continue into the distant future. Changing their direction is bound to be considered a betrayal of a promise, and few members of Congress are likely to vote for legislation that is bound to incur the wrath of masses of voters.

The combination of these pressures to maintain programs and the disincentives to cut them back provides much of the explanation why the national debt of the United States doubled in just five years to exceed $2 trillion in 1985. Much of the rest of the explanation for the debt is provided by the tax cuts of 1981, which were intended to stimulate the economy enough to eventually allow the budget to be balanced, and the rapid expansion of the military spending during the Reagan years (but actually beginning in the second half of the Carter administration). The resulting deadlock between demands for government funds and services and the insufficient resources needed to pay for them seems irresolvable from the vantage point of the mid-1980s—but it does make predicting the future of the role of government for the next decade and a half easier. With budget deficits so large (projected to be around $210 billion in FY1986) and the cost of servicing the aggregate national debt so monumental, the likelihood is small that the federal government will launch major new programs (or rapidly expand old ones) in the foreseeable future. This, therefore, is a second legacy of the Reagan presidency: Indirectly, through the deficit, it has changed the dialogue surrounding government from one of debating additions to the scope of government activity to a focus on how to maintain the functions and fund the programs that government has already assumed.

Given the deadlock between demands and resources, the rest of the 1980s—and probably the 1990s—is most likely to be characterized by fiscal stringency and policy deadlock, with government not launching any new major spending programs, but not terminating many either. To make matters more complicated, the new economic circumstances confronting America—that is, international competition and high technology—will create new demands on government to create programs that will allow it to work more closely with the private sector to compete effectively abroad and to facilitate technological development. These demands are bound to challenge policy makers to fashion new, low-cost arrangements to improve competitiveness without draining the public purse.

Few alternatives to this pattern are likely, but some longshots deserve brief mention.[6] First, the United States may be able to reduce defense spending by reaching new arms reduction agreements with the Russians. But the slow progress of the disarmament talks in the 1980s provides evidence of the difficulty of finding common ground on which to scale back military spending. Second, the deficit could be reduced in the way originally envisioned by supply-side economic theorists who predicted that the 1981 tax cut would produce a sustained period of economic growth that would eventually increase tax revenues to close the deficit. This alternative too seems unlikely, since the present debt would require a sustained growth pattern larger and longer than at any time in American history (or in anyone else's for that matter). A third possibility is a political realignment after the 1990 census that would result in the redistricting of the House of Representatives in favor of the Republicans. This could occur, but it would not necessarily mean that major programs would be eliminated. Given the weakness of the political parties in Congress and the strength of interest groups, it is quite likely that such a Republican majority would be almost as fragmented as a Congress divided along present lines and would be unable to work out a comprehensive restructuring of federal programs on a broad front.

A fourth alternative would be a reduction of interest rates on the national debt that would lower the annual cost of interest payments. To some extent this is already occurring as the rate of inflation stays low. But the annual deficit is high, and few economists expect the rate of inflation to stay in the 2 to 4 percent range forever. Furthermore, with such a large debt, high-interest government bonds and notes have the effect of causing large capital flows to the United States, raising the value of the dollar relative to other currencies and making exports less competitive in international markets. As a consequence, a large deficit means that even though interest rates may decline somewhat, the indirect effect on the total national debt is likely to cancel out large-scale savings from marginally reduced interest rates.

Finally, the cost of government can be reduced somewhat without affecting programs if the administrative overhead costs of government can be reduced. This entails expenses like personnel, equipment, travel, communication, and computer costs that are involved in coordinating, managing, and controlling government programs. These administrative overhead costs are, to be sure, a major expense of running the federal government, but they represent only a small fraction of total government spending, and cost-cutting efforts in these areas do not promise to yield sufficient savings to diminish the deficit appreciably. For example, in the social security program administrative expenses constitute less than 2 percent of the cost even though the Social Security Administration employs 83,000 people. Moreover, many of these overhead expenses are incurred in the servicing of clients who quickly let their representatives know if their service is threatened or if it actually deteriorates. Finally, many of these costs are associated with broad-scale efforts (such as elaborate personnel and auditing systems) aimed at assuring accountability and control. Although these control systems can undoubtedly be made more efficient, it is extremely unlikely, given the important function they serve, that they will be totally jettisoned.

In short, from the vantage point of the mid-1980s, it is unlikely that a way will be found out of the demands-resources deadlock short of a tax increase. Even The Balanced Budget and Emergency Deficit Reduction Act of 1985—Public Law 99-117 (The Gramm-Rudman-Hollings Act)—promises only to reduce the annual deficit by 1991, but not the national debt. If anything, the problem may become more severe if the aging population creates more demands on the federal treasury for traditional social programs, a recession or two occurs in the next decade and a half which requires either tax cuts or federal spending to stimulate the economy, heightened tension in international relations requires more defense spending, or a new wave of inflation eventually boosts the cost of financing the national debt.

The next decade and a half is therefore likely to be a period of risks and challenges, but no major change in the basic concept of the role of government will probably be forthcoming. Even if some services are "privatized," this is likely to occur on a provisional basis to enable the government to step back in if the privatizing arrangement fails to produce results as promised. But the deadlock over the issue of the role of government is not likely to characterize the way government goes about fulfilling its role. In the next fifteen years, changes in *how* government carries out policy are likely to be both dynamic and dramatic.

How Will Government Carry Out Its Role?

A third legacy of the Reagan presidency—and perhaps the one that will have the most lasting effect—has been to legitimize debate over the tools and techniques of policy implementation. The Reagan administration has brought into the open the full implications of the subtle shift in federal management over the past fifty years from direct service provision and production to greater dependence on "third party" service providers.[7] By insisting on greater reliance on contracting-out government responsibilities to private-sector service providers, the use of user fees for government services, and other alternative service delivery mechanisms, the Reagan administration has accentuated the trend away from the federal government's direct provision of goods and services. Furthermore, in its management of the executive branch—stressing greater central control from the White House and OMB over administrative rules and regulations and placing more political appointees at lower levels in the agencies and departments to direct policy—the administration has effectively centralized agency operations and minimized the autonomy of individual agencies and programs.[8] Finally, in its internal management of federal agencies the administration has pursued two strategies aimed at controlling and cutting costs. The first strategy has involved reducing "fraud, waste, and abuse" in the management of federal programs through active Inspectors General oversight of agency activity, while the second has emphasized modernizing administration through a variety of financial management and other cost-control techniques. The combination of these initiatives has resulted in the gradual transformation of federal operations over the course of President Reagan's first five years and promises to reshape the way the federal government carries out its role into the distant future.

Some of these changes merely reflect the fact that since World War II, the structure and functioning of the executive branch has been changing. While the popular image of the federal government is one of acres of clerks processing piles of forms, in reality the federal workforce is approaching the structure of a research and development firm. For example, in 1983, 55 percent of federal civilian employees had some college training, 16 percent had done some postgraduate work, 21,900 had Ph.D.s, over 150,000 had masters' degrees, and 15,532 were attorneys. Over the previous twenty years the number of engineers on the federal payroll increased by more than 50 percent to nearly 100,000, and the number of computer specialists increased by 600 percent to nearly 50,000.[9]

This profile reflects not only changes in our society but also in the federal government, which has been heavily oriented to scientific, engineering, and professional work since the New Deal and even before. That characteristic has been intensified, and the large-scale operations formerly staffed by clerks are now done increasingly by computerized equipment. The long-established practice of "contracting out," long evident in ship building, atomic energy development, and NASA, has been increased. The practice followed by the New Deal of turning over operations to state and local governments, and Great Society tendencies to rely on nonprofit organizations to get things done have also been increased. These arrangements allow federal agencies more flexibility and sometimes cost less than if their services were delivered by federal employees. In the 1980s, federal employees increasingly think, plan, analyze, evaluate, and dispense funds. Others, by contract or agreement, carry out federal policy. This change of tactics and responsibilities is reflected in the facts that from 1960 to 1983 the executive branch payroll actually declined as a percentage of the total federal outlays (from 13.8 percent in 1960 to 8.8 percent in 1983)[10] and that total federal outlays as a percentage of the GNP rose significantly (from 18.4 percent in 1960 to 24.8 percent in 1983).

This trend toward greater use of contracts and agreements by the federal government to carry out policy is likely to continue. As this occurs, over the next decade and a half, the federal workforce can be expected to become more professionally and scientifically based and probably much smaller. If current trends continue, some have suggested that the size of the federal workforce may be reduced as much as 20 to 25 percent. Most of the reduction that does take place will likely be due to new office technologies replacing secretaries, messengers, and other clerical employees, but some of it will also be caused by contracting-out and "privatization" aimed at capturing the efficiencies provided by competitive contracting of a variety of tasks. Another aspect of the contracting calculus could well be the growing need to hire highly skilled scientists, engineers, and technicians who cannot be attracted to federal employment for any appreciable length of time because the salaries they command in the market will exceed federal maximum rates.

Besides the attractiveness of contracting-out to cut costs and secure scarce technical talent, privatization and other means of indirect government activity are likely to remain appealing for a third reason: They are means to bypass the more stultifying and debilitating features of federal management systems. These features are unlikely to be liberalized in the near future. They have retained a certain permanency despite successive reforms of federal management because, whatever their faults, they have proven to have some beneficial effects. First, compared to other countries and other times, the federal government today is *remarkably honest* and relatively free of corruption. Granted there are instances of fraud, waste, and abuse, but they are small compared to the total of government spending and activity. Inspectors General are busy, but they have not had to prosecute many federal employees.

Second, polls of citizens show that the federal workforce is generally considered to be *responsive* to the public, even though many respondents said that bureaucracy as a whole is unresponsive and wasteful. This pattern of response reveals an ironic aspect of the U.S. system—Americans like their bureaucrats but dislike their bureaucracy—but it nevertheless suggests that management systems aimed at assuring responsiveness of federal employees have worked reasonably well.[11]

Third, substantial evidence shows that the productivity of the federal workforce is improving and that the system as a whole is reasonably *efficient* and *reliable*.[12] The constraints on the federal workforce imposed by rules, regulations, standardized procedures, and other controls limit flexibility, but they assure similar treatment for similar cases and machinelike processing of the vast number of cases handled by the federal government.

Yet despite these positive features, agreement is widespread that federal management systems have become so burdensome and constraining that they reduce rather than enhance effectiveness. This line of criticism argues that federal management systems, to assure reliability and central coordination and control, are expensive compared to private-sector staffing standards and have become so overregulated, overburdened, and stultifying that they constrain managers and choke off innovation and individual initiative, which are crucial in a rapidly changing society. The core of the problem, these critics charge, is that the management systems are too centralized, both within line agencies and between the line agencies and the central administrative agencies (i.e., OMB, OPM, and GSA).[13] Other critics charge that this problem has been exacerbated by the Reagan administration as it has sought to control management policy from the White House by using more political appointees to redirect policy in the agencies.[14]

Despite the criticisms that federal management systems are over-centralized, however, it is unlikely that much will be done about this problem in the next decade and a half. Several factors support this conclusion. First, as already noted, the prevailing system has provided the United States with some positive benefits—bureaucratic integrity, responsiveness, and reliability. Second, the benefits of control afforded by the present systems give individual presidents a powerful tool to help redirect policy.[15] Third, improved management has almost no constituency beyond the federal career managers themselves. For most Americans, the system is simply too complex to understand, and their stake in its improvement is too uncertain for them to focus their interest.

Therefore, it is reasonable to expect that the next three or four administrations will adopt a similar strategy for managing line agencies *but not for managing the totality of everything the federal government undertakes.*

Because of the importance of the government in facilitating the international competitiveness of American business and domestic economic development, government will need administrative tools that are not rigid, slow, or unimaginative, as control-oriented bureaucracies tend to be. It is quite likely, therefore, that the federal government will create a variety of public-private, special-purpose, hybrid organizations to carry out new programs or reshape old ones. These new organizations, which will range from government corporations to federally insured private ventures, are bound to widen the spectrum of management systems used by government.

At the same time, it is reasonable to expect that some of the standardization in management practices built into the old system will become modified in some select agencies, particularly those whose missions are not politically disputed.[16]

This will mean that the personnel, procurement, budgeting, and computer management systems of several agencies will be differentiated from those that cover most of the rest of government. As this occurs and the use of third-party service providers and mixed public-private enterprises gathers even more steam, the distinction between public and private organizations will become more blurred; executives and lower-level employees will move from one side to the other more frequently (aided in part by greater pension portability and formalized exchange programs); and notions of "public service" are likely to be extended beyond government to the nonprofit sector, voluntary organizations, and some public/private organizational arrangements.

Perhaps the Reagan administration's most lasting contribution to the organization and operation of the federal government will be the result of its efforts to modernize the "nuts and bolts" of management. Operating through several vehicles (including its first-term council on administration and management, its second-term domestic policy council, and OMB), the administration has focused efforts to improve how the federal government handles cash management, debt collection, real property, procurement, computer planning, travel, and other administrative overhead expenses. Some of these initiatives were begun in the Carter administration, others were generated by the General Accounting Office, and still others were stimulated (or publicized) by the Grace Commission, but it was not until the Reagan administration that they were broadly implemented. Although some people have charged that these efforts do not amount to management improvement in the broad sense and in reality are little more than "penny pinching," from a historical perspective one must conclude that the Reagan administration has initiated valuable, badly needed reforms in these areas that were overlooked in previous administrations. Furthermore, the administration's successes in these low-visibility but costly management areas are likely to encourage future administrations to carry on the modernization effort as new ideas and opportunities develop.

In sum, while that "what" of government (that is, its role) in the United States is unlikely to change much in the next decade and a half, the "how" (i.e., its structure and operations) is likely to undergo substantial change. This change will likely be in two directions: more central control over some parts of the executive branch and more decentralization and variation in organizational forms and operations in others. In addition, one can expect more privatization and more contracting-out, reflecting a distinctly American style of government—a way of having an ideological cake while also eating it. Such a system, broadly speaking, harmonizes with American individualism and antisocialist values and comports with customary American preferences for reliance on the private sector for goods and services.[17] In this evolving system of management, the question of "who" will do government's work will be problematic.

Who Will Do Government's Work?

A fourth legacy of the Reagan years for the future of American public administration has been to bring to a head some long-standing problems confronting the civil service system. Over the past five years, concern has grown rapidly about the quality, morale, and effectiveness of the federal civil service. Anecdotal and impressionistic evidence suggests that a serious problem exists and that it seems to be worsening. Although no one seems sure as to the precise nature and origin of the problem, agreement is widespread among informed observers of the civil service that the federal government has not established the mechanisms necessary to attract, educate, and retain the high-caliber career service it will need for the year 2000.

While most discussions of the civil service and its problems focus on the Senior Executive Service (SES) and equivalent levels—usually pointing out, for example, that more than 40 percent of the SES left government service from July 1979 through March 1983—evidence suggests that the problem goes deeper and spreads wider into the technical, scientific, and managerial corps that make up the bulk of the career service.[18]

In the opinion of some observers, the erosion of the human resource base of the federal civil service (i.e., the skills, morale, and commitment of the workforce) has been speeding up since the economic recovery of 1983.[19] Some federal agencies are having a more difficult time attracting and retaining high-quality personnel, and the morale of employees in the aggregate is quite low. For example, the Merit Systems Protection Board surveyed the 1,500 SESers who resigned (as distinguished from those who retired) from the federal service during the period July 1980 to June 1983. They found that 90 percent of the resignees left to assume higher-paying positions in the private sector. Another study by the Senior Executive Association in 1982 found that 80 percent of the respondents were concerned to a "great" or "considerable" extent about the morale among career employees. A more recent study by the Federal Executive Institute Alumni Association (FEIAA) rated morale at 3.6—down from 3.8 in 1983—on a scale from a low of one to a high of seven, far from high but higher than those conducting the survey said they expected.

The ambiguity of the morale surveys only complicates the difficulty of understanding what is happening to the civil service in the 1980s. On the whole, the available evidence suggests that the human resource base of the federal workforce is in decline. Convincing explanations for the decline are harder to come by. One thing is clear: The problem did not begin with the Reagan administration or President Carter's Civil Service Reform Act of 1978, nor will it likely end with a new administration in 1989.

It is reasonable to expect that few highly qualified and ambitious people want to work in a system that is perceived to be failing and which does not promise to be satisfying. This unhappy state of affairs has been noted by such disparate groups as the President's Private Sector Survey on Cost Control (The Grace Commission) and the National Academy of Public Administration. While they and other informed observers acknowledge that the federal civil service continues to attract and hold many well qualified and hard-working employees, some of whom achieve impressive results, by and large they view the system in pessimistic terms—pointing to an array of factors that combine to discourage individual initiative and encourage civil servants to take a narrow, "technocratic" perspective toward their work.

One factor that may be contributing to the poor morale of many federal employees today—and that may discourage the highly qualified and ambitious from joining their ranks in the near future—is the change in the missions of several domestic agencies. Particularly since 1981, budgetary cutbacks, program terminations, and a general decline in program activism have combined to reduce the sense of achievement that prevailed during the 1960s. Few people who have contributed to the creation, development, and growth of a program can be expected to approach its retrenchment with equal enthusiasm. Nor is it reasonable to suppose that adapting organizations and programs to cope with conditions of austerity will strike many potential federal employees as a rewarding challenge.

A related cause of human resource erosion—and another constraint on the adaptability of the civil service system—is the increased "politicization" of the higher civil service and the more extensive use of central controls by OMB through the budget and regulatory review processes to shape the policy agendas of departments and agencies.[20] By "politicization," critics mean the increased numbers and importance of political appointees at lower and lower levels in the agencies and the increased direction of the agencies by the White House. An often cited example of this trend occurred at the Office of Personnel Management under the leadership of Director Donald J. Devine. During his four-year term at OPM, the number of career professionals fell 18 percent, while the number of political appointees increased 169 percent.[21] Critics of this personnel policy argue that it amounts to a significant reduction in the policy roles of the top levels of the career civil service and with it an assault on the concept of "neutral competence," which previously guided civil service doctrine. Without some involvement in policy planning, these critics argue, career employees are kept ignorant of policy direction by short-term political appointees who often do not value their advice or institutional memory. This arrangement not only frustrates and confuses career employees but also increases the risk of mistakes, errors, and policy failures. While politicization may serve the interest of a president in the short run, these critics argue, it will prove unsatisfying and unworkable in the long run because the complexity of the administrative process requires that the roles of career and political appointees be interwoven—a partnership must exist between the cadres to assure sensible policy formulation and effective policy implementation.[22]

It should be pointed out that there is quite another view of this arrangement. Proponents of greater political control over the career civil service have observed that this system of administration has served President Reagan well, allowing him to redirect policy with more confidence that it will be implemented than were he to trust career bureaucrats. Because of this advantage, politicization, in one form or another, they argue, is likely to be the way of directing the federal executive branch for many years to come.[23] They also see the interweaving process as evolving into a new format for career-political relationships and responsibilities and doubt that morale problems, if any, will persist beyond the current generation of disappointed executive-level civil servants.

Much of the politicization of the executive branch—and other causes of low morale—has been attributed to the disappointing consequences of the Civil Service Reform Act of 1978 (CSRA) and its creation, the Senior Executive Service (SES). In the first two years after the SES was established, there was an excitement about the new system, which quickly turned to disappointment. First, Congress and the Carter administration came to believe that the SES bonuses were too generous and were given to too many people. Over the next several months, by law and regulation, the original provisions were amended by decreasing from 50 to 20 percent the employees eligible for bonuses. This was the first of many actions that slowly disillusioned the SES members. Second, the personal development plans promised by the CRSA were scaled down (e.g., in the first six years of the SES, only twelve senior executives used the sabbatical provisions of the act). Another disappointment to employees was the merit pay system for mid-level managers (GS 13-15), which was never adequately funded to provide attractive bonuses for high performers. Finally, reassignments and relocations, supposedly a positive feature of the new system, were sometimes used by the Reagan administration in its first years in a way that many SES members regarded as punitive—as a means to get them out of the way or to force them to retire.[24]

In combination, the SES and other features of the CSRA have been a disappointment to many federal employees and long-time supporters of the civil service. It has been perceived to be, in the words of one critic, "Carter's gift to Reagan" that enabled the latter to gain easy control over a bureaucracy made more vulnerable by the CSRA.[25]

It is important to note that these explanations for the perceived erosion of the civil service are largely internal to the federal government. External factors may be just as or more significant. For many government employees, policy redirection, politicization, and the disappointments of the CSRA may be less important factors bearing on their morale and commitment to remain in the federal service than the negative image of the civil servant in American society. This phenomenon has several explanations, the most obvious being the general antipathy of Americans since colonial days toward "big government" and "bureaucrats." To many citizens, "big government," "fraud, waste, and abuse," "bureaucracy," and "bureaucrats" are terms synonymous with a system of government—and of government spending—gone out of control. Both Presidents Carter and Reagan recognized and articulated this sentiment successfully in their initial presidential campaigns, and both came to Washington vowing to "clear up the mess."[26]

In such a political culture, it is remarkable that the federal government gets as many highly qualified employees as it does. Of course, given that roughly 2.9 million employees constitute the civilian federal labor force (including the Postal Service), the law of averages dictates that some are bound to be excellent. But that hardly explains why whole agencies attract and retain superior workforces. A better explanation is that the federal government has a monopoly or near monopoly on some interesting occupations. For example, professionals who want to work in meteorology, advanced archival techniques, space exploration, diplomacy, and intelligence have been unable to find many opportunities to practice their professions that compare with those available at NOAA, the Library of Congress, NASA, the State Department, or the CIA. As a consequence, the executive branch contains numerous "centers of excellence," especially in scientific and technical fields. For example, from 1968 through 1985, seven federal employees won Nobel prizes in medicine, and sixty federal employees are members of the National Academy of Sciences. Another explanation is rooted in social history. For many women, minorities, and first-generation college graduates, the corporate world has been seen as an alien place, while the civil service, with its social and ethnic diversity, affirmative action programs, and merit-based entrance and promotion systems, has been regarded as a socially comfortable place to pursue a career. Yet another explanation can be found in the expansion of governmental activity into new areas to contend with a variety of social problems, first during the New Deal and later with the programs of the Great Society. When one interviews government employees, many say they were attracted to federal service by the prospect of working to solve social problems through new federal programs. Many who took up employment at HUD, HHS, and AID, for example, were attracted to government service by their agencies' missions. Job security has also played a role in attracting and retaining federal employees. Until recently, reductions-in-force were a rare occurrence; federal employment has meant a relatively high degree of protection from the risks of layoffs. Finally, an even more utilitarian explanation exists: the chance to combine retirement credits gained through military service with the civilian retirement system has induced many well-qualified people to join and stay in the federal civil service. No matter what their initial motivation in joining the civil service, once there, many federal employees have advanced to more general management roles. As a consequence, over the years the federal government has enjoyed a cadre of well-qualified employees, many of whom have transferred among agencies, thereby enriching the capacity of the civil service as a whole.

If the assessments offered in several recent studies of the federal civil service are correct, this system of recruitment and retention has worked reasonably well in the past, but now there are some signs it may no longer be viable. According to agency recruiters, fewer highly qualified, technically trained college graduates are interested in federal employment. The perception, they report, is that more challenging work, greater flexibility, and higher rewards are available in the private sector. Furthermore, of the aforementioned factors accounting for the high quality of recruits attracted into federal employment in the past, almost all have lost some of their "pull." For example, in an era of greater government contracting, aerospace engineers can find plenty of challenges working for private contractors on DOD and NASA projects. Also, the barriers to corporate employment faced by women, minorities, and first-generation college graduates have been lowered. Moreover, the redirecting of federal policy away from social programs has channeled the interest of many "do-gooders" toward state, local, private-sector profit, and nonprofit social service agencies. Furthermore, reductions-in-force, furloughs, and position down-gradings have produced an environment of uncertainty around many federal jobs, creating an element of risk where security prevailed only a few years ago. Finally, according to recent studies, federal pay and compensation is trailing the private sector by an estimated 4 to 19 percent for comparable jobs and the disparity is growing larger every year.[27] Given these factors, it is hardly surprising that in a recent sample of the career members of the Senior Executive Service (the top 6,000 members of the civil service), 72 percent responded "no" when asked if they would recommend a career in the federal government for their children.[28]

The forces leading to erosion are unmistakable, and many of them seem to be inexorable, but the more important question is, what difference does it make? In other words, a civil service populated by highly trained, motivated, and well-deployed employees is preferable to one that is less so only if a lower-quality workforce can be shown to have undesirable consequences for government performance generally.

Perhaps the best explanation for the desirability of a high-quality civil service lies in the changing structure of the U.S. economy and government's likely role in it. In the new political economy into which the United States is moving, a rigid, poorly trained, unimaginative, and unmotivated civil service could be the cause of many episodes of policy failure. Especially significant will be those programs whose employees use high levels of science and technology in their work. These programs often have "life and death" consequences that are the product of seemingly minor decisions made by mid-level government employees. They suggest that a government populated by the "error prone" (be they ill informed, misinformed, lazy, or simply incompetent) can produce small administrative nightmares that add up to a general breakdown of government effectiveness.

In the next decade and a half—by the year 2000—the risks involved in the small decisions that mid- and upper-level federal employees will be called upon to make will be even greater. Not only is the economy of the United States becoming more complex and its technology more sophisticated, but the political pressures on government agencies will require more sensitive responses than in the past. A premium will need to be placed on having knowledgeable and savvy officials at the mid and upper levels of the bureaucracy, which in turn means that the federal workforce will need to attract even more skillful and committed employees than ever before. Yet current trends augur in the opposite direction. If they continue much longer, only a major overhaul of the system may be adequate to forestall serious consequences.

In the view of many observers, the most desirable overhaul of the system is one that would allow the federal government to evolve into an organizational system that is truly competitive in compensation, mobility, management systems, and innovative opportunities with the private sector. Such a reform, however, would be possible only if critical actors in the White House, Congress, the media, business, unions, and public interest groups reach some agreement about the magnitude and significance of the problem. But, in the 1980s, the alignment of these political forces seems to militate against compromise and change.

Since the mid-1960s, a fundamental transition has occurred in the political arena surrounding the federal civil service. Prior to that point, reforms of the civil service system were often motivated and guided by "good government" groups and associations of career civil servants espousing progressive notions of personnel management. In recent years, however, this coalition has given way to a new, more politicized and polarized alignment of friends and foes of the civil service. Perhaps the last vestige of the old civil service coalition was revived by Alan K. Campbell, the chairman of the Civil Service Commission under President Carter and later the first director of the Office of Personnel Management, in lobbying for the Civil Service Reform Act of 1978. Despite this brief throwback to an earlier era of relative consensus about the goals of civil service reform, the politics surrounding the civil service system for much of the past two decades—and particularly in the last five years—have been characterized by a high degree of polarization between the White House, with its hopes of cutting the size, cost, and autonomy of the federal workforce, and civil service unions and employee associations seeking to resist any erosion of employee pay, benefits, and perquisites.

In this contentious political context, a consensus-based approach to civil service reform aimed at promoting a more productive working environment to serve some concept of "the public interest" has largely disappeared. Potentially interested third parties—the business community, public interest groups, professional associations, etc.—have either been drawn into one or the other side or have fled the field, perhaps avoiding the risks of being "burned" by well-intentioned involvement. The consequence has been a change in the dialogue surrounding civil service policy from one of "management improvement" (i.e., to attract, retain, and better deploy an appropriately skilled and motivated work force) to one of confrontation and political stalemate (as exemplified by the militant words of OPM Director Devine who vowed "to bring the tanks up to the border" in order to make changes in the system).

The polarization of the civil service policy arena means that a broad-scale reform of the system is unlikely to take place in this decade. But without some reforms, the capacity and performance of the executive branch could well decline, suggesting that the civil service could become a "drag" on the economy.[29] In this respect, it is perhaps in the interests of the business community (which so far has been mostly silent on the issue) to take the initiative to bring the problem of civil service decline to the public's attention. In doing so, it could become a "third force" between the polarized factions to build a consensus behind reforms that would strengthen the system.

The president also has a major responsibility to assure that the system is not allowed to erode. A weak civil service stands as an impediment to the president's constitutionally-mandated responsibility to "take Care that the Laws be faithfully executed." It is not enough to control the system. To carry out his responsibilities, he and his successors must have a competent administrative apparatus. Therefore, it is the presidency that has the greatest stake in this issue, and a president who is committed to strengthening the civil service could do much to provide the leadership necessary to reform the system. Ignoring the issue or encouraging the processes that lead to erosion is to force the government to live on borrowed time and ignore the long-term consequences of a weakened civil service. Through presidential leadership, the public can be persuaded that a highly competent and motivated civil service is a public good that can be eroded through hostility, indifference, and neglect if not somehow revitalized from time to time through the infusion of new ideas, talent, and public support. Impressionistic evidence suggests that such a process of neglect and decline is now at work in the federal civil service. That this trend will be reversed and a countervailing process of revitalization launched seems—at least from the perspective of the politics of the mid-1980s—an unlikely prospect in the near future.

In the 1990s, however, the civil service will be called upon to be more technologically sophisticated, more schooled in the ways of the business community, and more savvy about emerging international economic trends and their implications. By then, deficiencies of the system and its weaknesses will be more apparent, creating an environment more amenable to broad reforms. By the year 2000, therefore, there is some chance that the civil service will be brought up to the challenges faced by government.

Will American Public Administration Be Ready for the Year 2000?

We come now to the bottom line: Will the federal administrative structure, systems, and workforce be able to meet the challenges of the year 2000? As the preceding discussion has shown, evidence supports both optimistic and pessimistic answers. On the whole, however, historic American optimism is likely to prove warranted. This conclusion is largely based on one important aspect of American government: When confronting crises and contingencies, the U.S. system has proved to be remarkably adaptive. When wars, domestic problems, and economic difficulties have posed a serious and pressing challenge, leaders have always emerged to pass laws and create administrative arrangements to grapple with the problem. There is no reason to expect that such a scenario will not play out again in the future, although there will no doubt be some temporizing of optimism and a keener recognition of the nation's fiscal and social limits.

Barring unforeseen events or politically improbable coalitions, the fiscal stringency that dominates public policy in the 1980s is likely to continue into the 1990s; public attitudes and our large national debt will continue to dictate a more constrained role for the federal government in domestic affairs. At the same time, however, one can expect a more diverse and dynamic array of government action. In the 1980s, the leaders of Congress and the executive branch are becoming more creative and more strategic managers. As a result, governments at all levels are making broader use of alternative organizational arrangements in their choices of service delivery and policy implementation strategies. The good news, therefore, is that government is likely to continue to be a large and positive force in American society; the better news is that it is likely to carry out its role in ways that minimize the negative aspects of bureaucracy, capture the advantages of joint public-private administrative arrangements, and borrow from the private sector the management techniques that can be appropriately transferred.

The bad news is that little evidence contradicts the assertions of those who believe that the quality of the federal civil service is eroding. But the problems of the civil service are not inherently unsolvable. Erosion can be stabilized—and even reversed—with a few structural changes in the rules and procedures used to attract and retain federal employees. Furthermore, proposed changes in the pension laws for the civil service may have the effect of encouraging a two-way flow of workers between the public and private sectors. Finally, contracting-out, government corporations, and other alternative service delivery arrangements can be seen as positive means of strengthening the talent pool available to government managers for carrying out their responsibilities.

The question remains, however, whether the federal government in the year 2000 will have an enhanced or diminished capacity to address issues of administrative management in an intelligent, integrated fashion. Since the late 1930s, the administrative apparatus of the federal government has been shaped by a widely shared administrative philosophy about the proper way to organize and administer operations and the role of its public employees in that arrangement. In the 1980s, considerable confusion prevails about these issues in both theory and practice. Without a clear doctrine based on guiding principles of organization and management, the executive establishment has evolved into a much more varied and complicated structure of governance that is increasingly using third parties, public-private hybrids, and indirect means to carry out national policy. Lacking the firm theoretical ground of an earlier era provided by such efforts as the Brownlow and first Hoover commissions, policy makers and government executives have tended to narrow the scope of their thinking to tackle more tractable, but nevertheless second-order problems. While this incrementalism may solve problems in the short run—and in the aggregate move government to a better fit with its problems and opportunities—it also creates problems and an uneasiness among many observers that these efforts lack clear direction. Unless there is a clearer resolution of the more central issues of what government should be doing, how it should be doing it, and who should be doing it, the debate over the focus and activities of the federal government will be increasingly dominated by grand ideologies that are inappropriate for the problems at hand. The result may be that the good work done to manage more narrow problems will get eviscerated by large-scale initiatives grounded in inapplicable theories of governance and public management.

This problem plagues all the developed democracies in the 1980s. Britain, France, Sweden, and Canada, for example, are struggling with austerity by redefining their roles and reshaping their administrative systems. The political leaders of these nations are reducing the scope of the public sector and the discretion traditionally provided to their civil servants. In part, this development can be explained by the fiscal problems of these countries and their retrenchment at the margins of the welfare state, but it also reflects some confusion about the operational practices of these governments.

It is in this context that we find a fifth legacy of the Reagan years: Besides opening up a discussion of alternative ends and means of government action, the difficulty which the Reagan administration has had in fashioning administrative tactics within the framework of conservative ideology suggests that neither liberal nor conservative—or for that matter "neoconservative"—approaches to public management provide complete guidance for arranging and managing the public sector in a mixed economy. This intellectual deficit, which seems likely to be even more apparent in the 1990s, promises to spur activity to fill it. Therefore, while in the 1980s one finds the intellectual study of public administration in the doldrums, the next decade and a half promises to be a much more lively period of debate and theory building.

Governments worldwide, including the United States, have changed in both their ends and means since the Brownlow and Hoover commissions—and will surely change more before the next century. To do so with a minimum of problems and errors, they will need a new, consistent doctrine to guide efforts to improve governance and management. Shaping such a doctrine is perhaps the central challenge confronting scholars and public officials in the next decade and a half and can be their most valuable contribution to the public interest of the future.

Notes

1. Many different terms have been used to describe the era we are entering, but consensus is remarkably high about what its main technical and economic shape is likely to be and how it will depart from the past. See, for example, Daniel Bell, *The Coming of Post-industrial Society* (New York: Basic Books, 1973); Michael Maccoby, "A New Way of Managing," *IEEE Spectrum*, June 1984, 69–72; and John Naisbitt, *Megatrends* (New York: Warner Books, 1982).

2. Stephen Skowronek, *Building a New American State: The Expansion of National Administrative Capacities, 1877–1920* (Cambridge, England: Cambridge University Press, 1982), 19–20.

3. Inaugural Address of President Ronald Reagan, 20 January 1981.

4. In at least one respect, however, President Reagan's approach to restricting the role of government has been contradictory. According to Lowi, rather than restrict government's role, "what Reagan was ultimately trying to accomplish was considerably more important to him than merely relieving corporations of some of their regulatory burdens. Reagan's goal as a conservative was to try to shift and extend government authority toward realms where government concerned itself with the morality of conduct." This has extended to Reagan's support for the thus-far unsuccessful "Right-to-Life" amendment to the Constitution, other antiabortion measures, his firm support of the proposed school prayer amendment, and his endorsement of firm discipline in the nation's schools. See Theodore J. Lowi, "Ronald Reagan—Revolutionary?" in *The Reagan Presidency and the Governing of America*, ed. Lester M. Salamon and Michael S. Lund (Washington, D.C.: Urban Institute, 1985), 38–39.

5. See Harold Wolman and Fred Teitelbaum, "Interest Groups and the Reagan Presidency" in *The Reagan Presidency and Governing of America*, ed. Salamon and Lund, 297–329.

6. For a discussion of several dozen ways to cut the deficit, see Congressional Budget Office, *Reducing the Deficit: Spending and Revenue Options* (Washington, D.C.: Government Printing Office, 20 February 1985).

7. Lester M. Salamon, "Rethinking Public Management: Third-Party Government and the Changing Forms of Government Action," *Public Policy* 29 (Summer 1981): 255–75; Frederick C. Mosher, "The Changing Responsibilities

and Tactics of the Federal Government," *Public Administration Review* 40 (November/December 1980): 541–47.

8. See Richard P. Nathan, *The Administrative Presidency* (New York: Wiley, 1983).

9. See Howard Rosen, *Servants of the People: The Uncertain Future of the Federal Civil Service* (Salt Lake City: Olympus Publishing, 1985), 13–30; and Kathy Sawyer, "Uncle Sam's New Look: A Workforce in Transition from Clerks to Technocrats," *Washington Post*, 4 August 1980, A1 and A7.

10. U.S. Office of Personnel Management, Workforce Analysis and Statistics Division, *Federal Civilian Payrolls, Fiscal Year 1950–1983*.

11. See Charles T. Goodsell, *The Case for Bureaucracy* (Chatham, N.J.: Chatham House, 1983).

12. See, for example, Rosen, *Servants of the People*, 164.

13. See National Academy of Public Administration, *Revitalizing Federal Management: Managers and Their Overburdened Systems* (Washington, D.C.: NAPA, 1983).

14. Edie N. Goldenberg, "The Permanent Government in an Era of Retrenchment and Redirection," in *The Reagan Presidency and Governing of America*, ed. Salamon and Lund, 381–404.

15. See Lawrence E. Lynn, Jr., "Manager's Role in Public Management," *Bureaucrat* 13 (Winter 1984–85): 20.

16. For a discussion of some of the conditions that support greater or lesser degrees of agency autonomy, see Richard E. Schmidt and Mark A. Abramson, "Politics and Performance: What Does It Mean for Civil Servants?" *Public Administration Review* 43 (March/April 1983): 155–60.

17. Raymond G. Hunt, "Cross Purposes in the Federal Contract Procurement System," *Public Administration Review* 44 (May/June 1984): 248.

18. See Goldenberg, "Permanent Government in an Era of Retrenchment and Redirection."

19. For a discussion of the concept of "human resource erosion," see Charles H. Levine, "Retrenchment, Human Resource Erosion and the Role of the Personnel Manager," *Public Personnel Management* 13 (Fall 1984): 249–63.

20. See Edie N. Goldenberg, "The Grace Commission and Civil Service Reform: Seeking a Common Understanding, " in *The Unfinished Agenda for Civil Service Reform*, ed. Charles H. Levine (Washington, D.C.: Brookings Institution, 1985), 69–94.

21. Goldenberg, "The Permanent Government in an Era of Retrenchment and Redirection," 396.

22. For a full statement of this position, see Chester A. Newland, "A Midterm Appraisal—The Reagan Presidency: Limited Government and Political Administration," *Public Administration Review* 43 (January/February 1983): 1–21.

23. See, for example, Nathan, *Administrative Presidency*, 74–76; Lynn, "Manager's Role in Public Management," 20; and Michael Sanera, "Imple-

menting the Mandate," in *Mandate for Leadership II: Continuing the Conservative Revolution*, ed. Stuart M. Butler, Michael Sanera, and W. Bruce Weinrod (Washington, D.C.: Heritage Foundation, 1984), 459–559.

24. U.S. General Accounting Office, *Detailed Statement for the Record by Charles A. Bowsher, Comptroller General of the United States, before the Subcommittee on Civil Service of the House Post Office and Civil Service Committee*, 7 November 1983.

25. B. Guy Peters, "Administrative Change and the Grace Commission," in Levine, *Unfinished Agenda for Civil Service Reform*, 19–39.

26. See Goodsell, *Case for Bureaucracy*.

27. See, for example, Hay/Huggins Company and Hay Management Consultants, *Study of Total Compensation in the Federal, State and Private Sectors*, Committee on Post Office and Civil Service, U.S. House of Representatives (Washington, D.C.: Government Printing Office, 1984); and Robert W. Hartman, *Pay and Pensions for Federal Workers* (Washington, D.C.: Brookings Institution, 1983).

28. Results of a survey conducted by the Federal Executive Institute Alumni Association, Draft Report, November 1984.

29. See Bernard Rosen, "Effective Continuity of U.S. Government Operations in Jeopardy," *Public Administration Review* 43 (September/October 1983): 383–91; and Irene S. Rubin, *Shrinking the Federal Government* (New York: Longman, 1985).

PART FOUR

Issues for the Future

9

Commissions, Cycles, and Change: The Role of Blue-Ribbon Commissions in Executive Branch Change

PATRICIA W. INGRAHAM

The ambivalence of American citizens toward their government has been frequently noted. Donald Kettl wrote, for example, that "as citizens, we cherish the ideal of limited government, but we demand that government solve our most pressing problems."[1] This discomforting tension has led to an almost continuous series of efforts to change and reform the federal government. A favored mechanism for identifying and advocating possible solutions to perceived problems with government and its operations has been the blue-ribbon commission—a group of distinguished citizens whose prestige will validate and legitimate the call for change. Commissions have come in various shapes and sizes; some have been congressionally appointed, while others have been appointed by the president. Still others have emerged from citizen concerns and fears.

Although these commissions and task forces have been created to analyze a wide variety of problems, one of the hardiest has been the issue of the organization and power of the executive branch. Moe argues that such groups study one perennial question: "Who should be held responsible by the electorate for managing the executive functions of the Federal Government?"[2] A closely related set of concerns have examined the various structures for achieving the "best" (read *efficient*) management. The "perennial question" has emerged so frequently that, by Moe's count, there has been a new commission or task force appointed to study executive reorganization on average every seven years for the past one hundred years.[3]

The continued reliance on reorganization, efficient management, and study commissions is somewhat odd, given the uncertain success of most past efforts.[4] Nonetheless, both the issue and the method continue to burn brightly. The report of the most recent study group, the National Commission on the Public Service (the Volcker Commission) was presented to President Bush shortly after his inauguration. Despite their perennial nature, however, study commissions have not been analyzed to any great extent. It is the intent of this chapter to provide a brief historical analysis of previous commissions and task forces, but to emphasize those that have emerged in the past twenty years. This group, and the view of government they present, are critical to our understanding of the potential for future change and reform.

Commissions and Governmental Reorganization

Background

Forty years ago, Herbert Emmerich noted that "federal reorganization is essentially a continuing process. It is going on all the time as a result of both internal and external pressures.... The occasional major reform efforts have the value of shock treatments for the rationalization of an organism which is subject to chronic imbalance...." [5] Emmerich's biological analogy is useful for understanding the complex interactions that stimulate and influence reform efforts. It is also useful for describing the evolution of theories and concepts that informed those efforts.

The first major efforts to reorganize the executive branch were instruments of Congress. In the late 1800s, both the Cockrell Committee and the Dockery-Cockrell Commission were created by, and reported back to, Congress. They were notable, Moe observes, not for "their substantive results, which were minimal, but [for] their attitudes towards the institutional Presidency and its relationship to the departments and agencies. Neither inquiry discussed the Presidential office nor what role that office might be expected to play in the improvement of the conduct of the executive branch." [6] The gradual shift from the supremacy of Congress to the view of the president as a true "chief executive" began in the very early 1900s.

The Commission on Department Methods
(the Keep Commission)

The formation of the Keep Commission in 1905 was the first move away from the existing orthodoxy. It was not a dramatic move; the Keep Commission did not, in fact, even publish a final report. The emphasis that its membership placed on internal management systems and on personnel administration, however, was a turning point that accurately reflected sentiments of the time. Van Riper writes that "the movement was toward concentration and centralization and the watchword was becoming 'economy and efficiency.'" [7] Theodore Roosevelt, who appointed the Keep Commission, also urged the Civil Service Commission to advocate and implement more modern and "businesslike" procedures in its activities related to federal personnel. [8] Arnold observes that "Roosevelt's action *assumed* that the

President ought to be responsible for the condition of administration and that he could plan and effect administrative reforms. The governmental context of national administration was turning upside down from its 19th century condition."[9]

The Commission on Economy and Efficiency
(the Taft Commission)

Even without a formal report, the Keep Commission had an impact by laying the groundwork for its almost immediate successor, the Commission on Economy and Efficiency (the Taft Commission). Authorized by Congress, but appointed by President William Howard Taft in 1910, the commission was the first to take a comprehensive look at the organization of the executive branch. It affirmed the central role of the president, primarily by examining budgetary processes and emphasizing the need for budgetary reforms. Characterizing the budget process as it existed in the early 1900s as a "more or less well digested mass of information," the commission observed that it was "submitted by agents of the Legislature to the Legislature for consideration of legislative committees to enable the Legislature both to originate and determine the policy which is to be carried out by the Executive during the coming budgetary period."[10]

The Taft Commission's recommendations included the creation of an executive budget process, a central bureau of the budget, and, within the Civil Service Commission, a bureau of efficiency. Again, however, the major impact of the commission's recommendations was in setting the stage for future action. The Bureau of Efficiency was established in 1916; the Bureau of the Budget was created in 1921. Both were firmly grounded in the economy and efficiency movements prevalent at the time. Both also saw their function as service to the president and to the more effective operation of the executive branch.[11]

The Joint Committee on Reorganization

The next major initiative occurred in 1920 when Congress created the Joint Committee on the Reorganization of the Administrative Branch of the Government. In 1921, the president was authorized one appointment to the committee. That appointment demonstrated the shifting balance of influence and power, for the single presidential appointment became the formative influence on the committee's report and recommendations. Although the presidential appointee was actually Walter Brown, a leading Republican and friend of the president, Secretary of Commerce Herbert Hoover played a major role. Arnold writes that "by far the largest influence in shaping the administration's reorganization program was Secretary of Commerce Hoover. He was the member of the administration who was most interested in reorganization."[12]

The committee's final report, informed as it was by what Arnold calls Hoover's "clear vision of administration,"[13] emphasized strengthening governmental performance, rather than achieving new economies, as Congress had initially intended. In addition, the emphasis on unity of purpose in government agencies and internal agency reorganizations to enhance the president's ability to direct clearly took another step toward centralization of the executive branch. The reforms were sold as benefiting Congress as well. Hoover testified before a congressional joint committee that reductions in expenditure were not as important as "the ability of Congress to handle expenditures with better comprehension and long view policies."[14]

The death of President Harding was also the death of strong support for the committee's recommendations. In what was already a pattern by 1924, the recommendations contained in the final report were not well received in Congress. The few that could be implemented without congressional action were implemented in Hoover's Department of Commerce, but only a small number of others were put in place. Nonetheless, the committee's strong commitment to the president as manager had an impact; Moe credits this contribution of the committee as important because it served as a "precursor of the Brownlow Committee in 1936."[15]

President's Committee on Administrative Management (the Brownlow Committee)

Although there was already a "commission tradition" and a clear trend toward strengthening the presidency prior to the establishment of the Brownlow Committee (the President's Committee on Administrative Management), that committee's activities and report have become landmarks. Rowland Egger described the Brownlow Committee's report as "the first comprehensive reconsideration of the Presidency and the President's control of the executive branch since 1787 ... [it] is probably the most important constitutional document of our time."[16]

The committee was created in the last year of Franklin Roosevelt's first term, a term characterized by strong presidential action and leadership but also by what Van Riper has called "one of the most spectacular resurgences of the spoils system in American history."[17] Many of the newly created New Deal agencies were exempt from the merit system; the president and his advisers followed a patronage system based on policy preference as well as partisanship in filling the many new positions available to them. This particular path to greater presidential control and direction led to a predictable public outcry: The League of Women Voters, the Junior Chamber of Commerce, a Commission of Inquiry on Public Personnel, and other groups demanded greater attention to merit. Roosevelt himself was becoming keenly aware of the need for good administration as well as better control.[18]

The president appointed the committee's three members—Louis Brownlow, Charles Merriam, and Luther Gulick—with the clear understanding that the report would be politically sensitive and that he would reject the recommendations if he and his advisers deemed them to be politically damaging. On accepting their appointments, the members of the Brownlow Committee assured the president that he would be "pleased" with their report. In appointing this carefully selected committee, President Roosevelt was "committing himself deliberately to a course of action, but one that he could control."[19] Given this rather suspect beginning, what was it about the Brownlow Report that caused it to be so significant?

The long-term impact of the Brownlow Committee reflects, at least in part, the clarity with which it defined the problem. The introduction to the report, for example, states:

> The efficiency of government rests upon two factors: the consent of the governed and good management.... Fortunately the foundations of effective management in public affairs, no less than private, are well known.... Stated in simple terms, these canons of efficiency require the establishment of a responsible and effective chief executive as the center of energy, direction and administrative management; the systematic organization of all activities in the hands of a qualified personnel under the direction of the chief executive; and to aid him in this, the establishment of appropriate management and staff agencies.[20]

This clearly directed approach, in combination with the presidential directive to provide him with a report that would be useful, produced a set of recommendations that were at once comprehensive and remarkably cohesive. Emmerich observes that, for the first time, the report enunciated a concept of "positive presidential management," as opposed to "sporadic supervision."[21] The recommendations included enlarging and strengthening the president's immediate staff, expanding and clarifying the merit system, making the Bureau of the Budget more directly accountable to the president, reorganizing the executive agencies into twelve major departments, and improving executive planning and fiscal management capabilities.[22]

As had other committees before it, the Brownlow Committee included a special appeal to Congress: "The preservation of the principle of full accountability of the Executive to Congress is an essential part of our republican system.... If the reorganization ... that we have recommended be carried out ... contradictory administrative policies which are so irritating to the Congress and so confounding to the people would be minimized. Thus, the accountability of the Executive Branch may be made sharp, distinct, and effective."[23]

Once again, Congress was not particularly interested. The Roosevelt imbroglio with Congress over the Supreme Court coincided with the release of the report; strengthening the president's powers was not high on the congressional agenda. In 1939, two years after the report was issued, Congress passed its own reorganization act. The president was given a limited reorganization authority and six presidential assistants. President Roosevelt used his new authority to create the Executive Office of the President and to move the Bureau of the Budget, the National Resources Planning Board, and the Central Statistical Board into it. Thus, another of the Brownlow recommendations was accomplished.

Given the broad sweep of recommendations in the report, however, it is fair to say that, even with these changes, the Brownlow Committee joined the ever growing list of committees whose primary impact would be in the future. That impact was two pronged. First, the Brownlow Committee greatly strengthened the case for a strong president with good central management controls. In doing so, it effectively altered the content of the reorganization debate. At the same time, its base assumption created a debate that remains with us today. Arnold writes of the Brownlow Committee that "its guise and language suggest an independent, neutral status of ultimate concern for good administration. *But the Brownlow Committee assumed that the interests of good administration and the President's interests were overlapping if not identical.*"[24] The validity of that assumption has been questioned in the intervening years; the questions remain critically significant today.

The First Hoover Commission

The first Hoover Commission was created by Congress in 1947. A combination of New Deal programs and the massive war effort had created a federal government with a large debt, overlapping agency structures and activities, and the major task of returning things to "normal." President Harry Truman requested and received new reorganization authority in 1945, but he, too, saw the need for the new commission. This reflected, in part, his belief that President Roosevelt had not been a strong manager and had left behind some serious managerial problems. It also resulted from Truman's lack of success in getting congressional approval for his reorganization plans.[25]

The first Hoover Commission was much more controversial than its predecessors had been. Many saw its formation as an attack on the New Deal, and the congressional appointment of Herbert Hoover as the first member did nothing to allay that fear. The need for a new look at the executive branch, however, was not in doubt. The foreword to the commercial publication of the first Hoover Report conveys some of the passion of the time: "the average citizen has become uncomfortably conscious of the vast size of our government. We all want and expect many services from the government, to be sure; but we are baffled by its magnitude, and frightened by its cost. Instinctively, we see a possible danger to democracy itself."[26]

Unlike the Brownlow Committee, which had operated under specific directives from President Roosevelt, the Hoover Commission was firmly under the direction of its chairman. Hoover's clear view of administration remained intact; it was necessary for some of his commissioners to move him beyond the views of the earlier joint commission to a view that more closely reflected the Brownlow Committee. Moe observes that "[Hoover's] primary goal had shifted from 'retrenchment' to the enhancement of the managerial authority of the President and his departmental secretaries. This shift in emphasis, begun before the election (of 1948), was merely reinforced by the results of the election."[27] The efficiency emphasis of the first Hoover Commission did not disappear, however; the final recommendations promised annual cash savings of over $3 billion.

The very broad scope of recommendations was made possible by the extensive use of task forces—there were twenty-four. Although Hoover played a very active part in selecting the chairs and members of the task forces, they operated rather independently of the commission. Moe observes, for example, that "there was no master plan guiding the mandate, operations, or timing of the reports of the several task forces."[28] He also notes that, again unlike the Brownlow Committee, few academics were associated with Hoover Commission activities; most of those involved were prominent business or professional leaders.

The Hoover Commission sent a series of nineteen reports to Congress. The final report was submitted in 1949. The reports included a total of 277 recommendations, which ranged from executive management to conduct of foreign affairs to federal-state relations. The commission recommended major changes in the organization of executive branch agencies and additional budgetary reforms. By virtually any measure, the first Hoover Commission was far more successful than any of its predecessors. Hoover estimated that 55 percent of the commission's recommendations were enacted.[29] Though other tabulations are more conservative, the record is impressive. What accounted for the difference in success?

There are at least three components to an answer. The first is that President Truman wholeheartedly embraced the recommendations. Despite its creation by Congress, Truman generally had confidence in the commission. Equally significant, he had come to trust Hoover. The president's commitment to moving as many of the recommendations as possible with the powers of his office contributed to a large part of the commission's success. Second, it is impossible to underestimate the influence of Herbert Hoover. His status as a former president, his understanding of the processes and problems of government, and his excellent political skills were all critical to the commission's success.

The third reason for the success is somewhat unusual. To support and lobby for the commission's recommendations, Hoover created the Citizens Committee for the Hoover Reports. With the motto "Better Government for a Better Price," the committee's activities were nationwide and very well publicized. Although, as Arnold notes, both the President and the Congress were wary of the committee, its influence was substantial and provided Hoover with great leverage as he continued to lobby for the recommendations of the first commission.[30]

The Second Hoover Commission

Encouraged by the success of the first Hoover Commission—or perhaps captured by it—Herbert Hoover lobbied both Congress and newly elected President Dwight D. Eisenhower for another commission in 1952. Eisenhower had already created an informal advisory committee to review previous reorganization reports and recommendations. Shortly after he assumed office, he created the President's Advisory Committee for Government Organization. Congress, however, had another interest: Reducing governmental expenditures and creating more efficient operations were high on its agenda. It created the second Hoover Commission in 1953. The second commission, also chaired by Hoover, was notable for the charge Congress gave it: This commission was directed to look into policy, as well as structure and organization. Moe describes the second commission in these terms: "The underlying premise, or as Hoover called it, the 'philosophy of the Commission,' was clearly that the Federal Government had grown too large and interventionist and that this trend needed to be reversed."[31]

The second Hoover Commission did not operate in the widely supportive environment of the first. Relations between Herbert Hoover and President Eisenhower were prickly. Even some commission members were critical of the scope of inquiry the commission assumed. The task force format was again adopted, but commission members did not serve on them. Again, there was considerable autonomy in the task force operation. The commission produced a total of twenty reports for Congress. The reports contained more than 300 recommendations. It is important to note, however, that President Eisenhower's Advisory Committee also continued to operate during this time. The reorganization activities undertaken by the president were informed by that group, rather than by the analysis or concerns of the second Hoover Commission.

There is a strong consensus among analysts that the second commission did not approach the first in terms of overall effectiveness. Part of the reason has been alluded to: the prickly relationship between the former president and the current president created suspicion on both sides. In addition, Hoover "invested his ego" in the second commission.[32] He was adamant that the Eisenhower administration give the reports top priority and essentially threatened the president with taking the case "to the people" (i.e., to the still operational Citizens Committee) if the administration did not respond adequately. Eisenhower's response was one of systematic analysis, rather than instant support; Congress approached implementing the recommendations with limited enthusiasm. Hoover continued to press for action, but to modest avail. Arnold describes the outcome in these terms: "The tense dance between the partisans of the Hoover Commission and the administration did not end in a neat climax; over time it simply ran down to a stop." [33]

Despite the failure to match the success of the first Hoover Commission, the second had its own achievements. Many of its more technical recommendations were, in fact, adopted.[34] In some areas, such as personnel and civil service, the second commission proposed substantial changes and laid the groundwork for future reform. The second Hoover Commission, for example, was the first to raise the issue of the relationship between political appointees and career civil servants. Similarly, it proposed, and argued strongly for, a cadre of top career managers with special status and recognition. The second commission also returned to the issue of better pay for the federal civil service. Its achievements, therefore, were very much in line with those of the commissions that had preceded Hoover I. Only in direct relation to the first Hoover Commission could the second be considered a failure.

The Task Force on Government Organization

Although President John F. Kennedy appointed an advisory committee on administration early in his presidency, the committee never met. The appointment of the next formal advisory group, the Task Force on Government Organization, occurred early in Lyndon Johnson's term. The task force, chaired by Don K. Price of Harvard, undertook a macro examination of the executive branch. High on its list of priorities was what one team of analysts labeled "protecting the president's hierarchical position." [35] The task force recommended major restructuring of cabinet departments. In line with the president's predilection for the rational planning systems being used at the Department of Defense, the Price task force recommended that greater analytical capabilities be built into the entire executive branch.[36] The task force did not have good access to the president, however; when its report was issued it "was sent to the President through his staff, but the indication is that it was given only cursory treatment at that level." [37]

In 1966, President Johnson tried again. This time, the task force was chaired by Ben Heineman, a private-sector executive. This task force had better access to the president, as well as a larger and more independent staff. The tasks faced by this group included sorting out the many programs and agencies that had sprung up around the War on Poverty and the Great

Society. In addition, the task force returned to the issue of strengthening presidential management capacity. Recommendations included reorganizing the Bureau of the Budget to improve program coordination and evaluation; the organization of departments by broad purpose and function, rather than the proliferation of narrow-purpose agencies; and a special executive staff for program coordination and review. This task force had the President's ear, and its earliest recommendations were acted on quickly. Most of the report, however, was issued in 1967. The President's energy and attention were by then riveted on Vietnam. The continuing work of reorganization would have to be carried on by the next president. And it was.

In Richard Nixon, the United States had a president who believed firmly that governmental effectiveness was "principally a matter of machinery."[38] Moreover, he departed from previous presidents in the extent to which he was willing to work with the existing "machinery." He came to office convinced that change was necessary and that it should occur as quickly as possible. It is significant to note that the objective of this change was better government, but better government of a particular kind: "President Nixon argued that the organizational principles he advocated had been 'endorsed' by the Brownlow and Hoover Commissions, but the underlying philosophy has its roots in Max Weber's ideas about bureaucracy and power relationships."[39] For President Nixon, then, improved executive management dealt not only with coordination and management but with control. His reorganization strategy was mapped out by a group of private-sector executives chaired by Roy Ash, president of Litton Industries.

A Turning Point: The Advisory Council on Executive Organization (the Ash Council)

The Ash Council was created in 1969. When announcing its creation, President Nixon stated that it would have direct and consistent access to him; the council was specifically directed to "examine the executive branch as a whole."[40] The council operated with a staff of about forty (the number fluctuated over its life span) and six "working groups." The council's activities also included task forces within many agencies and some interagency groups. Because the membership of these groups understood the fine points of government programs and structure, their primary task was to identify technical targets for improvement. Elimination of unnecessary regulations and guidelines, for example, was one objective.

For the council staff, there was a clear priority. Arnold writes that "from the beginning one topic was understood to be first on the agenda: the organization of the Executive Office for Management."[41] One of the first recommendations of the council was acted on almost immediately. In 1970, President Nixon submitted Reorganization Plan No. 2 to Congress.

That plan created the Office of Management and Budget to replace the Bureau of the Budget. Hart describes the major purpose of the new organization as ensuring "greatly improved executive branch responsiveness to presidential priorities."[42] One means of doing so was the placement of political appointees in top positions in the new organization. The increased reliance on political executives to supplement structural change was described by one of those executives, Richard Nathan, in *The Plot That Failed* and *The Administrative Presidency*.[43] While arguing that it is well within the rights of the president to utilize political appointees to the maximum extent possible, Nathan also notes that the need to do so is predicated on a fundamental distrust of the career civil service. This distrust was to become an inextricable part of Nixon management strategy. Of equal, or perhaps greater, significance, it was to become part of his heritage to future presidents.[44]

The Ash Council made far-reaching recommendations to the president. In the Executive Office, it recommended the creation of the Domestic Council, whose purpose would be to bring cabinet members and other top advisers concerned with domestic policies together in one high-level group. Since that group was located in the Executive Office and headed by a political executive, the structure gave the president much closer control over policy discussions and consideration of policy options.

The council also recommended sweeping reorganization of the agencies in the executive branch into four Super Departments: Natural Resources, Economic Affairs, Human Resources, and Community Development. In his 1971 State of the Union message, Nixon described the proposed reorganization in these terms: "I shall ask to change the framework of government itself—to reform the entire structure of American government."[45] The recommendations were accompanied by programmatic changes. To some extent, the block-grant programs created in the Nixon presidency accomplished programmatically what the reorganization hoped to accomplish structurally: They combined small, single-purpose categorical grants into broad, flexible-funding authorities. In combination, the Super Departments and the block-grant strategy *would* have dramatically altered the operation of the federal government. Once again, however, Congress was not inclined to approve a plan developed by the executive for his own purposes. Once again, also, larger events intervened. Watergate cut short the Nixon presidency, his efforts at reform, and—temporarily—the shift in power and authority to the president from Congress.

Arnold's commentary on the relationship between Nixon's excesses and the "managerial presidency" is important. He writes: "Nixon's ambitions for reorganization were not idiosyncratic; they were characteristic of the modern presidency.... The failure of reorganization's ambitions for control in the Nixon administration was not caused by the character flaws of the president; it was a failure of reorganization's ambitions per se. Reorganization's ideals as they had evolved by the early 1970s were unimplementable within the American system."[46] This perspective, shared by many analysts, is as important for its insightfulness as for its general exclusion from the efforts of the next two presidents to gain control of the executive branch.

President's Reorganization Project

Although Jimmy Carter came to Washington at a time of great skepticism about changing government, he was, by his very nature, a reformer. He had campaigned hard on the promise of cleaning up Washington and applying the lessons he had learned as governor of Georgia to the federal government. He had made a distinctly technical issue—civil service reform —one of the cornerstones of his campaign promises. Accordingly, he appointed the President's Reorganization Project very shortly after assuming office. It was housed in the Office of Management and Budget, but Carter himself was chair of the executive committee. With a budget of about $2 million, the Reorganization Project focused on reducing the number of government agencies, structural reform, budgetary reform, and personnel reform. Most of these tasks were specifically assigned by Carter. The most comprehensive reforms were targeted for the career civil service and the system that supported it.

To pursue the civil service reform design, Carter created the Personnel Management Project (PMP). Technically subservient to the Reorganization Project, the PMP was housed in the Civil Service Commission. The PMP operated with a network of nine task forces, staffed by about 120 people. The staff members of the task forces were largely career civil servants; career expertise and experience was further solicited through the Assistant Secretaries Advisory Group. The mandate was to propose comprehensive reforms; both Carter and the director of the Civil Service Commission, Alan Campbell, promised personal assistance in selling the reform to Congress.

The reform that emerged from this process was the comprehensive package that Carter had requested. Its very comprehensiveness ensured some internal tensions; among the most important were those between enhanced presidential control and greater protection of the merit system. The Civil Service Reform Act proposed, for example, to create the Senior Executive Service (SES). The SES would be an elite cadre of talented senior generalists whose management skills could be used wherever they were most necessary. The SES would also be much more amenable to political control because of performance evaluation, bonus, and mobility provisions in the act.

Carter's personnel reforms combined both structural and procedural changes. Campbell noted ten years later, "We did believe, and I still believe, that what we were trying to do would serve the interest of whoever was in power; and that there would be advantage taken of it in positive ways regardless of what happened on the political side."[47] The proposed reform was sent to Carter within four months of the creation of the PMP. The White House sent the package to Congress in March 1978. It was passed, with very few revisions, in October of that year.

Arnold's analysis of the Civil Service Reform Act notes its debt to the reform commission tradition: "The Brownlow Committee and both Hoover Commissions had called for major changes.... It was precisely the administration's ability to rely on those predecessors through the memory built into the experienced leadership of the Personnel Management Project that allowed Carter to plan a reform package within four months and then fight it successfully through Congress. It was the plan's virtue that its fundamental recommendations were not novel."[48]

Other Carter reorganization efforts were notably less successful. Budgetary reforms were short lived; Carter was successful in creating two new departments—Energy and Education—but was unsuccessful in reorganizing those that already existed. With the exception of civil service reform, the Carter reorganization effort received low marks from most observers. One, in fact, characterized it as "activity without purpose ... efficiency in search of popularity."[49] Further, Carter was not even able to enjoy the fruits of the civil service reform. The election of Ronald Reagan in 1980 introduced a different view of government; that view reemphasized the central role of presidential control and power. With few exceptions (e.g., the Senior Executive Service), President Reagan considered the Carter reforms toward that end trivial.

President's Private-Sector Survey on Cost Control (the Grace Commission)

Ronald Reagan's presidential campaign was waged against the federal government. In his first inaugural address he stated, "Government is not the solution to the problem. Government *is* the problem." Reagan's first term was an exercise in continuing the attack. As had presidents before him, but in much stronger terms, Reagan saw the need to control the career bureaucracy if he was effectively to reduce governmental involvement and activity. Reagan had a clearly defined strategy of centralized appointments, decision making, and budgeting. [50] The overall purpose, however, was to reduce the size and activity of government. As had other presidents before him, he turned to a blue-ribbon panel to assist and guide his efforts.

The President's Private-Sector Survey on Cost Control (PPSSCC) was created in 1981, but did not actually begin operations until 1982. The PPSSCC, more commonly called the Grace Commission after its chairman,

J. Peter Grace, eschewed broad reorganization in favor of straight cost cutting. Using about 2,000 corporate volunteers and many career civil servants detailed to provide it with information, the Grace Commission searched throughout government for "waste, fraud and abuse." In its report delivered to President Reagan in 1984, the commission said that it had identified ways of saving over $90 billion in personnel costs alone (over a three-year period). The title of the report, *War on Waste*, sums up both the basic assumptions and the recommendations in the report. Peter Grace, writing shortly after the report was issued, noted, "I have just spent the better part of two years as chairman of a commission looking into ineffiency and abuse ... in the Federal government. I am absolutely appalled at what we found."[51]

Although earlier commissions had stressed efficiency in government, among other things, the Grace Commission emphasized *only* efficiency. It recommended transferring many functions to the private sector, contracting-out whenever possible, reducing federal employee benefits and pay, and reducing the total number of federal employees. It included a number of agency-specific cost-cutting measures in its final report. The report was greeted with some skepticism by Congress, whose General Accounting Office immediately disputed the savings estimates claimed by the Grace Commission. President Reagan and the Office of Mangement and Budget, however, praised the report and implemented some of the recommendations that did not require congressional action. In addition, Reagan's "Reform '88," a government-wide efficiency program headed by OMB, relied on some of the Grace Commission findings in its initial activities.

The Grace Commission had another impact as well. Its flat-out attack on the career bureaucracy and government programs seemed excessive to many, who argued that such an attack did a serious disservice to the importance of government and governance. The Grace Commission was further questioned for its simplistic analysis of the problem. There was, for example, no case in which the federal government was described as different from the private sector. The Ash Council had been an earlier turning point in advocating presidential control of the bureaucracy; the Grace Commission became a turning point for its complete disdain for the bureaucracy and for government in general.

The National Commission on the Public Service
(the Volcker Commission)
The National Commission on the Public Service was a different kind of blue-ribbon panel. It was not appointed by either the president or Congress; indeed, it was formed because of a fear among its membership that neither the president nor Congress would address what was perceived to be a "quiet crisis" in the public service. That crisis was directly related to the

antigovernment bureaucrat bashing that had come to characterize presidential campaigns and rhetoric. It was related, too, to inadequate pay for many top career managers, to low morale, and to the politicization of the public service that had grown out of presidential efforts at increased control.

The National Commission on the Public Service was chaired by Paul Volcker, the former chairman of the Federal Reserve Board. Its membership included a former president, Gerald Ford, a former vice-president, Walter Mondale, the presidents of Harvard, Stanford, and New York University, Senator Charles Robb, and two former senators, Charles Mathias and Edmund Muskie. It also included members with long and distinguished public-service careers, such as Elliot Richardson, Rocco Siciliano, and Elmer Staats. It included representatives from the private sector, from Common Cause, and from organized labor. It was, in short, the most widely representative commission in that long tradition. The Volcker Commission was funded by private foundations. It is notable not only for the fine record of public service that its members represented but for its intention to act as *external* adviser to both the president and Congress, while officially representing neither one. It is notable as well for its efforts to restore some balance to presidential efforts at increased management and control. There was a clear sense that the "managerial presidency" and attacks on government had gone too far and that the quality of government suffered as a result.

Although the Volcker Commission was unusual in many ways, it was not the first such group to address the issue of presidential management and power. In 1980, for example, the National Academy of Public Administration created the Price-Siciliano Panel to examine the same problem. It, too, had distinguished leadership and membership; it also noted the cost of ever increasing centralization of power in the Executive Office. The report emphasized that while the managerial needs of the president were obvious, a "reliable base of nonpartisan, unbiased advice" was fundamental to effective political management and to "the presidency as a continuing institution of government."[52] The emphasis in both the Price-Siciliano report and that of the Volcker Commission was not on the broader issue of structural reorganization. It was on the more limited, but more fundamental, issue of the quality of the public service and the relationship between effective government and that service.

The Volcker Commission was created in 1987. It formed five task forces to examine the various dimensions of the "quiet crisis."[53] Each task force was chaired by a member of the commission and staffed by a part-time project director. Task force reports were made to the full commission; the final report, *Leadership for America,* did not contain all the recommendations from the task forces. The Volcker Commission recommendations echoed many of those of previous commissions and advisory groups. In the Brownlow and Hoover tradition, it recommended pay increases for some members of the career civil service. As had the Hoover Commissions and the Personnel Management Project, it recommended decentralization of managerial and personnel authority. Again like the Brownlow Committee and the Hoover Commissions, it advocated more attention to the education and training of career civil servants. The Volcker Commission broke new ground in recommending that the number of political appointments available to the president be fixed at 2,000, approximately 1,000 less than the 1988 total. The commission explicitly urged the president to abandon bureaucrat-bashing rhetoric and to speak instead of the value of the public service. The commission recommended formation of a special scholarship program to encourage able young people to pursue a public-service career.

How effective was this group of outsiders, distinguished though they were, in attracting attention to the commission's recommendations? The report was presented to President George Bush in March 1989. Shortly thereafter, the president (after noting how difficult it was to attract political appointees at current federal pay levels) forwarded legislation to Congress that requested a two-stage 25 percent pay increase for judges and top federal executives. After a major pay-raise debacle in Congress in early 1989, a new bill was passed in November 1989. The president delivered a strongly supportive address to members of the Senior Executive Service and spoke of the larger public service in laudatory terms. Both houses of Congress held hearings within six months of the report's release, and work was begun on the proposed scholarship program. Though an overall evaluation of its impact must be longer term, there is no doubt that the Volcker Commission was successful in placing the quiet crisis on both the presidential and congressional agenda. By doing so, it redirected the debate that has marched inexorably through commissions for the last fifty years: Effective management cannot be viewed only in terms of presidential power and control; it also must consider the career bureaucracy and the capabilities of its personnel.

Conclusion: What Difference Do Commissions Make?

The preceding review of commissions raises an inevitable question: If they are even moderately successful, why are there so many of them? There is an additional question: What is the appropriate measure of success? There are a number of possible answers to consider; perhaps all are partially true. Herbert Kaufman, for example, has described American governmental reform efforts as cyclical—a constant movement between the values of neutral competence, political responsiveness, and effectiveness.[54] Certainly the varying impact and legacy of the commissions mirror that cycle in some respects. Yet it is not possible to examine their history without becoming keenly aware of the constant quest for efficiency. Every commission to the time of the Brownlow Committee worked with efficiency as the primary value. The constant movement toward centralizing power in the presidency is efficiency in another guise—good management.

Despite its surface consistency, the ongoing quest for efficiency partially explains the large number of commissions because the president and Congress have generally defined "efficiency" in different ways. For presidents, the term has most often been equated with better management and increased authority in the Executive Office. For Congress, efficiency most often translates into reducing costs and streamlining government activities. As these two definitions jockey for position, the utility of having a blue-ribbon panel proclaim one to be correct becomes clear. Further, because definitions and priorities can shift with each major election, a cyclical need for new assessments is built into the system.

This cyclical characteristic has contributed to the development of two basic kinds of commissions. The first can be labeled "transformational." In these cases, a new definition of the proper balance of power between the chief executive and the legislature is still evolving. The commission's findings serve to clarify the status or stage of the evolution, as well as the need for its continuation. Certainly every commission to the time of Brownlow falls into the transformational category. History may determine that the Volcker Commission served this function by identifying the need for a new examination of the balance.

The second major kind of commission is the "ratifying" commission. These commissions have been created by presidents sure of where they wanted to go, but seeking wider justification of their chosen path. Brownlow falls into that category, as do both the Ash Council and the Grace Commission. In these cases, commissions provided specific components for an already determined presidential strategy. The first Hoover Commission probably falls into this category, but it is somewhat unusual because both the president and Congress agreed that a redirection was necessary.

Differing purposes have also created different measures and views of success.[55] For transformational commissions, success is nebulous and long term. Their impact is in shaping ideas and redefining the constitutional balance between the executive and the legislature. The gradual transformation of thought in the early part of this century, for example, culminated naturally in the statements of the Brownlow Committee: "canons of efficiency require the establishment of a responsible and effective chief executive as the center of energy, direction and administrative management...."[56] If the Brownlow Committee Report is viewed as an "important constitutional document," the earlier commissions, which created the foundation for Brownlow's success, must also be viewed as successful.[57]

One measure of ratifying commissions' success is the number of recommendations acted on by the president and/or the legislature. According to this measure, Hoover I is the most successful commission examined here. But that indicator is deceptively simple. The legislative record of the Brownlow recommendations, for example, is not extensive; the impact of the few recommendations that were adopted, however, was very significant. Further, Brownlow's imprimatur on the managerial presidency has been profoundly important. The experience of the Ash Council is somewhat similar. While many of the structural reorganization recommendations were not enacted, the creation of the Office of Management and Budget was very important.

The reality of absolute success or failure, then, is difficult to discern in the executive branch commissions examined here. Success or failure is a relative term and often very much in the eye of the beholder. By most measures, however, very few of the commissions were outright failures: Their findings shaped an important debate, placed items on the legislative agenda (however long term), and raised issues that the political actors to whom they reported could not. In the ever changing political environment in which these commissions operate, their very presence created a different level of debate. Even President Reagan's Grace Commission, which comes closest to falling into the failure category, had some impact. Debates about the applicability of private-sector measures to government were widespread; the operating assumption that "government was the problem" was seriously challenged. Reform '88, the major institutional legacy of the Grace Commission, began new efficiency initiatives throughout government.

Looking to the Future
The other chapters in this book attest to the continuing need to pursue effective management in government. Despite the difficulties of assessing success or failure outlined above, will the commission tradition continue to be a part of that effort? There are some signs that it may not. President Bush's failure to create the National Commission on Executive Organization, authorized by the bill creating the Veterans Department in 1989, for example, could be viewed as disillusionment with the practice. Moe writes, for example, that "President George Bush could divine no persuasive reason why he should initiate a study of either the executive branch or his Executive Office from an organizational perspective."[58] Moe concludes that as presidents and commissions have moved away from concerns with improved management and toward concerns with presidential power and control, guiding principles have been lost: "Presidential management is seen as a derivative of policy choices and has little intrinsic value apart from these choices. There are no organizational principles worth pursuing apart from

those that assist in the realization of a policy objective."[59] As a result, the potential for effective commission activity is attenuated.

Quite clearly, efforts at reform in the past twenty years *have* moved from concerns with effective management and accountability to an emphasis on control. Further, that emphasis has been guided by principles more clearly anchored in the private sector than in the public administrative tradition. Is Kaufman's pendulum now "stuck"? Will the president continue to pursue presidential power at the expense of better management? Probably not. Bush's failure to name the new commission is not unusual in the long tradition we have analyzed. In fact, the harmony between Harry Truman and the first Hoover Commission stands out as an unusual example of presidential and congressional cooperation. Despite the fact that a Democrat was succeeding a Democrat in the White House, the postwar years were an exceptional time. Both President Truman and Congress understood that. But 1989 was not such a time.

An additional difference in 1989 was the presence of the Volcker Commission. Although the reforms Volcker espoused were not high on the priority list of either the president or Congress, both understood that the commission could serve their purpose, even though it was not their creature. Responses to the Volcker recommendations in the first year suggest very strongly that this new kind of commission can have much the same impact as earlier transformational commissions: Some recommendations will become law (pay is the leading example), while others will become part of the long-term agenda. The terms of the debate will be altered, and the position of the pendulum will be examined. The controversial nature of some recommendations (reduction of political appointees is the leading example) ensures that they will be reexamined in the future.

In short, the reform commission tradition is likely to continue. The creative tension built into the American political system by the founding fathers has only been heightened by the complexity and scope of contemporary government. Constrained resources, dramatically different demographic patterns, and a new emphasis on the ability of the American federal government to compete effectively in the international arena, point to a very real need to render government more effective and efficient. As they have in the past, blue-ribbon panels will be part of the search for solutions. They are as American as apple pie.

Notes

1. Donald F. Kettl, testimony before the Subcommittee on Human Resources, Committee on Post Office and Civil Service, U.S. House of Representatives, Washington, D.C., 13 June 1989, 2.

2. Ronald C. Moe, *The Hoover Commissions Revisited* (Boulder, Colo.: Westview Press, 1982), 128. See also chap. 2.

3. Ibid., 7–12.

4. For a fuller discussion, see Peri E. Arnold, *Making the Managerial Presidency* (Princeton: Princeton University Press, 1986).

5. Herbert E. Emmerich, *Essays on Federal Reorganization* (University, Ala.: University of Alabama Press, 1950), 1–2.

6. Moe, *Hoover Commissions*, 8.

7. Paul P. Van Riper, *History of the United States Civil Service* (Evanston, Ill.: Row, Peterson, 1958), 191.

8. Ibid., 194–98.

9. Arnold, *Managerial Presidency*, 20. Italics added.

10. "Report of the (Taft) Commission on Economy and Efficiency: The Need for a National Budget," in *Basic Documents of American Public Administration, 1776–1950*, ed. Frederick C. Mosher (New York: Holmes and Meier, 1976), 76–81.

11. See, for example, the statement of General Charles Dawes, first director of the Bureau of the Budget, in *The Administrative Process and Democratic Theory*, ed. Louis C. Gawthrop (Boston: Houghton Mifflin, 1970).

12. Arnold, *Managerial Presidency*, 64.

13. Ibid., 65.

14. Ibid., 78.

15. Moe, *Hoover Commissions*, 10.

16. Rowland Egger, "The Period of Crisis: 1933 to 1945," in *American Public Administration: Past, Present and Future*, ed. Frederick C. Mosher (University, Ala.: University of Alabama Press, 1975), 71.

17. Van Riper, *History of Civil Service*, 315.

18. Ibid., 333–36.

19. Barry Karl, *Executive Reorganization and Reform in the New Deal* (Chicago: University of Chicago Press, 1963), 206.

20. "Report of the President's Committee on Administrative Management (The Brownlow Committee)," in Mosher, *Basic Documents*, 113–14.

21. Emmerich, *Federal Reorganization*, 80.

22. See "Report of the Brownlow Committee," in Mosher, *Basic Documents*, 116–31.

23. Ibid., 131–32.

24. Arnold, *Managerial Presidency*, 117. Italics added.

25. For excellent discussions, see ibid., chap. 5; and Moe, *Hoover Commissions*, chap. 2.

26. Preface to *The Hoover Commission Report* (New York: McGraw-Hill, 1949), vi.

27. Moe, *Hoover Commissions*, 27.

28. Ibid., 29.

29. Arnold, *Managerial Presidency*, 143.

30. Ibid., 154–59.

31. Moe, *Hoover Commissions*, 85.

32. Arnold, *Managerial Presidency*, 192.

33. Ibid., 200.

34. Ibid., 200–203.

35. See Emmette S. Redford and Marlan Blissett, *Organizing the Executive Branch: The Johnson Presidency* (Chicago: University of Chicago Press, 1981), chap. 7.

36. Arnold, *Managerial Presidency*, 240–43.

37. Ibid., 24.

38. Harold Seidman and Robert Gilmour, *Politics, Position, and Power*, 4th ed. (New York: Oxford University Press, 1986), 98.

39. Ibid., 99.

40. Arnold, *Managerial Presidency*, 277.

41. Ibid., 280.

42. John Hart, *The Presidential Branch* (New York: Pergamon Press, 1987), 79.

43. Richard Nathan, *The Administrative Presidency* (New York: Wiley, 1983).

44. Patricia W. Ingraham, "Building Bridges or Burning Them? The President, the Appointees and the Bureaucracy," *Public Administration Review*, September/October 1987, 425–35.

45. Richard M. Nixon, "State of the Union Message," *Public Papers of President Richard Nixon*, 51.

46. Arnold, *Managerial Presidency*, 302.

47. Alan Campbell, in "Forum on the Design of the Civil Service Act of 1978," U.S. Senate Subcommittee on Government Operations, Washington, D.C., March 1988, 35.

48. Arnold, *Managerial Presidency*, 334–35.

49. Ibid., 336.

50. See Seidman and Gilmour, *Politics, Position, Power*, chap. 6.

51. J. Peter Grace, *Burning Money* (New York: Macmillan, 1984), 5.

52. Hart, *Presidential Branch*, 194.

53. For a full discussion of the "quiet crisis," see Charles H. Levine and Rosslyn Kleeman, "The Federal Civil Service at the Crossroads," chap. 10 of this volume.

54. Herbert Kaufman, "Emerging Conflicts in the Doctrines of Public Administration," *American Political Science Review* 50 (December 1956): 1057–73.

55. I am grateful to Donald Kettl for very useful comments and discussion regarding comparative success or failure of blue-ribbon commissions.

56. "Report of the President's Committee on Administrative Management."

57. Egger, "Period of Crisis."

58. Ronald C. Moe, "Traditional Organizational Principles and the Managerial Presidency: From Phoenix to Ashes," *Public Administration Review*, March/April 1990, 129.

59. Ibid., 136.

10

The Quiet Crisis in the American Public Service

Charles H. Levine and Rosslyn S. Kleeman

It is obvious to many informed observers that the federal civil service is entering a new era. But how long it will last, what shape it will eventually take, and how well the federal workforce and government performance will fare in the future are surrounded by great uncertainty. Much of this uncertainty can be attributed to a lack of consensus among the policy makers responsible for shaping the size, composition, role, responsibilities, and working conditions of the civil service. Perhaps at no time since World War II has consensus seemed so far away. Old notions about how to organize and staff the government's workforce have given way under the weight of harsh criticism. Most new ideas about how to "fix" the civil service have proven politically or economically unfeasible or, like the Civil Service Reform Act (CSRA) of 1978, far more problematic than their proponents ever envisaged.[1] The result is a policy stalemate between Congress and the White House in which no one is developing a comprehensive and systematic approach to organizing and staffing the federal workforce. This, in turn, is helping to produce a civil service that many believe is unable to attract, retain, and appropriately deploy people with the skills and motivation needed for the tasks government faces now and in the next century.[2]

Indeed, the situation may be sufficiently dire that the civil service is experiencing what amounts to a "quiet crisis" that, if left unattended, could produce major breakdowns in government performance in the future.[3]

This situation suggests several questions: (1) What is the state of the civil service today? (2) Is its capacity in fact deteriorating relative to its tasks? (3) What ideas have been proposed for better aligning the federal government's workforce with its future requirements? (4) What is the likely feasibility and potential effectiveness of these ideas? And (5) given these feasibilities, what will be the likely shape of the civil service in the year 2000? These questions are not easily or conclusively answered, but they are at the core of the current debate over civil service policy.

This chapter addresses these questions by framing the issues involved and presenting available evidence to clarify trends and developments in federal workforce composition and personnel management policy. The picture is a complicated one. The data do not permit definitive answers to any of the questions, and people of different political persuasions may interpret "the facts" differently. Nevertheless, some evidence is sufficiently clear, and its implications potentially important enough, to merit serious scrutiny.

Background

The combined federal workforce numbered around 6 million employees in 1991: The uniformed armed services employed 1.9 million, the Postal Service around 811,000, the legislative and judicial branches about 65,000, and the executive branch about 3.1 million. Aside from the military and the Postal Service, by far the largest employer was the Department of Defense (DOD) with 1.0 million civilian employees. The next-largest employers were the Department of Veterans Affairs with 256,000; the Department of Health and Human Services (HHS) with 130,000, half of whom were in the Social Security Administration (SSA); the Department of the Treasury with 171,000; the Department of Agriculture with 130,000; the Department of the Interior with 81,000; the Department of Justice with 90,500; and the Department of Transportation with 69,000. Other employers with over 20,000 workers were the Departments of State and Commerce, the General Services Administration (GSA), the National Aeronautics and Space Administration (NASA), and the Tennessee Valley Authority (TVA) (see table 10.1).[4]

Of the federal government's 3.1 million executive-branch civilian employees, approximately 369,000 were under the Federal Wage System (FWS), which covers blue-collar occupations; about 38,000 were under the Veterans' Health Administration; and about 14,000 were in the Foreign Service. Most of the remainder, in professional, administrative, technical, and clerical (PATC) occupations, came under the General Schedule (GS) pay and classification system.[5]

In the aggregate, the federal workforce is obviously huge, but it is also socially and occupationally diverse, and its composition is steadily changing. The racial and gender composition of the workforce is perhaps one of the most noticeable social changes. For example, in 1965, blacks constituted 13 percent of the federal civilian workforce and women 34 percent. Almost all these people were clustered into lower-level clerical and non-professional jobs. By 1985, in contrast, minorities constituted 26 percent of the civil service and women 41 percent. By 1990, the minorities' share was 27 percent while the women's was 43 percent. Furthermore, by 1985, blacks occupied 5 percent of positions at the GS-GM-13 rank or above, and

TABLE 10.1
FEDERAL CIVILIAN EMPLOYMENT

	January 1986	July 1991
Executive Office of the President	1,606	1,828
Executive Departments	1,790,612	2,074,403
1. Department of Agriculture	108,705	130,438
2. Department of Commerce	35,238	38,121
3. Department of Defense	1,099,261	1,021,810
Other Defense Activities	94,660	99,617
Department of the Air Force	263,868	228,259
Department of the Army	392,880	367,764
Department of the Navy	347,553	326,170
4. Department of Education	4,805	5,153
5. Department of Energy	16,746	19,655
6. Department of Health and Human Services	133,855	130,668
7. Department of Housing and Urban Development	12,243	14,514
8. Department of the Interior	72,854	81,722
9. Department of Justice	65,005	90,589
10. Department of Labor	19,056	18,194
11. Department of State	25,139	25,736
12. Department of Transportation	62,175	69,273
13. Department of the Treasury	135,830	171,709
14. Department of Veterans Affairs	*a*	256,821

SOURCE: OPM Federal Civilian Workforce Statistics, Employment and Trends as of January 1986 and July 1991.

a. Formerly the Veterans Administration; became an executive department in 1989; see item no. 61.

	January 1986	July 1991
Independent Agencies	1,170,472	989,787
1. ACTION	507	430
2. Administrative Conference of the U.S.	23	23
3. Advisory Committee on Intergovernmental Relations	37	19
4. American Battle Monuments Commission	404	401
5. Appalachian Regional Council	7	9
6. Board for International Broadcasting	18	19
7. Commission of Fine Arts	7	7
8. Commodity Futures Trading Commission	404	614
9. Consumer Product Safety Commission	567	552
10. Delaware River Basin Commission	2	2
11. Environmental Protection Agency	13,169	18,452
12. Equal Employment Opportunity Commission	3,159	2,885
13. Export-Import Bank of the U.S.	342	363
14. Farm Credit Administration	281	530
15. Federal Communications Commission	1,884	1,852
16. Federal Deposit Insurance Corp.	7,125	21,939[b]
17. Federal Election Commission	236	261
18. Federal Emergency Management Agency	2,356	3,222
19. Federal Home Loan Bank Board	675	[c]
20. Federal Labor Relations Authority	278	242
21. Federal Maritime Commission	213	224
22. Federal Mediation and Conciliation Service	337	312
23. Federal Mine Safety and Health Review Commission	51	51
24. Federal Reserve System (Board of Governors)	1,532	1,569

b. Now includes employees of Resolution Trust Corporation.
c. Now the Office of Thrift Supervision.

TABLE 10.1 — *Continued*

	January 1986	July 1991
25. Federal Trade Commission	1,340	1,013
26. General Service Administration	25,725	21,174
27. Inter-American Foundation	63	74
28. International Development Cooperation Agency	4,860[d]	4,670[e]
29. Interstate Commerce Commission	827	623
30. Merit Systems Protection Board	420	315
31. National Aeronautics and Space Administration	22,122	26,314
32. National Archives and Records Administration	3,229	3,267
33. National Capital Planning Commission	50	44
34. National Credit Union Administration	588	939
35. National Foundation on the Arts and Humanities	582	591
36. National Labor Relations Board	2,526	2,119
37. National Mediation Board	57	54
38. National Science Foundation	1,675	1,265
39. National Transportation Safety Board	332	375
40. Nuclear Regulatory Commission	3,512	3,527
41. Occupational Safety and Health Review Commission	72	76
42. Office of Government Ethics	[f]	50
43. Office of Personnel Management	6,376	6,626
44. Office of Special Counsel	[g]	91

d. Includes AID (Agency for International Development).
e. Includes Overseas Private Investment Corporation, AID.
f. Formerly part of the Office of Personnel Management.
g. Formerly part of the Merit Systems Protection Board.

	January 1986	July 1991
45. Overseas Private Investment Corporation	153	h
46. Panama Canal Commission	8,459	9,020
47. Peace Corps	1,092	1,274
48. Pennsylvania Ave. Development Corp.	32	32
49. Postal Rate Commission	59	58
50. Railroad Retirement Board	1,621	1,794
51. Securities and Exchange Commission	1,915	2,411
52. Selective Service System	335	283
53. Small Business Administration	5,283	4,979
54. Susquehanna River Basin Commission	2	2
55. Tennessee Valley Authority	29,490	22,937
56. U.S. Arms Control and Disarmament Agency	263	216
57. U.S. Commission on Civil Rights	235	235
58. U.S. Information Agency	8,881	8,205
59. U.S. International Trade Commission	475	508
60. U.S. Postal Service	760,047	810,648
61. Veterans Administration	244,160	
Total, executive branch	2,962,690[i]	3,066,018
Total, legislative branch	38,439[j]	40,185
Total, judicial branch	18,280	24,675
Total, all branches	3,019,409	3,130,878

h. Now part of the International Development Cooperation Agency.

i. Does not include the Central Intelligence Agency, National Security Agency, Defense Intelligence Agency, and some small agencies and commissions.

j. Includes Congress, Architect of the Capitol, U.S. Botanic Garden, Congressional Budget Office, Copyright Royalty Tribunal, General Accounting Office, Government Printing Office, Library of Congress, Office of Technology Assessment, and U.S. Tax Court.

women held 12 percent of these jobs. According to 1990 statistics, women made up 19 percent of the GS-GM-13 to GS-GM-15 levels; all minorities occupied 13 percent of the GS-GM-13 to -15 positions; around 850 were in the Senior Executive Service (SES), nearly 11 percent of the total SES.[6]

Demographic changes alone do not account for all the shifts in the composition of the civil service. The occupational composition of the federal workforce is also changing. While the popular image of the civil service is one of acres of clerks processing mountains of forms, in fact the activities and structure of the workforce in many places now resemble those of a research-and-development company. Some educational statistics reflect this structure: Of the permanent white-collar workforce, about 65 percent have done some college work; over 35 percent have a bachelor's degree or above; about 7 percent have a master's degree; and about 2 percent have a Ph.D. (see tables 10.2 and 10.3).[7] Furthermore, the technical requirements of federal jobs have also changed. This is reflected by the rise in the number of engineers and computer specialists. Over the past twenty years, the number of engineers on the federal civilian payroll increased by more than 50 percent, to around 100,000; the number of computer specialists increased by more than 600 percent, to around 34,000.[8] Between 1985 and the year 2000, the greatest increases in federal white-collar nonpostal employment are expected to be in the following occupational groups: legal and kindred employees, medical and other health groups, biological sciences, and social sciences.[9]

This profile reflects technological changes in our society and in the federal government. Although the federal workforce has been oriented toward scientific, engineering, and professional work since the New Deal, that emphasis has been intensified. Furthermore, over the past twenty years, many large-scale clerical operations have been computerized. The established practice of contracting-out, long evident in shipbuilding, atomic energy development, and NASA, has increased. Turning over operations to state and local governments, and the Great Society's reliance on nonprofit organizations to get things done, has also increased. In the 1990s, federal civilian employees increasingly think, plan, analyze, evaluate, administer, and dispense funds. Others, by contract or agreements, carry out much federal policy.[10]

The shift away from federal employees' directly producing goods and services is captured by aggregate data on federal employment and expenditures. Between 1960 and 1985, the number of federal employees in civilian and postal jobs declined as a percentage of total U.S. employment from 3.7 to 2.75 percent. Over the same period, the executive branch payroll declined as a percentage of total federal outlays from 13.8 to 7.4 percent, while total federal outlays as a percentage of the GNP rose from 18.4 to 24 percent. Factors such as increased use of grants and contracts and direct

TABLE 10.2
EDUCATIONAL ATTAINMENT OF THE FEDERAL
CIVILIAN WHITE-COLLAR WORKFORCE

	October 1985	June 1991
Less than high school	35,500	30,981
High school diploma	513,700	399,976
Some college, no degree	361,300	390,542
Associate degree	63,800	83,473
Bachelor's degree	324,000	399,159
Postgraduate work	82,300	77,730
Master's degree	100,800	125,194
Post Master's degree work	20,800	19,292
Professional	36,100	41,529
Ph.D.	28,400	33,148
Other	2,300	104,169
Unspecified	15,800	14,020
Total	1,484,800	1,719,213

SOURCE: OPM, Office of Workforce Information.

payments to individuals in programs like social security and Medicare, help explain these changes.

The declining role of the federal government in the nation's and government's employment is suggested by aggregate data in federal employment. Between 1960 and 1990, federal employment per 1000 population declined from 13.1 percent to 12.2 percent. Federal employment as a percentage of all governmental units declined from 28.1 percent in 1960 to 16.7 percent in 1990.[11]

These shifts are also changing the shape of federal organizations and the distribution of its workforce. The large scale, pyramid-shaped organization with executives at the top, line supervisors in the middle, and armies of clerks at the bottom is giving way to more complicated arrangements of authority and communication. New organizations often have an "egg-shaped" form because they employ a larger number of middle-level professionals than clerks. This profile has been criticized by some as representing unnecessary "grade bulge" caused by "grade creep" and excessive promotions. Other explanations for its occurrence are that, in part, it reflects the growth in the number of professional and technical employees resulting from changing technology, legislated program changes (e.g., the creation of

TABLE 10.3

TOTAL CIVILIAN WHITE-COLLAR AND BLUE-COLLAR
WORKFORCE BY EDUCATIONAL ATTAINMENT

	October 1985	June 1991
Less than high school	274,800	66,155
High school diploma	570,600	580,044
Some college, no degree	395,900	461,607
Associate degree	70,100	98,620
Bachelor's degree	324,800	406,623
Postgraduate work	82,700	78,400
Master's degree	100,850	125,670
Post Master's degree work	20,850	19,336
Ph.D.	28,450	33,178
Professional (law/medicine)	36,100	41,574
Other	2,310	140,695[a]
Unspecified	20,400	17,786
Total	1,927,860	2,069,279

SOURCE: OPM, Office of Workforce Information.

a. The definition of "Other" has changed. It now includes workers with some occupational training, completed occupational training, six-year degrees, and work beyond the six-year degree.

new agencies such as the Environmental Protection Agency, EPA), and the necessity of employing large numbers of middle-level managers to coordinate contracts with organizations outside the federal government.[12] Some of these factors help to account for the profile of the federal workforce presented in table 10.4, which provides a picture of the workforce's grade and salary structure.

Another change in the federal workforce has been caused by Reagan administration shifts in policy and program priorities. The effect of these shifts on the distribution of the federal workforce is captured in table 10.5 (*page 218*). It is important to note that although full-time federal employment in nonpostal civilian agencies declined by 133,000 during the first five years of the Reagan presidency, increases of 153,000 in defense agencies, the Departments of State, Treasury, and Justice, and the Veterans Administration more than made up for the cuts. From 1985 to 1990, the number of nonpostal civilian-agency employees increased by 21,701. In fact, with the increase in the Postal Service of 121,000 during the first five years of the

TABLE 10.4
FEDERAL CIVILIAN NONPOSTAL EMPLOYEES
BY GRADE AND AVERAGE SALARY

	March 1985		September 1990	
Grade	Number	Average salary	Number	Average salary
GS-1	1,932	$ 9,523	1,374	$ 10,803
GS-2	14,972	10,748	4,910	12,832
GS-3	74,871	12,236	38,739	14,364
GS-4	161,259	14,272	136,202	16,508
GS-5	198,916	16,289	192,363	18,743
GS-6	92,677	18,467	102,814	21,149
GS-7	138,720	20,227	146,971	23,056
GS-8	29,619	22,885	32,364	26,227
GS-9	147,401	24,508	157,810	27,834
GS-10	30,456	27,632	29,238	31,957
GS-11	173,718	29,772	197,381	33,870
GS-12	177,754	36,082	211,433	40,822
GS-GM-13	117,478	43,523	141,201	48,869
GS-GM-14	60,013	51,714	75,378	58,106
GS-GM-15	29,806	61,505	35,822	69,909
GS-16[a]	723	67,957	445	77,539
GS-17[a]	145	68,700	42	78,200
GS-18[a]	73	68,700	22	78,200

			June 1991	
SES				
ES-1	374	61,296	595	87,000
ES-2	569	63,764	566	91,200
ES-3	1,092	66,232	1,099	95,300
ES-4	3,540	68,700	3,911	100,500
ES-5	925	70,500	1,263	104,600
ES-6	318	72,300	520	108,300
General Schedule	1,450,433	26,186	1,505,748	31,486
Wage System	417,578	23,288	368,582	
Other	135,613	34,413	160,516	

SOURCE: *Pay Structure of Federal Civil Service* (Office of Personnel Management, 31 March 1985); and *Executive Personnel Management Data* (Office of Personnel Management, 30 September 1985). Also, *Central Personnel Data File,* OPM, Office of Executive Personnel Data, June 1991.

a. These positions were moved by law into the SES as of fiscal year 1991.

TABLE 10.5
THE GROWING GOVERNMENT

	January 1981	January 1986	1981–86 numerical change	1981–86 percentage change	July 1991	1986–91 numerical change	1986–91 percentage change
Army	312,485	365,908	53,423	17.10	367,764	–27,615	–7.51
Army Corps of Engineers	34,063	29,471	–4,592	–13.48	326,170	–25,670	–7.87
Navy	317,163	351,840	34,677	10.93	228,259	–28,528	–12.50
Air Force	231,667	256,787	25,120	10.84	99,617	9,063	9.10
Defense Logistics Agency	45,321	52,591	7,270	16.04	25,736	243	0.94
Other Defense	32,291	37,963	5,672	17.57	171,709	33,177	19.32
State Department	23,521	25,493	1,972	8.38	90,589	25,463	28.10
Treasury Department	131,637	138,532	6,895	5.24	81,722	9,613	11.76
Justice Department	56,867	65,126	8,259	14.52	130,438	24,716	18.94
Interior Department	79,546	72,109	–7,437	–9.35	38,121	3,153	8.27
Agriculture Department	122,889	105,722	–17,167	–13.97	18,194	–111	–.61
Commerce Department	47,010	34,968	–12,042	–25.62	130,668	–6,502	–4.97
Labor Department	23,544	18,305	–5,239	–22.25	14,514	2,125	14.64
Health and Human Services	159,945	137,170	–22,775	–14.24	69,273	7,645	11.03
Housing and Urban Development	16,726	12,389	–4,337	–25.93	19,655	3,036	15.44
Transportation Department	71,641	61,628	–10,013	–13.98	5,153	388	7.52
Energy Department	21,692	16,619	–5,073	–23.39			
Education Department	7,538	4,765	–2,773	–36.79			

Environmental Protection Agency	14,927	13,852	−1,057	−7.20	18,452	4,600	24.83
General Services Administration	37,240	25,465	−11,775	−31.62	21,174	−4,291	−20.26
U.S. Information Agency	8,084	8,920	836	10.34	8,205	−715	−8.71
NASA	23,696	22,062	−1,634	−6.90	26,314	4,252	16.15
Office of Personnel Management	8,530	6,403	−2,127	−24.94	6,626	223	3.36
Panama Canal Commission	8,774	8,493	−281	−3.20	9,029	536	5.93
Small Business Administration	5,963	5,338	−598	10.07	4,979	−359	−7.21
Tennessee Valley Authority	51,841	29,359	−22,482	−43.37	22,937	−6,422	−27.99
Agency for International Development	6,157	4,940	−1,235	−20.00	4,847	−93	−1.91
Postal Service	655,748	777,078	121,330	18.50	810,648	33,570	4.14
Veterans Administration[a]	235,480	244,948	9,468	4.02	256,821	11,873	4.62
Total executive branch civilian employees	2,843,404	2,984,755	141,351	4.97	2,963,054	−21,701	−.73

SOURCE: 1981, 1986, 1991 OPM Civilian Personnel Data File.

NOTE: Figures for military services personnel include only civilians.

a. Now the Department of Veterans Affairs.

Reagan administration the size of the federal workforce grew by nearly 5 percent.[13] Although there was considerable discussion of continued cuts in federal programs, the workforce continued to grow after 1985 with increases of about 22,000 by 1990. Executive departments that showed increases of at least 5 percent between 1988 and 1990 included the Departments of Education, Transportation, Justice, and Commerce along with the EPA and NASA. Departments experiencing decreases included Treasury, Labor, Defense, and Interior.[14]

The changing requirements for the federal government's workforce suggest the importance of attracting an adequate supply of skilled workers into the civil service; of training, motivating and effectively deploying them once hired; and of retaining those with valuable skills through their most productive work years. As an employer, the federal government does not operate in a vacuum. It must compete for workers in dozens of occupational specialties and hundreds of locations. In some cases, it enjoys a monopoly position; in others, it faces a fully competitive labor market. In these cases especially, the federal government may be at a disadvantage when competing for talent and skills.

Inducements

Labor-market theory can be simple or complex depending on the problem at hand. Our problem is reasonably straightforward: How and with what effect does the federal government's package of inducements allow it to compete for labor? Simple logic suggests that if the federal government's key inducements are declining in value relative to its competitors, then their attractiveness must also be declining, and the workforce's capacity should show some evidence of erosion.

People choose occupations and work for organizations for a variety of reasons: to apply their skills to problems, to earn an acceptable level of pay and benefits, for advancement, for employment and income security, to work and live in an attractive location, for prestige, for comfortable working conditions, for a chance to assume challenging responsibilities, and to render public service—to mention only a few. Organizations, including federal agencies, shape their package of inducements to attract and retain a mix of employees with the talent, motivation, and skill necessary to tackle the work at hand.[15] Through the millions of career choices made yearly, people are sorted out, and organizations get staffed.

In studies dating back to the late 1940s, researchers have addressed the questions of who comes to work for the federal government and why. These studies reveal some interesting things about the federal workforce and the people it attracts. For example, the federal workforce has been shown to be remarkably representative of the general population in family background characteristics (i.e., religion, ethnicity, father's occupation, and place of birth). Attitude studies, while revealing a general progovernment orientation stronger than that of most Americans and (not surprisingly) strong support for the programs the agency administers, also showed a remarkable similarity between federal employees and the general population.[16] One significant area in these studies is the repeated finding that federal career employees placed a higher value on public service and a lower value on financial rewards than employees in the private sector.[17] Whether this is simply a product of employees facing the reality of pay and benefits of federal employment or a proclivity developed *before* they entered the federal government has not been firmly established.

Over the past fifty years, the federal government built a reasonably strong administrative capacity and in some areas a remarkably successful workforce. This occurred despite the fact that at no time during this period has the federal civil service been accorded the prestige of its European counterparts and the fact that the federal government has not taken as activist a position in domestic affairs as have European governments.[18] Given this situation, what factors helped the federal government attract a quality workforce?

Much of the explanation for the composition of the U.S. federal workforce can be found in our economic, political, and social history. It is important to remember that in the United States, in contrast to Western Europe, the private sector developed first during the nineteenth century. Not until this century did the federal government begin to take the initiative in areas of economic regulation, social welfare, and the provision of public goods.[19] Even in defense, until 1945 it was customary to maintain only a small full-time military capacity during peacetime. Several factors contributed to this posture: a historic distrust of strong central government rooted in the colonial period; a strong faith in laissez-faire capitalism; slow and cumbersome communication and transportation networks, covering an enormous geographic space; and a propensity toward "isolationism" in dealing with world affairs. In the twentieth century, isolationism became impossible, and communication and transportation systems underwent enormous improvements. Even Americans' distrust of central government and preference for market solutions to problems relaxed somewhat as the Great Depression, two world wars, and scientific and technical breakthroughs made it apparent that market solutions alone would not guarantee satisfactory levels of national security, economic prosperity, or scientific and technical development.

In several areas, the federal government became a monopoly supplier, and some interesting occupations grew up around government work. Some of these were scientific, others technical, still others administrative. But the important point is that in such areas as meteorology, applied astrophysics, intelligence, and diplomacy, government was seen as the best place to practice one's profession. In many other occupational categories, the facilities and equipment available to federal employees were simply so much better than could be found in the private sector or in universities that the federal government was seen as the most desirable place to advance one's professional career.

At the same time that the federal government was expanding its role and size, America's universities were also growing. For many first-generation college graduates from ethnic family backgrounds, the corporate world was unwelcoming. The federal government, with its merit system of examinations for hiring and promotion, was viewed as an attractive alternative.

The legacy of the "Progressive era" with its public-service ethic also contributed to the strength of the federal workforce. As government took on more social missions, "do-gooders" of all social backgrounds joined the civil service. The New Deal, the Fair Deal, the New Frontier, and the Great Society each gave government service a high social mission that brought legions of well-qualified people to federal employment, some at salaries well below those they might have commanded in the private sector.

Conditions of employment were also generally competitive with the private sector. For the risk-averse, reductions-in-force (RIFs) were rare and promotion rates were steady and even rapid during periods of program growth. For those with veterans' preference (who constituted almost 35 percent of the federal civilian workforce in 1986 and about 30 percent in 1990), there was special treatment in hiring and retention during RIFs and the chance to mix military and civilian retirement credits. Pay and pensions, if not downright generous, were at least reasonably competitive with those offered by the private sector. From the 1930s through the 1960s, the cost of living in Washington was closer to the national average than today, so federal employees in the nation's capital and in most other federal installations were able to maintain a middle-class life style on a single salary.[20]

As a result of these factors, for most of the past fifty years, the federal government has been able to recruit and retain a workforce capable of doing the tasks assigned to it. In some areas its workforce has been superb, in others less so, but on the whole its package of inducements attracted and retained the people it needed. And when its inducements did not keep pace with its competitors, special pay rates, training and education opportunities, the prospect of rapid promotion and responsibility, and other inducements combined with the special occupational attractions of federal employment to allow the government to compete with some success in even the most competitive markets.

Furthermore, the "nonportability" of the Civil Service Retirement System for those hired before 1 January 1984 had the effect of "locking in" federal employees who might otherwise leave government employment when the inducements became noncompetitive. The new Federal Employees Retirement System (FERS) is much more portable, however, and its holding power over employees is likely to be far less forceful. This alone may be reason for concern, but it is only one of several changes in government and its environment that, in the opinion of many people, have weakened or could potentially weaken the capacity of the civil service.

The Civil Service Reform Act of 1978

Before beginning a review of the problems of the civil service and of proposals for reform, it is important to place them in the framework provided by the 1978 Civil Service Reform Act (CSRA). The CSRA was intended to address long-standing issues surrounding the civil service system. By dividing the Civil Service Commission into the Office of Personnel Management (OPM), the Merit Systems Protection Board (MSPB), and the Federal Labor Relations Authority (FLRA), proponents of the act hoped to reduce some of the problems that came from the commission's serving as both a central management and a regulatory agency, in effect both judge and jury.

The CSRA also created the Senior Executive Service (SES) to replace most of the "supergrade" (GS-16 through -18) positions that made up the top management corps of the federal agencies and departments. The SES, which was to be the fulfillment of an idea originally proposed by the second Hoover Commission in 1955, was intended to provide its 7,500 or so members with opportunities for mobility, training, and bonuses for outstanding performance. The SES included both line and staff managers; scientists, engineers, and nontechnical executives; and career and political appointees (who were not to exceed 10 percent of the total SES membership and were ineligible for bonuses and appointment to certain positions reserved for career employees).

The act also introduced the "pay for performance" concept to mid-level managers (GS-13 through -15), who would earn annual merit pay based on favorable performance appraisals. Finally, the act gave OPM "demonstration authority" to approve up to ten agency personnel experiments at a time.

Eight years after the passage of the CSRA, its consequences disappointed many federal employees and proponents of the reform. First, the Congress and the Carter administration came to believe that SES bonuses were too generous and were given to too many people; they decreased the number of employees eligible for bonuses. Second, the personal development plans promised by the CSRA were scaled down; only a handful of senior executives were able to use the educational and sabbatical provisions of the act. Reassignments and relocations, supposedly a positive feature of the new system, were sometimes used by the Reagan administration in its first years in a way that many SES members regarded as punitive—as a means to get them out of the way or force them to retire. Another disappointment to federal employees was the merit pay system for mid-level managers, which never was funded to provide attractive bonuses for top performers. Finally, the demonstration authority given to OPM was approved for only one large experiment at two of the Navy Department's facilities, at China Lake and San Diego, California, and one small experiment at the Federal Aviation Administration.[21]

To compound these and several other problems with the CSRA, the Reagan administration's original appointee as director of the Office of Personnel Management, Donald J. Devine, took a decidedly negative view of what he considered to be excessive pay, benefits, and prerogatives of federal employees. During his four-year term, he reorganized the agency and shaped its policy priorities in ways that many critics thought "politicized" OPM and damaged the civil service. Rather than serve as an aggressive proponent of modern human resource management, as its supporters had hoped, OPM was viewed by many as a principal agent of what some people called the Reagan administration's "war on the bureaucracy."[22] While the criticism of the MSPB and its independent Office of Special Counsel was less severe, the board was criticized for failing to protect federal employees from merit system abuses.[23]

The perceived failure of OPM to implement the incentives provided by the CSRA for improving workforce performance or to provide the institutional leadership for improving personnel practices as originally envisioned by the CSRA's sponsors contributed to a sense of confusion among federal managers and policy makers about OPM's mission and its role in the federal personnel system.[24] Other factors have taken their toll on the capacity of the civil service in the 1980s, but the legacy of CSRA may be more profound because its disappointing consequences have produced an environment of suspicion and distrust among the major interests involved in the civil service policy arena—Congress, federal employee unions and associations, and the White House. In this context, broad reform, no matter how well conceived, will be very difficult to achieve.

Some Indications of Human-Resource Erosion

The capacity of a workforce is in large part determined by who it is able to hire; therefore, who is or is not coming into the federal service at entry level is of great importance. Several major changes have taken place during recent administrations that have greatly affected the hiring of new federal employees and in turn are bound to change the character of the workforce for many years. According to recent studies, recruiting practices that worked reasonably well in the past may no longer be attracting the quality of college graduates previously interested in federal employment. College graduates perceive equally challenging work, greater flexibility, and higher rewards to be available in the private sector.[25]

Also, women, minorities, and first-generation college graduates no longer face serious barriers to entering the private sector; in fact, they are now often sought out. In addition, the Reagan administration's attempt to cut back the size of the federal workforce—from the freeze announced at the president's inauguration to the frequent speeches by the director of the Office of Personnel Management, the message was loud and clear: Federal hiring, with the exception of the Department of Defense, was to be cut back. While RIFs and freezes have not been across the board in the civilian agencies, enough was heard about cutbacks to dissuade many recent college graduates from seeking federal appointments. Furthermore, with the redirecting of federal social programs to state, local, nonprofit, and private-sector agencies, many people who came to the federal government have been encouraged to look elsewhere. Recent surveys also report a decline in the perceived prestige of working for the federal civil service.[26] Frequent discussions during recent presidential campaigns of the "overpaid and underworked bureaucracy" also did little to encourage the "best and brightest" among college graduates to join the federal service.

Finally, according to recent studies, federal pay and benefits trailed the private sector in 1985 by an estimated 7 to 24 percent for comparable jobs, with the gap growing larger every year.[27] By 1990, the pay differential was 22 to 32 percent at GS-1 and 39 to 55 percent at GS-GM-15.[28] Thus it is hardly surprising that in a GAO survey of career executives who retired or resigned from the SES in fiscal year 1985, two-thirds of those responding would "advise" or "strongly advise" young people to seek employment in the private sector over the public sector, 11 percent favored the public sector, and 22 percent were undecided. Some said it depended on the person or the career choice.[29] Other surveys by the MSPB and the Federal Executive Institute Alumni Association (FEIAA) reported similar results.

Additional insight into the federal government's recruitment problems can be gleaned from a 1986 survey conducted by Edward Bewayo. Table 10.6 reports reasons that respondents gave for their choice of their first employer.[30] Bewayo's data suggest that in some areas such as "advancement opportunities," "use of wide range of skills," and "specialization opportunities," the federal government may be quite competitive with the private sector; in other areas, such as benefits, pay, and prestige, it may be operating at a disadvantage. Although Bewayo's study did not address the issue of public service, there is evidence from a study of college graduates by the Carnegie Commission that this factor is not widely or highly valued by the current generation of college students.[31] Another example: Of 1,500 Harvard graduates in 1985, only 3.3 percent planned to enter the federal gov-

TABLE 10.6

REASONS FOR CHOOSING A FIRST EMPLOYER

	Number of times mentioned	Percentage[a]
Advancement opportunities	75	16
Benefits	73	16
Use of wide range of skills	73	16
Pay	63	13
Challenging responsibilities	58	12
Job security	49	10
Company prestige	27	6
Informal, family-like working atmosphere	26	6
Specialization opportunities	8	2
Other reasons	18	4

SOURCE: Edward Bewayo, "What Employees Look for in First and Subsequent Employers," *Personnel* 64, no. 4 (1986).

a. Percentages were derived by dividing number of times mentioned by total number of responses (470). Percentages fail to total 100 because of rounding.

ernment immediately; at Harvard's Kennedy School of Government, where students have supposedly chosen to study for a career in government, only 25 percent of graduates of the two-year Masters of Public Policy program chose federal service.[32] (Although this percentage has not greatly changed, it may be somewhat misleading because recently about one-third of the graduates have been foreign nationals who are not eligible for federal jobs.)[33] Evidence from technical agencies—NASA, the National Bureau of Standards, and research arms of the Department of Defense—shows a lack of success in efforts to recruit scientists and engineers from the top quartile of universities based on quality rankings.[34] The National Institutes of Health (NIH) and the Department of Veterans Affairs have reported closing whole wards because of their inability to attract qualified nurses.[35]

The federal government has also taken actions that have discouraged new recruits. Besides general cutbacks, hiring freezes, and discouraging rhetoric, it has created confusing and frustrating processes for entry into the civil service. OPM has even closed some information centers and stopped distributing publications originally intended to help potential employees find their way through the maze of federal employment practices.

Some recruitment problems can be attributed to the abolishment of the

Professional Administrative Career Examination (PACE) as a result of a consent decree in 1981. The objective of the decree was to eliminate the adverse impact of PACE on the hiring of blacks and Hispanics for PACE-filled positions (95 percent of blacks, 87 percent of Hispanics, and 58 percent of whites failed the PACE examinations). PACE and its predecessor, the Federal Service Entrance Examination (FSEE), were used by the federal government for many years to establish the eligibility of college graduates with liberal arts and generalist majors for federal jobs, often in administrative staff functions such as program analyst, budgeting, personnel, or procurement.[36] As an interim replacement for PACE, OPM established a new Schedule B appointing authority to be used for the external hiring of entry-level employees. Approximately 4,000 appointments were made in both 1985 and 1986 under this authority. (This is out of a total of about 14,000 appointments a year to occupations formerly covered by the PACE examination.)

University and government placement officials cited as one of the greatest drawbacks in the Schedule B hiring process the lack of a government-wide application point for people who want information about or to be considered for a vacancy. Other problems come from Schedule B's authority being in the "excepted service": Persons hired could not be noncompetitively converted beyond the GS-7 level or reassigned to positions not covered by the authority. According to a GAO report, agency officials viewed the increased flexibility of Schedule B as an advantage in recruiting and selecting individuals, but cited problems with the requirement that applications had to go through agency headquarters to OPM's central office for clearance, lengthening the time it takes to process a job offer. Another problem mentioned was the increased opportunity Schedule B authority afforded for basing appointments on personal or political patronage.[37]

Another major change in recruiting came about with OPM's delegation to agencies of the authority to expand their employment of temporary employees. Under the new authority, agencies may make temporary competitive appointments from their own registers at GS-12 and below, for a year or less, and may extend these appointments without OPM approval for a period not to exceed four years. While appropriate for meeting short-term needs, some skeptics have expressed concern that in order to save money (temporary employees do not get retirement, health, and insurance benefits), the authority will also be used for filling permanent positions. Some fear that this practice could lead to productivity losses, increased training costs, and with the lack of commitment that comes from temporary employment, could result in the deterioration of the career workforce. OPM data do show that the number of temporary employees is growing and that more such appointments are being made at higher grade levels in professional, administrative, and technical positions.[38]

In 1990, OPM began using the Administrative Careers with America (ACWA) examination to replace PACE and Schedule B. It is too early to judge its success.

What of the problems of recruitment and retention for often mentioned shortage areas—scientists, engineers, accountants, and computer specialists? Inadequacy of pay is most frequently cited by agency officials as an obstacle in attempting to hire these categories of employees, and several legislative proposals have been introduced to remedy the pay comparability gap for these groups. According to several reports, very substantial differences exist between federal and private-sector wages in several occupational categories.[39] For examples, a PATC survey found the following:[40]

1. Chemists had the highest average pay gap, ranging from 33.1 percent at GS-12 to 57.3 percent at GS-5.
2. Buyers (acquisition and procurement specialists) had about a 45 percent pay gap at all grade levels.
3. Accountants' pay gaps ranged from 30.8 percent at GS-12 to 43 percent at GS-5.
4. Computer specialists and engineers had similar pay gaps (about 25 percent at entry increasing to 45 percent at GS-11), then the pay gap decreased, especially for computer specialists.
5. Clerical employees (clerk-typist, secretary) had the smallest average pay gap, ranging from 8.2 percent at GS-6 to 29.5 percent at GS-3.

Considering these serious pay differences, one would expect to find high quit rates for employees with the largest gaps. But the data do not support that conclusion. In fact, studies of public- and private-sector turnover rates yield the rather surprising finding that the overall turnover rate for the private sector in 1985 was 6.3 percent, while the federal government overall turnover rate was only 3.3 percent.[41] A 1989 survey by the Administrative Management Society reported turnover of 11.7 percent for private-sector office workers in industry in jobs similar to government workers'. The federal turnover rate for that group is about the same. Overall in 1990 the federal turnover rate was 6.3 percent. Furthermore, turnover statistics by occupations show that there apparently is no direct relationship between salary and attrition rates among federal workers. Although chemists had the *largest* pay gap with the private sector, they had the *smallest* quit rate. This was also true for engineers. Engineers had a relatively large pay gap, but their quit rate was relatively low. Conversely, clericals had the smallest pay gap but had the largest quit rate.[42]

There are several possible explanations for these findings. First, the nonportability of the federal retirement system for employees hired before FERS stands as a strong exit barrier to those with some time in the federal system. Second, some federal employees move across agencies, and these moves are not recorded in turnover statistics. As shown in table 10.7, when interagency transfers are added in, the turnover figure for federal employees rises to 6.3 percent.[43] Third, many federal functions have no private-sector counterpart where skills and knowledge developed in government might be applied. Fourth, the long-standing negative public attitude about government and the government workforce may be "spilling over" to affect the marketability of federal employees. Finally, if the federal government has become an attractive employer for less-qualified employees, as some people believe, there is little reason to assume that these same employees will become much more marketable after a period of employment in the federal service.

Comments of agency officials and available data indicate that employees' decisions to leave or remain with the federal government are also affected by other factors: advancement opportunities, the nature of work assignments, geographic location, health and retirement benefits, work environment.[44]

Are these factors applicable to the Senior Executive Service? Obviously, the pay gap is also an important factor at this level, but "salary com-

TABLE 10.7

QUIT AND TRANSFER PERCENTAGES, FY 1985, FY 1991

Occupation	Quit rate[a]		Transfer rate[b]		Total	
	1985	1991	1985	1991	1985	1991
Clerk-typist	13.8	11.9	6.9	4.5	20.7	16.4
Secretary	6.9	5.9	4.0	3.7	10.9	9.6
Engineer	3.3	c	1.3	c	4.6	c
Buyer	3.2	4.7	3.7	2.4	6.9	7.1
Computer specialist	2.8	2.2	2.3	1.7	5.1	3.9
Accountant	2.3	1.9	3.1	3.1	5.4	5.0
Chemist	2.3	2.7	.7	1.0	3.0	3.7
GS workers	5.2	4.4	2.1	1.9	7.3	6.3

SOURCE: Occupation Series Dynamics Report, *Full-time Permanent GS Equivalent, FY 1985* (Washington, D.C.: OPM, 1985); Occupation Series Dynamics Report, FY 1991.

a. Employees who resign from the federal government.

b. Employees who transfer to another federal agency.

c. No comparable figures are available because engineers are now listed under type of engineer (i.e., chemical, general, etc.).

pression" between grades is also a serious and recurring issue. Table 10.8 shows how both the pay gap and salary compression have affected the salary structure at NASA, an agency that constantly competes for talent with its own contractors and other high-technology firms.[45]

Low pay is not the only problem mentioned in studies of the factors that are affecting who comes into the top levels of the federal government. Concern also has been expressed about the need to rethink the Ethics in Government Act. Questions raised include whether the "open disclosure" requirement serves to deter conflict of interest or has the primary effect of discouraging those who prefer to keep their financial affairs private from entering the public service. Questions have also been posed about current "revolving door" provisions. A 1986 GAO study showed that 21 percent of former Defense Department employees working for defense firms worked on the same projects they handled for the government. Twenty-six percent of former federal employees working in private industry once made decisions while working for the Department of Defense that affected their current defense contractor employer. Although many former DOD employees are required to report if they are employed by defense contractors, the majority of those who are probably required to report did not do so. GAO therefore was recently unable to report the percentage working for defense contractors.[46] These practices create a serious dilemma: Will regulations designed to control conflicts of interest be made so restrictive that well-qualified people will not want to enter government service?

That each of these factors has contributed to the federal government's difficulty in attracting qualified people to federal service can be gleaned from comments from business executives who turned down senior-level government positions: "My future corporate career may be jeopardized";

TABLE 10.8

SALARY COMPRESSION AT THE TOP: SENIOR-LEVEL SALARIES,
NASA AND ITS INDUSTRIAL COUNTERPARTS

NASA position	NASA salary	Industry salary
Associate administrator	$72,000	$107,000–164,000
Center director	$72,000	$81,000–137,000
Program director	$70,000	$61,000–110,000
Project manager	$69,000	$56,000–$101,000
Project engineer	$52,000–68,000	$41,000–70,000

SOURCE: David Packard, "The Loss of Government Scientific and Engineering Talent," *Issues in Science and Technology*, Spring 1986, 130.

"Financial disclosure is too onerous"; "Divestiture means a large tax burden"; "Postemployment restrictions are too constraining."[47] Recent headlines of ethics violations seem only to have compounded the problem of finding the proper balance needed to avoid discouraging either long- or short-term public service and at the same time protect the public interest.

Of equal concern is the problem of retention of top officials. Much has been written about the number of current senior executives eligible for retirement and the effect of personnel policies and morale on their decision to stay or to leave federal service.

After an initial burst of retirements from 1979 to 1983, when 40 percent of the career executives who had converted to the SES in July 1979 left government (roughly 2,500), the rate of SES retirements has leveled off.[48] In large part, this reflects a decline in the numbers of SESers eligible for optional retirement, but it also reflects a change in the percentage of eligibles who chose to retire. Since fiscal year 1983, when 17 percent of those who were eligible retired, the percentage has risen; in fiscal year 1985, about 30 percent of those eligible for optional retirement did retire. In 1990, about 20 percent of all SES members were eligible for optional retirement.[49] The size and seriousness of the present pattern of retirements is captured by table 10.9 (*page 232–33*), which presents retirement rates in selected agencies for the first nine months of fiscal year 1986, and for May and June 1986, versus a corresponding period in 1985.[45] Fewer career executives left during 1990 than in any other year in the history of the SES, probably in anticipation of the January 1991 SES pay raise. The number of retirements is expected to remain low until 1994 when the "high three" years after the pay raise of 1991 are in effect.[50]

What factors affect retirement rates? In a 1987 GAO survey of all career executives who left the SES in fiscal year 1985, each recipient was asked to rate the importance or unimportance of fifty-four possible reasons for his or her decision to leave.[51] The top eight reasons, of "great importance" or "very great importance," were the following:

1. Dissatisfaction with top management
2. Unfair distribution of bonuses
3. Frustration with proposed and actual changes to compensation
4. Dissatisfaction with political appointees
5. Frustration with criticism of federal workers by press, politicians, or public
6. Unfair distribution of rank awards
7. Too few bonuses available
8. Dissatisfaction with agency management practices (i.e., amount of freedom given to manage job)

TABLE 10.9
RETIREMENT DATA FOR SELECTED AGENCIES

Agency	Total permanent workforce June 1986	Estimated number eligible to retire June 1986	Voluntary retirements October thru June		Percentage change
			FY 1985	FY 1986	
Army	360,000	24,046[a]	3,217[e]	3,914[e]	+22
FAA	45,800	5,124[a]	1,200	1,351	+13
FBI	21,000	466[a]	148	200	+35
IRS[f]	80,000	4,048[b]	1,410	1,641	+16
NASA	21,400	2,735[c]	460	564	+23
Navy	303,500	25,000[a]	5,962	5,650	−5
SSA	78,500	4,191[d]	1,125	1,204	+7
State	14,100	1,730[a]	228	267	+17

Agency	Voluntary retirements		Percentage change	Voluntary retirements		Percentage change
	May 1985	May 1986		June 1985	June 1986	
Army	285	520	+82	360	452	+26
FAA	109	109	+69	112	202	+80
FBI	16	37	+131	9	28	+211
IRS[f]	259	302	+17	139	219	+58
NASA	33	60	+82	51	112	+120
Navy	811	919	+13	670	751	+12
SSA	131	102	−22	94	138	+47
State	35	29	−17	37	50	+35

Agency	Total permanent workforce June 1991	Estimated number eligible to retire June 1991	Voluntary retirements October thru June		Percentage change
			FY 1989	FY 1990	
Army	226,265	14,235	3,788	3,314	−13
FAA	42,438	2,236	877	874	0
IRS[f]	120,816	4,965	1,128	1,424	+26
NASA	20,267	1,735	454	444	−2
Navy	167,246	8,609	2,701	1,926	−29
SSA	60,938	2,931	713	766	+7
State	4,148	220	45	28	−38

SOURCES: 1985 and 1986 data: U.S. General Accounting Office, *Federal Retirement: Retirement Data for Selected Agencies*, Fact Sheet for the Honorable Vic Fazio and the Honorable Michael D. Barnes, House of Representatives (Washington, D.C.: GAO-GGD 86-123FS, August 1986). 1989, 1990, and 1991 data: Central Personnel Data File. These figures pertain only to personnel covered by CSRS or FERS and compensated from the general schedule or its related pay systems, excluding those related to demonstration projects.

a. As of 30 June 1986.
b. As of 1 June 1986.
c. As of 30 September 1986.
d. As of 31 December 1986.
e. These figures do not include the months of October and November.
f. The IRS reported its retirement data on a pay period rather than a monthly basis. Thus its reporting periods are slightly different from those of the other agencies, but still cover the months of May and June.

It is noteworthy that these former career SES members identified the short terms of political appointees and their lack of qualification for their jobs as important reasons for their dissatisfaction. These reasons remain important today.

In addition to these findings, studies by the FEIAA and the MSPB's Merit Systems Review and Studies Group found that a great majority of federal career executives believed that the performance bonus system was not working well.[52] Among the problems they cite is the perception among career executives that too few bonuses have been awarded, and that those awarded have been unfairly distributed. The problem with the number eligible for bonuses arose shortly after the first year of the system when Congress, responding to complaints that bonuses were too generous, cut the number to be awarded from the 50 percent called for in the original law to 20 percent. Furthermore, although bonuses were expected to be based on performance evaluations, many executives have come to believe that factors other than performance, such as higher SES levels, have been used in making bonus awards, and that the bonuses have been used to compensate for low pay. Unhappiness also was expressed over the number of Presidential Rank Awards, the $10,000 and $20,000 bonuses for "meritorious" and "distinguished" executives. Although the law permits "distinguished rank" bonuses to be awarded to 1 percent of executives, and "meritorious rank" bonuses to 5 percent, a study by the staff of Representative Patricia Schroeder found that only half of the awards allowed had been given from 1980 to 1986. Close to the allowed number of distinguished and meritorious rank awards were given in 1990, however.[53]

Frustration has also been expressed over proposed and actual changes in pay and benefits. For example, for fiscal year 1986, the president proposed a 5 percent pay cut for federal employees, and a pay freeze was eventually instituted. For 1987, the president and his pay agent proposed a 2 percent pay raise, despite the government's own finding that private-sector pay increased over 4 percent during the previous year. In several other years, federal employees received raises that were less than increases in the cost of living. Health insurance benefits were also reduced, and a voucher system for health benefits was proposed that would cut the government's contributions by $5 billion over the next five years. Of further concern to federal executives has been the overall attitude of OPM toward pay and benefits. Besides proposing to cut pay, during recent years OPM also proposed drastic cuts in retirement benefits, including increasing the age for full benefits from fifty-five to sixty-five. In addition, the rhetoric and actions of some officials in the Reagan administration—and sometimes Congress—have been cited as contributing to a morale problem among career executives. The factors cited include the following: (1) the continued drumbeat from conservatives within and outside the administration to privatize and contract-out work performed by federal employees;[54] (2) workforce reductions, employment ceilings, and hiring freezes, often with little consideration for the number of employees needed to do the work required;[55] (3) the outcome of the air traffic controllers' (PATCO) strike; (4) the proposal, contained in tax bill pending before Congress, to rescind the "three year recovery rule," exempting federal employees' pension contributions from income taxes; (5) proposed drug-testing requirements for federal employees; (6) the present and potential impacts of the Gramm-Rudman-Hollings Act.

The result of these and many other actions was a growing perception among federal employees that they are unappreciated and underrewarded, which is affecting the morale and quality of the workforce at the entry level, among shortage groups, and at senior levels. The consequent erosion of the human-resource capacity of the federal workforce is an expected outcome of this process and raises a large question about what the future civil service will look like. Fortunately, since the appointment of Constance Berry Newman as director of the Office of Personnel Management in 1988, progress has been made in restoring the morale of federal employees. OPM's cooperation with the Congress to achieve passage of the Federal Employees Pay Comparability Act, the growing acceptance of FERS, and the lack of dramatic changes to the benefits systems have somewhat alleviated the uncertainties over pay and benefits created during the Reagan administration.

The Civil Service of the Future

The problems of the civil service have not gone unnoticed. Almost all observers agree that high technology, international economic competition, and the increasing complexity of sociotechnical systems have raised the costs of making mistakes. Systems are so complex and so tightly joined that a small error made by a single person or a small group may cascade to destroy a whole system.[56] This was true at the Three Mile Island nuclear plant and the *Challenger* disaster. Smaller mistakes occur daily. Examples include the revelations about health-care breakdowns at the Veterans Administration and the Navy's Medical Corps. Granted, only a small percentage of the government's functions carry life-or-death risks, but they are increasing in number.

Another side of the picture concerns lost opportunities. Increasingly, government agencies are called on to work creatively to solve problems and increase our country's economic competitiveness. To be effective in such areas as research and development and trade requires government to employ highly skilled and motivated people. While it is impossible to calculate what "opportunity costs" might be associated with a failure by government to assign highly qualified employees to these activities, such a practice could well produce a "chilling effect" on innovation and entrepreneurship, with negative impacts on the economy.

High-risk and entrepreneurial activities are but two extreme types of activity requiring highly trained and motivated employees. In almost all areas involving science, technology, international trade, and legal affairs, the government plays an important role. The problems government faces in domestic policy are increasingly complex as well. For example, responsible decision makers in agriculture, land management, environmental protection, and transportation all require more information and better analysis and advice to do their jobs properly. The costs of making mistakes may not be as high as in the scientific and international spheres, but they are important to those affected by them—social security and veterans' benefit recipients, regulated and audited companies, and those who indirectly receive government services in areas such as urban development and transportation. At the most abstract level, the legitimacy of government (i.e., its popular support) depends on a government perceived to be effective, just, and accountable. At a minimum, its workforce is expected to be contributing to those ends.

People concerned about the civil service and its ability to meet future challenges have proposed several solutions. They range from upgrading the workforce by improving pay, benefits, and responsibilities to "privatizing" large parts of the federal government's responsibilities and staffing many others with political appointees. In between are discrete proposals aimed at correcting what are perceived as small breakdowns and dysfunctions in civil service rules and practices. The potential and practicality of these ideas vary, but they each address serious problems facing the civil service today. Taken together, these recommendations provide a remarkably broad agenda of ideas for the future.

Reform Proposals

Proposals for reforming the civil service fit into three categories: (1) those that promise to cut costs and *downgrade* the career workforce (mostly emanating from conservatives); (2) those that propose to *upgrade* the compensation, status, and responsibilities of the career corps (emanating from advocates of a strong civil service and associations of civil servants); and (3) those that promise to go in *both directions* at the same time. Space does not permit a comprehensive and detailed analysis of every facet of these proposals and their variants, but it is possible to identify several of them and discuss their major features.

Proposals to Downgrade the Civil Service

Proponents of this strategy are usually in search of ways to cut the cost of the government's workforce. They often begin with the premise that federal workers are overqualified and overpaid because the functions of government are inherently simple and mundane. The workforce, including managers, should be structured and compensated to reflect these simple and mundane tasks. In this view, the abilities of the federal workforce should be "sufficient" to perform these tasks and no more.

Terry W. Culler, formerly associate director of OPM under Donald Devine, is representative of this school of thought when he argues that the government "should be content to hire competent people, not the best and most talented people."[57] He goes on to say that the federal government requires, in order to do its job, just about the present mix of technically qualified personnel. In fact, because of the vast supply of competent people in the labor market applying for government jobs, the federal government could pay less without adversely affecting the capacity of the workforce to perform present and future assignments. There is no need, in his opinion, to have a workforce that is more than "sufficient" to meet its routine requirements.

Culler extends his argument by asserting that the "best and the brightest" should not work in government but should be channeled into the private sector where national wealth is created. Others who support Culler's view of the civil service argue that policy-related work should be performed by political appointees; technical jobs should be staffed by well-paid contract employees; and where possible, other functions should be "privatized" either by turning government functions over to private firms or by creating quasi-governmental corporations.[58] This vision is in many ways at odds with the trends in the role and responsibilities of the federal government that have changed its workforce over the past fifty years. Culler's profile may indeed have existed before World War II, but, today, government tasks are far less routine and far more knowledge based—and the supply of skilled labor available to staff many of its jobs is by no means in surplus. Another glance at some aggregate statistics about the federal workforce should serve to underscore this point. Of the 1.5 million federal white-collar civilian employees in 1983, 137,443 were employed in medical, hospital, dental, and public health services; 55,536 were in biological sciences; 159,487 were in engineering and architecture; 43,307 were in physical sciences; 14,679 were in mathematics and statistics; 51,031 were in investigations; 18,919 were in quality assurance, inspections, and grading; 74,243 were in legal and kindred occupations; and 122,452 were in accounting and budgeting functions. In September 1989, of the 1.6 million federal white-collar employees, 141,766 were employed in medical, hospital, dental, and public health services; 61,252 were in biological sciences;

172,825 were in engineering and architecture; 43,504 were in physical sciences; 15,365 were in mathematics and statistics; 71,168 were in investigations; 19,236 were in quality assurance, inspections, and grading; 74,295 were in legal and kindred occupations; and 146,006 were in accounting and budgeting functions.[59] Clearly, this is a workforce heavily weighed toward technical competence based on educational attainments. These are people whose skills are not easily replicated.

What constitutes a "sufficient" workforce depends, of course, on one's definition of "sufficiency." Critics of the Culler position contend that sufficiency is determined by what the public expects the government to do and the technical requirements of those jobs. Once the people, through their representatives, assign the federal government responsibility for a function, they expect it to be done well. When the public expects the government to launch a complex space or defense system, or find a cure for cancer, sufficiency can become remarkably technical and sophisticated. These critics argue that for a complex function to be performed well, something more than a "sufficient" workforce staffed and managed by underpaid employees is required.

There are potentially costly subtleties involved in following a policy of downgrading the federal civil service. The costs may not be reflected simply in monetary terms or the risks of increased error, but might well have broader deleterious implications for the governance of the nation.

Proponents of greater privatization frequently argue not only that the federal government ought to do less but also that those public functions it must carry out ought to be assigned to "third parties"—private and non-profit contractors and grant recipients. More functions are, in fact, being assigned to nongovernmental organizations. As Lester Salamon has pointed out, however, this practice raises "serious questions of accountability because those who exercise public authority in these programs are only tangentially accountable to the elected officials who enact and oversee the programs."[60] Recent problems in NASA's space program point up the difficulties involved in assigning responsibility and accountability in an environment where an increasing percentage of public-sector decisions are made by third-party managers.

Almost as troubling to some is the current enthusiasm for turning government programs over to newly created public corporations. Sometimes motivated in part by a desire to avoid pay and benefit limits of the civil service system and central management control, these arrangements also tend to create unclear lines of accountability. Two recent examples of this phenomenon occurred at the Tennessee Valley Authority (TVA) and the Federal Savings and Loan Insurance Corporation (FSLIC). According to the GAO, the TVA circumvented the law by hiring a manager, through a contract with a private corporation, for its nuclear plants at a salary of more than $355,000 a year, nearly five times the legal ceiling for TVA employees. Although exempt from civil service rules, the TVA, a wholly owned government corporation, cannot legally pay its employees more than the salary received by a TVA board director. In a 4 April 1989 advisory legal opinion, GAO held that the supplemental plan for relocation incentive payments to top TVA managers that are clearly intended to circumvent TVA's statutory salary limitations are improper.[61] An even more involved maneuver occurred at the FSLIC. In pursuance of its statutory responsibility to liquidate the assets of troubled and mismanaged savings and loans in the private sector, the FSLIC, a public corporation, created a corporation whose director received a salary of $250,000 a year plus bonuses.[62] (The Office of FSLIC operations are now part of the Resolution Trust Corporation.) Meanwhile, Edward J. Gray, the FSLIC chairman, received a salary of $73,600. Needless to say, this technique for avoiding salary ceilings and central management control is being closely studied by other agencies. In the aggregate, and if carried to the extreme, such moves could produce what amounts to a piecemeal disintegration of the executive branch structure and salary system. To promote comparability in pay and benefits among the federal banking agencies and to avoid competition among them for qualified personnel, Section 1206 of the Financial Institutions Reform Recovery and Enforcement Act of 1989 was passed.

Undoubtedly the most provocative assertion in Culler's argument is that the "best and the brightest" should be steered away from government employment and toward the private sector where wealth is created. But his line of reasoning overlooks the important contribution that public employees make to "wealth creation" through the maintenance of a stable infrastructure of national defense, scientific and technical knowledge, and government housekeeping functions within which productive private-sector economic activity can take place. Culler's proposal would separate government work from those activities that contribute to GNP and diminish the significance and complexity of government functions. But even in the constricted concept of government held by economic conservatives like Milton Friedman, the environment for wealth creation requires certain minimum governmental functions, such as a capable national defense, an efficient revenue-raising system, skillful diplomacy, and a sound currency system.[63] Liberals would, of course, extend this list substantially, but the important point is that a model of government based, first, on a rigid division between public and private sectors and, second, on the presumption of a marginally competent government workforce simply misreads the current and likely future role of government—and its workforce—in our increasingly complex economic system.

Proposals to Upgrade the Civil Service

A more benign but perhaps equally unrealistic set of proposals has been advanced by advocates of a strong civil service, including unions, government employees, and several individuals with long association with the federal personnel system. As might be expected, most of these proposals are targeted on upgrading the pay, status, and responsibilities of the career civil service and on protecting their political neutrality, but some have also focused on the role and organization of OPM.

Some proposals for reforming OPM evidence a strong sense of nostalgia. For example, Bernard Rosen, formerly an executive director of the Civil Service Commission, has advocated a partial return to the past by changing the leadership of OPM from a presidentially appointed director to an independent, bipartisan, three-member board. According to Rosen,

> The record shows that the goal of attracting and retaining first-rate civil service employees has not dominated the policy decisions of OPM. *There is no reason to believe that this can again become and remain the number one goal unless the leadership of the central personnel agency has sufficient independence and partisan neutrality to be its strong advocate within an administration, with Congress, and with the public.*[64]

Two other former CSC officials, O. Glenn Stahl and James J. McGurrin, view the role ambiguity and occupational and political heterogeneity of the contemporary civil service as pervasive sources of weakness. They argue:

> The civil service is ill-defined and amorphous, with no clear or challenging service mission. No one is held accountable for trying to raise and keep it at a level of excellence. It has no active institutional, public, or media support. Its present low prestige fosters a poor reputation for impartiality, competence, and morality. Partisan, short-term presidential appointees have little or no interest in the long-range viability of the service. The SES suffers from a mixture of career executives and political hacks under the same umbrella.[65]

To improve this situation, Stahl and McGurrin offer four broad recommendations. Their first is that the president and Congress establish a commission of inquiry, a "Hoover Commission" for the civil service, to study the problem and formulate a strategy for change. Their second recommendation is to establish, in statute, a national Executive Branch Career Service that would develop a well-understood and shared mission among federal employees, as well as a shared sense of identity. Third, they advocate that "certain government wide merit system rulemaking authority should be transferred from the single-headed, politically conscious OPM to the three-member, bipartisan MSPB."[66] This authority would cover the rules that implement basic statutory merit priciples and prohibited personnel practices. Through this transfer of authority, Stahl and McGurrin would reduce OPM's policy-making authority as it affects the merit system, but maintain OPM's role in day-to-day service operations. Finally, they recommend that the government establish priorities for a comprehensive personnel management improvement program.

The Stahl-McGurrin recommendations are addressed in part to problems that were apparent to some observers before the CSRA, in part to problems that emerged after CSRA was implemented, and in part to problems that arose during the Reagan administration. Although they vary in detail and focus, their breadth and specificity are generally mirrored in recommendations proposed by employee associations, such as FEIAA, the Senior Executive Association (SEA), the Public Employees Roundtable (a coalition of thirty employee groups and professional associations), the Federal Executive and Professional Association (no longer in existence), the National Academy of Public Administration, and several others. It is impossible to cover these proposals in detail, and sometimes their recommendations conflict, and some are no longer applicable, but their overall themes are remarkably similar. Almost all of them speak to the following issues: the weakened concept of "public service" in the United States, the importance of protecting the merit principle in hiring and promotions, pay and pension comparability, relationships and boundaries between career and political appointees, education and training in public management, relationships and boundaries between contractors and civil servants, position classification, performance appraisal, the importance of encouraging a spirit of "professionalism" among federal employees, and the need for modern personnel practices and human-resource management techniques.

These ideas, often put forward in testimony before Congress, are generally presented as problems with one or more possible solutions. Most of these ideas are again discussed in the 1989 report of the National Commission on the Public Service (the Volcker Commission). While it is perhaps unfair to the groups involved because they do differ in some specifics, it is possible to summarize their recommendations in very general terms:

1. Strengthen the "public service ethic" through campaigns of public education in the media and in schools and colleges; organize public employees to combat politicians who engage in "bureaucracy bashing."

2. Reaffirm the "merit principle" by eliminating hiring and promotion practices for career positions not based on examinations; restrict use of Schedule B hiring authority; reestablish a general entrance exami-

nation for new college graduates to replace the old FSEE and PACE systems.

3. Reemphasize through congressional and presidential action the importance and value of the merit system and the "professionalism" and public-service orientation of the career workforce.

4. Adopt a "total compensation" approach for establishing real comparability with private-sector pay, pension, and benefits; use a cost-of-living approach to establish locality pay rates; sever the link between congressional pay and civil service pay in order to lift the pay cap; increase the percentage of SES members eligible for bonuses.

5. Reduce the number of nonpolicy-level political (Schedule C) appointments; separate political appointees out of the SES and more clearly delineate the roles, responsibilities, and authority of career and political appointees; restrict the use of political appointees in administrative roles (e.g., assistant secretaries for administration, budget and personnel directors, regional directors, and general counsels).

6. Increase education and training opportunities for all federal employees; require specific management training for all career executives appointed to the SES; promote more extensive training for political appointees.

7. Delineate more clearly the roles and relationships between employees of contractors and the career civil service; more carefully police procurement conflicts of interest and the practice of employing "in and outers" from industry in procurement decision-making roles; limit the use of temporary employees and consultants in permanent jobs.

8. Strengthen performance appraisal systems; where possible, relate individual performance to organizational performance; fill the majority of Performance Review Boards with career executives.

9. OPM, working in close cooperation with personnel specialists and line managers, should study and bring to the federal government modern methods of personnel management, human-resource planning, and productivity improvement used by the most progressive business firms. Before these practices are installed government-wide, OPM should sponsor extensive and carefully studied demonstration projects.

Some of these ideas are more practical than others, and some are more controversial than others; some are already reflected in regulation, but are not followed. Nevertheless, they are proposed as remedies to perceived deficiencies in the operation of the current civil service system forwarded by people who have previously been employed by, or who are currently working in, the federal government. Before critiquing these ideas, it is important to recognize that some of the problems they address are more tractable than others. So, for example, when national figures like Walter Mondale, Paul Volcker, and Alexander Trowbridge decry the decline of the "public service ethic" in American society,[67] progress has been made toward identifying and publicizing the problem, but not toward figuring out what to do about it.

The linkage between problems and proposed solutions also seems to be tenuous. For example, both Rosen's proposal to reorganize the leadership of OPM under a three-member, bipartisan commission and Stahl and McGurrin's recommendation to transfer the merit system functions of OPM to the MSPB would have the effect of greatly weakening the leadership role of OPM in promoting the improvement of federal personnel practices as originally envisioned by proponents of the CSRA. Without a strong OPM, opportunities to improve the civil service system might be less attainable. Furthermore, both Presidents Carter and Reagan found OPM to be a useful instrument of personnel management, and it is hard to imagine a future president supporting legislation that would, in effect, take a useful policy instrument out of his control.

Stahl and McGurrin's proposal for a new "Hoover Commission" for the civil service, like similar congressional proposals supported by Senator William Roth and Representative Frank Wolf, have not generated much enthusiasm. In several ways, the personnel report of the President's Private Sector Survey on Cost Control (the Grace Commission) encompassed many of the issues that such a Hoover Commission might address.

Furthermore, the lessons of two Hoover Commissions should not go unheeded. Standing behind the first Hoover Commission (1947–49) was a large body of well-supported doctrine around which a consensus could be built; its statutory achievements were substantial. By the time of the second Hoover Commission (1953–55), the broad consensus had deteriorated; its legislative achievements were minimal. A similar fate could well befall a commission on the civil service in today's climate. Not only is there little in the way of a widely supported civil service doctrine, but also the politics of the past six years suggest that a consensus behind even the most minor recommendations may fail to materialize. According to some, such an effort runs the risk of souring future presidents and Congresses on the commission idea even if, at some future time, a doctrine is more clearly formulated and a broad consensus exists.[68]

Stahl and McGurrin's third major recommendation would establish in statute the concept of a National Executive Branch Career Service. Such a service would have a well-understood mission, formally recognized members, "and it should be given a chance and challenge to develop proud traditions of political impartiality, professional competence, and rigorous ethical integrity in its conduct of day-to-day government business."[69] Presumably, such an arrangement would seal off the civil service from political appointees, including noncareer SES and Schedule C appointees, and from short-term "in and outers." It would resemble, more closely than the present system, the personnel systems used to staff most European governments.[70]

There are several problems with the idea of an Executive Branch Career Service. First, some people believe the particular strength of the U.S. system lies in its ability to merge career and political employees in workable short-term arrangements—that this arrangement prevents the career service from dominating policy at both the formulation and implementation stages, thereby defusing the threat and the criticisms of "bureaucratic government."[71] Furthermore, it has been argued that because career and political appointees are intermixed, frictions that might arise from their interaction are dissipated. Second, in many technical fields the use of short-term, temporary, nonpolitical appointees gives the government access to people with special skills, expertise, and experience who might not otherwise be attracted to a career in government service. Third, recent changes in the civil service retirement system would seem to augur strongly in the opposite direction from the Stahl-McGurrin proposal. By making the system more portable, the president and Congress have, in effect, declared that the civil service should be less costly to enter and exit and that a working-life career exclusively spent in the federal civil service should be an option, not a requirement of federal employment. Finally, a closed national civil service might collide with the strong identifications many federal employees have developed with their professions and their individual agencies. It is hard to imagine, for example, very many of the government's doctors, lawyers, engineers, and others with strong professional attachments identifying themselves as members of an entity like the Executive Branch Career Service. Likewise, employees in such agencies as the FBI, CIA, State Department, Forest Service, National Park Service, and NIH are unlikely to shift their strong organizational loyalties from their corps or services to a larger, amorphous entity.

It is impossible in this chapter fully to evaluate and critique all the proposals recommended by those who would upgrade the civil service, but several deserve brief scrutiny. Issues of pay and benefits are treated in some detail in the next section. Here we briefly treat (1) replacing the PACE examination for entry into the career service; (2) upgrading education and training; and (3) installing modern methods of personnel management, human-resource planning, and productivity improvement in federal agencies and departments.

General Entrance Examinations. Although PACE was a valuable tool for attracting college graduates with strong undergraduate records to the federal service, and promoted a sense of identity with the concepts of "public service" and "merit," it was susceptible to charges of discrimination against minority applicants. In 1981, OPM agreed not to challenge a court suit to the PACE examination and to substitute a series of job-related tests that could be validated as nondiscriminatory.

OPM was slow to develop such examinations. As of 1986, out of more than a hundred job-related categories, only seven tests were operational. Agencies needing to hire new college graduates resorted to using Schedule B hiring authority and an "extended temporary appointment" authority that limited their flexibility and, in the opinion of critics, resulted in the appointment and conversion to full-time career status of many marginally qualified people. Moreover, critics charged that the new examinations were for occupations that, while important and potentially interesting and rewarding, were difficult for liberal arts graduates and others unfamiliar with the federal government to learn about. As of 1986, OPM's seven examinations, which covered more than half the jobs previously filled through PACE, were in the following areas: computer specialist, tax technician, internal revenue officer, contract specialist, customs inspector, social security claims examiner, and social security claims representative. Rather than continue the use of Schedule B and temporary hiring authorities, many people recommended a return to a general entrance examination.

The PACE issue is a thorny one. It appears to be very difficult to assemble a written examination that will be totally immune to court challenge on grounds of discrimination. One might use "equal results" as a criterion for selecting those who qualify so that, for example, representative proportions of blacks, Hispanics, and whites who take the test are selected, but that practice might be susceptible to charges of "reverse discrimination." And it too could be overturned by the courts. Another approach would be to assemble examinations covering broader job categories, for example, "general administration," but those too might produce cultural biases. Finally, to get around the examination validity problem, the government might accept a variety of other accomplishments and tests to establish eligibility.

Replacing the PACE examination, six Administrative Careers with America (ACWA) examinations have been in place since 1990 and were being revised in late 1991. One-half of each examination is based on an Individual Achievement Record, a biodata inventory. The government at present may exempt those who graduate near the top of their college classes from general entrance exams through the Outstanding Scholar Program. In 1991 this program was becoming more widely used by agencies. OPM is also vastly expanding the prestigious but small (around 170 in

1985) Presidential Management Intern (PMI) program. The Volcker Commission recommended expansion of the PMI program from 400 to 1000. In 1991, there were 810 nominees and 343 finalists. But none of these ideas are certain by themselves to attract to the public service highly qualified college graduates.

Training and Education. It is almost an article of faith for supporters of the civil service to advocate more education and training for the federal workforce. Yet, since the passage of the Government Employees' Training Act of 1958, which enabled federal agencies to release employees for training programs at government expense, billions of dollars and millions of staff years have been spent on training and educational activities, with little evaluation of their effectiveness. Some critics complain that much of this money and time has been absorbed in clerical and technical training or has been misdirected toward training the wrong people in the wrong things. Others argue that although CSRA tried to remedy this problem, key personnel are not trained in public management before they are assigned or promoted to executive positions.

This second criticism is far more workable than the first because it is directed at three clusters of federal managers: (1) top political appointees who are offered, but sometimes have no time for, a two-week orientation program coordinated by the White House staff and held at Harvard's Kennedy School of Government; (2) scientists, engineers and other professionals who are often promoted to supervisory positions because of their technical competence rather than managerial promise or training; and (3) participants in the SES Candidate Development Program (CDP), who, although successfully completing the program, are often passed over for SES assignments in favor of people who have not gone through the program.

These practices have all been met with suggestions for reform from the public administration community. The program for political appointees, for example, has been criticized for being too short, too shallow, too political, too optional, and too temporary. To overcome some of these limitations, it has been proposed that the program be lengthened and required of all SES political appointees and subcabinet positions. Furthermore, instead of being staffed by Harvard faculty and coordinated by the White House, critics suggest that more realism and permanency would result if the program were staffed by experienced federal executives and coordinated by OPM.

Some of these ideas seem to have substantial merit, but there may be little to be gained from changing the program. For example, because of the prestige of the university, the Harvard program no doubt attracts many appointees who might otherwise pass up such a training program. Also, the Harvard faculty has people with high-level federal experience—as many, one suspects, as might be attracted to participate in an OPM-sponsored program. Moreover, given the recent history of OPM, there is no guarantee that under its supervision a program for political appointees would be any less partisan than the present program supervised by the White House. Further, given the length of time taken to complete the appointment process, requiring political appointees to attend a longer training program before they report for work is simply unrealistic. A likely scenario, if such a change were made, might be that people with the most important appointments would seek exemptions from the program and that the bulk of those attending would be those appointed to less significant jobs. Finally, there is the question of institutionalizing the program. Surely an OPM-run program is likely to have more permanency than a White House contract with Harvard, which can be delayed or dropped at any time. But there is no guarantee that future administrations will find the basic concept of the program of either Harvard or OPM the best training vehicle. Unless Congress decides otherwise, it is likely that the basic program curriculum and institutional arrangement will remain a matter of presidential preference. Since 1989, additional orientation programs have been added by OPM and the White House for both political and career executives. Presidential appointees attend a White House orientation program.

A second focus of concern for those critical of federal education and training programs has been the way scientists, engineers, and other technically and professionally trained employees are selected and educated for management positions. Critics charge that, all too often, these people are promoted to managerial positions solely on the basis of their technical competence, irrespective of their aptitude, experience, interest, or training in management. Sometimes the arrangement works out, sometimes not; at best, this selection practice depends on chance.

Proponents of change recognize that they are up against strong professional biases. Many scientists, engineers, and other professionals regard management education as little more than codified common sense that is unworthy of their time. Training in management and public policy, they reason, should be a very secondary criterion to technical competence in selecting professional leadership. Despite the strength of this point of view, in practice it has not dissuaded proponents of training who have urged that federal labs and agencies be required to train future managers and upgrade the administrative skills of people chosen for management positions.

Some criticism of the federal government's management training efforts was directed toward the Federal Executive Institute in Charlottesville, Virginia, and the federal management training centers at Kings Point, New York, Denver, Colorado, and Oak Ridge, Tennessee. Supporters of these training centers pointed out that attendees express high levels of satisfaction with the programs. Moreover, supporters argued, these training centers serve symbolic as well as functional purposes, such as reinforcement of the importance of management roles in the government. Others, while generally supportive of the centers, argue that the programs are too short and are attended too infrequently by too few federal managers. They also believed that when compared to the strongest corporate programs, the federal centers were underfunded and understaffed. Finally, they charged that changes in the title of the FEI directorship (from director to dean), reporting relationships, and the curriculum of the centers during the tenure of Director Devine compromised their political neutrality and reputation.

Under Devine's successor, Constance Horner, some of these criticisms were put to rest, and changes were planned. For example, the title and reporting relationships for the FEI director were upgraded. That official again had the title of director and reported directly to the deputy director of OPM, thereby signifying the institute's greater importance within OPM. Under Director Newman, FEI is part of a new Human Resources Development Group. The FEI director is now head of the Office of Executive and Management Development and has leadership responsibilities for FEI, the Executive Seminar Centers, the European Training Center, and other long-term development projects. Other aspects of the OPM management and executive-training programs, however, seem less amenable to change. It is questionable, for example, whether FEI or the other centers will be more generously funded in the near future or whether their programs will be greatly expanded and extended. Further changes were planned by OPM Director Newman for fiscal year 1992.

The Grace Commission took the view that the centers were costly and overstaffed and that one (Denver) was poorly located. A proposal to relocate the Oak Ridge and Kings Point centers in 1992–93 was approved by Director Newman.[72] An option mentioned in some circles was to close all the centers except FEI and to rely more heavily on universities and training programs provided by contractors and independent entrepreneurs. But others feared that strategy would not guarantee that appropriate training would be available or that federal managers and agencies would take advantage of the new offerings. Another proposal, in the opposite direction, was to create a National Civil Service Academy, independent of OPM, that would be similar in scope and funding to the Department of Defense's National Defense University. Those favoring this approach believed that it would signal a long-term commitment to civil servants. But this proposal failed to attract much support and has been opposed by OPM and universities involved in public administration education as an unnecessary duplication of their offerings.

A third important issue in training and education has concerned the workings of the SES Candidate Development Program (CDP). CDP was conceived as a way to prepare executives for a managerially oriented, mobile SES and as a major source for filling SES vacancies. After six years in operation, however, the CDP had not attained its goals. Whether its goals were unrealistic, given the breadth and diversity of the federal sector, or whether their implementation was misdirected is unclear, but it is generally agreed that the CDP was not a success. For example, of all candidates certified as eligible for SES, just 46 percent entered the SES as of March 1985. This percentage represented only 13 percent of all SES career appointments, making CDP far from a major SES entry; in fact, over a three-year period, agencies appointed five career SESers for every candidate selected for CDP. From July 1979 to September 1990 51 percent of the CDP's 1,257 graduates were selected for SES positions.[73]

Neither did CDP lead to more mobility among members of the SES. CDP did not encourage mobility among appointed candidates; about 5 percent entered SES in an agency different from the one selecting them for CDP, and fewer than 3 percent of candidates started CDP in an agency for which they had not previously worked. While agencies reported that CDP developed managerial competence, they noted that the candidates' technical competence was a main barrier to SES entry. Also, the situation produced a perverse irony: Some people doubted that CDP candidates represented the best, because so few entered the SES.[74]

In essence, a mismatch exists between the candidate enrolled in the CDP and the senior executives agencies seek. While technical competence clearly seems to be more important than managerial competence when agencies make SES appointments, in a recent survey over twice as many agencies claimed that they focused on managerial over technical competence in selecting candidates.[75] In short, many agencies seem reluctant to link CDP with the process for filling SES vacancies or to use CDP as a planning tool for expeditiously meeting SES needs.

The two primary proposals for change in these practices have generally been straightforward: (1) enforce the requirement that the SES candidate program be mandatory for all SES appointments; and (2) require successful completion of the candidate program for all promotions to the SES. Only in this way, according to proponents, will the integrity of the SES be maintained and the value of broad generalist training be established throughout government.

But old habits are hard to break. In most agencies there is a strong preference for promoting specialists familiar with a program's technicalities, personnel, and clients over generalists. In short, the idea that legitimate and potentially useful generalist skills can be learned in an SES candidate program has not won widespread acceptance at the top levels of most agencies.

OPM's Role in Personnel Management Improvement. A third important cluster of recommendations concerns the role of OPM in advancing modern methods of personnel management, human-resource planning, and productivity improvement throughout the federal government. The CSRA promised that OPM would function actively in these areas, and, under its first director, Alan K. Campbell, it strengthened its capacity to function as a strong central management agency, fostering improved personnel practices in the agencies. Under Director Devine, however, OPM reduced its staff and activities to basic personnel operations (e.g., investigations and pay and benefits recordkeeping). Lost, according to critics, was the momentum for promoting modern productivity and personnel management techniques in the agencies.[76]

This change in direction cost the government valuable time in finding, adapting, and testing methods for improving personnel management found useful in the private sector. To some observers, OPM's reluctance to use its research and demonstration authority and to investigate contemporary human-resource planning techniques left the federal personnel system "rudderless." Agencies, left to go it alone, were unable to gain OPM approval for significant modifications of their personnel systems. OPM's productivity improvement program, a growing feature of the agency under Campbell, disappeared under Devine and eventually was eclipsed by an OMB accountability-oriented productivity improvement program under the Reagan administration's "Reform '88" initiative.[77]

Under Director Horner's leadership, some facets of general overall leadership for personnel and productivity improvement slowly returned to OPM. Director Constance Berry Newman has also taken on a leadership role in personnel and productivity improvement. OPM now has an Office of Systems Innovation and Simplification to work with agencies and the Congress on both research and demonstration projects. The office holds quarterly meetings with federal agency representatives and publishes a quarterly newsletter of personnel research highlights and an annual strategic research agenda.

To summarize, those who would seek to upgrade the civil service have proposed remedies for many of the ills that they see in the present structure and operation of the government's personnel system. Some, who see CSRA as a failed reform built on faulty reasoning and bad-faith implementation, would turn the clock back to the era before the passage of CSRA in 1978. Others would keep the present structure, but would change large parts of the system, including the role and responsibilities of OPM. Whatever the proposed solutions, they share a common goal of improving the standing and quality of the federal workforce. Let us turn now to a third set of proposals, involving mostly pay and benefits, which promises to produce results in two directions at once—that is, to upgrade some parts of the civil service and to downgrade others.

Proposals That Would Upgrade and Downgrade
the Civil Service

Since 1975, when the Civil Service Commission issued its six-volume *Studies of Federal White Collar Compensation*,[78] three elements of the federal personnel system have dominated discussions of federal pay and benefits: (1) compensation comparability; (2) the general schedule (GS); and (3) retirement.[79] For the time being, many of the retirement issues seem to be solved with the passage of the Federal Employees' Retirement System Act of 1986 (FERS), which created a less costly and more portable three-tier system composed of social security benefits, a pension plan for federal employees, and a 401K option. Less successful have been efforts at resolving the total compensation and general schedule issues. Three new issues arose out of the Civil Service Reform Act of 1978: (1) the composition and compensation of the Senior Executive Service; (2) the effectiveness of merit pay plans for middle managers; and (3) the scope of collective bargaining and labor relations. Proposals related to these issues have provided much of the agenda for civil service reform since the passage of CSRA. Many of these proposals have potential consequences that promise to upgrade some parts of the federal workforce and downgrade others.

Proposals for total compensation comparability have long been discussed. Under the Federal Pay Comparability Act of 1970, employees' pay was governed by the principle that federal salaries should be comparable with pay for similar work in the private sector. Although there was an elaborate process for setting *pay* rates involving, among others, the Quadrennial Commission (known officially as the Commission on Executive, Legislative and Judicial Salaries), the Advisory Committee on Federal Pay, and the President's Pay Agent, there was neither a statutory policy to guide employee *benefit* determinations nor a systematic process for assessing the comparability of federal and private-sector benefits. Since benefits are a growing and increasingly important part of both federal and private-sector compensation, in recent years several reports have called for a comparability policy based on total compensation, including those issued by the GAO and the Rockefeller Panel in 1975, and a Carter administration task force in 1977.[80]

In response, the commission did considerable work to develop such a policy and submitted its proposal to Congress in June 1979. Congress declined to act on the proposed legislation.

Congress and OPM are watching the demonstration project testing the total compensation comparability concept. The House authorized the National Bureau of Standards (NBS) to conduct such a demonstration for 1,600 employees ranging from scientists to clerks beginning in fiscal year 1987. NBS, now the National Institute of Science and Technology, implemented this demonstration project in fiscal year 1988. Its 1991 evaluation suggests the agency is pleased with the project's success.

Over the years, several studies of federal pay have resulted in proposals to split up the general schedule, which covers about 1.4 million white-collar federal employees in 430 occupations. The Civil Service Commission report found that the practice of placing all occupational groups in a single general schedule had put too much emphasis on "internal alignment" (equalizing pay for jobs that an evaluation procedure deems to be equal) and too little on "external alignment" (paying rates comparable to those in the nonfederal sector).[81] The study recommended that the general schedule be split into four separate services, each with its own pay and classification system. The four services would be (1) clerical and technical (with 40 percent of the workforce); (2) professional and administrative (53 percent); (3) executive and managerial (2 percent); and (4) a special schedule (6 percent) covering medical, legal, and some other professional occupations.[82] The Rockefeller Panel, in its December 1975 report, endorsed the commission proposal and recommended locality pay for clerical and technical employees, and pay set on a nationwide basis for others.[83] The Carter task force in 1977 also endorsed this proposal, and a bill to establish locality pay was submitted by the Carter administration. At that time, Congress took no action; it wasn't until 1990 that Congress passed a locality pay bill.[84]

Much of the problem surrounding federal pay concerned the use of private-sector pay survey findings. Although required by the Pay Comparability Act of 1970, this information generally was ignored in setting federal pay rates. Fiscal year 1986 marked the eighth straight year that a president proposed, and Congress did not disapprove, lower pay increases than the comparability indicated by the survey data. The year 1990 marked the twelfth year of lower pay increases than indicated by the survey data. Because of the presidential use of alternative pay rates every year since 1978, general schedule salaries dropped significantly behind those in the private sector for similar levels of work. In March 1986, the difference, according to a survey, averaged almost 24 percent. In 1990 the *average* federal –private-sector pay gap was about 25 percent, with the gap in some areas believed to be over 35 percent.[85]

Even greater gaps occurred at the executive level. The Fifth Quadrennial Commission reported that the purchasing power of corporate executives' pay increased 68.5 percent between 1969 and 1984, more than doubling the gap between their pay and that of Level II executives. In 1969, the average corporate executive earned $140,000, or about three times the $42,500 earned by Level II executives. By 1984, the pay of Level II executives had risen only to $72,600, while private executives averaged over eight times that amount.[86]

Besides a decline in comparability, all officials covered by the Federal Salary Act experienced a decline in purchasing power. From 1967 to December 1985, the Consumer Price Index rose from a base of 100 to 318.5, meaning that it took $318 to purchase in 1985 what could be bought for $100 in 1967. Even though the real income of most Americans kept pace with inflation, and professions and private-sector executives experienced real gains, this was not the case for the 3,147 top federal executives, legislators, and judges, whose real income fell by approximately 40 percent.[87] The salary lag for federal officials was particularly problematic for recruiting people to move to high-cost-of-living areas like Washington, D.C., and for those with college-age children who faced the high cost of tuition.[88]

A cause for much of this problem was the statutory "linkage" between congressional and executive salaries and the salary-setting process, which reflected the reluctance of members of Congress to set off public reaction by voting themselves large increases.[89] Beginning with the Federal Salary Act of 1967, Congress sought to depoliticize the pay-setting process, but without much success. According to the Fifth Quadrennial Commission: "Commissions recommend salary adjustments, Presidents modify them, and Congresses, as often as not, reject them. The basic problem was the process."[90] To correct this problem, the Fifth Commission recommended a modified procedure adopted by Congress in 1985. Beginning in 1986, a one-time commission met to recommend salary adjustments to the president, whose recommendation became law unless overridden, within thirty days, by a joint resolution requiring a two-thirds vote of both houses. It was hoped that through this process the pay comparability gap and the cost-of-living lag could be closed—at least for the salaries of top officials covered by Quadrennial Commission recommendations.

Executive pay problems were greatly alleviated with the Ethics Reform Act of 1989, which provided for substantial pay raises in Executive Schedule pay. This made possible Executive Order 12736, which adjusted pay rates and allowances for SES members. Increases from 22 percent at ES-1 to nearly 30 percent at ES-6 began January 1991.

At lower levels, the federal white-collar "special rate" program helped agencies be competitive in certain occupations and labor markets. Under the program, pay rates above the general schedule are authorized when the government has a significant problem recruiting and retaining well-qualified individuals, and when the staffing problem is caused by substantially higher private-sector pay rates. The use of special rates is increasing; the number of special-rate positions rose from about 8,000 in fiscal year 1977 to almost 34,000 in March 1984 and to 37,000 in 1986. In 1987 the number of special rate employees increased dramatically to more than 127,000, primarily from the addition of thousands of clerical workers. By 31 December 1989 over 179,000 federal employees (13.8 percent of full-time permanent GS personnel) were receiving special rates.[91]

Primary reasons for the increase are these: (1) General schedule pay adjustments have been less than the amount needed to achieve comparability with private-sector salaries; (2) the adjustments have been equal across-the-board pay increases rather than by grade; and (3) geographic and occupational variations in private-sector pay are not recognized under the general schedule, meaning that despite the increasing overall lag in comparability, some federal employees continue to be paid over the going rate for their skills in some localities.

The comparability pay lag for workers covered by the general schedule resulted in a variety of congressional and administrative proposals to ameliorate the problem. Congress has considered six proposals for pay and personnel systems that remove groups of employees or whole agencies from the constraints of the general schedule pay system. Three proposals would establish new systems for paying personnel in the defense, intelligence, and acquisition work, and for scientists and engineers government-wide. Other proposals provide for entire agencies to create separate pay and personnel systems. The irony in these proposals is that each is required to be implemented at no additional cost, yet the reasons for the proposals stem from recruiting and retention problems directly attributed to the comparability pay lag. These problems worsened. In 1990, GAO reported that recruitment and retention problems posed a major risk of reducing the quality of government programs.

The proposals arise from a half dozen surveys and studies conducted in the last several years that purport to show that federal agencies apparently have been unable to compete with the private sector in recruitment and retention of employees. For example, in reporting its findings in the scientific and engineering area, the White House Science Council's Federal Laboratory Review Panel found that almost all the federal laboratories suffer serious disadvantages because of their inability to attract, retain, and motivate the scientific and technical personnel required to fulfill their mission.[92] In defense, it is perceived that there is a need to improve the management of procurement and to establish a better system for recruiting and retaining people of ability and initiative into key acquisition positions.[93]

In August 1986, an amendment to the defense authorization bill sponsored by Senators Quayle and Bingaman that would have created a separate salary scale for scientists, technicians, and acquisition personnel in the Department of Defense, and would have allowed up to 5 percent of DOD personnel to be paid above the salary cap, was defeated in the Senate by 52 to 44. If passed, the bill, originally recommended by the President's Blue Ribbon Commission on Defense Management, would have affected nearly half of the government's general schedule employees and allowed the salaries of around 50,000 DOD employees to exceed the salary cap.[94] Two other proposals were significant in this context. Already mentioned is the National Bureau of Standards' authority to test a new pay plan. Representative Frank Wolf and Senators Paul S. Trible and John W. Warner, all of

Virginia, submitted bills to make it easier for agencies to pay higher salaries to certain hard-to-recruit-and-retain employees. Needless to say, such moves prompted other agencies and occupational groups to seek similar treatment.

Pay

To address this situation, Congress passed the Federal Employees Pay Comparability Act (FEPCA) of 1990, which changed the way in which federal white-collar pay is set and adjusted in two basic ways. The first change concerned annual cost-of-living raises. Under FEPCA, annual pay adjustments will correspond to changes in the Employment Cost Index (ECI) for private-sector wages and salaries. In 1992 and 1993, federal white-collar workers are to receive the full ECI (unless the ECI is over 5 percent and is altered by the president in event of war or severe economic conditions). In 1994 and beyond, the adjustment will be the ECI minus 0.5 percent unless it is over 5 percent and is reduced to 5 percent by the president due to a national emergency or serious economic conditions.

The second major change will be locality-based salary adjustments, which are intended to narrow the federal-nonfederal differences within particular pay areas with at least a 5 percent federal-nonfederal pay gap. Locality pay is intended to bring federal salaries to within 5 percent of their nonfederal counterparts. In 1994, the locality payments will be 20 percent of the amount needed to bring federal employees to within 5 percent of nonfederal salaries in each pay area; in 1995 and in the succeeding seven years, the adjustments will be 10 percent of the amount needed to close the gap to 5 percent. At the end of this nine-year phase-in period in 2002, federal employees will be paid more nearly what their nonfederal counterparts are paid in the areas in which they work, thereby easing, it is hoped, federal recruitment and retention problems.

Until the initial locality adjustments begin in 1994, FEPCA authorizes the president to provide interim geographic adjustments of up to 8 percent in consolidated metropolitan statistical areas (CMSAs) where needed to address significant pay disparities and recruitment and retention problems. President Bush authorized 8 percent adjustments for the New York, San Francisco, and Los Angeles CMSAs in 1991.

The president was also given discretion in the payment of the locality increases. For example, if the amount of the 1994 payment exceeds $1.8 billion, the president may reduce the payment to $1.8 billion. He can reduce the 1994 adjustment below $1.8 billion if the nation is at war or in a recession. After 1994, the president has even wider discretion in locality payments.

In addition to the changes in the pay-setting process for annual and locality adjustments, FEPCA also authorized incentives such as recruitment bonuses, retention bonuses, and payment of travel expenses for job applicants. Higher salaries were also authorized for certain senior-level positions, critical positions, and certain highly qualified employees.

In 1986, there were several concerns about splitting up the general schedule. For example, if scientists and engineers are successful in splintering away from the general schedule and thereby able to upgrade their pay and benefits, it is likely that other groups, such as accountants and lawyers, who are also in short supply, will demand special treatment. Furthermore, removal of the higher-paid occupational groups from the general schedule would have had a dampening effect on the pay of the remaining occupational groups—mainly administrative and clerical employees including large numbers of women and minorities with little political influence. The result would be a civil service broken into the "haves" and the "have-nots," which may cause more problems than it solves in terms of morale, workforce relations, and collective bargaining. Finally, a move to separate DOD personnel from the general schedule would have forced interagency competition that, according to Senator Ted Stevens, former chairman of the Senate Governmental Affairs Civil Service Subcommittee, would have had the effect of "suctioning" out of other departments the technical and acquisition specialists universally in short supply.[95]

Another plan for changing the general schedule attracted the support of President Reagan. The administration proposed the Civil Service Simplification Act of 1986 extending the basic concepts of the Navy's China Lake demonstration project to the rest of the civil service. In essence, this plan would have allowed OPM to extend authority to agencies and installations to move from the GS system of narrow pay bands, rigid job classifications, and almost automatic "step increases" and promotions, to wide pay bands, flexible classifications, and more extensive use of pay-for-performance. If enacted, the Simplification Act would have greatly widened the scope of managerial authority in recruiting, hiring, and assigning employees to jobs and awarding employee raises and promotions.

While the Simplification Act was attractive to many people, and employees and managers at China Lake (and the Navy's Ocean Systems Command) showed support for its basic concepts, it had some potential drawbacks.[96] First, the Simplification Act, as proposed, was to be "expenditure neutral"; that is, whatever raises result from future pay increases must come out of a common (and fixed) pool of salary increments. That means that employees would have been divided into higher and lower categories of performance and that raises would have varied. It also means that, unlike China Lake, where personnel costs have been estimated to be 5 to 6 percent higher than they would have been without the experiment, some people would have to take no or very small increments in order for others to receive substantial rewards. Second, the China Lake plan places a great deal more authority into the hands of managers for determining the value of jobs and performance. Some feared that this change would have placed employees at an unfair risk because many managers are simply not very good at recognizing performance. Third, some charge that the Pay Simplification Act would have directly undermined the role of personnel classification specialists and that by compromising their function as a fair and equitable instrument of the merit system, the basic underlying structure of the civil service system would have been compromised. Finally, some critics argue that the Navy's China Lake facility is a unique environment and that its isolated location (in the desert), unusual workforce (largely engineers), and specialized tasks (weapons research) have had a large impact in determining its success. They wonder whether a different combination of location, workforce, and tasks would produce the same results. Generally these people argue for a "go slow" approach; OPM should experiment further with the China Lake idea and at the same time sponsor more demonstrations to test other proposals. By 1991, OPM was moving away from supporting new demonstration projects and was using some of the lessons learned in proposing change in classification and performance management.

Some of these proposals relate to altering the structure of the SES, in particular to reduce the size of the SES by (1) removing noncareerists, (2) removing all but top executives, and (3) removing scientists and engineers from its ranks. A 1985 GAO study found insufficient evidence to support any of these proposals.[97]

The proponents of an "all-career SES" believe that including both career and noncareer members in SES increases tension between the two groups and creates the potential for politicization of the executive branch. GAO found that tension between career and noncareer executives has been a long-standing concern, and one not limited strictly to the question of structure. And although the total number of political appointees at the SES level has increased somewhat, the legal limits on the number of political appointees allowed in SES (10 percent) has been maintained.

Another form of criticism came from the Grace Commission, which recommended a large pay increase for government executives, but asserted that SES was too large and contained too many individuals who were not "true executives."[98] Even though GAO found a few individuals who do not warrant executive status, in general it found little reason to support a wholesale reduction in the size of SES.[99]

Several other groups have suggested that the scientists and engineers who make up over a third of the SES be removed from the SES and placed in a special service. However, GAO found little hard evidence to support the contention that the federal scientific community is experiencing detrimental effects by being included in the SES. Several sources suggested that the difficulties involved in recruiting and retaining scientific and technical employees is not unlike those affecting the entire civil service.[100] In spite of this reasoning, several concerned groups have introduced legislation to create a separate "Senior Scientific Service." Since the executive pay raise of 1991, no proposals to restructure the SES have been suggested.[101]

There are also concerns with the merit pay system—established by the Civil Service Reform Act of 1978—which fundamentally changed the manner in which most federal managers and supervisors in GS-13 through -15 are paid. Following CSRA, merit pay employees were no longer guaranteed the full annual, within-grade, and quality-step increases that their GS counterparts received. Instead, these employees received a reduced annual salary adjustment and competed with other employees for merit pay increases based on their performance in their jobs. According to former President Jimmy Carter, the merit pay system and cash awards program were intended to put "incentive and reward back into the Federal system. . . . From now on, promotions and pay increases will be a sign of jobs well done."[102]

Merit pay, however, has not worked as well as its designers had expected. Numerous problems and inequities have emerged under the system. A GAO report identified a myriad of shortcomings that have plagued the system and have undermined its effectiveness, not only as a fair and equitable pay-for-performance system, but also as an impetus for stimulating quality performance in the federal sector generally.[103]

To administer merit pay, agencies placed employees in organizational groups called "merit pay pools" whose composition was determined by agency management. Employees' increases were paid out of a fixed merit pay fund made up of a maximum of one-half the annual salary adjustment plus an amount equal to the within-grade and quality-step increases pool members would have received had they remained under the general schedule. Performance appraisals formed the basis for agencies' merit pay decisions. Employee performance was assessed according to the degree with which individuals did not meet, met, or exceeded performance standards established at the beginning of the appraisal period.

Of the many problems that have emerged under merit pay, several stand out: (1) Nonperformance-related factors have had an unwarranted impact on the sizes of employees' merit increases. As a result, merit increase amounts have varied considerably among and within agencies, even for employees with the same grade and rating. (2) Negative perceptions of merit pay have developed even among the top performers, who received the largest payouts. Often cited complaints have focused on inconsistencies among raters; the distribution of ratings within a merit pay pool among the various performance levels; the composition of grades and types of employees in the merit pay pool; and agencies' formulas for distributing increases.[104]

GAO found that many problems of merit pay center on performance measures. Despite slight improvements in the quality of performance standards over a two-year period, less than half the standards reviewed by GAO contained objective performance measures, and many did not distinguish between performance levels.[105] Also, employees expressed dissatisfaction with the amount of input they had in setting standards and objected to managers establishing identical standards for different jobs. In addition, although CSRA required performance standards to be communicated to each employee at the beginning of the appraisal period, many employees did not receive their standards until several months after the appraisal period began.

To correct several of these difficulties, in November 1984 Congress replaced merit pay with the Performance Management and Recognition System (PMRS). PMRS retained the "pay for performance" principles of merit pay by requiring that employees receive pay increases and performance awards based on the quality of their performance. But PMRS included new formulas to make PMRS salary increases fairer than those under merit pay. In addition, PMRS required that employees rated at the top level actually receive performance awards and that employees rated one and two levels below be considered for awards. The designers of PMRS expected that these legislative changes would help ensure a fair and workable pay-for-performance system for the government's managers and supervisors.

By 1991, PMRS had not gained government-wide acceptance yet the system was extended by the Congress until September 1993 (Public Law 102-22). This law established a PMRS review committee to advise the OPM on policy and system changes to enhance performance management and recognition of federal managers. A Pay for Performance Labor-Management Committee was also established by FEPCA to advise OPM on ways to strengthen the link between pay and performance for general schedule employees. Both committees were to report to OPM Director Newman. Newman has also taken several actions to examine and attempt to improve pay-for-performance systems. The study she commissioned from the National Academy of Sciences has been widely used in attempting to find solutions for revising the performance management systems for government employees.[106]

Finally, the pay-setting process has proven to be a disappointment to federal unions. From 1962 until 1978, federal labor-management relations evolved under a series of executive orders that recognized the right of federal employees to join (or refrain from joining) employee organizations and defined the scope of negotiations. Before the Civil Service Reform Act of 1978, labor-management policy making was divided between the Federal

Labor Relations Council, composed of the chairman of the Civil Service Commission, the secretary of labor, the director of the Office of Management and Budget, and the assistant secretary of labor for labor-management relations. CSRA consolidated those policy-making functions into the Federal Labor Relations Authority and placed existing labor-relations policies into law. As a result, the unions hoped that the scope of bargainable activities, including some pay decisions, would broaden and that organized sectors of the federal workforce would have a greater impact on policies that affected them.

This has not been the case. The scope of federal bargaining remains narrow when compared to the private sector or to state and local governments. The federal wage system, under which most blue-collar employees are organized and represented by unions, provides for co-participation of labor and management in setting rules for the required private-sector wage surveys, but this hardly constitutes what advocates of unionization mean by full collective bargaining. Some past legislative proposals were meant to broaden the scope of bargaining. The Oakar bill (H.R.4738), for example, would have allowed GS union employees in a selected agency to have a say in pay decisions under one of the proposed demonstration projects. But resistance to this provision of H.R.4738 and declining union membership combined to suggest that proponents of full collective bargaining for federal employees were a long way from achieving their goal. No action was taken on the Oakar bill. Changes based on results of a 1991 GAO study on labor-management relations and 1991 hearings before the House Committee on Post Office and Civil Service were to be considered by Congress in 1992.

Capturing all the issues involved in federal pay and compensation (for example, comparable worth) is nearly impossible, but some themes continue to recur in proposals advanced by members of Congress, the administration, and public employee interest groups, even since FEPCA was passed. No matter what interest is represented, most proposals have one thing in common: They seek to find ways of designing a compensation system that will balance costs (and, in some cases, equity) against the need to recruit and retain an appropriately skilled and motivated workforce. It is a balance that is hard to find because no one knows with certainty what "an appropriately skilled and motivated workforce" looks like or how an increment (or decrement) of compensation contributes (or detracts from) that end. Nevertheless, if FEPCA does not solve recruiting and retention problems, then at least a partial fragmentation of the system can be anticipated. If this indeed comes to pass, then it is likely that some occupational groups and agencies can be expected to be upgraded, while others will be left behind.

Four Futures at the Crossroads

In his seminal work on the civil service, *Democracy and the Public Service*, Frederick C. Mosher divides its history into six time periods, each with its own blend of merit and patronage: (1) government by "gentlemen" (1789–1829); (2) government by the "common man" (1829–83); (3) government by the "good" (1883–1906); (4) government by the "efficient" (1906–37); (5) government by "administrators" (1937–55); and (6) government by "professionals" (1955 to 1982, the date of publication).[107] Each of these periods reflected changes in American society, shifts in the political and technical demands on government, and the development of ideas about how to run a civil service. Each left behind a legacy of concepts, statutes, and practices that affects the way today's civil service policy is conducted.

By the end of the 1980s, the same forces caused a shift toward some new structural alignment. Although it is impossible to label this new period, and the people who will define it in statute (i.e., Congress and the president) had not grappled with it in a comprehensive fashion (preferring instead to deal with pieces of the system), it is possible to identify trends in practices and in proposed and recent legislation that hint at where the civil service system might be headed.

Five trends, in combination, seem capable of shaping the civil service system into a qualitatively different configuration than that which dominated Mosher's most recent era, "government by professionals."

1. The increasing use and acceptance of an "administrative presidency" strategy to staff and direct top positions in the civil service.[108] Such a strategy makes more extensive use of short-term political appointees in all aspects of policy, truncates the top of the civil service career ladders, and limits the responsibilities of career employees to what are primarily technical tasks. The success of the Reagan administration in using political appointees to control the administrative machinery of government is a lesson that is unlikely to be lost to future presidencies.[109]

2. The increasing use and acceptance of the concept of "pay for performance" at all levels of the federal civil service. Beginning with the CSRA of 1978, the use of incentive pay schemes, such as bonuses for the Senior Executive Service and merit pay for middle managers, has been increasingly incorporated into proposals to increase salaries. While these programs are difficult to administer and are not popular with civil servants, they have been strongly endorsed by the Carter, Reagan, and Bush administrations and by outside groups like the Grace Commission and the U.S. Chamber of Commerce. There appears to be a strong likelihood that more ex-

tensive pay-for-performance schemes will cover a greater percentage of federal jobs in the future.

3. The increasing freedom of entry and exit into the federal service facilitated by the new Federal Employees' Retirement System. The greater portability of the retirement system means that present and prospective federal employees can move in and out of government employment without incurring a large financial penalty. Pension reform is likely to create a new openness in the civil service; people will move in and out of federal employment at several stages in their working careers. It also means that federal pay, benefits, and working conditions must keep abreast of private-sector opportunities or the federal government will lose its most marketable personnel to the private sector.

4. The increasing numbers of minorities and women in the federal workforce is another trend with potentially profound implications for the future. Given the explosion of educational opportunities for minorities and women over the past twenty years and the growth of "two-career" and female-headed households, the growth of their numbers in the federal workforce should not be surprising—it is mirrored to some extent in large corporations. But studies of pay and benefits have found that in the aggregate, minorities and women are better paid in the federal government than their private-sector counterparts.[110] Whether this reflects well or poorly on the federal system or the private sector, or simply represents the benefits of affirmative action and equal employment opportunity programs in the federal government, is less important than the simple fact that as long as the gap in rewards and opportunities exists, the federal government will continue to attract a disproportionately larger share of educated minority and female workers. If minority and female employment trends continue, however, and the pay and benefit gap between private and federal employment for minorities and women does not narrow, it might generate proposals to decrease the pay and benefits package for certain agencies and occupational groups where large numbers of women and minorities are employed.

5. There is increasing support for proposals that would have the effect of "splintering" the civil service into several separate pay schedules and formulas. This includes proposals to "privatize" large portions of federal workforce functions; to create a series of public corporations outside the civil service system; to create permanent pay rates and salaries above the pay cap for scientists, engineers, procurement, and acquisition specialists and other occupations in scarce labor markets; and to break up the general schedule into different pay schedules for administrators, clericals, and other professionals. Opponents of these

proposals argue that if such divisions occur, the concept of a National Executive Branch Civil Service—no matter how fragile it is today in practice—will be lost forever. Nevertheless, the idea of separating agencies and occupational groups from the unitary general schedule, by one means or another, is attractive to several agencies and occupational groups with advocates in Congress.

Some of these five trends promise to produce a stronger civil service; others threaten to weaken the capacity of the federal government. At this time it is impossible to predict if and how they will coalesce and, therefore, what their combined impact might be. It is possible to describe some alternative futures and to make some guesses about their probabilities.

Alternative Futures—Views in 1986

Two questions overarch much of the current debate about the civil service: (1) Should the pay, benefits, and responsibilities of civil service jobs be competitive in all respects with comparable jobs in the private sector? and (2) Should the civil service be a unitary entity (with small variations for special occupational categories), or be splintered into many different systems of pay, benefits, and other conditions of work based on markets for different occupations and localities? From these two questions four alternative futures for the civil service come to mind: (1) a noncompetitive, unitary system; (2) a competitive, unitary system; (3) a competitive, splintered system; and (4) a dual system, fully competitive in places and noncompetitive in others.

A Noncompetitive, Unitary System

This is what some critics say we have now. In this arrangement, salary caps, comparability gaps, and the tight interlocking of occupations into a single general schedule with only minor exceptions for "special rates" and special services causes a general erosion in the quality and morale of the civil service. In the words of Representative William Ford, former chairman of the House Committee on Post Office and Civil Service, and Representative Mary Rose Oakar, such an arrangement may make the federal government an "employer of last resort."[111]

It is hard to imagine this situation continuing far into the future. While employee groups with less marketable skills will no doubt attempt to "lock in" the more marketable occupations into a unitary general schedule with the hope of "ratcheting-up" the entire pay schedule, the more marketable employee groups and their agencies will likely continue to attempt to break out of the general schedule. This struggle promises to produce at least a partial breakup of the system.

A Competitive, Unitary System

Such a system would continue to use a single general schedule for most federal employees. It would allow a few exceptions for occupations covered by special rates and "locality pay" for lower-level clerical and technical employees. It would also use a "total compensation" approach to setting wages and benefits. Salary caps and other artificial constraints on market wages would be relaxed. "Pay for performance" would be extended, and pay bands would be widened.

At first glance, this would seem the most likely outcome of current maneuvering in the civil service policy arena because it represents incremental adjustments in the present system. But the scenario appears to be an unlikely outcome for several reasons, not the least of which is that it promises to be very costly. Moreover, if such a system is based on a large-scale ratcheting-up of the salaries of the whole general schedule, it will likely produce substantial distortions in the real wages and benefits paid to different occupational specialties relative to their private-sector counterparts. These factors suggest that government-wide civil service based on a fully competitive, unitary system is an unlikely possibility in the long run.

A Competitive, Splintered System

This alternative future has two versions, a conservative and a liberal one. In the conservative vision, the federal government's functions would be radically reduced in size. Large portions of the government's work would be contracted-out to the private sector or managed by government corporations. The remaining federal employees would be paid at market wages, meaning that some would get substantial raises in pay and benefits, while others would have wages and benefits gradually reduced. Artificial constraints to market prices, such as salary caps, would disappear. For those who would remain in the much smaller civil service, their wages, benefits, and prerequisites would float on a comparability and pay-for-performance basis.

The feasibility of this alternative depends on several things happening at once, not the least of which is the willingness of the president and Congress to move large portions of the federal government into semi-independent status and manage its workforce through a highly diversified set of public, semipublic, and private personnel systems. Therefore, even though there are currently many proposals to privatize different federal functions, given the areas in which the bulk of the federal workforce is employed —defense, security-related agencies, and national "housekeeping" activities—it is hard to imagine political support building for the kind of radically decentralized system that this scheme implies in the aggregate. In short, despite its attractiveness to some conservatives, this alternative future must also be considered a long shot.

The liberal vision of a competitive, splintered system shares with the conservative vision the notion that federal employees should be paid market wages; while some would get substantial raises in pay and benefits, others would be allowed to lag behind at market rates. But that is where the similarities end. The liberal vision leaves little room for privatization or the creation of public corporations and rejects proposals radically to reduce the size of the federal workforce. The concepts of "locality pay" and "pay for performance" would be extended, but with tight controls over managerial discretion. Furthermore, the scope of collective bargaining would be extended to encompass bargaining over pay and benefits. Finally, a few liberals would even support modest reductions in the size of the federal workforce as a tradeoff for higher wages.

This vision must also be considered a long shot, for several reasons. First, Congress has shown little sympathy for removing the pay cap. Second, the principal supporters of this vision, federal employee unions, express some concern that it might negatively affect their members by producing large wage disparities between senior executives and scientists and engineers on the one hand, and clerical and other nontechnical white-collar employees on the other. Third, supporters of locality pay hedge their enthusiasm because they are fearful that it might be used to lower wages in areas where the cost of living is less rather than increase wages in high-cost-of-living regions. Fourth, collective bargaining for pay and benefits might appeal to Congress on a small demonstration basis, but it is unlikely that it will generate much support on a general and permanent basis throughout government. Finally, the tradeoff of a smaller workforce for raises for those who remain has questionable administrative logic that is likely to be apparent to even its most ardent advocates. Such a plan assumes that agencies can increase productivity at a rate equal to declines in personnel. Recent experience with RIFs and cutbacks in staffing levels suggest that this is no easy task. For all these reasons, the liberal vision of the federal workforce of the future seems very unlikely to come about.

A Dual System

If present trends continue, there is a substantial chance that the civil service system will break up into what amounts to a dual structure. To say this is to assume that the stalemate over a comprehensive civil service policy will continue and that Congress and the president will reform small pieces of the system one at a time. Under such a process, the civil service system seems likely to break into two parts, the haves and the have-nots, gradually fraying first the edges and then the core of the present system. The division of the system will come from a combination of forces, including (1) the realization of some limited privatization and public corporation schemes; (2) the breakaway of scientists, engineers, and perhaps lawyers, accountants, contract managers, and acquisition personnel from the general schedule; and (3) separation of whole agencies that will be able to muster the political strength to break away. At the other extreme will be employees without professional status and political clout, such as administrative staff specialists and clericals, and agencies without large constituencies and powerful advocates. They can be expected to gradually float downward in pay, benefits, and perquisites compared to colleagues able to break away from the general schedule. The outcome, therefore, is likely to be a mixture of some up and a few down; that is, a dual system that is fully competitive in some places and not competitive for top-quality employees in others.

Whether this most likely outcome will best serve the national interest is a matter of some debate. That will really depend on whether such a dual system produces flexibility in the "right" places so that the federal workforce has the necessary human resources to do its most important jobs while keeping personnel costs down. It also depends on whether the fragmentation of the system will be so complex that it cannot be managed in an accountable fashion and whether pay disparities between occupation and agencies eventually create demands for greater equity. If these problems arise—and it is likely that they will—it is a safe bet that a decade or two from now, strong counterpressures for reform will be generated for greater unification and standardization of the civil service system. Perhaps, the policy choices at that crossroad—and their potential consequences—will be more apparent than they are today.

Outlook for the Future

Despite the fact that no one of the predicted futures has occurred, many segments of the scenarios are in place. And although in some respects the crisis has abated and much progress has taken place, many questions remain.

Has the image of federal employment improved so that the best and brightest of young people will be attracted to federal service? Are the OPM initiatives to encourage college graduates to enter federal service sufficient to meet the competition from state and local governments and the nonprofit and private sectors? Will the Federal Employees Pay Comparability Act of 1990 provide added incentive for young people to enter federal service and those in crucial occupations to remain? Has the much improved senior executive pay provided enough inducement for senior employees to remain in the government? Will training and development for federal employees be adequate to ensure necessary improvements in government productivity? Will the flexibilities in the Federal Employee Retirement System mean higher turnover rates?

Much will be decided in the near future as the OPM and Director

Newman implement the many initiatives and as political campaigns address the values and contributions of the employees who execute what the federal agenda requires.

Notes

1. For a comprehensive review of the Civil Service Reform Act of 1978, see Patricia Ingraham and Carolyn Ban, eds., *Legislating Bureaucratic Change* (Albany: State University of New York Press, 1985).

2. For this statement, see Charles H. Levine, ed. *The Unfinished Agenda for Civil Service Reform: Implications of the Grace Commission Report* (Washington, D.C.: Brookings Institution, 1985).

3. The use of the phrase "quiet crisis" to describe the current state of federal personnel policy comes from two sources: *The "Quiet Crisis": A Report by the 1984–85 Commission on Executive, Legislative, and Judicial Salaries* (Washington, D.C.: Government Printing Office, 1986); and Carl Brauer, "The Quiet Problem of Public Service," Center for Business and Government, John F. Kennedy School of Government, Harvard University, unpublished paper.

4. Office of Personnel Management, *Federal Civilian Workforce Statistics, Employment and Trends as of July 1991.*

5. Office of Personnel Management, *Pay Structure of the Federal Civil Service; Federal and Civilian Workforce Statistics,* March 1990.

6. Office of Personnel Management, Office of Workforce Information, *The Status of the SES, 1990.*

7. Office of Personnel Management, Office of Workforce Information.

8. See Howard Rosen, *Servants of the People: The Uncertain Future of the Federal Civil Service* (Salt Lake City: Olympic, 1985), 13–30; and Kathy Sawyer, "Uncle Sam's New Look: A Workforce in Transition from Clerks to Technocrats," *Washington Post* (4 August 1980), A1, A7.

9. Office of Personnel Management, *Civil Service 2000,* table 1-5.

10. Rosen, *Servants of the People.*

11. *The Budget of the U.S. Government, FY1992.*

12. General Accounting Office, *How Certain Agencies Are Implementing the Grade Reduction Program,* Report to the Honorable William D. Ford, Chairman, Committee on Post Office and Civil Service, House of Representatives (Washington, D.C.: GAO-GGD 86-33, January 1986).

13. See "Workforce Is Up 5 Percent in 5 Years," *Washington Post,* 30 April 1986.

14. Office of Personnel Management, Office of Workforce Information.

15. The concept of an "inducements-contributions bargain" holding organizations together has been at the center of academic thinking about public ad-

ministration since it was first formulated in Chester Barnard, *The Functions of the Executive* (Cambridge: Harvard University Press, 1938); see also Herbert A. Simon, *Administrative Behavior,* 2d ed. (New York: Free Press, 1957); and James D. Thompson, *Organizations in Action* (New York: McGraw-Hill, 1967).

16. See, for example, Reinhard Bendix, *Higher Civil Servants in American Society* (Boulder: University of Colorado Press, 1949); W. Lloyd Warner, Paul P. Van Riper, Norman H. Martin, and Orvis F. Collins, *The American Federal Executive* (New Haven: Yale University Press, 1963); Franklin P. Kilpatrick, Milton C. Cummings, Jr., and M. Kent Jennings, *The Image of the Federal Service* (Washington, D.C.: Brookings Institution, 1964); John J. Corson and R. Shale Paul, *Men Near the Top: Filling Key Posts in the Federal Service* (Baltimore: Johns Hopkins University Press, 1966); David T. Stanley, Dean E. Mann, and Jameson W. Doig, *Men Who Govern: A Biographical Profile of Federal Political Executives* (Washington, D.C.: Brookings Institution, 1967); Kenneth John Meier, "Representative Bureaucracy: An Empirical Analysis," *American Political Science Review* 69 (June 1965): 526–42; Kenneth John Meier and Lloyd G. Nigro, "Representative Bureaucracy and Policy Preferences: A Study in the Attitudes of Federal Executives," *Public Administration Review* 36 (July/August 1976): 458–69; Joel D. Aberbach and Bert A. Rockman, "Clashing Beliefs Within the Executive Branch: The Nixon Administration Bureaucracy," *American Political Science Review* 70 (June 1976): 456–68; and Hugh Heclo, *A Government of Strangers: Executive Politics in Washington* (Washington, D.C.: Brookings Institution, 1977).

17. For a review of some of these studies see Hal G. Rainey, "Perceptions of Incentives in Business and Government: Implications for Civil Service Reform," *Public Administration Review* 39 (September/October 1979): 440–48. See also Eric Yoder, "Studies Find Workers Rank Pay Below Job Opportunities," *Federal Times,* 29 July 1985, 8.

18. For a recent comparative discussion of these issues see Bruce L.R. Smith, ed., *The Higher Civil Service in Europe and Canada: Lessons for the United States* (Washington, D.C.: Brookings Institution, 1984).

19. See Thomas K. McCraw, "Business and Government: The Origin of the Adversary Relationship," *California Management Review* 26 (Winter 1984): 30–56.

20. Given the decline in purchasing power of federal salaries over the past fifteen years, and the presence of around 360,000 federal civilian employees in the Washington metropolitan area, it should not be surprising that the Washington area leads the nation in two-career families and working women.

21. For a critique of the implementation of the CSRA see Edie N. Goldenberg, "The Grace Commission and the Civil Service Reform: Seeking a Common Understanding," in Levine, *Unfinished Agenda for Civil Service Reform,* 69–101.

22. The belief that there was a "war on the bureaucracy" during the first Reagan term was sufficiently widespread that OPM Director Devine felt the

need to deny it. See Murray Comarow, "The War on Civil Servants," and Donald J. Devine, "There Is No 'War on Civil Servants,'" *Bureaucrat* 10 (Winter 1981–82).

23. See, for example, Bernard Rosen, "A Disaster for Merit," *Bureaucrat* 11, no. 4 (Winter 1982–83): 8–17; and "Crisis in the U.S. Civil Service," *Public Administration Review* 46 (May/June 1986): 207–14.

24. See Chester A. Newland, "A Midterm Appraisal—The Reagan Presidency: Limited Government and Political Administration," *Public Administration Review* 43 (January/February 1983): 1–21.

25. See, for example, the testimony before the Subcommittee on Civil Service, Post Office, and General Services, Senate Committee on Governmental Affairs, presented at the Hearings on S.1327, to Permit Special Pay Rates in Areas Experiencing Recruitment and Retention Problems; S.1727, the Federal Science and Technology Revitalization Act of 1985; and S.2082, the Defense Acquisition Enterprise and Initiative Act of 1986, 15 April 1986.

26. U.S. Merit Systems Protection Board, *The 1984 Report on the Senior Executive Service* (Washington, D.C.: MSPB, December 1984); and *FEIAA Newsletter*, no. 83 (April 1986).

27. See *Report of the President's Pay Agent*, August 1986; U.S. Department of Labor, Bureau of Labor Statistics, *National Survey of Professional, Administrative, Technical, and Clerical Pay*, March 1986, *Bulletin 2243* (Washington, D.C.: Government Printing Office, August 1986); also Hay/Huggins Company and Hay Management Consultants, *Study of Total Compensation in the Federal, State and Private Sectors*, Committee on Post Office and Civil Service, U.S. House of Representatives (Washington, D.C.: Government Printing Office, 1984); and Robert W. Hartman, *Pay and Pensions for Federal Workers* (Washington, D.C.: Brookings Institution, 1983).

28. GAO-GGD 91-63FS.

29. GAO-GGD 87-106FS, 12 August 1987.

30. Edward Bewayo, "What Employees Look For in First and Subsequent Employers," *Personnel* 64, no. 4 (1986).

31. Frank Newman, *Higher Education and the American Resurgence* (Princeton: Princeton University Press, 1985).

32. Jonathan Karp and Susan Benesch, "Shunning the Job-Hunt Maze: Civil Service Loses Career Appeal for Recent College Graduates," *Washington Post*, 27 August 1986, A17.

33. Office of Career Services, Kennedy School of Government, Harvard University, October 1991.

34. Some data are contained in internal agency memoranda made available to the author. Other data are contained in reports to individual members of Congress and in applications for "special rate exemptions" to OPM. One report is David Packard, "The Loss of Government Scientific and Engineering Talent," *Issues in Science and Technology*, Spring 1986, 126–31. See also "Study of Scientists and Engineers in DOD Laboratories," done under contract to the Institute for Defense Analysis, 1990.

35. Judith Haveman, "Lacking Qualified Nurses, NIH Is Closing Beds," *Washington Post,* 22 August 1986. See also GAO-GGD 91-117.

36. Bernard Rosen, "A Disaster for Merit," 9–10.

37. GAO-GGD 85-18, 10 December 1984.

38. See *New Authority to Make and Extend Temporary Appointments* (Washington, D.C.: GAO-GGD 86-111BR, July 1986).

39. *Report of the President's Pay Agent,* August 1986.

40. Ibid.

41. *Occupation Series Dynamics Report, Full-Time Permanent GS Equivalent, FY 1985* (Washington, D.C.: OPM, 1985).

42. GAO-GGD 87-37. See also GAO-GGD 89.

43. Office of Personnel Management, *Occupation Series Dynamics Report, Full-Time Permanent GS Equivalent, FY 1985, FY 1991.*

44. Congressional Budget Office, *Employee Turnover in the Federal Government* (Washington, D.C.: CBO, February 1986).

45. Packard, "Loss of Government Scientific and Engineering Talent," 130.

46. GAO-NSIAD 86-71, 4 March 1986; see also GAO-NSIAD 89-221.

47. Ibid.

48. See Edie N. Goldenberg, "The Permanent Government in an Era of Retrenchment and Redirection," in *The Reagan Presidency and the Governing of America,* ed. Lester M. Salamon and Michael S. Lund (Washington, D.C.: Urban Institute, 1985), 381–404.

49. General Accounting Office, *Federal Retirement: Retirement Data for Selected Agencies,* Fact Sheet for the Honorable Vic Fazio and the Honorable Michael D. Barnes, House of Representatives (Washington, D.C.: GAO-GGD 86-123FS, August 1986); see also Office of Personnel Management, *The Status of the SES, 1990.*

50. Ibid.

51. GAO-GGD 87-106FS.

52. MSPB, *1984 Report on the Senior Executive Service;* and *FEIAA Newsletter.*

53. Judith Haveman, "President Seems Bashful About Managers' Bonuses: Program Underused, with Minimal Fanfare," *Washington Post,* 7 May 1986. See also Office of Personnel Management, *The Status of the SES, 1990.*

54. See Dale Russakoff, "Deficit Worries Bolster New Push for 'Privatization,' " *Washington Post,* 13 January 1986, A11.

55. See Irene S. Rubin, *Shrinking the Federal Government* (New York: Longman, 1985); also Haynes Johnson, "The First Federal Agency: Career of Frustration—Problems Spread Across the Civil Service," *Washington Post,* 25 August 1986, A1, A10.

56. Charles Perrow, *Normal Accidents: Living with High Risk Technologies* (New York: Basic Books, 1984).

57. Terry W. Culler, "Most Federal Workers Need Only Be Competent," *Wall Street Journal,* 21 May 1986, 33.

58. For a review of this and other positions on "privatization," see Ronald C. Moe, *Privatization: An Overview from the Perspective of Public Administration,* Congressional Research Service, Report No. 86-134 (Washington, D.C.: 30 June 1986).

59. Office of Personnel Management, Office of Workforce Information, *Occupations of Federal White-Collar and Blue-Collar Workers,* September 1989.

60. Lester A. Salamon, "Rethinking Public Management: Third-Party Government and the Changing Forms of Government Action," *Public Policy* 29 (Summer 1981): 261. See also Frederick C. Mosher, "The Changing Responsibilities and Tactics of the Federal Government," *Public Administration Review* 40 (November/December 1980): 541–47.

61. Legal opinion—GAO-B222334, 2 June 1986; also GAO-RCED 89-137BR.

62. "Chief Executive Named at New Federal Agency," *New York Times,* 28 January 1986.

63. Milton Friedman, *Capitalism and Freedom* (Chicago: University of Chicago Press, 1962); and Milton Friedman and Rose Friedman, *Free to Choose* (New York: Harcourt Brace Jovanovich, 1980).

64. Rosen, "Crises in the U.S. Civil Service," *Public Administration Review* (May-June 1986): 213.

65. O. Glenn Stahl and James J. McGurrin, "Professionalizing the Career Service," *Bureaucrat* 15 (Spring 1986): 14.

66. Ibid., 15.

67. Remarks of Walter F. Mondale at the dedication of the Hubert H. Humphrey Center, Minneapolis, Minnesota, 27 May 1986; remarks of Paul A. Volcker before the Harvard Alumni Association, Cambridge, Mass., 15 May 1985; and Alexander B. Trowbridge, "Attracting the Best to Washington," *Harvard Business Review,* March-April 1985, 174–78.

68. See Ronald C. Moe, "A New Hoover Commission: A Timely Idea or a Misdirected Nostalgia?" *Public Administration Review* 42 (May/June 1982): 270–77.

69. Stahl and McGurrin, "Professionalizing the Career Service," 14–15.

70. See Smith, *Higher Civil Service in Europe and Canada.*

71. See, for example, Newland, "A Midterm Appraisal—The Reagan Presidency."

72. President's Private Sector Survey on Cost Control, *Report on Personnel Management* (Washington, D.C.: PPSSCC, 1983).

73. General Accounting Office, *Agencies Use of the Candidate Development Program,* Report to the Chairman, Subcommittee on Civil Service, Post Office and General Service, Committee on Governmental Affairs, United States Senate (Washington, D.C.: GAO-GGD 86-93, July 1986). See also Office of Personnel Management, *Status of the SES, 1990.*

74. Ibid.

75. Ibid.

76. Goldenberg, "Grace Commission and Civil Service Reform."

77. For a description and analysis of this program, see Peter M. Benda and Charles H. Levine, *President Reagan's Productivity Improvement Program: Déjà Vu, Fresh Start to an Old Story, or Lasting Reform*. Congressional Research Service, Report No. 86-895 (Washington, D.C.: 15 April 1986).

78. Civil Service Commission, Bureau of Policies and Standards, *Studies of Federal White-Collar Compensation* (Washington, D.C.: CSC, October 1975).

79. Hartman, *Pay and Pensions for Federal Workers*, 77–107.

80. Ibid.

81. Ibid.

82. Ibid.

83. *Report to the President's Panel on Federal Compensation* (Washington, D.C.: Government Printing Office, 1975).

84. *Personnel Management Project*, vol. 1, *Final Staff Report* (Washington, D.C.: President's Reorganization Project, 1977).

85. Bureau of Labor Statistics, National Survey of Professional Administration, Technical, and Clerical Pay, March 1986.

86. *The "Quiet Crisis": A Report by the 1984–85 Commission on Executive, Legislative, and Judicial Salaries*; Brauer, "The Quiet Problem of Public Service."

87. Ibid.

88. For further analysis of this problem, see Robert W. Hartman and Arnold R. Weber, eds., *The Rewards of Public Service: Compensating Top Federal Officials* (Washington, D.C.: Brookings Institution, 1980).

89. Roger H. Davidson, "The Politics of Executive, Legislative, and Judicial Compensation," in Hartman and Weber, *Rewards of Public Service*, 53–98.

90. *The "Quiet Crisis": A Report by the 1984–85 Commission on Executive, Legislative, and Judicial Salaries*; Brauer, "The Quiet Problem of Public Service."

91. GAO-GGD 90-118, September 1990. See also GAO-GGD 90-117, September 1990.

92. *Report of the White House Science Council, Federal Laboratory Review Panel* (Washington, D.C.: Office of Science and Technology Policy, Executive Office of the President, May 1983).

93. See, for example, David Packard, statement before the Subcommittee on Compensation and Employee Benefits, U.S. House of Representatives, 10 June 1986.

94. See Judith Haveman, "Pentagon Pay Plan Rejected by Senate: Goal Was to Attract Civilian Employees," *Washington Post*, 12 August 1986, A4.

95. Ibid.

96. "Personnel Management Project Verifies Non-Civil Service System," *Aviation Week and Space Technology*, 20 January 1986, 85–86.

97. GAO-GGD 86-14, October 1985.

98. President's Private Sector Survey on Cost Control (J. Peter Grace, Chairman), *War on Waste* (New York: Macmillan, 1984).

99. GAO-GGD 86-14, October 1985.

100. Ibid.

101. One proposal would create a separate service for all "professionals" in the federal government; Federal Executive and Professional Association, *Career Professionals in the Federal Service—Navigators of the Ship of State* (Washington, D.C.: FEPA, 23 August 1985).

102. President Carter at the signing ceremony for the Civil Service Reform Act of 1978, 13 October 1978.

103. GAO-GGD 81-1, 26 March 1984.

104. Ibid.

105. GAO-GGD 86-79FS, 16 May 1986; GAO-GGD 87-28, 21 January 1987.

106. National Research Council, *Pay for Performance: Evaluating Performance Appraisal and Merit Pay* (Washington, D.C.: National Academy Press, 1991).

107. Frederick C. Mosher, *Democracy and the Public Service,* 2d ed. (New York: Oxford University Press, 1982).

108. See Richard P. Nathan, *The Administrative Presidency* (New York: Wiley, 1983).

109. There are widely different perceptions of the efficacy of this approach. For example, Hugh Heclo, "A Government of Enemies?" *Bureaucrat* 14 (Fall 1984): 12–14; and Michael Sanera, "Implementing the Mandate," in *Mandate for Leadership II: Continuing the Conservative Revolution,* ed. Stuart M. Butler, Michael Sanera, and W. Bruce Weinrod (Washington, D.C.: Heritage Foundation, 1984).

110. Steven F. Venti, "Wages in the Federal and Private Sectors," paper prepared for the National Bureau of Economic Research Conference on Public Sector Payrolls, Williamsburg, Virginia, 15–17 November 1984. Other studies that conclude that the federal wage-setting process distorts salaries upward are Sharon Smith, *Equal Pay in the Public Sector: Fact or Fantasy?* (Princeton: Princeton University, Industrial Relations Section, 1977); Jack Meyer, *An Analysis of Federal Pay* (Washington, D.C.: American Enterprise Institute, 1983); and Office of Personnel Management, *Reforming Federal Pay: An Examination of More Realistic Pay Alternatives* (Washington, D.C.: OPM, December 1984).

111. Remarks of the Honorable William D. Ford, U.S. House of Representatives, 13 March 1986; and opening statement of the Honorable Mary Rose Oakar, *Oversight Hearing on Pay,* 19 March 1986.

II

The State of Merit in the Federal Government

Patricia W. Ingraham
AND
David H. Rosenbloom
with the research assistance of
John P. Knight

> The merit system, by raising the character and capacity of the
> subordinate service, and by accustoming the people to consider
> personal worth and sound principles, rather than selfish interest
> and adroit management as the controlling elements of success in
> politics, has also invigorated national patriotism, raised the stand-
> ard of statesmanship, and caused political leaders to look more to
> the better sentiments and the higher intelligence for support.
> —The Eaton Report to President Rutherford B. Hayes, 1879

The Problem

For over one hundred years, the American civil service has been guided by
merit principles. Those principles, underpinning a system intended to protect federal employment and employees from partisan politics, were simple
and direct: fair and open competition for federal jobs, admission to the
competitive service only on the basis of neutral examinations, and protection of those in the service from political influence and coercion. The system that has grown from these principles, however, is not simple and
direct. Today, rules and regulations related to federal personnel administration fill thousands of pages. Today, the federal government's merit system
does not work. These procedures have created a system in which the
recruitment, testing, and hiring of employees is often conducted independently of those who will manage and be responsible for the employees' per-

formance. The personnel function is often viewed independently—indeed, often in isolation—from management concerns and priorities. Many continue to define merit only in terms of entrance to the federal service through centralized neutral and objective examinations, but in a diverse and complex society, tests alone are not an accurate measure of merit. It is abundantly clear that the construction and administration of such examinations create as many problems as they solve. Many federal managers argue that the time spent trying to understand the system overshadows whatever benefits the merit system provides.

In 1978, President Jimmy Carter declared that there was "no merit in the merit system." Others have argued that there is no system in the merit system. Incremental laws and procedures, accumulating over a one-hundred-year period, have created a jerrybuilt set of rules and regulations whose primary emphasis is on negative control of federal personnel, rather than on a positive affirmation of merit and quality in the federal service. The design of a system intended to screen large numbers of applicants for a limited number of positions is outdated and inappropriate for contemporary technology and the changing demographics of the twenty-first century. The elimination of the discriminatory Professional and Administrative Career Examination (PACE) in 1982 demonstrated how entrance procedures should not look, but failed to specify how they should. The gradual accretion of often conflicting objectives, rules, and regulations has created, not a coherent national system of merit, but a confusing maze of procedure. At the same time, the long-term effectiveness of the federal government rests on the ability to recruit and retain a quality workforce. The many restrictive components of the contemporary merit system severely inhibit that ability. Merit has come to signify a narrow and negative focus on positions and jobs, rather than competence, accountability, and effective public service.

It is not the intent of this chapter to propose or endorse specific reforms, although there are many. Instead, the purpose is to describe the disjointed evolution and current state of the federal merit system—the status quo from which future reforms must proceed. Very clearly, those reforms cannot build on a clear and coherent foundation, for no such foundation exists. Future reforms, therefore, must address fundamental questions: What does "merit" mean for contemporary federal personnel administration?[1] What are the critical components of a merit system for the future? Is it possible to replace rules and regulations with flexibility and discretion for federal personnel, but still to ensure accountability and responsiveness to the public and to elected officials? Without this fundamental analysis, current proposals for reform may only contribute to the system's baggage; the ability of the federal government to be an effective and competitive employer will not be addressed.

The Origins

The passage of the Pendleton Act in 1883 began the process of creating a civil service based on merit for the American national government. Strongly anchored in the experience of the British civil service, the American system nonetheless reflected uniquely American politics and government. The public excesses of the patronage system were viewed as a national disgrace and as a serious burden on the presidency. The assassination of President James Garfield by a demented office seeker dramatically demonstrated the problem. The glut of office seekers in Washington and their constant demands on the president and his staff created other problems; they reportedly led President Abraham Lincoln to request, when he contracted smallpox, that all the office seekers be sent to him, for "now I have something I can give to each of them."[2]

The passage of the legislation reflected political realities as well. There were strong civil service leagues in many states. They had successfully placed personnel reform on the agenda for the 1882 congressional elections. The support expressed for reform in those midterm elections ensured that it would become a national issue. Political demands, however, were tempered by a serious constitutional question: Did the creation of a centralized personnel system and Civil Service Commission violate the powers of both the president and Congress over personnel matters?[3]

The dilemma posed by the political need to act and questions of constitutional legitimacy produced a classically political solution: The initial legislation covered only 10 percent of the federal workforce. But Congress granted the president power to include additional federal employees in the classified civil service by Executive Order. Patronage would be controlled, but slowly. Van Riper notes, "If the act permitted an orderly retreat of parties from their prerogatives of plunder, it made possible as well the gradual administrative development of the merit system."[4]

At the heart of the new merit system was one fundamental principle: Admission to the classified civil service would be *only* through open competitive examinations. Unlike the British system, which relied on formal academic training, the American system hailed the practical American spirit; the examinations would focus on common sense, practical information, and skills. The examination system would be designed to provide all who desired federal employment a fair, equal, and objective opportunity to enter the civil service. The act created decentralized Boards of Examiners to administer the tests and specified that they "be so located as to make it reasonably convenient and inexpensive for applicants to attend before them."[5]

The American system also differed from its British heritage in its definition and treatment of neutrality. Very clearly, political neutrality was to be a hallmark of the new classified civil service. The need for a competent civil service that would serve either political party well was widely accepted. At the same time, neither members of Congress, the president, nor the reformers were willing to commit to the British tradition of an elite higher civil service whose members were active participants in policy debates. Policy participation was not viewed as a legitimate administrative function. For the American civil service, neutrality was a protection against politics, but also an exclusion from policy. Herbert Kaufman offered the following assessment: "the civil service was like a hammer or a saw; it would do nothing at all by itself, but it would serve any purpose, wise or unwise, good or bad, to which any user put it." [6]

The Growth of the Classified Service

The origins of the merit system in the federal government are important for a number of reasons. First, because the system had a purposefully limited beginning, growth could, and did, occur in an unplanned and unpredictable way. Second, the system was formed in a way designed to gather the largest possible number of applicants for a limited number of government jobs. The "fair and open competition" principle was interpreted from the outset to be national competition for what were then largely Washington-based jobs (postmasters were not included in the original legislation). The system was, in short, designed to be a screening system and was based on the fundamental assumption that there would be many more job seekers than jobs. Further, since most positions would be in Washington, centralizing the personnel function within the Civil Service Commission made good sense. Third, despite the emphases on objective merit and free and open competition, the Pendleton Act included provisions whose intent and impact was to attenuate those emphases. The act specifically noted, for example, that veterans were to continue to be given preference in federal hiring, a practice that had been formally established in 1865. In addition, the Pendleton Act reaffirmed the nation's commitment to a geographically "representative" federal workforce, an emphasis first articulated during George Washington's presidency. Merit, veterans' preference, and geographic representativeness did not necessarily coincide, even in 1883. In the ensuing years, veterans' groups, in particular, have often pursued objectives clearly at odds with those of federal personnel experts and managers.

Finally, the provision for presidential determination of increased coverage did not remove politics from the development of the civil service system; instead, it ensured that the growth of "merit" would be dependent on political cycles. Presidents who chose to extend the merit system often came under attack from their own parties for doing so; each extension of civil service coverage meant fewer patronage appointments and fewer payoffs for party loyalty. As a result, commitment by presidents to merit and the classified civil service fluctuated dramatically in the early years. Generally, presidents such as Theodore Roosevelt (also a former civil service commissioner) who succeeded a president of their own party found advancing merit to be somewhat easier than those who did not. President William McKinley, for example, included 1700 additional employees in the classified service by Executive Order, but also exempted about 9,000 employees through rollback and new exemption procedures.[7] Woodrow Wilson took the reins of a federal government that had been controlled for sixteen years by Republicans. Despite his association with the National Civil Service Reform Association, the Wilson administration was under intense pressure for patronage. President Wilson said of this pressure, "The matter of patronage is a thorny path that daily makes me wish I had never been born."[8]

Congress, too, retained a keen interest in patronage. As new governmental tasks and functions were approved, Congress could choose to place the jobs created outside the classified service. From the time of the first Wilson term to the New Deal, that option was often pursued. It was pushed to new heights—this time at presidential initiative—in Franklin Roosevelt's New Deal. The experience of the civil service in the New Deal years is treated differently by different analysts; Van Riper, for example, offers an exceedingly harsh assessment. More pragmatically, Kaufman notes that Franklin Roosevelt managed to "kill two birds with one stone," when he "put into effect all of the programs and projects he considered vital for the welfare of the country. And he excepted the positions in these agencies from the classified service, thus enabling him to fill many of the patronage demands threatening the merit system."[9] In any case, prior to Roosevelt's election in 1932, approximately 80 percent of federal employees were in the competitive civil service. By 1936, that proportion had declined to about 60 percent.[10]

The percentage of the federal workforce under merit protection gradually increased during and after World War II. That time period also saw notable efforts to bring cohesion to the previously haphazard development of the civil service system. The Ramspeck Act in 1940, for example, gave the president the authority to eliminate existing exemptions, including those created by the Pendleton Act. By 1951, about 87 percent of total federal employment was in the classified service.[11] The percentage expanded still further throughout the 1960s and 1970s, so that, by 1980, well over 90 percent of the federal workforce was covered by civil service laws and regulations.

The Growth in Complexity

The Pendleton Act itself contained the seeds for the disjointed growth, internal contradictions, and enormous complexity of the American merit system. The very limited initial coverage and the presidential power to extend merit created "blanketing in" procedures. As each new group of employees was thus included in the system, employees who had been appointed by patronage became members of the merit system. As the Civil Service Commission noted, "Although the practice represents a deviation from the merit principle, it makes future appointments to the 'blanketed in' positions subject to merit rules."[12] In addition, the provisions for veterans' preference flatly repudiated the merit principles that applied to everyone else in the competitive system. It was not until 1953, for example, that veterans were required to achieve a passing score on the competitive examinations before having their five- or ten-point veterans' preference added.[13] All other applicants, of course, were not considered for federal employment if they failed the examination.

Hiring

There were other deviations from merit principles. Almost from the beginning, the Civil Service Commission divided the classified civil service into "competitive" (competitive exam required), "noncompetitive" (noncompetitive exam required) and "excepted" (no exam required). Schedule A authority, which exempted from examination some positions that were technically within the classified service, formalized these distinctions. Until 1910, all noncompetitive and excepted categories were lumped under Schedule A authority. In 1910, Schedule B was created to include all noncompetitive positions. In 1953, an Executive Order from President Dwight Eisenhower removed confidential and other policy-sensitive positions from Schedule A and placed them in the newly created Schedule C, whose intent was to permit the president greater numbers of political appointees in policy-sensitive posts (as well as in other lower-level positions, such as chauffeurs and receptionists).[14] Although Schedule A authority is now used primarily for appointing in specialized professions such as law and accounting, Schedule B authority became the primary vehicle for federal hiring in the period immediately following the abolition of PACE. Because federal hiring during this period was limited to a few major agencies with the greatest employment needs, most federal agencies had no systematic hiring authority available to them and little, if any experience with Schedule B. In 1985, one of the last years of heavy reliance on Schedule B, 98 percent of all appointments under the authority were made by nine of the twenty-one largest departments and agencies.[15] The use of Schedule C, although fairly limited initially, has also expanded in the past twenty years, primarily at upper grade levels.[16]

It is also important to consider the large number of special authorities under which federal agencies now hire. Reliance on such authorities (as well as on Schedule B) was necessitated by the abolition of the Professional and Administrative Career Examination (PACE) in 1982. PACE, which replaced the earlier Federal Service Entrance Examination (FSEE), had provided a single centralized means of recruitment and entry for many federal jobs. When PACE was abolished with no replacement, it became necessary for the Office of Personnel Management (OPM) and the many federal agencies to fall back on existing limited authorities and to use them for purposes for which most had never been intended.

Temporary appointment authority, intended to simplify hiring and separation, as well as to limit the expansion of government, is one such special authority. Temporary appointments have increased substantially in both numbers and duration in recent years, particularly since 1984, when the OPM permitted expansion of their use. Of equal significance, methods of appointing to temporary positions have increased dramatically. At the present time in the federal government, there are *thirty-five* ways to appoint to temporary positions alone.[17] Part-time appointments are an additional option; they, too, are not consistently made through competitive examination procedures.

Direct-hire authority was created for hard-to-hire occupations such as engineers, nurses, and scientists. Direct-hire appointments are made on the basis of unassembled examinations. In 1989, a new direct-hire authority was created for Vietnam veterans. The Outstanding Scholar authority permits on-the-spot hiring of college graduates who have completed four-year degrees with a GPA of 3.5 or better. Simplified hiring procedures also exist for affirmative-action hires, for returned Peace Corps volunteers, and for students enrolled in the Cooperative Education Program, among others. A precise and current list of the many authorities available to federal employers is difficult because the OPM has not updated and distributed such a list since 1980. It is important to note, however, that in 1989, 45 percent of federal career appointments were made under provisions that delegated either examining or hiring authority (or, in some cases, both) to the individual agencies. Another 25 percent were direct-hire appointments in hard-to-hire occupations, while about 15 percent were specialized mid- to senior-level appointments for which there was no register. Only about 15 percent of the appointments were made through "traditional" civil service procedures; that is, through centralized examination or from central registers administered by OPM.[18]

Finally, the federal merit hiring "system" is made more complex by the inclusion of entire agencies (FBI, CIA, Postal Service) in excepted authorities and by the creation of separate but parallel merit systems in others (TVA, for example). The Foreign Service operates with a separate system; so too does the Public Health Service. In some organizations, such as the Department of Health and Human Services and the State Department, more than one system is in place.

In 1978, major civil service reform legislation was passed. A centerpiece of Carter administration domestic policy, the Civil Service Reform Act of 1978 (CSRA) was intended to simplify federal personnel policy through decentralization and delegation, as well as to increase the accountability and responsiveness of federal employees through performance appraisal and evaluation. CSRA created financial incentives linked to performance for top career executives and mid-level managers. The act created the Senior Executive Service (SES) in an effort to make the senior management cadre of the federal career service more flexible and more responsive. It codified federal labor-management practices for the first time, reaffirmed the federal government's commitment to representativeness and affirmative action, and provided new protection for whistleblowers. The act abolished the Civil Service Commission and replaced it with the Office of Personnel Management, the Merit Systems Protection Board, and the Federal Labor Relations Authority. These new institutions were to be leaders in shaping a new and more coherent federal personnel and human resource management strategy.

Because CSRA was the first comprehensive reform of the civil service in nearly a hundred years, expectations for improvements were high. In fact, however, many of those expectations have not been met.[19] This is due to a modest understanding and shallow level of support for many of the reforms; the new political environment of the Reagan administration also had a profound impact on many of the primary implementation activities. The budgetary cutbacks in the early years of the Reagan administration accompanied implementation of critical components of the reform. Much of the political rhetoric accompanying proposed policy changes was directed at the career bureaucracy: the "permanent government." Morale was very low. Delegation, decentralization, and simplification proceeded in fits and starts; attention was again paid to this issue only because the abolition of PACE removed the major central means of recruiting and testing for the federal service.

Most significantly, however, for all its emphasis on greater clarity and simplicity in the federal merit system, the Civil Service Reform Act did not replace the tangle of procedures related to federal personnel practices. In many respects, it merely added another layer of complexity and confusion to an already complex system. Decentralization and delegation of recruiting and hiring, for example, is not simplification if 6,000 pages of rules, regulations, and guidelines remain in effect. The ability to understand and monitor such a system is extremely difficult, and probably impossible in the absence of any central guiding principles and objectives. The ability to understand and manage effectively in such a system is made even more difficult when other characteristics of the federal personnel system are considered.

Classification and Compensation

Classification of federal employees was formally authorized in 1923 with the passage of the Classification Act. This legislation not only classified positions according to duties and responsibilities but also assigned salary levels to those positions. It therefore established in law the principle of nationally uniform compensation levels. The act was passed shortly after the Budget and Accounting Act of 1921, and clearly fell under the umbrella of the economy and efficiency movement so prevalent in government at that time. Van Riper notes that "the Bureau of the Budget [created by the 1921 act] tended to emphasize economy at the expense of almost everything else. But the pressing need for careful estimates of personnel and personnel costs, if any budget was to really mean anything, stimulated further concern with the standardization ... of federal wages and functions." [20]

The administration of the new act was supervised by a newly created Personnel Classification Board.

In addition, the act established in law the American principle of "rank in job," rather than the European practice of "rank in person." This meant that the salary or wages for each job was determined solely by the position and by the necessary qualifications for that position, not by the personal qualifications of the person filling the position (although presumably they matched fairly closely). Finally, the act institutionalized the very specialized nature of the American civil service. The jobs to be classified were narrow and specific; again, in keeping with the economy and efficiency movement, flexibility and discretion were limited whenever possible.

Although an analysis of the Classification Act's effectiveness in 1929 indicated that it had not created a "consistent and equitable system of ... pay for positions involving the same work," [21] there was no additional reform in this area until 1949. There were, however, fairly consistent calls for change during that twenty-year period. The Commission of Inquiry on Public Service Personnel noted in 1935, for example, that "the most obvious fault to be found with all classifications made on the American plan is their complexity—the great number of classes and occupational hierarchies that are set up. What seem to be the most trifling differences in function or difficulty are formally recognized and duly defined...." The commission noted further that "classifications of such complexity are to be condemned because of the fetters that they place upon department heads in the management of their business." [22]

The Ramspeck Act extended the Civil Service Commission's authority for classification to the entire field service in 1940; in 1945 a presidential order directed the commission to begin that task. By that time, the commission was responsible for about half of the total federal civil service positions. [23] The complexity of the federal personnel system was now much in evidence. The absence of a comprehensive wage-and-salary policy had become a notable problem. The final report of the first Hoover Commission detailed the issues related to pay and personnel and concluded: "Probably no problem in the management of the Government is more important than that of obtaining a capable and conscientious body of public servants. Unfortunately, personnel practices in the federal government give little room for optimism that these needs are being met." [24]

In 1949, at least partially in response to Hoover Commission recommendations, the Classification Act of 1949 was passed. The act created the "supergrade" system, which preceded the Senior Executive Service, and simplified the occupational series by merging the previous five into two. The Classification Act of 1949 is important for another reason: It marked an early point on what has now come to be considered the "cycle" of centralization and decentralization in federal personnel policy. Excessive centralization of classification activities was perceived to be a major cause of an overly rigid and slow system. As a result, the 1949 act delegated classification authority for positions below the supergrades back to the agencies. It gave the Civil Service Commission postaudit review authority for those delegations. With other authority such as examining still residing with the Civil Service Commission, with very limited experience in classification activity at the agency level, and with extensive central regulations and procedures still governing the activity, however, this delegation set the precedent for others to follow. Authority was gradually pulled back into the commission until, when the Civil Service Reform Act of 1978 was written, excessive centralization was again perceived to be the problem.

Despite the centrality of classification activities to federal personnel policy and pay, classification has not been thoroughly analyzed since before the passage of the 1949 act. In the intervening forty years, the procedures and regulations associated with classification—most notably the classification and qualification standards[25]—have become seriously outdated and burdensome. The Merit Systems Protection Board recently found, for example, that 63 *percent* of the white-collar classification standards currently in use were issued before 1973.[26] In addition, for the 1982-84 period, OPM declared a moratorium on writing new classification standards and the problem was exacerbated. Because grade levels flow directly from classification and qualification standards (or they *should*), the link between these standards and pay is immutable. Obsolescent standards inevitably influence the ability to determine fair pay for an occupation or grade. There are more than 900 occupations in the federal classified service and over 30 different pay systems. The links between the two cannot be ignored in reform, and simplification or total redesign of federal classification schemes is also necessary.

The Civil Service Reform Act of 1978, which did not address the issue of pay, did give the Office of Personnel Management authority to delegate classification activities to the agencies. It did so, however, without addressing or eliminating the plethora of rules and regulations that had accumulated over the years and without directly reforming the Classification Act of 1949. As noted earlier, this failure to address the procedural "baggage" added yet another layer of complexity to a very murky system. To date, OPM has limited such delegation to a very small number of demonstration projects. "Reform" of classification and qualification standards has occurred primarily through efforts to write "generic" standards, which provide greater flexibility. Without a fundamental reexamination of classification procedures, however, other efforts at personnel and pay reform necessarily remain somewhat tangential to change.

Training and Development

Training and development of the federal workforce has had a somewhat checkered history. Although a limited number of agencies created education and training programs for their employees, general direction and support was clearly lacking until the passage of the Government Employees Training Act of 1958. Indeed, Van Riper notes that, before 1940, "the excess of applicants compared to available jobs had suggested to both Congress and many administrators that extensive in-service training programs were essentially wasteful." [27] The very limited supply of labor during World War II mandated that federal personnel policy include provisions for training and retraining of federal personnel. At the end of the war, however, many of these activities were cut back or eliminated. The training void was duly noted by the first Hoover Commission and, partially in response to the Hoover Report, President Truman directed the Civil Service Commission to attack what the commission itself called the "curse of excessive specialization." [28] By most accounts, this attack garnered only modest results.

During the presidency of Dwight Eisenhower, whose military training convinced him of the benefits of the enterprise, training began to achieve more credibility. In Eisenhower's first term, the Federal Training Policy Statement was issued. This directive advocated formulation of training plans and emphasis on employee development opportunities. The Civil Service Commission was given lead responsibility for these training efforts. In 1958, during the second Eisenhower term, his administration followed up with the Government Employees Training Act of 1958. Although passage of the act involved intense political negotiation, this act legitimized the training function and provided funds for training and centralized training programs. In its 1974 report, *Biography of an Ideal*, the Civil Service Commission argued that the provisions of the 1958 act "make the training function in the United States Government the envy of even the most advanced of nations." [29] That statement was undoubtedly an exaggeration in 1974; it is clearly not accurate today.

Like much else in the federal personnel system, training and development have not grown in a systematic and coherent way. Despite the provisions of the 1958 act (which has never been revisited), training has remained a fairly low priority. In times of budget cuts and constraints, training costs are often the first to be eliminated from the budget. In its report to the National Commission on the Public Service, the Task Force on Education and Training said, "There are significant shortcomings in federal government human resource policies. Government agencies spend far too little on training of all kinds and concentrate their efforts on meeting narrow, short-term needs. The area of greatest concern is the plainly inadequate attention paid to the development of management and executive leadership in the civil service." [30]

The Civil Service Commission and, later, the Office of Personnel Management, did not develop a government-wide training strategy until Constance Newman assumed the directorship of OPM in the Bush administration. Financial support for training at both central and agency levels remains very limited. At the same time, the need for training and retraining has never been more clear. The demographics of the twenty-first century, changing skill demands, and dramatic technological progress all point to new development needs. Merit and competence are inextricably intertwined.

The Courts and the Merit System

In the 1970s and 1980s, the federal judiciary played a substantial role in defining and redefining the merit system. The Supreme Court, in particular, has been an ardent supporter of two historical tenets of merit: (1) depoliticization of the public service, and (2) assuring that operational definitions and applications of merit in public personnel administration are strongly job related.

Depoliticization

A major goal of the merit system has been to remove partisan politics from public personnel management. George William Curtis, a leading nineteenth-century civil service reformer, noted that the merit system made it possible to take "the whole non-political public service out of politics." [31] The effort had two prongs: to prohibit public employees from taking an active part in partisan political management and campaigning, and to eliminate patronage hiring and dismissal from the public service. The Supreme Court has embraced both elements of depoliticization.

The effort to remove public employees from partisan politics has been most generally embodied in the first and second Hatch Acts (1939 and 1940) and in various state and local equivalents. The first Hatch Act applies only to federal employees; it prohibits them from using their "official authority or influence for the purpose of interfering with or affecting the result of an election," or from taking an "active part in political management or political campaigns." The second Hatch Act applies similar restrictions to state and local government employees whose positions are at least partially funded by the federal government. These measures carve out a legal and political status for public employees that is remarkably different from that of ordinary citizens. While partisan political participation is considered virtuous for citizens generally, it is simply illegal for public employees. Not surprisingly, both acts have been subject to challenge in the courts on the grounds that they violate the First and Fourteenth Amendment rights of public employees. They have also been attacked for vagueness because both acts lack a comprehensive definition of the activities they proscribe.

The constitutional arguments against the Hatch Acts and similar political neutrality statutes have filled volumes of law reviews and many court briefs. In 1973, however, the Supreme Court seemed to put the constitutional issues to rest in an opinion that strongly supported depoliticization of the public service and afforded Congress great latitude in seeking to achieve that end. In *U.S. Civil Service Commission* v. *National Association of Letter Carriers (NALC)*,[32] the Court held:

> We unhesitatingly reaffirm ... that Congress ... has the power to prevent [federal employees covered by the first Hatch Act] from holding a party office, working at the polls and acting as party paymaster for other party workers.... Our judgment is that neither the First Amendment nor any other provision of the Constitution invalidates a law barring this kind of partisan political conduct by federal employees.
>
> Such a decision on our part would no more than confirm the judgment of history, a judgment made by this country over the last century that it is in the best interests of the country, indeed essential, that federal service should depend upon meritorious performance rather than political service.

The *NALC* decision effectively allows Congress to take virtually any reasonable steps to remove the federal service from partisan political activity. The Court went even further in supporting depoliticization when, in *Elrod* v. *Burns* (1976),[33] it ruled patronage dismissals from ordinary public-service positions *unconstitutional*.

Elrod concerned the constitutionality of patronage dismissals from the Cook County, Illinois, Sheriff's Office. The discharged employees claimed that their First and Fourteenth Amendment rights to freedom of belief and association had been violated. A majority of the Supreme Court's justices agreed that the dismissals were unconstitutional, but the Court was unable to reach a majority opinion as to precisely why.

The issue was more fully clarified in *Branti* v. *Finkel* (1980),[34] in which the Court came close to "constitutionalizing" merit. In assessing the patronage dismissal of two public defenders in Rockland County, New York, Justice John Paul Stevens, speaking for the Court's majority, reasoned that patronage dismissals are unconstitutional unless "the hiring authority can demonstrate that that party affiliation is an appropriate requirement for the effective performance of the public office involved." As Justice Lewis Powell argued in dissent, however, the only logical alternative to a patronage system is one that is merit oriented: "Many public positions previously filled on the basis of membership in national political parties now must be staffed in accordance with a constitutionalized civil service standard that will affect the employment practices of federal, state and local governments."

An important aspect of the *Branti* ruling is that the Court reasoned that merely labeling positions "policy making" or "confidential" is not enough to justify patronage dismissals from them. In practice, this means that some traditional public personnel classifications, such as "excepted" and "exempt," will no longer be synonymous with "at the pleasure" of the political official at the head of an agency or government.

In sum, the Supreme Court has been very sympathetic to the nineteenth-century civil service reformers' ideal of taking politics out of the public service and the public service out of politics. It has declared that patronage dismissals will generally be unconstitutional and has held that the Constitution can easily accommodate restrictions on public employees' partisan political activities. At the same time, it must be noted that Congress has recently raised questions about the overall utility of the Hatch Act and about its infringement on the rights of public employees. Each of the last several sessions has seen the introduction of legislation intended to roll back Hatch provisions. Those in favor of reform argue that federal employees are severely disadvantaged by the inability to participate in politics on their own behalf. Those opposing reform argue that continued political restrictions on federal employees are essential to maintaining any semblance of a merit system. It is important to note that the strength of the proreform group has increased recently; in fact, some observers predicted reform of the Hatch Acts before the end of 1990.[35] The Supreme Court's view of such legislation, should it pass, could be an important redefinition of merit.

Making Sure That the Merit System Assures Merit

A second aspect of the judiciary's involvement in public personnel administration has concerned the very meaning of *merit*. Here, too, the thrust of judicial activity has been two pronged.

All merit systems afford covered employees protection against arbitrary, capricious, illegal, or unconstitutional dismissals. These same systems provide for dismissals in the interests of the efficiency of the public service. During the aftermath of the loyalty-security programs of the late 1940s and early 1950s, the federal judiciary began to look more closely at the government's claims that particular dismissals promoted efficiency. In *Board of Regents* v. *Roth* (1972),[36] the Supreme Court held that public employees are constitutionally entitled to procedural due process protection when dismissals abridged their constitutional rights or liberties, damaged their reputations, seriously impaired their future employability, or infringed upon a property interest, such as tenure, in their jobs. By 1985, the Court had expanded the application of due process considerably. In *Cleveland Board of Education* v. *Loudermill*, [37] it found that a public employee had a "property right" in a job because the Ohio civil service statute made him a "classified civil service" employee, who was entitled to retain his position "during good behavior and efficient service."

Constitutional due process in dismissals from the civil service does not necessarily require elaborate procedures. It does require that the government, as employer, state its reasons for the dismissal and allow the public employee to try to rebut its claims. Once the record contains each side's perspective, review by an administrative official or a court is generally possible. Unsubstantiated claims that dismissals will promote efficiency have been vulnerable to successful challenge. Thus, where there is a merit system, the government cannot simply purport that dismissals serve efficiency objectives; it must demonstrate conclusively that they do so.

The federal judiciary has also sought to assure that merit systems yield merit by requiring, under some circumstances, that standard civil service examinations be strongly job related. In a series of cases beginning in the early 1970s, the courts have held that employment practices having a negative impact on the employment interests of members of minority groups and women are illegal unless they are valid in the sense of being job related.[38] These rulings have been under the Civil Rights Act of 1964, as amended, and the Constitution's equal protection clause (limited to the public sector). There have been numerous instances in which public agencies have been unable to demonstrate sufficient job relatedness to make the practices at issue legally or constitutionally acceptable. One remedy that the judiciary may impose in such cases is quota hiring from among qualified minority-group members for a limited period of time, as in *United States* v. *Paradise* (1987).[39]

These cases have forced public-sector jurisdictions to rethink their definitions and applications of merit principles and to attempt to eliminate cultural bias in their hiring and promotional procedures. In *Johnson* v. *Santa Clara County* (1987),[40] the Supreme Court accepted a broad definition of merit that included an effort to establish a socially representative work-force. It specifically embraced the principle that exam scores do not have to be the sole determinant in promotions. Instead, jurisdictions are free to consider a range of factors, including sex and minority-group status. In *Johnson*, the Court noted that merit systems can be flexible because "there is rarely a single, 'best qualified' person for a job. An effective personnel system will bring before the selecting official several fully-qualified candidates who each may possess different attributes that recommend them for selection." [41]

Thus the federal judiciary and the Supreme Court have strengthened two aspects of the merit system. They have protected depoliticization by upholding regulations prohibiting federal employees from engaging in partisan political activity. They have required depoliticization by finding that patronage dismissals from the public service will generally be unconstitutional. The courts have also strengthened the merit system by requiring that dismissals, selections, and promotions done in the name of merit actually embody merit.

The Merit System and Merit Principles

This, then, is the procedural and legal environment of the contemporary federal "merit system." The remarkable growth of complexity in both the environment and the system has been reflected in restatements of the underlying principles: Not surprisingly, there are more merit principles today than there were in 1883. After a long period of formal silence about what the merit principles actually ensured, they have been enunciated in legislation twice in the past twenty years. In 1970, the Intergovernmental Personnel Act formally listed the merit principles for the first time:

1. Hiring and promoting employees on the basis of relative ability, with open consideration for initial appointment.
2. Providing fair compensation.
3. Retaining employees on the basis of performance, correcting inadequate performance and separating those whose inadequate performance cannot be corrected.
4. Training employees as needed for high quality performance.
5. Assuring fair treatment of applicants and employees in all aspects of personnel administration without regard to political affiliation, race, color, national origin, sex, or religious creed, and with proper regard for their privacy and constitutional rights as citizens.
6. Protecting employees against partisan political coercion; and prohibiting use of official position to affect an election or nomination for office. [42]

It is worth noting that the Intergovernmental Personnel Act, by using the lever of federal funding, applied these merit principles to state and local governments, just as the second Hatch Act had earlier prohibited state and local employees from partisan political activity.

In 1978, the principles were restated and somewhat redefined again in the Civil Service Reform Act. Now there were nine, much more complex, principles:

1. Recruitment should be from qualified individuals from appropriate sources in an endeavor to achieve a workforce from all segments of society, and selection and advancement should be determined solely on the basis of relative ability, knowledge and skills, after fair and open competition that assures that all receive equal opportunity.
2. All employees and applicants for employment should receive fair and equitable treatment in all aspects of personnel management without regard to political affiliation, race, color, religion, national origin, sex, marital status, age, or handicapping condition, and with proper regard for their privacy and constitutional rights.
3. Equal pay should be provided for work of equal value, with appropriate consideration of both national and local rates paid by employers in the private sector, and appropriate incentives and recognition should be provided for excellence in performance.
4. All employees should maintain high standards of integrity, conduct, and concern for the public interest.
5. The federal workforce should be used efficiently and effectively.
6. Employees should be retained on the adequacy of their performance, inadequate performance should be corrected, and employees should be separated who cannot or will not improve their performance to meet required standards.
7. Employees should be provided effective education and training in cases in which such education and training would result in better organizational and individual performance.
8. Employees should be (a.) protected against arbitrary action, personal favoritism, or coercion for partisan political purposes, and (b.) prohibited from using their official authority or influence for the purpose of interfering with or affecting the result of an election or a nomination for election.
9. Employees should be protected against reprisal for the lawful disclosure of information that the employee reasonably believes evidences (a.) a violation of any law, rule, or regulation, or (b.) mismanagement, a gross waste of funds, an abuse of authority, or a substantial and specific danger to public health and safety.[43]

Whatever else might be said about the merit principles as we near the year 2000, they are no longer simple and straightforward. Even the principles without their baggage do not provide clear guidance to the federal manager or personnel director who seeks to ensure merit within the overarching objective of effective service delivery. Further, the principles themselves now contain conflicting purposes and objectives. They are more comprehensive, but they are much, much more confusing.

Coping with the Merit System

How do federal managers deal with the constraint, confusion, and complexity of merit as it exists today? In an effort to examine this question, staff members of the National Commission conducted a series of interviews with personnel directors and others in agencies that have made extensive and recent use of existing hiring procedures. Representatives from different agencies, different regions of the country, and central and field offices were interviewed to determine whether and where differences in attitudes toward merit existed. Many persons interviewed requested confidentiality. To honor those requests, no persons or agencies are identified in this chapter. In the interviews, commission staff focused on entrance to the federal service, rather than on promotion once inside.

Two findings from our interviews are paramount: first, there continues to be remarkable support for the merit *principles*. Second, there is almost unanimous dissatisfaction with the merit *system*. Furthermore, although there is strong support for reforming and removing what many refer to as the "procedural baggage" of the merit system, there is a continuing awareness of the potential for political and other abuse of the merit system and for the need for some protection of career employees and positions. There was, nonetheless, a very strong conviction that federal personnel directors and other federal managers, left on their own, would actively pursue merit. One group of managers said, "If the slate were clean, most of the agencies, most of the time, would create procedures that make good sense. Those procedures that they would re-create would look like the merit principles." [44]

Other managers affirmed this commitment, but emphasized that both the definition of merit and the means of pursuing it need to be examined. Arguing that managers must focus on purpose, not problems, one personnel director said, "The merit system has come to be a way of life, but we must remember that the principles are the basis." [45] Another noted that merit "is confused and it is struggling, but it is there. The system, however, is beyond repair; it needs to be totally rethought. Delegating bad procedures to us does not solve problems; we need to go back to the fundamental principles and guidelines." [46]

The central agency personnel directors interviewed were unanimous in their assessment that the basic design of the current merit system is not appropriate for either current or future recruiting and hiring needs. One director said, "The days of national recruiting are over; the reality is that if you waste the time advertising nationwide, you lose the opportunity to hire the people you really need." [47] Representatives of an agency noted for its innovation and foresight in relation to personnel summarized the situation in these terms: "the goal is to find the best person for the job. The principles are fundamental and they shape the process, but you cannot control merit in a centralized way.... The system is arcane and archaic and we have not done a good job of articulating the new realities." [48]

The interviews uncovered strong differences between central agency staff and field staff in relation to the status of merit. The view of the merit system as archaic and procedure bound was echoed in the field office interviews, but those interviews reflected serious concerns about protecting merit as well. One manager put it in the following terms, "The merit system has little credibility ... only a few remaining bureaucrats and a few conscientious managers are keeping it from being totally disregarded." [49] Another manager said, "Until merit is defined as something other than test scores, we will continue to reach merit goals, but the quality of the workforce and the quality of the work, will go steadily down." [50]

Underlying many of these concerns is the conviction that while the merit system does not work well or consistently anymore, no coherent replacement or direction has been advanced. Without that replacement and additional guidance, field managers fear replacing even an unworkable system. Indeed, a recent report of the General Accounting Office found that in the face of extensive decentralization and inadequate central-to-field communication, many field managers simply did not know how they were supposed to operate in relation to merit. There has been virtually no systematic monitoring of field experience and precedent; GAO found that even keeping adequate records was problematic. [51]

Overall, then, while there continues to be strong support for the fundamental principles of merit, dissatisfaction with and confusion about the current system is high. Further, the split between central agency personnel and field personnel in terms of how well agencies are coping in the current environment is cause for concern. The inability, or unwillingness, of central personnel to trust and train other personnel in their own agencies is damning evidence of the problems with merit today. The problem highlighted by National Commission interviews has been noted elsewhere. A recent MSPB survey reported that "personnel specialists view delegation of authority from agency personnel offices to line managers somewhat less favorably than they view delegation from OPM to agencies. Whereas 83 percent of respondents believe that delegation of authorities from OPM to agency personnel offices can lead to improved personnel management, only 60 percent believe the same is true of delegation from personnel offices to line management." [52]

It may be that, lacking confidence in field managers, central agency personnel have failed to take the responsibility of decentralization and delegation seriously. The same may be said of the Office of Personnel Management. The ensuing lack of reporting and monitoring is a serious deficiency that needs to be corrected. A more accurate record of experience with decentralized merit is necessary for effective reform. In addition, the need for training and education—about the new environment, the new accountability, and the new responsibility—is very clear. It must be given high priority.

Conclusions and Recommendations

Today, neither the essential definition of merit nor fundamental merit principles is clear. Merit cannot mean, as one would assume from examining the system, excessive constraint and blind obedience to a nearly unintelligible maze of procedure. No manager or personnel director can work consistently or effectively in a system defined by over 6,000 pages of rules and regulations. One hundred years of accumulated rules and regulations are the baggage of merit. They do not clarify and define; they obscure. The current system essentially assumes that public managers must be coerced into meritorious behavior; there is no presumption that, left to their own skills and conscience, members of the federal service will nonetheless pursue quality and effective service.

The basic components of the system continue to reflect demographic realities of the late nineteenth century. For many federal agencies, many occupations, and many regions of the country, the contemporary reality is that personnel systems cannot screen out potential employees, but must gather them in. Demographic projections for the next twenty years demonstrate very clearly that to be competitive in these activities, the federal government must be flexible, aggressive, and innovative. The current system is set up precisely to discourage such qualities.

Key components of the current system have not been reexamined for many years. Classification and training are leading examples. A crazy quilt of rules and regulations, patched together as new needs and demands appeared over the past hundred years, provides false assurance that important protections are in place. Rhetoric creates both complacency about the status quo and an unnecessarily negative view of the career civil servants the system is intended to protect.

Today, it is inconceivable that a major nation could govern well, resolve social and economic problems, or play an effective global role in the absence of a strong civil service that is well integrated into its political in-

stitutions and culture. Throughout the world, national civil services are being reformed and restructured. Virtually everywhere, government is considered a tool for formulating and implementing public policies. But as Alexander Hamilton noted two centuries ago in *The Federalist Papers,* "the true
test of a good government is its aptitude and tendency to produce a good
administration."

Good government in the United States requires much better public administration. There is no doubt that public personnel administration, always the cornerstone of public administration, must be redesigned—or perhaps designed for the first time—if the United States is to meet the challenges of the present and the future. There is no "quick fix" for the civil
service and public administration. There is a dramatic need to decide, for
the first time in over a hundred years, what kind of public service the
American national government needs and deserves. Proceeding from that
base, future reforms must provide the map and the tools for a new system.

Notes

1. Throughout this chapter, "merit" is defined primarily in terms of entrance to the federal service. Very clearly, promotion and protection of employees' rights are also part of the merit mosaic. Both, however, are worthy of separate treatment.

2. Civil Service Commission, *Biography of an Ideal* (Washington, D.C.:
CSC, 1974), 28.

3. Paul P. Van Riper, *History of the United States Civil Service* (Evanston,
Ill.: Row, Peterson, 1958), 106.

4. Ibid., 105.

5. The Civil Service Act of 1883 (Pendleton Act), *Statutes at Large of the
United States of America,* vol. 20, p. 403, sec. 3.

6. Herbert Kaufman, "The Growth of the Federal Personnel System," in
The American Assembly, *The Federal Government Service* (New York: Columbia University Press, 1954), 36.

7. Stephen Skrowronek, *Building a New American State: The Expansion
of National Administrative Capacities, 1877–1920* (New York: Cambridge
University Press, 1982), 70–71.

8. Woodrow Wilson, quoted in Van Riper, *History of Civil Service,* 234.

9. Herbert Kaufman, "Growth of Federal Personnel System," 39. For Van
Riper's dissenting view, see Van Riper, *History of Civil Service,* chap. 13.

10. See the Civil Service Commission, *Biography of an Ideal,* 66.

11. See the discussion of the Ramspeck Act and its implementation in Van
Riper, *History of Civil Service,* 344–46.

12. Civil Service Commission, *Biography of an Ideal,* 49.

13. Ibid., 89.

14. Van Riper, *History of Civil Service,* 207.

15. Merit Systems Protection Board, *In Search of Merit: Hiring Entry Level Federal Employees* (Washington, D.C.: MSPB, September 1987), i.

16. The greatest increase occurred in the Carter presidency; the elevated levels from that administration were increased still further under President Reagan. See Patricia W. Ingraham, "Building Bridges or Burning Them? The President, the Appointees and the Bureaucracy," *Public Administration Review,* September/October 1987, 425–35.

17. This number is based on research conducted by the U.S. Navy, Office of Civilian Personnel.

18. Data from the U.S. Office of Personnel Management, Office of Career Entry.

19. For extensive discussion of CSRA, see Patricia W. Ingraham and David Rosenbloom, Co-Editors, "Symposium on Ten Years of Civil Service Reform," *Policy Studies Journal,* Winter 1989.

20. Van Riper, *History of Civil Service,* 298.

21. Ibid., 304.

22. Lucius Wilmerding, Jr., *Government by Merit* (New York: McGraw-Hill, 1935), 57.

23. See Van Riper, *History of Civil Service,* 426–27.

24. *Final Report of the First Hoover Commission,* in *Basic Documents of American Public Administration, 1776–1950,* ed. Frederick C. Mosher (New York: Holmes and Meier, 1976), 210.

25. Standards are the tools actually used to describe a job and the necessary qualifications for it. The Merit Systems Protection Board notes that "typically, each occupation is covered by a standard that describes the work of the occupation at various grade levels ... to function, the classification process must bring together three elements—position descriptions, classification standards, and human judgment—to arrive at appropriate conclusions.... OPM's qualification standards determine what skills are needed and evaluate whether candidates who apply are basically qualified to perform the work." Merit Systems Protection Board, *OPM's Classification and Qualification Systems: A Renewed Emphasis, A Changing Perspective* (Washington, D.C.: MSPB, November 1989), 6–7.

26. Ibid., 12.

27. Van Riper, *History of Civil Service,* 380.

28. Ibid., 432.

29. Civil Service Commission, *Biography of an Ideal,* 97.

30. Task Force on Education and Training, National Commission on the Public Service, *Investment for Leadership: Education and Training for the Public Service* (Washington, D.C., 1989), 120.

31. George William Curtis, *The Situation* (New York: National Civil Service Reform League, 1886), 17.

32. 413 U.S. 548 (1973).

33. 427 U.S. 347 (1976).

34. 445 U.S. 507 (1980).

35. For a full discussion of the issues surrounding Hatch reform, see chap. 2 of this book.

36. 408 U.S. 564 (1972).

37. 470 U.S. 532 (1985).

38. See David H. Rosenbloom, "What Every Public Personnel Manager Should Know about the Constitution," in *Public Personnel Administration*, ed. Steven Hays and Richard Kearney (Englewood Cliffs, N.J.: Prentice-Hall, 1990), 49–52, for a brief recent analysis.

39. 94 L. Ed.2d 203 (1987).

40. 94 L. Ed.2d 615 (1987).

41. 413 U.S. 548 (1973).

42. This summary of the principles contained in the Intergovernmental Personnel Act is taken from Civil Service Commission, *Biography of an Ideal*, 99–100.

43. P.L. 95–454, 13 October 1978, Civil Service Reform Act of 1978, Title I.

44. Personal interview, National Commission on the Public Service staff, February 1990.

45. Ibid.

46. Personal interview, National Commission on the Public Service staff, March 1990.

47. Ibid.

48. Personal interview, National Commission on the Public Service staff, February 1990.

49. Telephone interview, National Commission on the Public Service staff, December 1989.

50. Ibid.

51. General Accounting Office, *Federal Recruiting and Hiring* (Washington, D.C.: GAO, May 1990).

52. Merit Systems Protection Board, *Federal Personnel Management Since Civil Service Reform* (Washington, D.C.: MSPB, November 1989), 10.

APPENDIX

Charles H. Levine: Selected Works

Books

Expertise and Democratic Decision Making: A Reader. Edited with Peter M. Benda. Washington, D.C.: Government Printing Office, 1987. Prepared for the Task Force on Science Policy, Committee on Science and Technology, 99th Congress.

Fiscal Stress and Public Policy. Edited with Irene S. Rubin. Beverly Hills, Calif.: Sage, 1981.

Managing Fiscal Stress. The Crisis in the Public Sector. Editor. Chatham, N.J.: Chatham House, 1980.

Managing Human Resources: A Challenge to Urban Government. Editor. Beverly Hills, Calif.: Sage, 1977.

The Politics of Retrenchment: How Local Governments Manage Fiscal Stress. With Irene S. Rubin and George G. Wolohojian. Beverly Hills, Calif.: Sage, 1981.

Public Administration: Challenges, Choices, and Consequences. With B. Guy Peters and Frank J. Thompson. New York: HarperCollins, 1990.

Racial Conflict and the American Mayor: Power, Polarization, and Performance. Lexington, Mass.: Heath/Lexington, 1974.

Readings in Urban Politics. Edited with Harlan Hahn. 2d ed. New York: Longman, 1984.

The Unfinished Agenda for Civil Service Reform. Editor. Washington, D.C.: Brookings Institution, 1985.

Urban Politics: Past, Present, and Future. Edited with Harlan Hahn. New York: Longman, 1980.

Articles

1988

"The Assignment and Institutionalization of Functions at OMB: Lessons from Two Cases in Workforce Management." With Peter M. Benda. In *New Directions in Budget Theory,* edited by Irene S. Rubin, 70–99. Albany: SUNY Press.

"The Centralization-Decentralization Tug-of-War in the New Executive Branch." With Michael G. Hansen. In *Organizing Governance: Governing Organization,* edited by Colin Campbell and B. Guy Peters, 255–82. Pittsburgh: University of Pittsburgh Press.

"Human Resource Erosion and the Uncertain Future of the U.S. Civil Service: From Policy Gridlock to Structural Fragmentation." *Governance* 1, no. 2 (April), 115–43.

"Reagan and the Bureaucracy: The Bequest, the Promise, and the Legacy." With Peter M. Benda. In *The Reagan Legacy,* edited by Charles O. Jones, 102–42. Chatham, N.J.: Chatham House.

1987

"Career Success in the Future: Five Pattern Changes in the 1980s." *Bureaucrat,* Spring, 37–39.

"The New Shape of the Civil Service." In *Governing,* edited by Roger H. Davidson and Walter J. Oleszek, 305–12. Washington, D.C.: CQ Press.

1986

"The Federal Government in the Year 2000: Administrative Legacies of the Reagan Years." *Public Administration Review,* May/June, 195–206. Selected for the Marshall E. Dimock Award of the American Society for Public Administration.

"OMB and the Central Management Problem: Is Another Reorganization the Answer?" With Peter M. Benda. *Public Administration Review,* September/October, 379–91.

"OMB's Management Role: Issues of Structures and Strategy." With Peter M. Benda. In *Office of Management and Budget: Evolving Roles and Future Issues,* edited by Robert S. Gilmour and Roger L. Sperry, 73–145. Washington, D.C.: Government Printing Office, February. Prepared for the Committee on Governmental Affairs, U.S. Senate, 99th Congress.

"President Reagan's Productivity Improvement Program: Deja Vu, Fresh Start to an Old Story, or Lasting Reform?" With Peter M. Benda. Congressional Research Service Report No. 86–895, April 15. Also published in *Public Productivity Review* 10, no. 1 (Fall): 3–26.

"The Reagan Administration and the Intergovernmental Lobby: Iron Triangles, Cozy Subsystems, and Political Conflict." With James A. Thurber. In *Interest Group Politics,* edited by Allan J. Cigler and Burdett A. Loomis, 202–20, 2d ed. Washington, D.C.: CQ Press.

"Workforce Management at OMB: Issues of Functional Assignment and Institutionalization." With Peter M. Benda. In *Office of Management and Budget: Evolving Roles and Future Issues,* edited by Robert S. Gilmour and Roger L. Sperry, 305–33. Washington, D.C.: Government Printing Office, February. Prepared for the Committee on Governmental Affairs, U.S. Senate, 99th Congress.

1985

"The Family as a Coproduction Unit: Some Second Thoughts." *Urban Resources,* Summer, 21–23.

"Police Management in the 1980s: From Decrementalism to Strategic Thinking." *Public Administration Review,* Special Issue, November, 691–700.

"Reforming Federal Personnel Management: The Search for New Balance." In *The Unfinished Agenda of Civil Service Reform,* edited by Charles H. Levine, 1–14. Washington, D.C.: Brookings Institution.

"Triviocracy: Sayre's Law Revisited." With Frederic D. Homer. *Policy Studies Review,* November, 241–51.

"Where Policy Comes From: Ideas, Innovations, and Agenda Choices." *Public Administration Review,* January/February, 255–58.

1984

"Retrenchment, Human Resource Erosion, and the Role of the Personnel Manager." *Public Personnel Management,* Fall, 249–64.

1983

"Citizenship and Service Delivery: The Promise of Coproduction," *Public Administration Review,* Special Issue, December, 178–87.

"Fees, Tolls, and User Charges: A Bibliography." *Policy Studies Journal,* June, 730–52.

"Fiscal Stress and Local Government Adaptations: Toward a Multi-Stage Theory of Retrenchment." With Irene S. Rubin and George G. Wolohojian. In *Research in Urban Economics,* vol. 3, edited by Vernon Henderson, 253–303. Greenwich, Conn.: JAI Press.

Testimony on *Programs and Activities of the Economic Development Administration.* U.S. Congress, House Subcommittee on Investigations and Oversight of the Committee on Public Works and Transportation, 98th Congress, 1st session, November 30, 58–89.

1982

"Managing the End: Death and Dying in Public Organizations." With Irene
S. Rubin. *Public Management,* March, 18–20.
"Managing Organizational Retrenchment: Preconditions, Deficiencies, and
Adaptations in the Public Sector." With Irene S. Rubin and George
G. Wolohojian. *Administration and Society,* May, 101–31.
"Retrenchment and Human Resource Management: Combating the Dis-
count Effects of Uncertainty." With George C. Wolohojian. In *Pub-
lic Personnel Administration: Problems and Prospects,* edited by
Steven W. Hays and Richard C. Kearney, 175–88. Englewood Cliffs,
N.J.: Prentice-Hall.

1981

"The Centralizing Effects of Austerity on the Intergovernmental System."
With Paul L. Posner. *Political Science Quarterly,* Spring, 67–68.
"The Hazards of Going It Alone." With Richard D. Schmitt. In *Perspec-
tives on the Limitation on Taxing and Spending in the Public Sector
in the United States,* edited by Charles B. Tyer and Marcia W. Tay-
lor, 219–58. Columbia, S.C.: Bureau of Governmental Research and
Service, University of South Carolina.
"The Hidden Hazards of Retrenchment." *Bureaucrat,* Fall, 34–36.
"Managing Public Sector Retrenchment: Headaches and Heartbreaks." In
Managing Fiscal Limitations, edited by Gunther G. Kress, 13–22.
Davis, Calif.: Institute of Governmental Affairs, University of Cali-
fornia, Davis.
"Resource Scarcity and the Reform Model: The Management of Retrench-
ment in Cincinnati and Oakland." With Irene S. Rubin and George
G. Wolohojian. *Public Administration Review,* November/Decem-
ber, 619–28.
"State Targeting on Urban Fiscal Problems: A View from Below." With
Irene S. Rubin. *Urban Interest,* Fall, 73–82.

1980

"Doing More with Less: Some Problems and Alternatives in Cutback Man-
agement." *Management Aids,* Spring.
"Economic Growth, Decline, and Policy Change." With Irene S. Rubin. In
Fiscal Stress and Public Policy, edited by Charles H. Levine and
Irene S. Rubin, 11–20. Beverly Hills, Calif.: Sage.
"Management Decisions in the Face of Budget Constraints." In *Proceed-
ings of the National Urban Policy Roundtable,* edited by Harrington
Bryce, 15–16. Washington, D.C.: Academy for Contemporary Prob-
lems.

"The New Crisis in the Public Sector." In *Managing Fiscal Stress,* edited by Charles H. Levine, 3–12. Chatham, N.J.: Chatham House.

"The Politics of Urban America and the Study of Urban Politics." With Harlan Hahn. In *Urban Politics,* edited by Harlan Hahn and Charles H. Levine, 1–45. New York: Longman.

"Response to Fiscal Stress: A Model and Plan for Research." With Irene S. Rubin and George G. Wolohojian. In *Selected Papers from the 1980 Annual Meeting of the Council of University Institutes for Urban Affairs,* edited by Harvey K. Newman. Atlanta: Georgia State University.

"Retrenchment, Uncertainty, and Human Resources: Combating the Discount Effects of Bleak Future." With George G. Wolohojian. In *Public Personnel Management: Problems and Prospects,* edited by Steven W. Hays and Richard C. Kearney, 192–213. Columbia, S.C.: Bureau of Governmental Research and Service, University of South Carolina.

"State Executive Branch Reorganization: Patterns and Perspectives." With James L. Garnett. *Administration and Society,* November, 227–76.

1979

"Cutback Management in an Age of Scarcity: Hard Questions for Hard Times." *Intergovernmental Personnel Notes,* January-February, 11–14.

"Facing Up the Hard Times Ahead: Cutback Management in an Age of Scarcity." *Maryland Alumni Magazine,* Spring, 18–20.

"How Cities Cope with Shrinking Funds." *Council Policy Leadership Program Special Report,* 3, 22. Washington, D.C.: National League of Cities, May.

"Managing the Cutback Process." In *Bridging the Revenue Gap,* edited by S. Kossak, 35–40. Washington, D.C.: National Association of Counties.

"More on Cutback Management: Hard Questions for Hard Times." *Public Administration Review,* March/April, 179–83.

"Public Management: First Approximations." *International Journal of Public Administration* 1, no. 4: 179–83.

1978

"Organizational Decline and Cutback Management." *Public Administration Review,* July/August, 315–57. Selected for the William E. Mosher Award of the American Society for Public Administration.

1977

"Collective Bargaining in Municipal Governments: An Interorganizational Perspective." With James L. Perry and John J. Demarco. In *Managing Human Resources,* edited by Charles H. Levine, 159–99. Beverly Hills, Calif.: Sage.

"Interorganizational Analysis: An Analytical Handle on the Complexity of Service Delivery Systems." With Robert Berne. *Urban Affairs Quarterly,* March, 411–22. Also in *The Politics and Economics of Urban Services,* edited by Robert L. Lineberry. Beverly Hills, Calif.: Sage.

"Managing the Human Resources of City Government in the Post-Reform Era." In *Managing Human Resources,* edited by Charles H. Levine, 9–22. Beverly Hills, Calif.: Sage.

"On Evaluating Journals." *Bureaucrat,* Summer, 77–82.

"Technology and the Governance of the Health Care Industry: The Dilemma of Reform." With Martin A. Strosberg and Alfred Mauet. *Journal of Health Politics, Policy, and Law,* Summer, 212–26.

1976

"Comparing Public and Private Organizations." With Robert W. Backoff and Hal G. Rainey. *Public Administration Review,* March/April, 233–44.

"An Interorganizational Analysis of Power, Conflict, and Settlements in Public Sector Collective Bargaining." With James L. Perry. *American Political Science Review,* December, 1185–1201.

"Leadership: Problems, Prospects, and Implications of Research Programs Aimed at Linking Empirical and Normative Modeling." *Policy Studies Journal,* Autumn, 34–41. Also in *Public Administration and Public Policy,* edited by H. George Frederickson and Charles R. Wise, 53–60. Lexington, Mass.: Heath/Lexington.

"Macro-Micro Interfaces in Leadership Research." *Organization and Administrative Sciences,* Summer/Fall, 49–57. Also in *Leadership Frontiers,* edited by J.G. Hunt and L.L. Larson, 49–57. Kent, Ohio: Kent State University Press.

1975

"Organizational Design: A Post-Minnowbrook Perspective for the 'New' Public Administration." With Robert W. Backoff, Allan R. Cahoon, and William J. Siffin. *Public Administration Review,* July/August, 425–35.

"The Public Personnel System: Can Juridical Administration and Manpower Management Coexist?" With Lloyd G. Nigro. *Public Administration Review,* January/February, 98–107.

"Public Sector Unionism: Theory and Methodology." With James L. Perry. *American Politics Quarterly,* April, 209–14.

"Unrepresentative Bureaucracy." *Bureaucrat,* April, 90–98.

1974

"Beyond the Sound and Fury of Quotas and Targets." *Public Administration Review,* May/June, 240–41.

"Urban Conflict as a Constraint on Mayoral Leadership: Lessons from Gary and Cleveland." With Clifford L. Kaufman. *American Politics Quarterly,* January, 78–106.

1972

"Black Entrepreneurship in the Ghetto: A Recruitment Strategy." *Land Economics,* August, 269–73.

1969

"The Dilemma of the Black Businessman: A New Approach." *Indiana Business Review,* March/April, 12–26.

1968

"Maximizing the Benefits of Summer Work Programs for Graduate Students." *Public Personnel Review,* October, 231–34.

1967

"Poverty and Public Policy: An Administrative Approach." *Collected Papers in Political Science,* Fall, 101–12.

Monographs

Cutback Management in Criminal Justice. With H. Jerome Miron, Mark D. Corrigan, and Edward J. Pesce. Washington, D.C.: National Institute of Justice, 1981.

"Cutting Back the Public Sector: The Hidden Hazards of Retrenchment." Stene Chair Inaugural Address, November 1981.

Managing the Pressures of Inflation in Criminal Justice. Coauthored with several others. Washington, D.C.: National Institute of Law Enforcement and Criminal Justice, 1979.

Proceedings of the Conference on University-State Relations. Edited with George G. Wolohojian. College Park, Md.: Bureau of Governmental Research, University of Maryland, 1980.

The Quiet Crisis of the Civil Service: The Federal Personnel System at the Crossroads. With Rosslyn S. Kleeman. Washington, D.C.: National

Academy of Public Administration, December 1986. Revised by
Kleeman in 1992, appearing on pp. 208–73 of this volume.

Report of the Ad Hoc Panel on Attracting New Staff and Retaining Capability During a Period of Declining Manpower Ceilings. Washington, D.C.: National Academy of Public Administration Foundation, 1973.

Strategic Management for Law Enforcement Agencies. Washington, D.C.: National Institute of Justice, September 1985.

TRIM: Causes and Consequences. With Richard D. Schmitt and George G. Wolohojian. College Park, Md.: Bureau of Governmental Research, University of Maryland, 1981.

Symposium

Editor, "Symposium on Organizational Decline and Cutback Management." *Public Administration Review,* July/August 1978, 315–57.

Agenda for Excellence

Peter M. Benda is Program Associate for Public Policy with the Pew Charitable Trusts in Philadelphia. He has taught at the University of Virginia and Swarthmore College.

Colin Campbell, s.j., is the head of the Graduate Public Policy Program at Georgetown University, where he is University Professor in the Martin Chair.

Patricia W. Ingraham is professor of public administration and political science at Syracuse University's Maxwell School of Citizenship and Public Affairs. She previously taught at the State University of New York at Binghamton.

Donald F. Kettl is a professor in the Department of Political Science and the LaFollette Institute of Public Affairs at the University of Wisconsin–Madison. He has also taught at Columbia University, the University of Virginia, and Vanderbilt University.

Rosslyn S. Kleeman is the U.S. General Accounting Office's Director of Workforce Future Issues.

Donald Naulls is a member of the political science department at Saint Mary's University in Halifax, Nova Scotia.

Lloyd G. Nigro is a professor in Georgia State University's Institute of Public Administration.

James L. Perry is a professor at Indiana University, Bloomington. He teaches in the School of Public and Environmental Affairs.

James P. Pfiffner is a professor of government and politics at George Mason University. He received his Ph.D. in political science at the University of Wisconsin–Madison.

Hal G. Rainey is a professor in the Department of Political Science at the University of Georgia. He previously taught at Florida State University.

William D. Richardson is an associate professor of political science at Georgia State University.

Barbara S. Romzek is the chair of the Department of Public Administration at the University of Kansas. She received her Ph.D. from the University of Texas at Austin.

David H. Rosenbloom is Distinguished Professor of Public Administration at the American University's School of Public Affairs.